AN AFRICAN BOURGEOISIE

RACE, CLASS, AND POLITICS IN SOUTH AFRICA

AN AFRICAN BOURGEOISIE

Race, Class, and Politics in South Africa

by LEO KUPER

New Haven and London, Yale University Press, 1965

Designed by John O. C. McCrillis,
set in Garamond type,
and printed in the United States of America by
The Colonial Press Inc., Clinton, Massachusetts

Library of Congress catalog card number: 64–20925

The author acknowledges with thanks permission
from Faber and Faber and from Curtis Brown, Ltd.,
to quote copyrighted material from *Down Second
Avenue,* by Ezekiel Mphahlele.

To my brother Simie

Contents

PART IV

The Organizational Milieu

Conclusions

ILLUSTRATIONS

following page 238

Plate *1*. Sports officials lead their football teams onto the playing fields. Courtesy of Zonk.

Plate *2*. Elite of the African bourgeoisie caged in the Treason Trial. Courtesy of *The World*.

Plate *3*. Honoring a graduate. Courtesy of *Ilanga Lase Natal*.

Plate *4*. Routine police raid. Courtesy of *Natal Daily News*.

Plate *5*. Experiments in Africanization: The Minister of Bantu Administration and Development fosters African idiom.

Plate *6*. Experiments in Africanization: Revival of traditional costume by wives of African political leaders. Courtesy of *New Age*.

Preface

Bourgeoisie may seem a pompous word for the African professionals, traders, and senior government and municipal clerks who are the subject of this study. It may also carry the quite misleading implication that there is a well-defined class structure in the African communities of South Africa, consisting of a bourgeoisie and a proletariat, and that by some mysterious process of enclosure, the bourgeoisie comprises all persons following the above occupations and no others. Nothing so definite, rigid, or classificatory is here intended. Little is in fact known of the structure of urban African society in South Africa. There has been some interest in the economic and political role of African professionals and traders, their wealth, patterns of consumption, style of life, and moderating or revolutionary tendencies. But this interest has been expressed in very general observation and speculation, or it has been colored by surprise and exaggeration, as if the emergence of strata differentiated from a general mass of impoverished and poorly educated African workers were a sport of evolution. At this pioneering or frontier stage of research, it seemed convenient to explore a narrow segment of African class structure from the firm base of a few occupations. And I chose occupations akin to my own, in which I knew many Africans and could hope for greater ease of communication. *Bourgeoisie* may thus be regarded here as a shorthand reference for these occupations.

However, I clearly intend more by the term bourgeoisie. I apply it specifically to the "upper" occupational strata of African society. And in the use of the word, for which I offer some justification in Chapter 1, I want to suggest a struggle by rising groups against privilege resting on the traditional basis of birth, the aristocratic prerogative of race. I want also to convey significance and a rather special status, based on the fact that these men belong to the circles from which, in other territories in Africa, many of the leaders are drawn, and that in different circumstances they would furnish the presidents, the international statesmen, the ministers plenipotentiary, and the new men of wealth. There is a pathos in their position, in the contrast between the narrow restraints and low status of systematic racial discrimination in a society dominated by White settlers, and the almost boundless opportunities for power and fulfillment in the independent African states. The study deals then with some of the potential leaders in South African society, given a radical change in the structure of racial domination.

The problem of political change, from the perspective of the African bourgeoisie, is one of my main themes. Political philosophy and action are so interwoven with racial attitude and racial structure in South Africa that political alternatives may be rephrased largely in the language of race relations; for example, the political theory and practice of the ruling doctrine of apartheid is a theory of race relations and a structure of racial domination. From this point of view, political choice lies between the extremes of racialism and racialization (in the sense of maximum emphasis on racial and tribal and ethnic entities as the units of social organization and cultural differentiation) and of nonracialism (understood as a relatively random social and cultural distribution of members of different races). Concretely, the African bourgeoisie may accept apartheid, strive for African domination, seek some form of partnership or other balancing of racial interests, or work toward what its members sometimes describe as a nonracial democracy, implying a system based on the racial anonymity of the individual as distinct from a racial democracy, whatever that may be. And linked with these alternatives are choices as to means, violent or nonviolent, with presumably some sort of affinity between racialism and violence, and between nonracialism and nonviolence.

Equating political solutions with race relations may seem to introduce a naiveté, a bourgeois bias toward eliminating certain choices, such as that between communism and capitalism (though no doubt these too have their affinities, with probably a greater hospitality toward racialism in capitalist society). But in fact these choices are mostly subordinated by the African bourgeoisie to the issues of race relations. In any event they have not been omitted from the study.

Discussion in terms of choice suggests the language of self-determination in a United Nations charter, or that the African bourgeoisie is the political decision maker in South Africa, whereas in fact the situation is so firmly structured and the African bourgeoisie so subordinated that there is little immediate freedom of choice. The highly effective massing of laws and of force at the present time is designed to exclude all choices other than apartheid, and to deny Africans a creative or otherwise significant political role. Immediate, if not long-term, policy may be largely determined by the situation itself. Thus campaigns may be conducted in the spirit of nonviolent resistance, because violence would be foolhardy, or, conversely, sabotage and violence and terrorism may be used not from conviction or preference, but as the only seemingly efficient means of change. If the conclusion is drawn that only an appeal to racial sentiment will mobilize sufficient power for the overthrow of White domination, then there may be a challenge to a long-established political ideology of nonracialism, or an attempt to reconcile incitement to racialism as a technique with nonracialism as a goal. The theme of African perspectives on political change must thus be set in the context of specific conditions and trends within South African society, relative to the issues of racialism and nonracialism, violence and nonviolence, and bearing on the degrees of freedom officially permitted Africans. This I attempt in Part I.

Part II deals with the class manifestations associated with the occupations selected for study. Only a limited aspect of class analysis is presented. There is no attempt to analyze African society into a system of classes, with clearly delineated boundaries between each class, and well-defined principles for placing each member of the society into an appropriate class. This would be too rigid a model even for a relatively stable and homogeneous Western industrial society, and certainly it is for the African sector of South African society, where rapid social change transforms traditional structures and creates new structures under the impact of Western urban industrial forces and political domination. In any event, it would be a most ambitious enterprise in the present state of our knowledge.

My approach is limited to a process of class differentiation within the African communities, which I trace mainly at the level of the professionals and traders, though this inevitably introduces wider aspects of class differentiation as the "bourgeoisie" reacts to other segments. It is further limited by the selection of the city of Durban, with its largely Zulu-speaking African population, as the field of empirical research from which I move outward to South African society in general. Specifically my approach was to ask whether what I have called the bourgeoisie is simply an occupational classification, conveying no more than certain objective differences implicit in the occupational structure, or whether there are social correlates to this occupational classification of a type generally associated with social class. In particular, are the social origins of the bourgeoisie distinctive, indicating some depth over the generations to occupational difference, some crystallization of inherited inequality? And has the bourgeoisie elaborated the objectively given occupational differences into a distinctive style of life, with special patterns of association and claims to prestige made manifest in conspicuous consumption, and imbued with some measure of class consciousness?

Class formation among Africans cannot be analyzed simply as an attribute or correlate of the occupational differences between them. It must be related to the overall structure of South African society, and to the transition of Africans from a tribal system to a system of racial domination. The classes emerge out of the tribal matrix, and develop in the context of a racially structured society. Inevitably there is interaction between tribe, race, and class, each of which may provide a basis for association and loyalty. And inevitably, in the context of this interaction, class differences are seen from the most varied perspectives, dependent on the specific situation and the identifications of the actors. It is with these themes that Part II deals—the objective and subjective correlates of occupational differentiation, in a context of restratification from rural tribal society to urban plural society, and amidst the varied perspectives of tribe, race, and class. I have, however, excluded the more sealed-off areas of domestic life, in which urban and traditional, bourgeois and working class, Africans might be expected to have different patterns of family relationships and domestic routine.

The approach in Part III—The Occupational Milieu—is more detailed and more specific. The unit of analysis is now the occupation, and the chapters are devoted to particular occupations or clusters of occupations. Some order has been imposed by a separation into two sections, the intellectuals and the traders. This is not too arbitrary, since the professional and trading occupations are in many respects patently heterogeneous, and a divergence in the educational, religious, and parental background of professionals and traders is shown in Part II. Indeed in some studies of African class structure in other territories of Africa, sociologists have been reluctant to consign the educated and the traders to the same class category because of the marked differences in many aspects of their lives and life chances. For the time being, the comprehensive category of bourgeoisie is replaced either by the individual occupation, or, more broadly, by a classification into intellectuals and traders, and the analysis moves to the distinctive and common elements in the occupational milieus, with special emphasis on aspects relevant to race attitudes and political choice.

The space devoted to a particular occupation is no measure of my judgment as to its significance in the structure of African society. In general, there is extended analysis of the more populous occupations, such as teachers, nurses, and traders. By contrast, the discussion of the small number of African lawyers and doctors is condensed, though I hope without sacrifice of emphasis on the significance of these occupations as symbols of African achievement and as entitlement to eminence and leadership. In the case of the senior state and municipal employees, the somewhat cursory analysis reflects difficulty of rapport, not lack of significance. On the contrary, these occupations are highly significant, and it would be unrealistic to exclude them in any discussion of the upper strata of African society. Historically, African officials have played an important role in the relations between the White rulers and their own conquered people. Civil service occupations were one of the prerogatives of educated Africans, and conferred high prestige among them. To some extent these qualities persist, but with the heightening of racial conflict and the instrumental role of the African official in the subordination of his people under apartheid, the occupational milieu of

African civil service has become highly charged with ambivalence. In a situation in which the African civil servant may readily be branded as a traitor by his own people, or dismissed as disloyal or punished as subversive by the Government, and at a time of emergency, rioting, and arbitrary arrest, rapport is not readily established.

Much of the analysis in Part III is directed to the institutional context of the different occupations, more especially to the extent of harmony and tension between the institutional context of a particular occupation and other institutions of the society. There is a sharp contrast, for example, between the institutional context of the teaching profession under the apartheid policy of Bantu Education, and that of the ministry in the English-speaking churches. Bantu Education may be thought of as an intermediate or intercalary institution, functioning for Whites as a political institution by means of which apartheid policy may be imposed on Africans, and functioning for Africans as their only institution for formal education. Policy is directed toward harmonizing the African school system with a racial organization of all other institutional structures in the society, so that the economic, political, residential, welfare, recreational, and educational aspects of African life are integrated in a racially distinctive way of life. The English-speaking churches, on the other hand, stand dogmatically opposed to many of the practices in other institutional orders of contemporary South African society, since they aspire to be interracial, not merely multiracial, and since they reject racial discrimination as morally repugnant. Thus at the level of dogma or theory, the English-speaking churches are in a state of tension, and the African schools in a state of harmony, or projected harmony, with the main institutional orders. At the level of organization and ritual, however, the practices of these churches are more consistent with the practices in the wider society. Discrimination in the salaries of African school teachers and the segregation of African education find their counterpart in discrimination in the stipends of African ministers and in segregated worship. Conversely, the theoretical adjustment of African education to other institutional aspects has been accompanied by many disturbances in the African schools, though not necessarily by way of cause and effect.

It is in these varied combinations of tension and adjustment between institutional structures that some of the distinctive features of the occupational milieu of teachers, ministers, nurses, doctors, and civil servants are found, as well as some of the ambiguities in their status and prestige. Ambiguity in the position of the African teacher arises in part from the different expectations of the White bureaucracy, which employs him, and of his own people, who depend on him for Western skills. The ambiguity in the position of the African minister in English-speaking churches arises in part from the conflict between the doctrinal rejection of racial discrimination in all social spheres, and, at the same time, its routine practice within the church community itself. Indeed, the very fact of African advancement conflicts with many aspects of South African society and therefore creates ambiguity. In a society in which the most cultivated of urban Africans is required, under the pass laws, to bear documentary evidence of his right to be out at night after the curfew hour, and in which there is gross and systematic discrimination in all major aspects of life, the very concept of African scholar, African intellectual, African lawyer, and African doctor is ambiguous.

The occupation of trader introduces a different type of tension within the structure of South African society and its dominant ideology. To some extent, in theory at any rate, the occupations of African teacher, nurse, doctor, or clergyman can be given a racial definition and harmonized with apartheid. The teacher may be regarded as one who conveys African education, the doctor and the nurse as concerned with African disease and health, and the clergyman as dedicated to the curing of African souls. But it is more difficult to give a racial definition to trading and to conceive of the African trader as serving the African consumer, when the trader accumulates in the process such nonracial or at any rate non-African commodities as money, profit, and capital. Or to phrase the matter differently the White teacher serving White students is hardly in competition with the African teacher in an African school, whereas the African trader, by virtue merely of his carrying on as a trader, deprives the White trader of prospective profit.

From this inevitable competition, many dilemmas arise. For the Government, there is the insoluble problem of encouraging African trade in African areas as part of the promise of separate development and at the same time restricting its growth, lest the rise of an African trading class diminish the political power or the economic potential of the Afrikaners. For the African trader, there is the ambivalence between the promises of apartheid and the massive and burdensome reality of control and domination. Lacking in capital and experience, a newcomer in fields of established commercial enterprise, the African trader may feel a compelling need for protection from competition by way of a racial monopoly of trade in his own areas, or indeed with his own people. But a government which represents the interests of Whites, and more particularly the interests of an Afrikaner petite bourgeoisie, can only grant a token monopoly of such large opportunities for profit. Hence the African trader may see in racialism the path to salvation, but a racialism under African auspices, not Afrikaner. There may be special circumstances in the social context of African trade as compared with African professional life which drive sentiment and action with greater force toward racialism.

Part IV deals with the problem of choice from a different point of view, that of the organizational milieu, or, more precisely, the milieu of the voluntary associations. Even that term is not very precise, since I have included under it the statutory bodies—in which Africans are free to participate if they wish—and the churches. It is to a large extent in the major associations that the chaos of individual interpretations and inclinations becomes ordered into explicitly formulated alternatives of choice and action; and it is through the organized activities of these associations that powerful influences may be exerted toward racialism or nonracialism, and violence or nonviolence. At the same time, the associations provide the bourgeoisie with an arena in which to display their prowess and exalt their status. Two of the main themes of the study—the expression of occupational status and the problem of political choice—are thus drawn together in this section.

The main growth of formal associations takes place in the cities, where the basic pattern of life for Africans is laid down by the White authorities. They control or profoundly influence the character of African formal associations. Hence the relationship of Africans to Whites, that is to say the broader context of race relations, is crucial to the analysis of the organizational milieu. From this point of view, associations may be distinguished either as paternalist under White control, or as independent, which is to say substantially under African control (though not completely, since White domination is pervasive). This distinction has implications for the type of leadership and also for the choice between racialism and nonracialism—or rather the relative emphasis, as elements of both racialism and nonracialism are likely to be present in the same association. The racial composition is also relevant, since associations in which membership is interracial, racially exclusive, or a combination of the two, may be expected to exert different influences on the pattern of race relations either by withholding opportunity for contact or by providing varied social contexts for the experience of racial contact. So too, the relationship of the association's goals to the status quo—whether conservative of White interests, aimed at promoting social change in favor of Africans, or neutral but with a potential for change—bears directly on the problem of political choice.

My purpose is not to survey the whole range of African associations but rather to gain some insight into the organizational milieu of the African bourgeoisie, with particular reference to political choice. I have selected the predominantly African associations for detailed discussion, though I mention other types of association briefly in Part IV and also incidentally elsewhere in the study, as, for example, the interracial churches in the discussion of the occupational milieu of African ministers. The opening analysis of paternalism, in the context of the African Advisory Board to the Durban City Council, focuses on an episode, seemingly quite minor, which nevertheless provoked a boycott by the

African members, and reveals the forces of attraction and repulsion which act upon them. A study of the Advisory Boards offers some insight into the nature of the intercalary institutions established by Whites for the governance of Africans with their participation, and into the nature of the intercalary position of the Africans who man them. The Boards function within the framework of apartheid, but seem likely to induce an explosive combination of dependence on the White man and racialist rejection of him which is by no means conducive to the maintenance of apartheid. I cannot say whether this is characteristic of the many intercalary structures established by the Government, or under what conditions these structures may be expected to promote racialism or some measure of racial cooperation.

The remaining studies are of independent associations in sport and politics, the former permitted, indeed encouraged under certain conditions, and offering the relatively secure opportunities for leadership denied in the largely forbidden field of politics. Partly for this reason, considerable political energy may be expended in the struggles for leadership within the sports associations. The study of the Durban and District African Football Association (Chapter 22) shows marked oligarchical tendencies and acute tensions over leadership, finally resolved by fission. Paradoxically, sports associations with racially exclusive memberships actively promote nonracialism in sport. The crucial factor in this development appears to be the readiness of the international sports associations to apply sanctions against racialism in sport. By contrast, the United Nations offers far less effective encouragement of nonracialism in South African politics. In the final chapter of this section I analyze the pressures which impel the African political organizations toward violence and racialism.

This leads to the conclusion, in which I attempt to assess the specific role of the bourgeoisie and suggest that racial civil war is by no means inevitable. Sometimes it seems to me that the South African conflict is essentially an international conflict, as was the Spanish Civil War; that forces outside South Africa help to sustain White racialism and to nurture Black racialism; that these different forces of international racialism are preparing for a trial of strength with South Africa as the battleground. Peaceful solutions may be found by international agreement, within the framework of the United Nations.

This research was carried out in a time of troubles, or perhaps I should say in a time of acute troubles, since trouble seems endemic in South African society. I started field work toward the end of 1958 and continued until July 1961. The material I have gathered relates mainly to this period, though I have included relevant changes to 1964. These years seem to me a sort of watershed of revolutionary change.

They include massive disturbances, both urban and rural, spontaneous and politically directed; the establishment of a Republic and the withdrawal from the British Commonwealth of Nations; the declaration of a state of emergency, and indeed virtually a continuing state of emergency, as measured by the increasing assumption and exercise of arbitrary powers in the form of banning, exile, arrest without trial, house arrest, and proscription of political organizations. They also include preparations for violent conflict, with increasing mobilization of arms and men by the South African Government, the growth of sabotage and terrorism, and the beginnings of a Pan-African organization for the forceful liberation of Africans in South Africa.

These tensions and conflicts are part of the texture of this research, and not simply matter for observation and analysis. Situations of crisis illuminate hidden aspects of a relationship and may encourage voluble communication. They may therefore be of help in gaining qualitative insights of some depth, which was my major interest. But crises also raise barriers and introduce influences and distortions, the effects of which are difficult to assess. In any event, I had no choice, because of the continuing nature of the crises. Most of the teachers, for example, were interviewed during a period when the country was in a declared state of emergency. The alternative would have been to wait for less disturbed times. But these have not yet arrived. Indeed, I would suppose that the difficulties of communication have grown rather than diminished over the last few years.

This study continues earlier research interests. Arriving in Durban during the Defiance Campaign against Unjust Laws in 1952, I immediately became absorbed in the possibility of nonviolent change toward a democratic society. Later, assisted by my colleagues Hilstan Watts and Ronald Davies,[1] I analyzed the racial ecology of Durban, partly to explore the plans for the compulsory segregation of racial groups and partly to establish a basis for systematic sociological research in Durban. In *Durban: A Study in Racial Ecology* is to be found a description of the city and of the demography and ecological distribution of its peoples, based on the 1951 census. The concern with the problem of nonviolence persists in the present book, where the issue of violence is posed more sharply and urgently, reflecting the movement toward violent conflict. At the same time, *An African Bourgeoisie* further explores the sociology of Durban and of South Africa from the perspective of a particular segment of the population.

There begins to accumulate a body of sociological research in Durban —a study of race relations in an interracial neighborhood by Margo

---

1. Leo Kuper, Hilstan Watts, and Ronald Davies, *Durban: A Study in Racial Ecology* (New York, Columbia University Press, 1958).

Russell,[2] an analysis of the conversion of Indians to Catholicism by Teresa Currin,[3] and a study of sport and politics by Bernard Magubane.[4] Hamish Dickie-Clark is completing a study of the marginal situation of Coloreds in Durban and Fatima Meer is completing a work on suicide in Durban. Hilda Kuper[5] has contributed an anthropological study of the Indians of Natal; there are studies by economists in the Natal Regional Survey of population, life, and labor; and an interdisciplinary analysis of an African urban location by the Institute for Social Research of the University of Natal.[6] Apart from wide gaps in knowledge of the White population, a basis has been laid for more intensive research, and I hope that the sociological exploration of Durban will continue. The city has much to offer the sociologist: its varied economic bases as a port, a holiday resort, and an industrial and commercial center; its diversity of groups, with Africans numbering about 175,000, Coloreds almost 27,000, Indians 221,000, and Whites 185,000 (according to the final figures given for the 1960 census); and the almost infinite variety of its patterns of culture and situations of culture contact.

I could not have carried out this research into the African bourgeoisie but for help from African friends and, above all, the help of my research assistants, Bernard Magubane and Anthony Ngubo. Their views and insights appear throughout the book. I acknowledge my special thanks to them; to Margo Russell, Edna Miller, and Carlene Tanigoshi for help in checking manuscripts and processing materials; to the Department of Sociology and Social Work, University of Natal; to the Department of Bantu Administration, Durban; to the South African National Council for Social Research and the Institute for Social Research of the University of Natal for financial assistance; to the University of California, Los Angeles, for assistance in the final preparation of my manuscript; to Jane Olson and Elizabeth Swift for the editing of this book; and to my wife Hilda, who took over the inquiry into the nursing profession when I failed to make headway, and who has contributed the chapter on nurses and, always, much interest and encouragement.

L. K.

Los Angeles, California
August 1964

2. "A Study of a South African Interracial Neighbourhood," unpublished thesis for the master's degree (University of Natal, 1961).

3. "An Exploratory Study of the Roman Catholic Indian Minority, with Special Emphasis on the Sociological Aspects of Conversion," unpublished thesis for the master's degree (University of Natal, 1962).

4. "Sport and Politics in an Urban African Community," unpublished thesis for the master's degree (University of Natal, 1963).

5. *Indian People in Natal* (Pietermaritzburg, University of Natal Press, 1960).

6. *Baumanville, A Study of an Urban African Community* (Cape Town, Oxford University Press, 1959).

PART I

The Setting: Dilemmas of Choice

CHAPTER 1

An African Bourgeoisie

THE BOURGEOISIE, in Marxist theory, is the class which owns the means of production—and consequently wields political power—by control of the state and the propagation of the ideologies which promote its domination. Its basis is private property and the exercise of full civic rights in the protection and enhancement of that property. There are also psychological overtones to the term—an individualism flowing from enterprise rooted in private property, a respect for the laws which secure the established order, and a complacent system of ideas, a stockade against new and creative thought. In popular usage, the term suggests sober virtue and respectability resting on the solid mahogany of possessions. The proletariat stands in conflict with the bourgeoisie, opposing the private property from which the bourgeoisie derives its power, the state which is the instrument of that power, and the individualism which would frustrate a challenge to the bourgeoisie by means of the mass organization of workers.

Different levels may be distinguished within the bourgeoisie. There are the large landowners, the big industrialists and merchants, the bankers and financiers, and the chief executives of the giant economic corporations. They control the means of production, and embody the power and the splendor of the bourgeoisie. Attached to them and to the system from which they draw high rewards are the new categories of managerial and technical experts. And finally there is the petite bourgeoisie, set apart from the working class by its white-collar occupations and from the owners by its small stake in property and power. This category includes the petty traders, the professionals, the clerks, and the salesmen. In theory, the petite bourgeoisie aligns itself with the owners, aspires to their values, and keeps aloof from the working class. In certain circumstances, however, as the class conflict intensifies, sections of the petite bourgeoisie may combine with the proletariat in a revolutionary struggle.

Against this background, it may seem a verbal fantasy to describe as a bourgeoisie the African traders, professionals, and clerks with whom this study deals. The word itself was strange to some of the delegates at the annual conference of the Natal African Teachers' Union in 1961, and interpreted as "Bush Swazi." Their property rights are weak, in the sense that not much sanctity attaches to the little property they own. Even these meager rights they cannot protect—far less can they build a structure of power on the basis of private property. Their lack of property is linked with political subordination. Secure and remunerative employment may be regarded as a form of bourgeois property, but African employment is basically insecure and, on the whole, not very remunerative. It is difficult for Africans to maintain respectability under the pass laws, which control their freedom of movement and subject them to routine raids and surveillance by the police. And they have little incentive to respect the laws which encompass their inferiority, or to give their loyalty to a society which denies them the full enjoyment of their achievements.

They may seek fulfillment and emancipation in their own separate areas, along the lines of the South African Government's policy of apartheid, but the promise of industrial and commercial development, of thriving cities, of a series of independent states in the small backward rural African areas is brought by the Messiah of another nation. The Messianic prophecy in Judaism arose from a people suffering under foreign domination: this is its natural seedbed. In South Africa, there is the added unreality that the creator of the Messianic prophecy for the African peoples is, in many ways, the agent of their suffering. Emancipation, its tempo, conditions, and limits, lie in the discretion of an alien group of rulers, preoccupied with power, self-interest, and self-preservation. And the new world of the prophecy is the old world of African chiefs, an anachronism for educated and urban Africans in a continent of independent nation states.

Alternatively, Africans may seek fulfillment through evolutionary change in the structure of South African society. This was the hope of the early African leaders, as they manned their deputations and framed their petitions to the rulers, and as they modeled themselves on the pattern of the cultivated, moderate, bourgeois gentleman. The racial barriers would be raised and the doors would open to those who qualified by the standards of Christendom and of Western civilization. In this way, the area of liberty would gradually extend. Instead, the doors have been closed by the seemingly granite wall of racial separation, and the area of liberty has contracted. Racial definitions dominate the social situation, discriminating implacably between the life chances of the different racial groups, and breeding competing racialisms.

Mosca[1] writes that

1. J. H. Meisel, *The Myth of the Ruling Class* (Ann Arbor, University of Michigan Press, 1958), p. 147.

the absolute preponderance of a single political force, the predominance of any oversimplified concept in the organization of the state, the strictly logical application of any single principle in all public law are the essential elements in any type of despotism, whether it be a despotism based upon divine right or a despotism based ostensibly on popular sovereignty.

Certainly the consistent application of the ideology of racial separation in South Africa has been accompanied by a great inflation of the powers of the state. In particular, the lives of Africans are comprehensively regulated, their degrees of freedom narrowly defined. Protests seem ineffective, whether spontaneous in the form of mass murmurings and riots, or closely planned, as in the symbolic strikes and the mass demonstrations and marches. New laws and the more efficient mobilization of force control these challenges, which serve, then, on the one hand to perfect the machinery of domination and on the other hand to move the struggle for power in a more revolutionary direction.

None of these circumstances favor the label of bourgeoisie for any segment of the African population. Indeed, *proletariat* might seem more appropriate for all Africans. Color is the main basis for stratification. In some ways, the entire White group is a bourgeoisie in relation to Africans. White manual workers and petite bourgeoisie identify with the industrialists, financiers, and landowners in domination over the non-Whites. They share common and valuable rights in this domination, which secures to them the best work opportunities, high rates of pay, and other material rewards, prestige, and power. There is no parliamentary party representing labor. The parliamentary struggle is largely between groups of preferential White shareholders over the dividends, and some of the nuances, of domination.

Africans similarly share a common destiny in many essential respects. Neither education nor wealth emancipates them from the indelible racial status. Lack of property combines with political subordination to fix the seal of hereditary inequality. Its source is transparent to many African leaders— not an immutable divine dispensation or law of nature, but very secular and changeable social institutions. Law and justice are no manna falling from Heaven to the faithful supplicant, but a measure of the distribution of power. Salvation lies in the wresting of power from the oppressors by means of the organization of the internal resources of the oppressed.

The relations between the racial groups suggest elements of a proletarian struggle in the contemporary South African scene. But the class struggle is only one of many strands. To identify the racial conflict with conflict between White bourgeoisie and Black proletariat would obscure as much as it illuminates. The races do not confront each other as solid antagonistic blocs. Cooperation and interdependence are more marked than conflict and separation. Social relationships extend across the racial barriers, weaving complex and varied patterns of interracial contact and creating common interests transcending those of race. Even the policy of racial separation, by virtue of its inner contradictions, forges new links and new mechanisms of integration.

Shared privileges and common domination do not guarantee the unity of the rulers. There is an uneven distribution of power among the members of the ruling White group. Not all Whites display the lineaments of gratified desire. The special interests of different language groups, industrialists, religious denominations, and educators disturb solidarity under the policy of racial separation. At the political level, a few White "bridge builders" identify with non-Whites in revolutionary struggle, or experiment with new formulas for evolutionary change toward democracy or with modifications of the ruling ideology. At other levels too, there is more diversity of behavior in race relations. Greater rigidity has its counterpart in greater flexibility. Around the superficially solid core of racial separation is a fluid area of discovery and change. Subtle new forms of paternalism veil the old patriarchal paternalism and obscure the self-interest of the father. Desegregation attracts a variety of White sponsors and displays unexpected facets— petrifaction and flux, unity and diversity.

There is no easy unity for Africans, either, no solid identity of interests, whether defined objectively or from an African point of view. A wide gulf separates the traditional from the Westernized. Depending on the perspective, the system of Bantu Authorities introduced by the Government promises the chiefs a restoration of power or destroys the last vestiges of their power. The Bantu Affairs Department of the central Government offers some opportunity for educated Africans, but only to serve an ideology of racial separation which many of them reject as a frustration of their hopes. African ministers of religion may seek fulfillment as leaders of separatist churches, or identify with radical political movements, or concentrate on the hereafter, or work against discrimination in the White-dominated churches to which they belong. Traders, independent professionals, teachers, nurses, civil servants, clerks, migrant laborers, and other manual workers have their distinctive occupational interests.

Only in the very general sense of freedom or emancipation can the objective interests of Africans be described as identical, and even then it is by no means clear what proportion so perceive their interests. Certainly there is divergence in the interpretation of ends and in the selection of means. At the more specific level of immediate life chances and style of life, the occupational groups described here as a bourgeoisie show many of the characteristics conventionally associated with a social and economic class. A common subjection has not stifled class differentiation within the African community, nor has the low ceiling placed on their achievements prevented Africans from drawing distinctions among themselves. This is not a unique phenomenon, as is demonstrated by rivalry for prestige between scheduled castes in India. Since the range of differentiation is narrow, the distinctions drawn are more fine, sometimes appearing to the outside observer as distinctions without difference. Perhaps the rejection by the dominant group, the strength of the pressures toward an equal subordination, and the limited scope for achievement stimulate, under certain conditions, differentiating tendencies rather than the reverse.

A variety of characteristics differentiates the bourgeoisie of this study. The parental background of the educated is distinctive. To be born of educated parents enhances life chances among Africans as it does in the wider South African society. In terms of rewards, the foremost among the African bourgeoisie, with some exceptions, may rank little higher than the least among the Whites. But their modest earnings are still sufficient to raise them above the general level of the African community and to permit qualitative differences in their style of life. In public life, their opportunities may be more limited than those of an uncultivated White man, but the educated have a better understanding of urban industrial society and of the modern state than the mass of Africans and occupy many of the command positions in African society. Their roles as leaders, their higher earnings and education, and their mode of life patterned on that of the White middle class promote ease of association within their own ranks and give rise to subjective sentiments of class differences.

This social awareness is heightened by the structure of race relations in South Africa and by the simultaneous use of two conflicting systems of evaluation:—the achievement of status by individual effort and the ascription of status by race. Within the African community, achievement in the fields of education and trade is sufficiently rare to win an exaggerated recognition and prestige. Within the wider society, in relations with the dominant group, race as the main criterion of status divests African achievement of true significance. There is thus both an exaggeration and a frustration of achievement. Furthermore, the contacts of the African bourgeoisie with Whites are mainly at the level of the lower strata of petty officials and policemen, so that the higher racial status but low achievement of the Whites confronts the higher achievement but low racial status of the Africans. The resulting tensions engender a more acute awareness of social disabilities precisely within the class of the African bourgeoisie.

The same consequence flows also from the circumstance that it is this class which has provided many of the new leaders in the independent

African states. These leaders have achieved international recognition by virtue of the importance of Africa in the struggle between America and Russia rather than the power of the states they rule. Their world stature, derived partly from race—precisely the fact that they are Africans—accentuates the anguish of hereditary racial inequality in South Africa. The pressure for social change is felt most keenly by the African bourgeoisie. The lives of the peasantry and the proletariat are not likely to be radically transformed in the near future. The bourgeoisie, on the other hand, has the world to gain if the conditions in other parts of Africa could prevail in South Africa.

The term bourgeoisie is thus chosen not only to describe the upper occupational categories in African society with certain tendencies to class formation but also to emphasize in terms of social change and prospective power their role at the apex of subordination. It is their interests which will shape African action and aspiration, perhaps along evolutionary lines through the raising of the color bar and progressive recognition of achievement. Or the bourgeoisie, thrown back on the African masses by the denial of entry into the dominant society, may interact with them to forge a nationalist movement with the goal of African domination, in which case the development would be from political power to bourgeois property, and not from property to power. Or the bourgeoisie may be divided, and sections may seek fulfillment in a revolutionary struggle aimed at the creation of a socialist state and the destruction of bourgeois property.

CHAPTER 2

Mass Murmurings

THE MANY CRISES in the years of my research, 1959 to 1961, seemed
the precursors of revolutionary change. The crises open with the spontaneous violence of disorganized masses. They end with the calculated
violence of the saboteur. And they include, with rising tension, the
massacre at Sharpeville, the march on Cape Town, the declaration of
a state of emergency, "insurrection" in the Transkei, withdrawal from
the Commonwealth of Nations, inauguration of the Republic of South
Africa, and the massive suppression of anti-Republic demonstrations
on that occasion.

My diary of events in the second half of June 1959, based on a
summary of newspaper reports, mainly in Natal, opens with the following items:

> June 16, 1959, *Natal Daily News:*[1] Cato Manor Emergency Camp
> Welfare and Development Board objects to the appointment of a
> White clerk to replace an African clerk at its monthly meetings.
> African chairman says it is contrary to Government policy. Meet-
> ing adjourns as no agreement can be reached.

> June 17, 1959, *Natal Mercury:* Demolition of Tin Town (in Cato
> Manor, Durban) reveals 25 liquor stills. The profit from liquor
> sales is one of the main reasons why people do not want to leave
> Cato Manor. Police raids have had little effect. Officials favor a
> ration of White liquor being granted.

> June 18, 1959, *Natal Mercury:* Two hundred African women
> armed with sticks and pick handles storm Cato Manor Beer Hall,
> smashing pots, spilling beer, stoning police. Chase African men
> out of beer hall, saying they should get liquor from the women and
> not from the beer hall. Police sent to disperse the crowd. Mr.
> Bourquin [Director of Durban's Bantu Administration Depart-
> ment] says women are seeking retaliation for the destruction of
> stills under Cato Manor slum clearance scheme.

1. Now the *Daily News*. I have retained the old name throughout, as also in the case of the
Golden City Post, which has been changed to *Post*.

June 18, 1959, *Natal Daily News:* "Large numbers" of African women demonstrate outside Cato Manor, Dalton Road, and Victoria Street beer halls. These three beer halls closed. Three thousand women baton charged at Cato Manor, by several hundred police armed with Sten guns, rifles, and submachine guns, after a parley with the Director of Bantu Administration, Durban. Women say they will picket all beer halls in Durban and Pinetown tomorrow. Women smash beer containers and spill 1,000 gallons of beer at Victoria Street, warning men not to patronize the beer halls. Two hundred women pelt male drinkers at Dalton Road Beer Hall with mugs and hit them with sticks. Tear gas used against crowd at Dalton Road. Mr. Bourquin says that the disturbances are not solely a retaliation for the destruction of Cato Manor liquor stills. Natal employers agree that an immediate improvement in the lot of unskilled African labor is required.

June 19, 1959, *Rand Daily Mail:* Fifteen thousand Africans camp in hills, singing anthems and chanting, surrounding the area where earlier police opened fire on 5,000 African women, and again on crowds of advancing Africans. Fires burning all over Cato Manor and Chesterville. Municipal buildings and recreation hall at Chesterville, medical clinic and schools burnt. Women shouting to men "Don't be cowards. Kill them [the police]." Attempts made to destroy electricity supply to Cato Manor Beer Hall. Road block set up by rioters. Cars and buses being halted and searched. Deputy Commissioner of Police says situation is "electric and fluid." Search lights erected overlooking Cato Manor. White officials evacuated from Bantu Administration offices in Cato Manor.

June 19, 1959, *Natal Daily News:* Eight-hour wave of arson, destruction, and pillage began at 4 P.M. on June 18 after police baton charged women at beer hall, and dispersed them. Attacks were then directed against municipal buses, African- and Indian-owned buses being allowed to pass. Destroyed or damaged [particulars given in *Natal Daily News* of June 30, 1959]—seven of the eleven Cato Manor community welfare huts, Lutheran Church, offices of Bantu Administration at Cato Manor, and security police barracks, all Indian shops except one, as well as garage, municipal clinic, and X-ray office, all municipal shops occupied by Africans, with the exception of one or two, burned or looted, doctor's consulting and dispensing rooms damaged, Chesterville Community Center. Official death roll—four men from gunshot wounds, thirteen with bullet injuries, eleven with injuries from other causes. Saracens [armored cars used by the police] are moved from Grahamstown to Durban.

A year later, in mid-June 1960, the country is in a state of emergency, proclaimed by the Governor-General on April 1, 1960, because, in his opinion, it appears that "circumstances have arisen in the areas specified in the attached Schedule which seriously threaten the safety of the public and the maintenance of public order, and the ordinary law of the land is inadequate to enable the Government to ensure the safety of the public and to maintain public order." A proclamation on April 2 provides for the mobilization of a portion of the citizen force. The situation is analogous to martial law. Many thousands lie in gaol, detained without trial as political prisoners, or rounded up and secretly sentenced in gaol for infringements of the pass and related laws.

My diary carries the following items:

> June 16, 1960, *Natal Daily News:* A member of the Malan Liquor Commission says that Cato Manor and Sharpeville disturbances persuaded the Commission to amend their report, making provision for Africans to buy spirits.
>
> At the Commission of Inquiry into the Sharpeville disturbances, Advocate Kentridge attacks the police on nine points.
>
> 1. Officers made no attempt at nonviolent dispersal of crowd.
> 2. They did not warn the crowd to disperse.
> 3. They did not warn that force would be used if the crowd did not disperse.
> 4. They failed to supervise and control their men.
> 5. They took no steps to ensure that the shooting would be limited if it did start.
> 6. Constables shot without orders.
> 7. Constables shot to kill (eight women and ten children were among those killed).
> 8. The shooting was indiscriminate and continued after the crowd turned and ran.
> 9. There was no need to fire and no justification for police conduct.
>
> June 17, 1960, *Natal Daily News:* Sharpeville inquiry ends with address by the Attorney-General for the Orange Free State. He claims that the demonstration was entirely organized by the Pan-Africanist Congress, and that the people had no intention of being arrested. Police evidence showed that the crowd shouted "Police Dogs! Unless you arrest us all, we will burn down your building," and "Cato Manor!" [Nine policemen had been murdered in Cato Manor on January 24, 1960.] The police officers must be vindicated—they saw the position and knew the danger.

June 19, 1960, *Sunday Times:* Report on hut burning in the Transkei. Police vans move into the Transkei, smoldering with unrest. Rebel leaders mainly illiterate tribesmen. No man goes unarmed at night.

June 20, 1960, *Natal Daily News:* Fresh outburst of hut burning at Bizana.

June 21, 1960, *Natal Mercury:* Government appoints team of experts to investigate unrest in the Transkei. Strong police patrols maintained. Mr. Stanford, parliamentary representative of Africans in the Transkei, says that he has repeatedly warned the Government of the almost total refusal of Africans in the Transkei to accept the Bantu Authorities system.

June 21, 1960, *Natal Daily News:* The Minister of Bantu Administration denies that the trouble involves Bantu Authorities. The Chief Bantu Commissioner for the area says agitators have fomented misunderstandings about the Bantu Authorities system.

June 22, 1960, *Natal Mercury:* Chief Bantu Commissioner says that a period of peace is expected, and that there is no violence in the Bizana, Flagstaff, or Lusikisiki areas since he addressed a series of meetings some days ago. In his view, it is an exaggeration to suggest that there is unrest in the Transkei from the Kei to the borders of Natal: there are occasional faction fights throughout the territories and these have been going on for years. The disturbances in Eastern Pondoland are purely tribal.

June 24, 1960, *Natal Mercury:* Hut burning continues in Bizana. Police, Saracens, and helicopters continue to patrol. Rumors of the resignation of the Paramount Chief Botha Sicgau in favor of his brother are officially denied.

The following year, in mid-June 1961, the country seems quiet as its peoples again take up the normal routines of life which had been threatened as much by the Government's mobilization of violence as by the planned non-White "stay at home" demonstration against Government policy. It is a period of brief calm after the catharsis of hope and fear, triumph and anguish.

The extent of political motivation, that is to say, the presence or absence of political planning and objectives, provides a rough basis for grouping the major racial conflicts of this period. At one extreme is the murmuring of the masses—although the word "murmur" is a euphemism for much violence—and at the other extreme, the specifically political campaign. In this chapter, I discuss the spontaneous action of the African masses; in the next, the political campaigns and the dilemma of political choice of means.

In the murmuring of the masses, the reaction is provoked by some specific incident. It is spontaneous—the similar reactions of people in the same social situation. A somewhat amorphous pattern of action begins to emerge and attracts participants, who achieve a measure of cohesion under the pressure of events. During this process, self-selected leaders may appear, bloom for a brief period, and then fade again into obscurity.

The forms of action taken in these spontaneous racial conflicts are surprisingly stereotyped. It seems reasonable to expect that since deep emotions are aroused, their expression would be varied, wayward, and unpredictable, and yet in South Africa the expression of open racial conflict appears to be narrowly confined. Perhaps the explanation is that the deeper the emotion, the more limited the range of action, since the imaginative calculation of alternatives would be excluded.

Conventions seemingly govern spontaneous violence. Protracted disturbances among the racial groups in Durban are almost certain to include at some stage the stoning and burning of buses by Africans, even when the issue is in no way related to the transport service. Similarly, police action is a regular component, often in the form of the sudden and violent dispersal of mass demonstrations. Characteristically, race riots in South Africa involve the police and Africans, since the police are the main agents of racial aggression, to which the African reaction is likely to be the destruction of government and municipal property in the locations (the segregated, often fenced-off areas of living to which urban Africans are largely confined) and sometimes of schools and churches.

The stereotyping of violence may be explained partly by the influence of past actions in a relevant context, such as Africans burning Indian-owned buses in the anti-Indian riots of 1949, or the boycott by African women of the beer halls introduced to Natal in 1928. These actions become part of the experience of the masses, and are established in the repertoire of violence and of protest. The people become conditioned to a specific pattern of stimulus and response. A more far-reaching explanation is that the situation is so controlled and so structured that the possibilities of action are severely restricted. Suppose that Africans living in a location are deeply aggrieved, and that they have demonstrated in mass and suffered violent dispersal by the police. How are they to act if they turn to violence? The only weapons readily available to them are stones, matches, and such sticks and domestic articles as have not been confiscated under the laws forbidding the possession of dangerous weapons. They can stone, burn, pummel, or break down.

The agents of their suffering will usually be well-protected, well-armed, or far removed from the location. Violence may be directed against the police or against such Whites as happen to be near the scene of the disturbances, but, in general, members of the White group are not likely to be present or vulnerable. Violence thus turns from persons to property. In much the same way that the workers initially attacked the machines, and not the bourgeois conditions of production, so too Africans, in these spontaneous outbursts, are not attacking the system of racial domination or its representatives but the concrete symbols of domination, and indeed any of the accessible works of the White man. They burn the offices of the Bantu Administration, they set on fire buses belonging to the Durban City Corporation, they sometimes settle private scores, and in the process they also destroy churches, schools, and clinics which serve the community.

There is nothing in this behavior to suggest that Africans are in any way strange or different or barbarous, as White observers are often inclined to think. There is nothing baffling about "the senseless manner in which these people have destroyed the things that have been provided for their own good," contrary to the views of the Durban police commandant during the beer hall disturbances (*Sunday Tribune*, June 21, 1959). Certainly the behavior is senseless, but it is perfectly intelligible. How else could the aroused passions be discharged, if not in the destruction of the White man's property? What other avenues for action were open?

The police and the Government hold the initiative, and can experiment freely and innovate. They have certainly improved the machinery for domination. They have borrowed new techniques from totalitarian regimes, such as mass trials, imprisonment without trial, secrecy, mystification, and terror. The police are armed with more efficient weapons for wounding, mutilating, and annihilating in mass. The vast armory of penal laws offers an equally destructive potential. Criminal sanction, armored cars, and machine guns have replaced the rifles of the early conflicts, while the disarmament of Africans largely reduces them, from shield and assagai, to natural objects and domestic appliances.

And yet official action has the same stereotyped quality as the violence of the African masses. Presumably over the long period of contact, well-tested techniques for the handling of Africans have crystallized into traditions and rituals of domination, to which the single-minded application of the doctrines of apartheid lends a sacred rigidity. Move and countermove are highly predictable, following a few set patterns. It is like a game of chess, played on a board with a few squares and a few simple chessmen. An unconventional gambit, the march of 30,000 African demonstrators on a central police station in Cape Town at the end of March 1960, almost transformed the pattern of South African race relations. And so too, in the future, the intrusion of some new element from the outside world, or the creative use of new forms of conflict within South Africa, might gain for the Africans a surprise victory. As it is, the institutional structure of South African society appears strong enough to contain the conventionalized forms of racial conflict.

The many murmurings of the masses in the period under survey include a series of disturbances initiated by the beer hall demonstrations with which this chapter opened, a number of rural episodes originally involving tanks for the dipping of cattle but spreading to other issues, and the murder of nine policemen at Cato Manor, at that time a vast straggle of shacks which housed fully half the African families in Durban. They are described as murmurings because they are not motivated politically, and tend to be spontaneous and unorganized, but political aspects do enter in. Africans have a major asset in their relatively large numbers, and the hopes of African leaders for internal change rest on the political education and organization of the African masses. Realistically, African politicians must identify with the masses during a disturbance, or become alienated from them. They must seek to give constructive political direction to actions which might otherwise turn to self-destruction and disillusionment.

Moreover, the line between the political and the nonpolitical is not easily drawn. Political decisions affect the very basis of subsistence. Apartheid laws regulate in comprehensive detail much of the routine of African life and awaken many resentments. The incident which provokes a disturbance may arise from a specific grievance, but this is embedded in a common matrix of grievances, widely felt and increasingly articulated. Hence the demonstrators may move rapidly from the initial issue, such as the brewing of beer, to the issues of low wages and control over influx into the town, and to the general rejection of the White man. This is not necessarily evidence that the professional politician is at hand. The total nature of apartheid impels in that direction. Its systematic application ensures an impact throughout the country, establishing a common basis of experience and suffering, which results also from the compulsory removal of townsmen to the rural areas. Apartheid is a political baptism even for the unsophisticated.

The beer hall disturbances started at Cato Manor. The destruction of stills immediately before the events gave some plausibility to the charge that responsibility lay with the shebeen queens, who market illicit liquor. In fact, liquor raids and prosecutions were among the main grievances voiced by the women. They complained that the permits given residents to brew a limited amount of beer served as traps, because the people with whom residents enjoyed their drink, even their own sons, were arrested, charged, and fined. And since it was not the Zulu custom for men to drink on their own, they went to the municipal beer halls and were picked up by the police on their way home, losing in fines what remained of their meager earnings.[2] However, the grievances extended far beyond the issue of beer drinking. They included low wages, the demolition of homes, deportation of residents on loss of employment, and lack of opportunity for the young people.

The Director of the Durban Bantu Administration Department felt that the women did not really understand the nature of their grievances, that they emphasized symptoms rather than root causes.

> Even the women who started off this tragic course did not express their grievances in terms of bare, basic and intrinsic facts. They have talked about Kafir beer and illicit liquor, transport and housing, shack removals and influx control, the keeping of live-stock and the keeping of husbands, gambling dens and of shebeens. They have talked about those subjects as if they mattered for their own sakes. Only here and there did the real, naked reason break to the surface—money or rather lack of it. . . . The basic and ultimate reason is an economic one. The poverty of the urban Bantu; the discrepancy between his earning capacity and his cost of living; his inability to meet the demands of modern times in a city modeled on the Western way of life; his inability even to meet the barest necessity of life, to feed, clothe, educate and house him-self and his family [*Natal Mercury*, June 24, 1959].

Poverty was certainly a crucial issue, aggravated by a policy of shack demolition and the withholding of capital expenditure in an area which Africans were required to evacuate; aggravated too by continuous liquor raids, pass raids, and the application of influx control, based on the assumption that Africans are merely temporary residents in the urban areas. More fundamentally, the issue was one of racial domination and discrimination. It is characteristic of this type of movement that the demonstrators react to specific and tangible aspects. Where a political protest movement concentrates a campaign on a symptom, such as the pass laws, the campaign is usually a tactical maneuver in a strategy directed against the system itself, and there is a deliberate element in the selection of target. In the spontaneous movements, the actors are absorbed in the immediate and associated grievances, and it is these which make the direct emotional impact and dominate perception.

There are many indications of the spontaneous and unsophisticated nature of the beer hall movement. The first woman to speak for the demonstrators outside the Cato Manor Beer Hall was neither an elected nor a recognized leader; she took the lead because silence followed the Director's request that the women state their case. Later, by invitation,

---

2. In 1961, the Liquor Amendment Act removed the prohibition against the purchase of liquor by Africans from bottle stores, but shebeens persist.

she attended a meeting of the African National Congress, and was much impressed. It was the first time, she explained in an interview, that she had been to a church meeting where they spoke about the grievances of the people. In another demonstration, the women demanded to see the Corporation. When forty White and thirty Black policemen arrived, the women refused to hand over their weapons. "They swung their sticks in the face of the policemen, and lifted their dresses to the policemen as they danced. Their attitude was threatening" (*Natal Mercury*, July 16, 1959). Tribal dancing and other traditional maneuvers, and the inability to distinguish between a church meeting and a political gathering, reflect the political naiveté.

The destruction of property followed a baton charge against the women, in the conventional gambit. Juveniles and *tsotsis* (destructive gangs of young African men, rejected by the society) became active in arson and pillage. Apart from the destructive climax, however, the movement was remarkable for the dominant role of the traditionally subordinate Zulu women. An unconscious expression of this subordination emerged in an interview with one of the Cato Manor women who complained that the police had beaten them. "No one has the right to beat a woman, only her husband," she stated. For the most part, in the more controlled phases of the movement, the men were deliberately excluded, and the women acted and spoke for themselves. In the context of the traditional minority status of the Zulu woman, who is almost always under the guardianship of her father or husband or husband's relative, the militant emancipation of the women in these movements suggests the beginnings of a suffragette movement. And there was a certain contagion—the same pattern of beer hall demonstrations spread widely among the women of Durban and further afield.

The involvement of the women meant the deeper involvement of the men. They were embittered by the baton charges against the women, by their arrest and imprisonment. They were shamed by the militant role of the women, by the imputation that they were allowing them to fight their battles because police action would be less violent against women than against men. But above all, women represent the home. During the Cato Manor disturbances, the women sang: "You touch women, you touch grinding stones." The militancy of the women threatens the family hearth. In consequence, political consciousness has been heightened among the Zulu people.

While the beer hall demonstrations were spreading outward, together with an occasional stoning of municipal buses, and while the women were being arrested and tried, tension began to develop in the rural areas of Natal. Again women led the movement: they destroyed cattle and dipping tanks because they were obliged to maintain them without reward—a characteristic violent murmuring. Direct political action was, however, interwoven with this movement—deputations demanded a minimum wage of £1 per day for the men, the abolition of pass registration for women, and the relaxation of influx control and taxation.

The most serious disturbance was at Harding in rural Natal. Tribesmen marched on the town to free their women, who had been convicted for destruction of government property in protest against a land resettlement scheme. Some farmlands were burnt, and the White population armed itself against the tribesmen. At St. Faith's, near Port Shepstone, more than 1,200 African women armed with sticks and clubs demonstrated against the poll tax and influx regulations. African men who came too close to the women were driven away. Police stood by, armed with Sten guns and rifles, bayonets fixed. They were joined by two Saracens, which the women received with derision. The *Natal Mercury* of August 18, 1959, carried pictures of emotional and militant tribal dancing, of the police and armored cars drawn up in a line facing the women, and of a lone African woman waving her stick in defiance of a Saracen. The demonstration was led by an African woman doctor wearing the colors of the African National Congress. Chanting, tribal dancing, frenzy, prayer, deputation, and Congress songs provided a strange potpourri of tradition, culture change, and political baptism. Meanwhile at Maritzburg, African boys set fire to schools in a minor reverberation of the Cato Manor disturbances.

According to a newspaper report, by August 21, 1959, more than 10,000 women, excluding those in the Cato Manor demonstrations, had taken part in the disturbances, and 624 Africans, mainly women, had been sentenced to a total of 168 years of imprisonment and/or fines totaling £7,130 (*Natal Mercury*, August 21, 1959). And the movement was still active. In October, a peaceful deputation to the Government's commissioner at Ixopo complained of the burden of taxation and influx control. The women were told to submit their grievances to their men, who would then inform the tribal chief, and the tribal chief would pass on their complaints to the commissioner. The commissioner insisted on the use of the correct bureaucratic channels, in accordance with a directive from the Secretary of the Bantu Affairs Department. Discussions should not be held with the masses of women and their so-called leaders, but with recognized chiefs and responsible male leaders. The recognition of women's demonstrations on the lines favored by Whites, among whom women enjoy a different status, could only have the harmful, dangerous effect of undermining the structure of the community (*Natal Daily News*, August 21, 1959). The Secretary clearly did not view the emancipation of women as part of the Government's policy of modern tribalism.

A White police contingent arrived, armed with pickhandles, sjamboks, and Sten guns (according to a report in the *Golden City Post*, October

11, 1959). The women were ordered to disperse. They knelt in prayer, but apparently without immediate effect on the officials or the Almighty, since they were summarily sentenced at an improvised open-air court to individual fines of £35 or four months' imprisonment. Bail money was raised after part of the period of imprisonment had been served, and the sentences were later set aside on appeal.

Mopping-up operations by the police and the courts gave further occasion for demonstrations, sometimes peaceful, sometimes violent, but always extending the political involvement of the masses. The murder of nine policemen in Cato Manor on January 24, 1960, was not related to the disturbances: a chance occurrence during a routine liquor raid inflamed the masses. But the trial itself gained a certain political significance. For many Africans, the murder of the policemen had something of the quality of reprisals during a state of war. They felt that the accused were the police force and the oppressive Government, that these were ultimately responsible.

The nature of the mass disturbances, their sudden eruption, the excitation by the women, the high passion of mob action, and the pervasiveness of suffering make violence inevitable and difficult to control. African political leaders condemned the violence and sought to restrain their people, to direct their activities in a politically constructive way. They recognized, however, the circumstances provoking violence. The African chairman of the Locations Combined Advisory Boards of Durban, commented that

> the African women of Natal have demonstrated that the sufferings endured by many families cannot be described in constitutional words. It is the voice of oppressed people who have no other means of voicing their grievances before the governments of the land . . . I do not blame them. I lay the blame at the door of the multiplicity of the laws and their regulations, which are harshly administered by men who do not show sympathy. Men and women in urban areas and rural areas suffer and feel the same.

One of the demonstrators expressed the point more graphically: In destroying a dipping tank, the people had written a letter which the Government would read (*Drum*, October 1959, p. 24).

The difficulty is that the African people have no effective constitutional means for lightening their burdens. Deputations may help to forge unity. They may inform the world of the disabilities of the non-Whites. As Chief Luthuli, President of the African National Congress, expressed it, "A child that does not cry may die unnoticed, carried by its mother on her back." But the cry to assuage suffering, the reasoned petition, and the gentlemanly deputation have been of little avail in South Africa. Their use implies the belief that certain universal sentiments of justice, morality, and compassion can be evoked by a proper appeal. Reason and morality undoubtedly do exert an influence on the relationships between groups. They appear, however, to be related to the distribution of power. Where it is relatively even, discrimination is hardly feasible and is likely to be repugnant to reason and morality.

Systematic discrimination in South Africa is not accidental, an unfortunate oversight, a moral lapse. It is a deliberate policy, justified as being necessary to the survival of the White man, and it protects a massive superstructure of privileged opportunities for wealth, power, and prestige. Principles of justice and morality have been redefined so as to provide an ethical foundation for the system. It will be changed by a demonstration of strength when the racial groups are joined in conflict, not by an appeal to morality. Deputations and petitions may readily be interpreted as weakness. Like the act of kneeling in prayer before a deity, they imply voluntary submission, prostration before the rulers.

The violence of the mass disturbances, on the other hand, is a raw display of power. Petitions may evaporate in the correct bureaucratic channels, while dramatic action and violence evoke an immediate response. During the beer hall disturbances, for example, the Director of the Durban Bantu Administration Department and the Natal Chamber of Industries spoke of the need for higher African wages. So as to avoid the impression that riots bring higher wages, the Durban Chamber of Commerce gave added support only later, in October 1959. The impression remains, however, that violence may be more effective than nonviolence. This has been one of the major issues facing African leaders. What are the relative advantages and disadvantages of violence and nonviolence? And if violence is more immediately effective, can its use be justified?

CHAPTER 3

Dilemma of Choice: Violence–Nonviolence

FOR MANY YEARS, the main African political organizations followed a policy, or strategy, of nonviolence. Over the last decade in particular, they experimented with a variety of militant nonviolent techniques—mass demonstration, boycott, civil disobedience, and the withholding of labor. Where violence attended the campaigns, it was not by design; the typical reaction of mass violence was often provoked by the forceful intervention of the police.

The selection of specific issues in these campaigns was related to the need for mass appeal and their relevance to the ultimate goal of liberation. Pass laws, which restrict freedom of movement, limit the right to seek work, and impose a curfew, were an obvious target. They lay the foundations for White domination and continuous police surveillance of African life—they place the stamp of office routine on midnight raids and mass arrests and give legal sanction to rule by force. At the same time, the African masses perceive the pass laws as a major cause of their suffering, and their support is generally assured in anti-pass campaigns.

Other issues of major political significance to the leaders may fail to evoke a response from the masses. This is the inevitable difficulty of working downward from the top. Most African leaders are drawn from the educated bourgeoisie, and they often become absorbed in ideological issues remote from the interest of the workers. The remedy might be found in a continuous ferment of activity on the model of a doctor armed with pillboxes and injections. Something will be specific, something will take, something will succeed in innoculating against mass apathy and in injecting political sophistication. But the result may be disillusionment, not political fervor, as greater repression follows the nonviolent campaigns. The masses may become estranged from the leaders and reject disciplined political action, a situation conducive to sporadic mob violence.

Where the movement develops spontaneously, the involvement of the masses is assured. The leaders might therefore allow the Government the initiative in provoking mass action by its policies. Mass action,

however, is often a source of embarrassment to the leaders, especially
when expressed in violence and on issues of little or no political relevance. Since the leaders must identify with their people, they are obliged
to give the issues political significance and at the same time to resolve
the problem of both rejecting and sympathetically interpreting the
violence.

The most favorable combination of circumstances for African political action is a spontaneous movement of the people against one of
the supporting pillars of the system, which ensures the participation of
the masses as well as their emotional involvement in politically significant issues. This occurred in Pondoland, eastern Transkei, and assumed
the dimensions of an insurrection against Bantu Authorities.

The system of Bantu Authorities consists of a promise and a reality.
The promise is the creation of independent Bantu states or Bantustans
on the model of the independent states of Africa. In them there will be
no laws to restrict soaring aspiration. Africans will serve their own
people as doctors, lawyers, dentists, engineers, teachers, administrators,
industrialists, and merchants, and they will shape their own destiny,
giving expression to their unique ethnic essence. Only the date for this
self-realization remains uncertain, though preparatory steps toward self-
government, in the form of a Legislative Assembly with specified
powers, have been taken in the African rural reserve of the Transkei,
ostensibly by way of preamble to the Promised Land.

An elaborate ritual attends the conception and parturition of Bantu
Authorities. There are the Commissioners-General appointed by the
Government, the black jackets and pinstripes of an ambassadorial priesthood; the ceremonial investiture of chiefs, with a traditional exchange
of gifts—animal skins to the White officials, briefcases to the Black
chiefs—and bread and circuses in the form of slaughtered beasts and
beer; and there are the hymns to tribal glory sung by White trouba-
dours. Here the power of the White man is displayed in a comic opera
of equality with the Black man, indeed of homage to his tribal essence.
Here backward tribal reserves are in a state of Messianic transformation
to satellite bucolic Ruritanias.

The reality is more mundane and more immediate. Under the Bantu
Authorities Act of 1951, the Government's policy is to establish a
pyramid of authority in the African areas—district, tribal, regional, and
territorial authorities. The selection of personnel is effectively controlled
by the Government. Chiefs are given the positive inducement of increased powers and the negative inducement of avoiding deposition and
banishment. During the period from January 1, 1955, to July 18, 1958,
thirty-five chiefs or headmen were deposed for a variety of official
reasons, including ill health, mental abnormality, conviction on a criminal charge, addiction to alcohol, dereliction of duty, weak administra-

tion, and generally unsatisfactory conduct over a long period.[1] These official explanations are difficult to assess, since the powers of deposition are arbitrarily exercised. Eccentricity and an inclination for drink and leisure in a chief who supports Bantu Authorities may appear as abnormality, drunkenness, and gross neglect in one who opposes the system. In any event, the establishment of Bantu Authorities coincided with the deposition of several chiefs and headmen, and the impression is widely current that deposition and banishment are the penalties for opposition. This is a sufficient deterrent for all but the most brave or the most diplomatic of chiefs.

Moreover, the increased powers of the chiefs, and especially their repressive powers, though real enough, are wielded by the direction of an alien group. The chief does not rule his people, with the aid of his council, in the traditional manner. He rules by the indulgence of a foreign government, administering its policies and its laws, and accountable to its bureaucracy. Chiefs are effectively relegated to the lower levels of this foreign bureaucracy, forming the base of the bureaucratic pyramid.[2] It is on this domesticated role of the chiefs that Bantu Authorities rest. In the towns, the policy is that tribal ambassadors and Bantu Urban Councils be established to provide a mechanism for linking the urban African to the tribal states in-process-of-becoming. They are to be the urban replicas of the chiefs and of the Bantu Authorities, showing the same combination of qualities—the mirage of high responsibility and the reality of bureaucratic subservience.

Bantu Authorities and the Bantustan policy are thus directed toward a revival of tribal chieftainship, albeit domesticated and modernized, at a time when the institutional basis of chieftainship and the traditional system of reciprocity between chief and subject, on which loyalty rested, have long been undermined by foreign conquest, urbanization, and industrial employment. The policy is to retribalize Africans and to fragment them into separate tribal entities, self-policed, introspectively detached from each other and from the White man's world, and self-perpetuated by the insemination of tribal ardor.

Acceptance of Bantu Authorities implies for Africans acceptance of a temporary status in all areas outside the reserves: the model is that of the citizens of a foreign country entitled to temporary employment under a special visa. It implies the renunciation of stable rights in the cities and developed areas, in the industry and the wealth built on

1. *A Survey of Race Relations in South Africa, 1957–1958* (Johannesburg, South African Institute of Race Relations), p. 60.

2. The following report illustrates the generally subordinate role of chiefs: a Zulu chief, head of the Zungu tribe, was found guilty on two counts of disobeying the lawful order of the Chief Bantu Affairs Commissioner of Natal and of showing "insult and disrespect" for the Bantu Affairs Commissioner at Mahlabatini, Natal (*Natal Daily News*, June 20, 1962).

African labor. And it implies the abandonment of aspirations for full participation in the modern industrial society of South Africa and the reversal of a long-cherished political goal, that of a broad, national unity in place of divisive tribalism. The Bantustans might be accepted as an expedient, a base from which to strike at White domination, but this could be a dangerous expedient, since it plays with the sentiments of tribesmen and the ambitions of chieftains.

When the disturbances arose in Pondoland, the Government immediately denied that the Pondos were striking against the system of Bantu Authorities and laid the blame on outside agitators. Congress leaders promptly repudiated the charge. Both moves are conventional. For the Government, the charge of outside agitation immediately introduces the specter of communism, of professional politicians exploiting the masses for their own personal ends. There is the further implication that the people are content until misled by false propaganda. The magic formula thus exonerates the Government, eliminates the issue of policy, and transforms it into a problem of exorcising the devil. The chiefs and the common people are incited against the political leaders, playing on the antagonism of the traditional authorities for the new elite and of the uneducated for the educated. Oppressive action is justified so as to protect the masses against their real enemies.

This is a recurrent theme in the speeches of the Minister of Bantu Administration.

> There are people who would destroy this, your own system [i.e. Bantu Authorities and Bantustans], who would do away with your chiefs and councillors; people who even make use of women in order to create chaos. . . . I see White, Yellow and Black people among those to whom I have referred. . . . They push your people—even women—into the fire with fine words and promises and then they sit in the shade of the trees and laugh. These people must be destroyed [extracts from a speech by the Minister to Zulus at Eshowe].

The Editor of the *Ilanga Lase Natal* comments that "this may have given the people concerned the dangerous impression that all opposing the chiefs are deadly enemies or, in the Minister's flowery language, 'the wolves and the snakes' " (November 14, 1959). On another occasion, the Minister admonished:

> I want you to remember that these people [i.e. the "agitators"] are becoming a real threat to the chiefs. They say they do not want chiefs. They say they do not know you. By these words they show that it is they who desire to become the rulers of the people.

This matter is a real challenge to you who are chiefs [*Natal Mercury*, May 6, 1960].

Understandably, chiefs may be persuaded. Thus Chief Kaiser Matanzima, at that time the prospective first Prime Minister of the Transkei, declared his belief in the divine appointment of the chiefs of Eastern Tembuland, his conviction that the Tembu accepted separate development "as a doctrine and a religion," founded on the traditional way of life in the Transkei, and his rejection of communists, "who were like 'dirty flies' and who polluted the system of the traditional rule in the Transkei" (speech at the installation of a brother chief, as reported in *The Star*, Air Edition Weekly, October 6, 1962).

It would be reasonable enough, though dangerous, for Congress leaders to accept the charge of agitation. Why should they not agitate? Are they to accept discrimination and subordination without protest, as the immutable destiny of the non-White peoples? In any event, they consistently repudiated their very necessary role of political agitation, perhaps with justification, in the early stages of the Pondoland movement. The effect has been to counter Government propaganda that the system works smoothly and justly and to assert that, on the contrary, the complaints of the people arise from intolerable suffering and that the system is immoral.

Both parties thus contend at the level of moral values, maintaining the public illusion, favored by politicians, that they are personally indifferent to the struggle for power. A curious by-product of this contest is the acceptance of the spontaneous reaction of unenlightened masses as a measure of policy. The masses are regarded as a litmus paper of morality, changing color under injustice. Or perhaps a closer analogy is to the wisdom of the innocents. Yet manifestly, the masses may submit to injustice without protest, or explode in violence against valuable community services.

The facts indicate that the Pondos were indeed reacting against the Bantu Authorities system. There is, for example, the testimony of witnesses as to the causes of the disturbances. When the police station commander at Bizana appeared before a government commission of inquiry, he testified that the trouble was due to the application of Bantu Authorities (*Natal Mercury*, August 12, 1960). An adviser to the Paramount Chief in Eastern Pondoland was of the same opinion (*Natal Daily News*, August 17, 1960), as were other witnesses at the inquest into the deaths of Pondos by police action at Ngqusa Hill. At a meeting of four thousand Pondos in Lusikisiki to hear the findings of the commission of inquiry, the spokesman for the Pondos declared that they did not want Bantu Authorities (*Natal Mercury*, October 14, 1960).

The actions of the Pondos were even more eloquent. Violence was not haphazard. It was directed against the property and person of officials and supporters of Bantu Authorities. The insurgents burned the huts of councillors, headmen, and chiefs. They murdered pro-Government chiefs and headmen, including the brother of the Paramount Chief of Eastern Pondoland, allegedly because he led police armed with Sten guns in an attack on a meeting of Pondos (*Drum,* January 1961, p. 22). They established "mountain committees," a new system of authority in embryo, replacing the Bantu Authorities and the traditional authority of the chiefs. According to one report:

> A Chief or headman who becomes part of the Bantu Authorities system is branded as a stooge or "impimpi." These "abangcatshi" [traitors] or "abathengisi" [sell-outs] are summoned to the villagers' courts to face charges of pro-Government activities. Those who ignore the summons see their kraals burnt down. The kraal burnings are warnings that the Government men are outcasts from the life of the tribe and must quit the area. . . . A man accused by a village court of support of a Bantu Authority is fined, then forgiven, if he repents his stand. But those who persist in their support of Bantu Authorities are hounded from the villages [*New Age,* October 6, 1960].

Some chiefs, not surprisingly, sought Government protection or went into hiding. They had accepted Government schemes which their people rejected, and they were now in danger of losing their lives. One chief commented: "The Paramount Chief has on occasion had to go and live in the bush because he found his enemies were surrounding him to kill him. We also literally live in the bush because we have accepted Government schemes which are opposed by the people." Another said: "People waylay you somewhere and kill you." [3]

There was certainly sophisticated leadership among the insurgents. The campaign included a refusal to pay taxes (since there should be no taxation without representation), a boycott of the census, an occasional boycott of White traders, and the smuggling of a petition to the United Nations. One letter protested against the concentration of police in the Bizana area when the findings of the commission of inquiry were to be presented, on the ground that the Pondos could find no justification "for the galvanisation and concentration of the police in our area. We deplore and deprecate this uncalled-for show of strength. We want to make it quite clear that should an unfavourable situation crop up, the Government will have to shoulder the blame. Our policy is that of peace and friendship among races" (*New Age,* October 13, 1960).

But there is nothing to suggest that the movement was simply fo-

3. "Report on Unrest in Pondoland," South African Institute of Race Relations, RR. 152/60.

mented from the top downward. Rather, it seems that political direction was given to the spontaneous rejection by Pondos of policies affecting their daily lives—agrarian reform by way of agricultural betterment schemes, increased taxation, influx control, and the imposition of levies, including levies for Bantu Education. Chiefs and other Pondo officials serving in Bantu Authorities became identified with the Government and its policies. Hatred was thus directed against them, perhaps with greater ferocity because these were their own people, not aliens. There were also abuses of their new powers by the chiefs, and reprisals against the common people, steeping the struggle in the anguish of civil war and sealing in blood the opposition to the Bantu Authorities.

The remoteness of the rural areas; the distance both physical and intellectual which separates many of their inhabitants from the forum of world opinion; the possibility of excluding outside contact by an iron curtain; all these factors may incite a government to brutality. In Zeerust (1957), Sekhukuneland (1958), and Pondoland (1960), the South African Government violently suppressed the movements its own policies had nurtured. But suppression—the assumption and exercise of extraordinary powers, as in Pondoland, the mobilization of police and armored cars, and the killing of tribesmen—disturbs the self-confidence and self-righteousness of the rulers, and arms the subjects with weapons in the ideological battle.

Liberation movements have their heroes, their martyrs, and their holy days. As the people meet to mourn or celebrate past events, their leaders recall brutal episodes of repression, bloody testimony of immoral rule, and they feel united by a common suffering, and renew their determination to achieve freedom. For leaders of an older generation, the evocative episodes were Bulhoek, Bondelswarts, and Witzieshoek. For the young men, they are Zeerust, Sekhukuneland, Ngqusa Hill, and Sharpeville. As the rural insurrections mount, as each group accumulates its local tragedies, and as the major catastrophies become national symbols, the backward rural populations (the despair of African leaders) move out toward the politically sophisticated campaigns of their urban brethren.

The specifically political campaigns culminated, after a decade of militant activity, in two major campaigns, one in 1960 against the pass laws by the newly formed Pan-Africanist Congress, and the other by the Congress Alliance, in 1961, against the inauguration of a republic without reference to the wishes of the voteless non-White majority.

The African National Congress, in association with its political allies, initiated most of the activity during this decade. In 1952, the Defiance Campaign against Unjust Laws, a movement of civil disobedience influenced by the philosophy of Mahatma Gandhi, marked a new phase of militant, coercive struggle on a multiracial basis, replacing the representations, deputations, and supplications of the past. A period of intense political propaganda preceded the adoption of a declaration of human rights by the Congress of the People in 1955. This Freedom Charter provides the ideology of the Congress Alliance, consisting of the African National Congress, the South African Indian Congress, the South African Coloured Peoples Organisation (now Congress), the Congress of Democrats, and the South African Congress of Trade Unions. Since 1955, African women have shown massive resistance against the extension of the pass laws to them. In 1958, non-Whites voted in the country's general elections, not through the ballot box, which was virtually closed to them, but by a stay-at-home demonstration designed to dissuade the electorate from returning the National Party to power and to draw attention to suffering under low wages and apartheid laws. Throughout the decade, the Congress Alliance organized mass demonstrations, the observance of days of mourning and of human rights, "all-in" conferences, and a variety of boycotts (the most successful boycott, however, was the spontaneous nonpolitical Alexandra bus boycott in 1957).

The Congress Alliance emphasized nonviolence and racial cooperation in its struggle for a democratic society. Its most characteristic technique was the stay-at-home campaign, a symbolic struggle for power through the demonstration of the numbers who will withhold their labor for one day or more in response to a call by Congress. The struggle is fought by move and countermove to maximize or minimize the mobilization of supporters. No single campaign was conceived as decisive. Reliance was placed rather on the mounting strength from the cumulative effects of continuous campaigning. The strategy was to mobilize the non-White masses by increasing their involvement in planned activity.

The backwardness of the African rural population and the low educational standards of urban Africans impede programs of mass mobilization. Much African energy is committed in the struggle for a bare subsistence and in the immediate bread-and-butter issues, the blinkers of sheer survival. The life fate of Africans is by no means one of unrelieved gloom. Satisfactions from their own community life and the interest and stimulus in new urban and industrial experience somewhat blunt the sharp anguish of their suffering. And long periods of foreign domination have molded habits of submissiveness which are not readily discarded, so that spontaneous eruptions against authority come more easily than deliberate subversion.

In these circumstances, the tempo of political education would have been slow, but for the policies of the Government. The totalitarian nature of the Government's plan ensures that its impact is felt by all sections—men and women, townsmen and tribesmen, the old and the young, the pensioner and the schoolchild. The rigid application of a single principle permits little relaxation for the mitigation of suffering, few exceptions for the relief of hard cases. And the overwhelming conviction that White interests should prevail renders discrimination against non-Whites a matter of indifference, or perhaps rather a virtue as necessary to the survival of the White man and his way of life. In any event, discrimination is so blatant, and policies are made so abundantly explicit, that Africans cannot help but perceive the hand of the Government and of the White man in their sufferings. The Government has thus quickened the political awareness of the African masses. And yet the Congress Alliance has not been able to exploit this growing awareness. Some of the campaigns were successful as demonstrations, but, with the possible exception of the women's campaign against the passes—and, at that, passes have now been issued to African women —they achieved few concrete gains which might be set against the sacrifices of the participants. Indeed, the debit items mount as the campaigns provide the occasion for greater repression.

The reasons for these negative results lie partly in the power of the Government and its techniques of control, partly in the resilient structure of South African society, which has been able to contain severe conflicts without disruption, and partly too in the organization of the Congress movement. There was a great stereotyping of ideologies, propaganda, and campaigns, which may have been inevitable, given the varied composition of the Congress Alliance and the nature of its appeal, directed toward the African masses. Much of the political activity was surfaced and platitudinously proclaimed. The leaders were known, there being a deliberate policy of publicly building national leaders as symbols of unity and of inspiration. Precisely, then, because the struggle had developed its well-defined idiom, its rigid etiquette, and precisely because the movement had a well-defined and highly visible leadership, the task of the Government was eased. It had no difficulty in anticipating the course of the Congress campaigns and in emasculating its leaders. The campaigns were predictable and the leaders known. Even the violence which often erupted against the express wishes of the leaders followed the predictable pattern of the spontaneous mass movements, police aggression, and African retaliation— understandably so, because the same people were involved. There was some manifestation of violence turned inward, as groups of Africans sought to compel participation in the stay-at-home demonstrations or boycotts. But whether the violence was turned inward or outward, mass disturbances imposed the need to restore law and order and gave a certain legitimacy to forceful suppression.

The overwhelmingly superior power of the state was demonstrated in the final campaign of the Congress Alliance against the inauguration of the Republic. The campaign was advertised and organized in the conventional manner, with fair warning and ample opportunity for anticipatory action. The Government staged a massive display of force, launched mass raids, and assumed and exercised new powers of arbitrary arrest. Many employers exerted pressure to ensure that their workers would not take part in the campaign. The issues may have been somewhat complex for many Africans; in any event, they lacked the resources to withstand pressure from employers. The display of state power could not fail to impress, and there had been many similar campaigns, perhaps disillusioning in their consequences. Whatever the explanation, the Congress campaign failed to muster sufficient support for an impressive display of strength.[4]

The 1960 campaign of the Pan-Africanist Congress introduced new elements. The mode of action was conventional, indeed it was a deliberate duplication of the 1952 civil disobedience campaign by the African National Congress against the pass laws. Africans presented themselves at police stations and surrendered their passes, inviting imprisonment. The police massacre at Sharpeville and illegal police assaults on Africans in the streets and locations of Cape Town enhanced the political and moral significance of the campaign. They were not planned by the Pan-Africanist Congress, however, and are not new in South African history.

The innovations lay in the grandiose conception and the urgency of the campaign. Liberation was to be almost immediate—not "in our lifetime," as the older leaders proclaimed, but in 1963, and initiated by so massive a movement against the very basis of White domination that the system would crumble. Although the campaign itself was nonviolent in the traditional manner, the Pan-Africanist leaders did not accept nonviolence as a matter of principle, a commitment for the future. They projected an image of themselves as brave and resolute men, part of a great movement shaping the destiny of the African continent. They appealed frankly to African nationalism and, perhaps less frankly, or more ambiguously, to African racialism.

The campaign achieved mass support in some parts of the country. It reverberated in the world press. And, momentarily, it threatened the South African Government, perhaps because the political branch of the police did not seriously observe the Pan-Africanist Congress, being conditioned to a struggle with the traditional enemy, the Congress Alliance. The climax, the march of 30,000 Africans to a Cape Town police station in the vicinity of the Houses of Parliament, would have

4. Congress leaders have made statements to the contrary, claiming substantial support and a powerful demonstration.

been even more threatening if leaders had not come forward to assume responsibility. As the German sociologist Georg Simmel [5] explains:

> if a mass rebels against an authority, the authority gains an immediate advantage if it succeeds in causing the mass to choose representatives who are to lead the negotiations. At least, the overwhelming, smashing onslaught of the mass, as such, is broken in this fashion; for the moment, the mass is checked by its own leaders in a way in which the authority itself can no longer succeed. The mass leaders exert the formal function of the authority, and thus prepare for the re-entrance of the authority into its dominating position.

African leaders face a dilemma of choice. They have struggled unsuccessfully, within the framework of the constitution, for an extension of rights and a redistribution of power. They appear temporarily to have exhausted the potentialities of nonviolent struggle. Either the techniques have proved ineffective, or they require, for successful use, a more massive organization. It is precisely this development which the Government frustrates, by consistently harrassing and indeed outlawing non-White political organizations. Inevitably interest turns to violence as an alternative, perhaps more effective, means of change, and to an assessment of the conditions under which the military power of South Africa might be challenged. There is relevant experience of the effective use of violence in other White settler states, such as Kenya and Algeria, and much deprivation in South Africa to incline Africans toward violence. Meanwhile, the use of sabotage and terrorism indicates that some Africans have already made this choice. Indeed, sabotage groups may multiply and fragment and splinter like the innumerable small African Christian sects. If the trend is toward violence, an even more intense racialism will be generated. African leaders now confront the issues of anarchic violence, revolutionary violence, and racialism.

5. Kurt H. Wolff, *The Sociology of Georg Simmel* (Glencoe, Free Press, 1950), pp. 281–82.

CHAPTER 4

The Compulsions of Racialism

THE EARLY CALVINISTS carried out the rationalization of life for the greater glory of God. Not desiring the world, they nonetheless conquered it. The latter-day Calvinists of South Africa have substituted the comprehensive racialization of life, though hardly, it would seem, for the glory of God. Profoundly desiring to conquer their world, they appear to be losing it.

Superficially, the South African policy of racialization (apartheid) seems rationally enough adjusted to the ends of Afrikaner nationalism. I am assuming the not unnatural desire of Afrikaner nationalists to maintain their political power, and to convert it into wealth and prestige. Of course, this is not the expressed aim of apartheid. Political parties rarely acknowledge their concern with power, and they propagate the belief that it is indecent, cynical, and Machiavellian to analyze their activities in these terms. The Afrikaner nationalists are no exception. Racialization is presented in the somewhat curious altruism of a mission to preserve White civilization against Black barbarism, Christian capitalism against atheistic communism, and the God-given differences between races and nations against the miscegenating lusts of integration. Material self-interest happily coincides with both the will of God and the duty of self-preservation.

The maintenance of Afrikaner power obviously depends on the maintenance of the separate identity of Afrikaners as a political group. They are a majority of the White population, and hence of the voters. Monopoly of constitutional power requires the continued supply of voting fodder, bearing the nationalist cross to the ballot paper. The solution lies between the sheets for numbers—though this is hardly necessary during the next generation—and in the insemination of racial solidarity by the Afrikaner churches and schools in an alliance sanctified by the rituals of nationalism: the basis of Afrikaner power thus rests on the racialization of the Afrikaners.

The racialization of one group in a multiracial society may perhaps imply the racialization of other racial groups, in much the same way as the presence of a single class or caste implies the organization of the society on class or caste lines. Exclusive racial sentiment would seem to require some counterpoint to bring out its own inner harmony, though this could be found outside the territorial limits of the society. Within the boundaries of the society, the racialism of one group may be expected to provoke the racialism of other groups, where their members are present in large numbers, and thus extend racialization.

Quite apart from these considerations, however, the presence of a large non-White majority in a ratio of about four-to-one, drives the nationalists toward the comprehensive racialization of the society. They control the constitutional power to legislate the social pattern, and are thus able to relegate non-Whites to an apolitical category; non-Whites are objects of bureaucratic regulation, not agents of legitimate political action. Compliance with the prescribed legislative pattern is enforced by an increasing armory of penal sanctions and other, more lethal weapons; but there remains the danger of non-White unity, and a revolutionary challenge to the whole structure of power. If, however, barriers could be maintained between White and non-White, and equalizing processes aborted; if non-Whites could be fragmented into racial and tribal groups; and if each non-White group could be imbued with ethnic pride and exclusiveness, by much the same devices as succeeded with the Afrikaners, then Afrikaner power would rest on a natural self-perpetuating process of racialization, and everyone, not least the Afrikaners, would live happily ever after—at any rate, for a while.

At the same time, the policy can be administered in a moral capsule. The main ingredient is the supreme value of the ethnic group. Each group is endowed with its own unique quality, its own soul, its own destiny. The greatest fulfillment for the individual lies in subordination to the group, and the greatest fulfillment of the group in the realization of its destiny. The Afrikaners are therefore offering each non-White group a revelation of its destiny; they are freely offering what the Afrikaners themselves desire most fervently. The destinies are different, that is all:—the cities, industry, commerce, the developed areas of South Africa, and some four-fifths of its land for the Whites, and the rural, underdeveloped, and periurban areas for the non-Whites; a modern, Western, wealthy democracy for the Afrikaners, and an Afrikaner tribal revivalism and modernization for the Africans.

The difficulty about all this predestination is that it rests not on the inscrutable and incomprehensible will of God, but on the all too obvious and comprehensible material self-interest of the Afrikaner. For some strata in African society, the ideology may be persuasive; for many, it is too transparent to beguile, and they reject it totally. For others, it becomes a means of political maneuver to be cynically manipulated for personal gain, or indeed for the subversion of the system.

This contradictory strand, this boomerang from one's own weapons, affects not only the ideology but the whole policy of racialization. The underlying conception of society appears to be superficial. Enacted law does not automatically become custom. Society is not plasticine, to be pummeled into crude shapes; there are limits to its remodeling by fiat. Rule by Saracen and machine gun may exact too high a price and provoke counterviolence. Racialization is not a Calvinist Bible, which can be opened and closed as the spirit moves. It is not a process which can be arrested at any moment and petrified into a monumental pattern, like Lot's wife, head turned to the past. It is not a sluggish stream, to be canalized for the irrigation of the White man's vineyards, maize fields, or orchards. Racialization is turbulent, intractable, and passionate. The humiliation may still devour, the bitterness still corrode, when the insults have been avenged a thousandfold.

The fuel for racialization is a heightened consciousness of race, shaped by the apartheid laws. These laws impose racial separation, or provide for control of racial contact, in almost every conceivable human relationship, from physical intimacy to shared religious or intellectual experience. Recent racial legislation affects marriage, "illicit carnal intercourse," proximity between neighbors and traders, inclusion on a common electoral roll, the reservation of work opportunities, industrial conciliation and trade unions, school and university education, occupation of premises for homes, worship, and medical care, or even briefly, for recreation, refreshment, and public assembly. In consequence, the racial concept becomes increasingly weighted with social and cultural connotations.

Race consciousness is given an intense emotional quality by a system of punishments and rewards. The control of race relations is enforced by penal sanctions. Marriage, sex, living in a home, trading, working, studying, healing, welfare work, going to a cinema, eating, playing golf, and attending a meeting are not in themselves criminal offenses in South Africa, but they may become so if they involve forbidden race relations. The primacy of the racial criterion is thus emphasized in the daily indispensable routine of living under the threat of punishment as a criminal.

On the positive side, rewards provide additional incentives. Racial separation in South Africa is highly discriminatory, and, with few exceptions, immediately rewarding to those who impose it. Moreover, such laws as the Group Areas Act, providing for residential and commercial segregation, offer new and handsome dividends in the racial partitioning of South Africa, and the reservation of occupations provides a systematic basis for favored treatment in employment. Race and an

aggressive consciousness of race may be as valuable an asset as entre-
preneurial skill and technical training.

As the range of racially defined situations extends, more and more
persons are involved. Most Whites are committed in one way or another
—as participants in plans for the racial redistribution of property and
opportunities for unearned wealth under the Group Areas Act, as
employers of non-White labor, domestic and other, and so on, in many
of the contexts described above. New occupational opportunities are
opened in state and local administration, and rewards of office stimulate
conscientious devotion to racialism. Outside of administration, organizations providing services on an interracial basis are obliged to re-
examine, and perhaps modify, their policies in the light of the new
racial laws, and even those who oppose these laws become more racially
conscious under conditions where interracial contact savors of deliberate defiance.

Non-Whites are equally affected with Whites. Administration and
legislation relates not only to broad categories of non-Whites but also
to their subdivisions—Colored, Malay, Chinese, Indian, and, in the
case of Africans, linguistic and tribal subdivisions. Increasingly, the
linguistic or ethnic group is the unit of administration for Africans, as
for example in the revival of tribal authority in the rural areas and in
the settlement by segregated linguistic groups in the towns and in the
new universities. Reward and punishment reinforce the system. Penal
sanctions inevitably fall more heavily on the non-Whites, and their
punishment is augmented indirectly by the redistribution of resources,
as in the Group Areas Act. But there are rewards too—not only ficti-
tious as in the lavish promise of separate development but real also, as
in the opening of new occupational opportunities in tribal administration, in social services, in the economic expansion of the country, and
in the development of the reserves.

Inevitably, political activity follows the lines of racial cleavage, expressed in legislation and propagated by it. The Government virtually
represents the Afrikaner people and the interests of Afrikaner domination, and derives its dynamic force from racial conflict. The official
opposition represents English-speaking White people and a minority of
Afrikaners, and the interests of the English-speaking in an equal share
in White domination. The non-White political groups are largely confined to extraparliamentary activities directed against White domination. Political activity, pressure toward conservatism or toward revolution, is largely racial, and serves to heighten racial consciousness.

In these circumstances, there is little likelihood that the people of
South Africa will lose their "sense of color," as members of the Government sometimes phrase it. Race has become a primary, immediate ele-

ment of perception. Race consciousness proliferates throughout the society, and a vast bureaucracy transforms it into the routine of office.

Within the White group, race consciousness is channeled in the antagonistic direction of race prejudice by unfavorable stereotypes of other races, and by policies and ideologies which create or intensify competition between the races.

The many racial laws in South Africa shape an image of other races which is compounded of unfavorable qualities—unfitness as a marriage partner, neighbor, and so on. Legislative policy and national administration make racial competition for the resources of the country public and patent, as under the Group Areas Act, where the redistribution of property in favor of the White population proceeds with great deliberation by way of public hearings and semijudicial procedures. The racial ideology of the dominant group, in one of its most general formulations, rests on the basic incompatibility of the races and the inevitability of conflict between them when in contact. A race must dominate or be dominated; or, to express the theory in less general terms, the non-Whites will use their numbers to dominate the Whites if given the opportunity. The survival of the White man and his way of life depends, therefore, on White paramountcy in areas where they live together (which is to say, discrimination against non-Whites in all material respects) or on territorial separation.

These laws, policies, and ideologies presumably encourage conflict in racial contact, since there is an ideological expectation of conflict. Race consciousness is canalized in a sharply antagonistic form by both the concept and the reality of races in competition for power and wealth, while discrimination is invited, since self-preservation is assumed to depend on withholding from the subordinate races, as far as possible, any opportunities which might contribute to their power as competing groups.

Discrimination itself serves to heighten racial prejudice. The main apartheid laws seek to eliminate primary contacts as far as possible, excluding, however, the master and servant relationship. Secondary contacts, that is to say, formal, remote contacts, are confined to discriminatory situations, or are highly impersonal and fleeting. In consequence, the White man finds himself consistently in a position of superiority. This routine experience may be expected to reinforce sentiments of superiority. Moreover, a realistic basis for these sentiments of superiority is ensured by discrimination itself, which severely limits the opportunities for development of members of the subordinate races. It is natural that, in these circumstances, the White man should seek to maintain his social superiority, and perhaps to enhance it, by further discrimination.

Apartheid therefore sets in motion a self-perpetuating process, the chain reaction of racialization. Race consciousness in the White group is heightened by increasing emphasis on the criterion of race in the routine of living. It is molded into racial prejudice and racial discrimination by official legislated encouragement in the form of rewards and punishments. Increasing racial prejudice seeks expression in an intensified discrimination, and the extension of discriminatory practices stimulates racial prejudice. Prejudice feeds on discrimination, and discrimination feeds on prejudice, unleashing a racial arrogance which threatens the society.

There are further consequences, of a dehumanizing nature. Apartheid rests on the preponderance of a single idea. Salvation, but in this world, is to be sought in the separation of the races. Max Weber argued, in his discussion of the Protestant ethic, that the preoccupation of the early Calvinists with the salvation of their souls developed in them a ruthless self-confident, self-righteous personality and a lack of sympathy for the poor and unfortunate, whose sufferings were regarded as evidence of a lack of grace. So too, in apartheid, there is an indifference to the sufferings of the non-Whites. Sacrifices are imposed and justified because they serve the ends of racial separation, which is to provide the opportunity for each God-created ethnic group to fulfill its own unique mission. While the early Calvinists derived their self-righteousness from the doctrine of predestination, the Afrikaner nationalists find it in the sanctification of the group, the moral elephantiasis of nationalism, and in the crusade for self-preservation and the preservation of White civilization.

The routine and continuous exercise of extensive powers over the lives of others may also be dehumanizing. What were the effects on the personality of the Nazi official who, in the course of his duties, decided the fate of the many thousands of inmates in the concentration camps? And what stamp is laid on the personalities of South African influx control officials who decide whether Africans are to be given the opportunity to work in the urban areas, or whether they are to be returned to their rural poverty and despair? And how are the police molded by the routine of mass raids, the magistrates by the administration of discriminatory laws, and the general White population by habituation to non-White suffering? It is possible that a warm sympathy within one's group may be combined with a callous indifference to the human qualities of others, but it seems more likely that there will be a general brutalization, an undermining of the concept of justice and of the feeling for humanity.

The dominance of the apartheid idea results in the pervasiveness of racialism throughout the society. The same patterns ramify. The Government relies on the Group Areas Act, providing for racial segregation, to control interracial activities. So too, some of the White English-speaking members of the Methodist Church Conference sought to rely on the Group Areas Act when faced with a challenge by Africans for leadership of the Church, as did the South African Golf Union when a leading Indian golfer first wished to compete in the South African Open Golf Championship. The Government considers that in principle Africans should largely finance their own social services. Even English ministers of religion may justify unequal salaries on the ground that African congregations should support their own ministers. There is a general discrimination in salaries against non-Whites. There is also discrimination in English-speaking churches.

Issues quite remote from race are invaded by racialism. If a nurse behaves irresponsibly, it becomes immediately relevant that she is African, and evidence that Africans cannot be entrusted with responsibility. Much as crystals form around a foreign body dropped into a saturated solution, so racialism crystallizes in South Africa around seemingly irrelevant issues. The society is saturated in racialism. The overwhelming importance of race impedes the perception of a common humanity.

Economic interests accentuate the racial divisions, and reinforce the denial of a common humanity. Racial separation is not an end in itself, but a means for conserving and promoting racial privilege. Specific laws (such as the Group Areas Act and the reservation of types of employment for a particular racial group), function to enrich the White man, while the whole structure of apartheid laws serves to maintain his dominant position, both economically and politically.

Two important consequences for race relations flow from this. First, the groups which impose and support apartheid or White domination, and which wield political power—i.e. the Afrikaner nationalists and to some extent the Whites in general—are numerous, and their economic interests must first be satisfied. Pareto[1] writes: "The more numerous that [ruling] class is, the greater the evils resulting from its domination, because a large class consumes a larger portion of wealth than does a class restricted in size." It therefore becomes impossible to allocate sufficient resources to non-Whites, and in this way to win from them extensive support for the system. Even though Africans are sometimes accorded opportunity for wealth, their earnings mostly fall below a modest subsistence level. Really substantial inducements in the form of a redistribution of wealth, or of opportunities for wealth, are inconceivable without revolutionary change in the structure of power. Apartheid sets the material interests of the racial groups in sharp conflict. Only if nations friendly to the South African Government could be persuaded to finance

1. Meisel, *The Myth of the Ruling Class*, p. 181.

the development of the African reserves would it be possible to allocate significant resources to Africans within the framework of apartheid.

A second consequence is that a certain ferocity is injected into race relations by the innumerable economic interests of the White settlers. This appears to be a characteristic of White settler societies. It is especially marked in South Africa where the National Party represents the numerous descendants of a large poor White population; small men entering the civil service, industry, and commerce; workers paid at civilized rates and protected from non-White competition. The system offers them privilege and opportunity. High rewards are within their grasp. But precisely at this turn of most favorable fortune, they are beset with fear. The growth of independent African states, the events in Kenya, Congo, Angola, and Algeria give a realistic basis for insecurity. This is a crucial combination—uncertainty about the future at the moment of fulfillment. And the Whites may be expected to defend their material interest with the same violent aggression as the colons in Algeria.

The system of apartheid has stimulated, among the Whites, a racialism which moves to extremes, and provokes a counterracialism among the non-Whites. The apartheid laws create a systematic discrimination against non-Whites in almost every sphere of life. Discrimination may be based on consent. Our picture of traditional Hindu caste society is over-simplified, but there were certainly elements in Hindu thought which facilitated the acceptance of inequality—such as the religious sanctions for social differentiation and the doctrine of moral responsibility for one's social situation in society (the doctrine of Karma). Religious beliefs also gave hope for the future, rendering inequality more acceptable. By fulfillment of duties in this life, a man might improve his position in the next. In other societies, too, for a variety of reasons and social philosophies, discrimination and inequality were regarded as the natural or divine order of things.

None of these philosophies, which might mold consent to inequality, is, however, accepted in South Africa. Whatever its practice may be, the Government does not justify inequality in its propaganda. On the contrary, it proclaims a policy of creating independent African states. Bantu States are offered as a solution by which equality, self-determination, and independence may be secured to Africans in carefully defined and regulated linguistic subgroups.

Nor do the churches justify discrimination. The English-speaking churches increasingly attack the imposition of social inequality as "un-Christian." Even the Nederduitse Gereformeerde Kerk, which stands in a more intimate relationship with apartheid than the early Calvinists with capitalism, does not offer scriptural sanctification for the policy of legally enacted inequality. In its statements, the discriminations of apartheid are regarded as an interim and regrettable necessity in the realization of ultimate justice.

> The Nederduitse Gereformeerde Kerk has made it clear by its policy and by synod statements in the past that it can justify and approve of the policy of independent distinctive development [i.e. apartheid], provided it is carried out in a just and honourable way, without impairing or offending human dignity. The Church has also accepted that this policy, especially in its initial stages, would necessarily cause a certain amount of disruption and personal discomfort and hardship, for example in connection with the clearing of slums. The whole pass system must be seen in this light [*Dutch Reformed Church Monthly Newsletter*, Mid-April, 1960.].

From a religious point of view, this means the sanctification of sinful means for the sake of an uncertain future. Considerations of this sort undoubtedly lie behind a recent statement made by the delegations of the Nederduitse Gereformeerde Kerke of the Cape Province and the Transvaal to the conference of World Churches to the effect that: "the church had a responsibility to test the policies of the state in the light of the Word of God. If complete territorial separation was impossible, then full rights, including political rights, could not be indefinitely withheld from those Bantu living in white areas" (*Dutch Reformed Church Monthly Newsletter*, March 1961). There is recognition that if present discrimination is to be tolerated for a just future, then religious sincerity demands an honest confronting of the possibility of realizing this future. From a social point of view, the issue is not simply that of a temporary personal discomfort occasioned by such desirable programs as slum clearance, as suggested by the first quotation, but the uprooting of hundreds of thousands of people under Group Areas and Black Spot removals, and a massive burden of discrimination.

There is thus no ideology which nourishes systematic inequality, save as a temporary expedient, to be judged by the speed with which it is discarded. Separation is justified, but not inequality. And the rejection of racial discrimination by non-Whites is shown clearly in the campaigns against Unjust Laws and in the vast numbers of statutory offenses committed by Africans. It is evasive to place responsibility, as the Government does, on agitators, whether communists, liberals, progressives, Anglican churchmen, English newspapermen, or interfering busybodies from overseas. There are many other sources of the desire for freedom. Respect for human dignity and the concept of the equality of all persons, irrespective of race, color, or creed, are part of the contemporary world ethos, proclaimed in the policies of non-White peoples. They will not be eliminated in South Africa by shock therapy in the form of treason trials, mass arrests, banishments, bannings, house arrests, torture, routine midnight raids, states of emergency, and Bantu Education. Indeed, local experience suggests that these sufferings merely heighten the determination to achieve equality. Nor can the treatment of members of a racial group be confined within the boundaries of a single nation. Why should Africans in South Africa accept discrimination as Africans when members of their racial group are governing independent states?

Important consequences flow from the fact that the ideal of human equality is firmly established in the consciousness of large numbers of non-Whites, and that discrimination does not rest on their consent. Discrimination is imposed on racial grounds. It is imposed by one race on another race. Hence each act of discrimination constitutes a direct racial aggression, and the resentment against the discriminations is inevitably expressed in racial terms.

Discrimination by Whites provokes the reaction of non-White racialism, more particularly African racialism. And thus the self-feeding mechanism of racialization is completed. Apartheid stimulates a heightened racial consciousness among Whites and channels it in the direction of racial prejudice. This racial prejudice expresses itself in discrimination and is in turn intensified by discrimination. Prejudice and discrimination feed on each other, engendering extremism. Since the system does not rest on consent, Africans increasingly react with a counterracialism. The more extreme the racial actions of Whites, the more embittered the racial reactions of non-Whites. As the non-Whites move from mass murmurings and protest to organized revolt, insecurity besets the White group, aggravating the racial antagonism. The Whites respond with increasing repression, and the struggle moves into a revolutionary phase. Racialization has ceased to be an instrument of policy, and now threatens the structure of Afrikaner domination.

CHAPTER 5

Intimations of Nonracialism:
Racial Integration by Separation

RACIALIZATION is a dominant process in South African society, but there is also a process of racial integration. Indeed, the South African choice, in terms of political goals actually pursued, is not between racial separation and racial integration, as the alternatives are normally phrased. It is between different modes of integration.

Integration may be conceived on the model of "nonracialism," in which each individual has the right to participate fully and as an equal in all spheres of social activity: in other words, race is irrelevant, and the unit of integration is the individual. Or the unit of integration may be the racial group, not the individual, in which case there is a variety of models. Thus different spheres of activity may be distinguished, and a policy advocated of, say, economic integration but social separation. Or the model may be that of a racial partnership or a balance of power between the racial groups. Or racial integration may rest on stratification, with the subordinate racial groups either leveled or themselves differentially ranked.

The various modes of integration may be ordered in a continuum, ranging from the present policy of maximum emphasis on racial groups as the units to be integrated to the disappearance of race as a criterion and maximum emphasis on the individual as the basic unit, the variable being the degree of emphasis on the group. Alternatively, the continuum may be conceived as extending from maximum racial discrimination (or stratification) to racial equality, the variable being discrimination. The Government's policy of apartheid (racial separation), *considered in its practical implications rather than in its ideological formulations,* is in fact a policy of integration by means of racial stratification. The unequal racial units are to be systematically coordinated into a functioning whole. So-called separation between White and non-White is largely an intellectual device to define the units, their role in the total social system, and their manner of relationship in different spheres, although as between the non-Whites themselves there is an attempt to raise real vertical barriers against unification.

From the point of view of the Government, the most important areas for control are the political and economic. In these fields, the Government pursues a policy of integration by stratification. Indeed, the same policy is applied to the general pattern of social relations. Apartheid is in fact a very tightly knit system of integration, extending to numerous aspects of the lives of the groups involved.

Politically, non-Whites are removed from the major sources of national power—the vote and direct representation in Parliament. Only Colored voters in the Cape Province still have the right to elect four White representatives to the House of Assembly. A high level of integration is sought administratively by the delegation of non-White affairs to special departments of state. In the case of the White population, control is distributed among many departments, with a division of function according to type of activity. For the Coloreds and Indians, on the other hand, separate Departments of Coloured Affairs and of Asiatic Affairs have been established, and the trend of policy is to centralize control over Coloreds and Indians in these departments. Their scope is defined in racial terms, not functionally. African affairs are already largely centralized in two departments, the Department of Bantu Administration and Development, and the Department of Bantu Education. Hence the administrators are in a position to implement policy toward non-Whites in a systematic and unified way.

The system of Bantu Authorities, with its promise of self-governing African linguistic communities, developing along their own lines, would appear to be a departure from the general principle of centralized bureaucratic control; and so it may prove in the future.[1] But at present, it is essentially an administrative device for harnessing the traditional tribal authorities to the state machine, and for absorbing the chiefs into the state bureaucracy. The potentially disruptive forces of tribal authority, and of tribal traditions in conflict with the requirements of a modern industrial state, are thus controlled. Tribalism is integrated into the total social system, and the African majority, which might otherwise threaten and indeed overthrow the established order, is fragmented —at least in theory.

The political system provides a basis for almost total racial integration. Education for Africans can be harmonized with their prescribed political and economic status, with the system of tribal and White authority, with the idealization of tribal life, and with the philosophy and practice of apartheid. The same general principle of harmonious development

1. It is still early to assess the new constitutional developments in the Transkei: the indications are that the Transkei and its leaders will not be easily contained within the framework of apartheid.

within a predetermined framework can be applied to the other non-White groups. Moreover, the heads of the racial bureaucracies are in a position to coordinate the affairs of the different racial groups with each other and with the total racial strategy of the Government. Greater consistency of control may be expected from a bureaucracy than at the parliamentary level of compromise between contending interests.

Integration of economic activity is also based on the stratification of racial groups, on the differentiation of role by the criterion of race. This is most marked in the public sector. In Natal, for example, in the Provincial Architects Department, Africans were employed as general laborers, cleaners, and messengers; Indians as gardeners for semiskilled work, sirdars, and tractor and lorry drivers; while Europeans held the administrative positions. On the railways, there was a clear racial demarcation of posts. In the Local Health Commission, the general principle was that Indians should be employed to serve in Indian communities, Africans to serve in African communities, save that rough labor in all communities was reserved for Africans, and the higher administrative and executive positions for Europeans. To an appreciable extent, roughly similar patterns of racial differentiation prevail in the private economy. Europeans hold the managerial, executive, and skilled occupations; Africans the unskilled and to some extent the semiskilled; while Indians and Coloreds fall somewhere between the Africans and Europeans. This racial organization of the economy was beginning to change as a result of rapid industrialization. The powers assumed by the Government to reserve occupations for particular racial groups have provided the legal means for restoring the pattern, at any rate in those circumstances where the privileged position of the White worker might be threatened.

By contrast, integration in a free economy (considered as an ideal type), is based on the mobility of labor, capital, and resources, and on freedom to contract. The society is a unit from the point of view of employment, in the sense that competitive wage rates prevail throughout by virtue of the mobility of workers who would otherwise move to areas of higher remuneration (other factors being equal). It is a unit in terms of investment, in the sense that capital and resources are not restricted to particular areas or particular uses, but move freely into enterprise in any area or any sector. It is a unit in the sense that all members of the society, regardless of race, may be brought into all manner of contractual relations with each other, and that each sector of the economy is responsive to changes in every other sector.

In the racially ordered economy of South Africa, on the other hand, there are extensive restrictions on the geographical mobility of African and Indian labor, and on the occupational mobility of all non-Whites. There are limitations on the use of capital in terms of area, race, and type of investment. Freedom to contract is limited by reference to the race of the contracting parties and the nature of the contract. And as for the sensitive interrelations between sectors of the economy, a poor harvest in the African reserves has limited repercussions on the general economy, save to ensure a supply of migrant labor—which is guaranteed in any event by the poverty of the reserves.

A further distinction between a free economy and a racially organized economy may be phrased as follows. In both types, there is economic stratification of positions and of occupations, in the sense that these positions and occupations carry different rewards and prestige. In a racially organized economy, the stratification of positions is likely to be more extreme, with greater differences in the rewards for skilled and unskilled work, where the former is reserved for the racially dominant, and the latter for the racially subordinate group. And the same positions may be rewarded differently because of the race of the incumbent, as for example, in the case of European, Indian, and African teachers with the same qualifications. Both economic systems then are stratified. In a free economy, however, there is open recruitment. Theoretically, no rigidities restrict the mobility of workers: recruitment is based on the universally applicable criteria of aptitudes and training. In the racially controlled economy, there is a stratification of the groups which provide the potential recruits to the economy. The particular criterion of race becomes central, so that members of the different racial groups are recruited at different levels of the economic hierarchy, and the different levels themselves are highly stratified.

This added element of stratification does not imply a lack of integration, provided of course that sentiments of injustice do not threaten the entire system or the privileges of the White group. Even then, conflicts may give rise to mechanisms which more firmly integrate the system, as, for example, the machinery of industrial conciliation. The conflicts are contained within the system and the threat of disruption removed. Thus, the Labor Boards established by the South African Government are designed as a means of resolving labor disputes between employers and their African workers, while at the same time impeding African use of the challenging power of trade union organization.

Indeed, racial stratification in South Africa may assist the process of integration, if integration is conceived as involving the precise interweaving of the parts into a functioning whole. Control over the movement of Africans and the systems of influx and efflux control and of labor bureaus permit, in theory, the exact integration of African labor into the economy. African labor can be treated as a commodity and fed into the economy in the precise quantities and qualities desired, without any redundancies in the urban areas. Surplus workers will move out of sight into the reserves to provide a labor pool for new or changing demands, and their poverty will not be a charge on the industrial areas. This is a most exact form of economic integration.

Apart from the political and economic integration of the racial groups, there is the broader problem of integrating the wide range of social relationships, both formal and informal, into the system of apartheid, and of securing a measure of agreement on supporting values. It would seem fantastic to attempt to integrate such varied bonds between individuals and groups. And yet this is precisely what the apartheid laws seek to accomplish: the harmonizing of social relations with the over-all ideology. The laws move in a planned way through the range of human contacts, controlling and regulating both the racial identity of the parties and the content of the relationship between them.

The model for social relationships in societies with a minimum of hereditary stratification of races is presumably the same as for a free economy or a democratic political system—the mobility of the individual and his freedom to participate in all manner of relationships. There are no special norms governing interracial relationships, and members of different races are distributed randomly in social groups. Companionship with schoolmates, spiritual affinity with fellow worshippers, and shared occupational interests stimulate loyalties cutting across those of race, and supporting a common value system.

In a racially stratified society, a consistent pattern of inequality in social relationships between members of different races may be expected to promote appropriate common values, since contact on the basis of inequality reinforces the sentiments supporting inequality. Where contacts begin to develop on a basis of equality, there is a challenge to the whole system of stratification, since the experience of equality in a particular situation negates the assumption of a general inequality. Hence the maintenance of racial stratification requires the integration of social relationships within one consistent pattern. If this were acceptable to all the groups, then presumably there would be a self-perpetuating system. Failing acceptance, the policy must be imposed by force, or a new supporting value system must be created. Both methods have been adopted by the South African Government. The volume of repressive laws and the application of force have rapidly increased, while educational policy is directed toward the forging of a common value system. The increased interest of the Dutch Reformed Church in the evangelization of Africans also has the potential function of inculcating the appropriate apartheid values.

The policy of total integration by separation has been applied since 1948, but the pattern is not yet established. There are inherent contradictions. Africans are promised the establishment of independent African states within the boundaries of South Africa, yet power is increasingly centralized, and the rights of the individual are increasingly curtailed. In these circumstances, it is inconceivable that the Government would simultaneously follow a policy of decentralizing power and extending individual rights. There is little reason to believe that authoritarian states wither away by a process of self-immolation. And yet the myth of independence engenders a measure of reality. The Government, by virtue of the sheer force of its own propaganda and the hostility of the outside world is obliged to lay the foundations for a façade of independence, while some chiefs, by accepting the myth as reality, are unleashing a truly separatist movement. An ideology to sustain apartheid unleashes forces which may destroy it, though no doubt the National Party calculates that it is not threatened by tribal Africanism, but only by national Africanism.

A large urban housing program for Africans accompanies the preservation of the urban and developed areas of South Africa for the Whites. Separation of the races in theory means, in practice, the increasing urbanization and industrial employment of Africans. Racial conflict sharpens and threatens to disrupt the entire system. Indeed, the contradictions of apartheid are widely pervasive. And there is much evidence to suggest that they arise because present policy is incompatible with the structure of South African society in many essential respects.

This incompatibility may be assessed by the number and the nature of the laws passed to lay the basis for racial separation. If miscegenation were foreign to the structure of South African society, there would not have been any need to define miscegenation between White and non-White as a criminal offence. So too, if the White group had enjoyed a monopoly of amenity and profit in the urban areas, there would have been less demand for the spatial separation of the races. Hence the Immorality Amendment Act, prohibiting miscegenation, and the Group Areas Act, providing for the compulsory segregation of the races, are evidence of the incompatibility of apartheid with the structure of South African society.

The laws passed since the accession of the National Party Government provide controls for almost every conceivable social situation involving members of different races—marriage; "illicit carnal intercourse"; proximity between traders and neighbors; inclusion on a common electoral roll; school education for Africans (and now for Coloreds); industrial conciliation machinery for Africans; trade unions; reservation of occupations; control of contact in trade; control of contact with Africans in schools, hospitals, clubs, places of entertainment, public assemblies, and churches (under certain conditions); occupation of premises for a substantial period of time; university education; partaking of refreshments; and (pending) all aspects of African life and work. The wide range of these laws, and the penal sanctions they incorporate, demonstrate the extensive incompatibility of racial separation with the nature of South African society.

Campaigns and their objectives, disturbances and their causes, yield further measures of incompatibility. Since the 1952 campaign against the systematic application of racial separation, that is, the Defiance Campaign against Unjust Laws in which over 8,000 non-Whites voluntarily served prison sentences, there has been a continuous succession of protest campaigns, following set patterns, and persisting despite mounting repressive action. At the same time, disturbances have become endemic, from the East London riots in 1952, through the series of conflagrations in Durban at Cato Manor, to the destruction of African life by the police in Sharpeville, and assault and murder in the tribal area of Pondoland. The systematic attempt by the Government to impose a totally integrated pattern of race relations throughout the country has had the effect of drawing in wider and wider circles of protest and despair. Even the most improbable segments of the population have become involved—African women in rebellion against low wages, liquor raids, and the beer hall system, and rural Africans in revolt against influx control and the role of the chiefs as Government servants.

Increasing rule by force is further evidence of the incompatibility of Government policies. If these policies were compatible, the ultimate power of the State would not be evident: the populace would hardly be aware of the State's armory of violence. As it is, force is so manifest that even small African children in Cato Manor readily distinguished between the Saracen armored car and the troop carrier. Police with submachine guns appear at public gatherings, and even on the university campus. During the stay-at-home demonstration by non-Whites, at the time of the inauguration of the Republic, troop carriers and soldiers with bayonets drawn were to be seen traveling along the peaceful holiday Esplanade of Durban.

There has been a whittling away of civil liberties, proscription of organizations, long treason trials of innocent people, midnight raids and arrests, and the terror of secrecy and mystification. Men and women are deported, banished, banned, and imprisoned without trial, and now they are condemned to the "civil death" of house arrest, "interrogated," or tortured. The declaration of a state of emergency has set the pattern for the arbitrary suspension of the rule of law. The police are armed with Saracens and improved weapons for killing people. Military forces are mobilized for police duties. Refugees flee the country along established escape routes and seek asylum in other countries. There are the beginnings of a government or governments in exile. All this indicates that systematic racial stratification so conflicts with current trends in South Africa that it can only be maintained by the extraordinary use of force. And as a result, opposing forces are released.

The process of imposing racial separation has unleashed racialisms which seem to threaten the disintegration of South African society. These racialist reactions are inevitable because the official policies are grounded in racialism, are incompatible with certain trends in South African society, and do not rest on consent. At the same time, new adjustive mechanisms are arising to contain the threatening conflicts. These structures cross racial lines and bring together individuals on the basis of a community of interest, not as representatives of racial groups. In other words, racial policies have stimulated not only a massive reaction of racialism, but also some movement toward integration on a nonracial basis.

The opposition to the official policy of racial separation is not confined to a single group. On many issues, Whites and non-Whites have come together, finding shared values and an identity of interest. New patterns of organization are emerging to resolve racial conflicts, to promote better understanding, and to plan for a shared future, such as the multiracial conferences of churches and the multiracial political organizations. There has been a slight breach of the taboo against joint political action with non-Whites. The founding of two political parties with membership open to all racial groups, the Liberal Party and the Progressive Party, coincided with the systematic application of racial separation. The multiracial church conferences and the multiracial political parties are a response to the threatened conflict of racialisms. The threat of disruptive racialism promotes new forms of nonracial integration.

A further stimulus in the same direction is the common subjection of racial groups to the total plan. Resentment against the attendant discrimination forges new links. This is most marked among non-Whites, though White persons are not exempt from its influence.

Political developments among the Colored people demonstrate the complexity of the new alignments. Traditionally, the Coloreds have identified with the White group, since the Whites are at the apex of the system of stratification, and the Coloreds enjoyed the highest racial rating and privileges among the non-White groups. Coloreds tended to accept their position as appendages of the Whites, and to guard their privileges by maintaining an extreme social distance in relation to Africans. This is beginning to change as a result of new discriminations against the Colored people, which were motivated partly by the total nature of the plan for racial differentiation, and partly, perhaps mainly, by the fear that the Afrikaners might merge into the Coloreds, with whom they had already intermingled their blood. For some of the same reasons that Coloreds maintained their exclusiveness in relation to Africans, the National Party Government is increasing the social distance between Whites and Coloreds, so that Coloreds now find difficulty in maintaining their traditional attitudes. The result has been a movement among Coloreds toward cooperation with Africans. This change so conflicts with their traditional attitudes that it is difficult to assess its significance. It may be a passing phase with only a small section of the Coloreds drawn into enduring relationships with Africans, or it may be extensive in its effects and inaugurate a basic reorientation in racial attitudes. In any event, some new links will be forged between Coloreds and Africans.

Indians are particularly threatened by the competing racialisms of Afrikaners and Africans, since they are a small minority, with a few conspicuously wealthy men, and with some commercial interests to which the new trading classes in both the African and Afrikaner communities aspire. The promise by the Government that Africans would enjoy a monopoly of trade in their own areas has helped to focus African commercial antagonism against Indians, who had largely pioneered this trade. There is much hostility, latent, but sufficiently near the surface to be readily inflamed by African or White politicians. The 1949 African riots in Durban emphasized the vulnerable position of Indians, and their need to forge closer links. At the political level, the South African Indian Congress worked as a member of the Congress Alliance, which included the proscribed African National Congress, the South African Coloured People's Congress, the South African Congress of Trade Unions and the Congress of Democrats (also proscribed).

Cooperative approaches by Coloreds and Indians involve the Africans themselves in new interracial contacts. There is some reciprocity— Africans derive help from the greater political experience and resources of the Indian political leaders, and strength from non-White unity. These new political relationships act as a measure of restraint on African racialism. At the nonpolitical level, there is increasing contact, with visiting of homes and the forming of friendships. And some significance should be attached to the assistance Indian lawyers have rendered African political leaders by making available to them facilities for legal training.

The sociological principle involved in these tendencies toward non-White integration is the unifying effect of a common subordination. The Government has chosen to reduce the hierarchical distance between the non-White groups. Suffering a common subordination, sections of the non-White groups are showing signs of drawing together. Such are the antagonisms and prejudices between them that the strongest pressure was needed to forge political cooperation. Apparently the Government provided this. The aversion felt for the Government by some members of the non-White groups is seemingly greater than the aversion they feel for each other. In direct contravention of its goals, apartheid is effecting a measure of non-White unification which might otherwise have been delayed for decades.

In the field of sport, non-White integration is most advanced. Here integration derives from what Georg Simmel described as the appeal to a higher tribunal. Sport in South Africa was organized almost entirely on racial lines (White, Colored, African, Indian), with White sportsmen monopolizing the opportunities to represent their country in the Olympic games and other international contests. Since recognition of national sporting bodies rests with the international tribunals, and since a national body cannot be representative of a country if it practices racial discrimination, non-Whites had valid grounds for demanding either the removal of discrimination in the bodies controlling South African sport, or the disaffiliation of the White sports associations from the international organizations. But the non-White sporting associations could hardly appeal to the nonracial charter of the international tribunals while they themselves were organized on racial lines. Hence, with the hope of international recognition acting as a spur, there is now—though beset with many difficulties—a process of racial disintegration, and of reintegration on a nonracial basis. These new patterns of social relationship, once established in a joint struggle, are not likely to be bounded by the world of sport.

The consequences extend further. The White sporting associations are threatened with disaffiliation from the international organizations. They are unwilling to integrate on a nonracial basis, or they claim that they cannot legally do so. At the same time, they are obliged to demonstrate that they are representative of all the groups, if they are to meet the charges of racial discrimination. Hence, White sports administrators are motivated to sponsor separate non-White sports associations linked to the White organizations in a manner compatible with apartheid, or in other ways to demonstrate their active concern for non-White sport. In the process, non-Whites are detached from the main body of non-White sportsmen, creating non-White disunity, but at the same time, White sportsmen are obliged to enter into new relationships with members of other races, and new loyalties temper the opposition between solid racial blocs.

In the field of religion, changes within the English-speaking churches demonstrate the varied pressures toward nonracialism. There is first the need to eliminate racialism in any organization which opposes racialism, the same need which promoted nonracial integration in the non-White sports organizations. The English-speaking churches now experience this need. They oppose the policy of enforced racial separation, and they suffer under its application, by the loss, for example, of their African schools. However, segregatory practices and discrimination prevail in many of these churches. This poses a dilemma, expressed by the Rev. E. W. Grant, then President of the Methodist Church of South Africa, at a multiracial conference of churches in 1949 (virtually at the inception of apartheid as official policy).

But when it (a Church) is confronted by a system which checks the growth of individuals, which divides citizens into mutually exclusive groups whose bounds are determined by differences of class or race, or which creates in the underprivileged a grievous sense of injustice, the Church can effectively raise its voice in judgement only if it is achieving within itself an inter-racial unity which embraces every sphere of its activity.

It was to resolve this dilemma that the conference arrived at the following conclusions:[2]

(1) the Church not only has the right to speak on matters that concern society, but it is its duty to do so. There are times when it would be wrong for the Church not to speak. (2) In doing so, however, we appeal to our fellow Christians to recognise that if the Church has the duty to protest against wrong, it does so most effectively if it demonstrates the right within its own life.

Churchmen, in all sincerity, are thus turned inwards to a scrutiny of their own segregatory and discriminatory practices.

At the same time, the racial conflicts in the wider society affect relations within the church, and influence churchmen to seek reconciliation. They cannot be indifferent to the sufferings and conflicts of their non-White members outside the church, nor indeed to the more militant demands of non-Whites for equality inside the church. This reinforces the pressure for internal reform arising from theological considerations and considerations of personal integrity. Hence some churches begin to narrow the gap between what they profess and what they practice, and seek to achieve greater and more equal integration.

The influence of the world community of churches, the higher tribunal of the conscience which transcends local problems, operates as a further mechanism for integration on a nonracial basis. Rejection of racial separation by the churches of the world influences local South African churches which regard themselves as members of this wider community. And support by the world community of churches in the struggle of the South African churches may be expected to encourage reorganization in conformity with generally acceptable models of Christian conduct.

These pressures operate in the same way as the pressures on the non-White sports organizations when they appealed to the international tribunals. They do not arise where organizations are isolated from the outside world, and want nothing from it. A purely separatist African church can presumably foster a spirit of African nationalism and exclusiveness within its own severely bounded environment without ide-

2. *The Christian Citizen in a Multi-Racial Society* (Cape Province, Christian Council of South Africa, 1949), pp. 13–14.

ological strain or ambiguity. To some extent, the Afrikaans-speaking churches, notwithstanding their non-White membership, have fulfilled this role for Afrikaner nationalism, though by no means in complete isolation. When the pressures of outside opinion become too strong there is always the possibility of withdrawal and separatism.

The recent withdrawal of the Afrikaans-speaking member churches from the World Council of Churches is a movement in the direction of Afrikaner separatist churches. The close identification between the Afrikaner churches and the State may have fostered the illusion of sufficient strength to take a stand independent of the world. But it is an illusion. The Afrikaner churches still regard themselves as members of the world community of churches; ecumenical work will no doubt continue; and in any event the rejection of apartheid by some of their dominees indicates that the defences were penetrated before the barrier of withdrawal was raised. It is not likely to stand for long. According to a report in *The Star* (Air Edition, June 20, 1964), the Nederduitse Gereformeerde group of churches will send a strong multiracial delegation to the General Assembly of the World Alliance of Reformed Churches in August 1964.

The World Council of Churches is only one manifestation of the higher tribunals of the conscience. These include the United Nations and other international organizations, the world press, the declaration of human rights, and a world ethos of racial equality. And they must be regarded not as an external force only, but as a force within South African society itself, shaping nonracial integration.

The pressures toward nonracialism, or at any rate toward more varied and individual forms of race relations, act also on the National Party Government and its supporters. They arise from the application of apartheid policy, as one of its paradoxical consequences. Thus a policy declaration by some Colored leaders of closer alignment with Africans, carrying implications of desperate antagonism to apartheid amongst the most loyal supporters of the White group, stimulated new approaches by some of the National Party intelligentsia. There is a demand for closer and less discriminatory relations with the Coloreds, extending also to Indians, who have in the past been particular anathema to the National Party. This is not necessarily motivated by any Machiavellian intention to divide and rule, but by an automatic response to the danger of a non-White bloc united in its hostility to the Whites.

Some measure of conflict with other groups is necessary to promote the solidarity of Afrikaner nationalism. It is difficult to assess to what extent conflict is desired for its own sake, or as a means to an end. The general plan is for the establishment of Afrikaner nationalism, as a bureaucracy, in the command posts of the society, and for the peaceful government of other racial groups in the spheres allotted to them. Conflict provides the dynamic force for implementing the plan, but it must not be a conflict of such magnitude that it threatens Afrikaner survival.

The danger of a growing unity and antagonism among the non-Whites obliges the National Party to seek friends and influence. Firm links must be established with loyal supporters in other racial groups—there must be a display of friendship for them and concern for their aspirations. The curious development of ambassadorial offices and protocol in the backward tribal areas is a concrete, albeit theatrical, exhibition of friendship and respect.

White solidarity represents another possibility, a replacement of Afrikaner nationalism by White racialism, or the taking in of a partner. Many English-speaking Whites feel the need for a strong White government in a period of turbulent African nationalisms. Some are attracted to the National Party by the desire to end the wasteful conflict between English and Afrikaner, or hope for personal advantage. Others draw nearer the non-Whites in an exploration of social relationships and political solutions. There is thus further fragmentation of the solidity of an ethnic group, and a crossing of the ethnic barriers. Afrikaner nationalism begins to draw in members of the English-speaking group into new alliances, which must inevitably modify Afrikaner nationalism, even if the process is largely an Afrikanerization of English adherents.

Hastening the spread of relationships between individuals of different races is another inherent contradiction in the policy of apartheid. Its imposition requires the establishment of many new interracial structures in education, religion, and administration. Teachers with the right value systems are needed in the African teacher training and university colleges. In consequence, graduates of the Afrikaans universities must now relate themselves to their new African pupils, and missionaries from the Dutch Reformed Churches, as a more intense policy of evangelization is pursued, will be obliged to relate themselves to increasing numbers of African converts. Presumably education of the African student is also education of the Afrikaner teacher, and evangelization of the heathen is also, in some measure, or sometimes, an evangelization of the missionary. The totalitarian nature of the plan for racial separation, requiring control of most aspects of life, ensures the wide penetration of African life by Afrikaner nationalists. Many of the contacts depart from the model of the master-servant relationship, and introduce new experiences of other races, breaking through set patterns in a multiplicity and variety of relationships. The more intensely the policy is applied, the greater is the probability that loyalties will conflict with the solidarity of separate groups, especially that of the Afrikaner nationalists.

Many forces thus contribute to lay the basis for integration on a nonracial pattern. The process suggests a dialectic, the policy of integration by racial stratification stimulating a movement for nonracial integration. Afrikaner nationalism provokes African nationalism, and the impending clash stimulates a re-examination of the consequences of exclusive racial (or ethnic) nationalism in a plural, multiracial society, preparing the way for the broader synthesis of an inclusive South African nationalism. The heavy toll of conflict engenders striving for peaceful solutions. It is almost as if every action produced an opposite reaction.

Where there is an appearance of the operation of dialectical forces within the society, the cause must be sought in the structure and values of the particular society. In South African society, varied factors create counterforces to the policy of integration by racial separation, and encourage new forms of racial integration.

First, there is the interdependence of the racial groups, built up in some areas over hundreds of years. Varied patterns of social relationships have been established, slowly changing with the structure of South African society. Interdependence has been magnified by the increasing urbanization and by the division of labor, which has resulted from industrialization. The disturbances created by the new laws, which are designed to impose a uniform pattern conflicting with established relations, reverberate through the society.

Then there is the balance of power between Whites and non-Whites. The Whites are a large minority group, over three million in number, highly organized and armed: they cannot be driven into the sea. The non-Whites are too substantial a majority to be subjugated by policies they reject, and they are strengthened by the emergence of the new independent states. The racial groups in South Africa must arrive at an accommodation. And finally, there is the world ethos of racial equality. It is a major force in South African society. Plans for the racial re-segregation of Indians through a massive redistribution of population have only been partly implemented. The Indians of South Africa, to all appearances a small vulnerable minority and an obvious scapegoat, can appeal to the United Nations and know that they will have the support of most of the nations of the world. The violent suppression of demonstrations provokes world condemnation, restraining future acts of violence. The English-speaking churches of South Africa draw strength not only from their faith but concretely from the communities of fellow believers in other countries. Boycotts and condemnation in the United Nations affirm nonracialism, and provide sanctions against racial discrimination. Many aspects of South African life are permeated with the egalitarian values of the outside world. Adjustment to these values is essential, and the creation of Bantustans is an attempt by the Government to find a solution acceptable to other nations.

It is by virtue of these varied elements—interdependence, conflicting loyalties, the demographic relationship of the racial groups, and outside pressures—that the policy of integration by racial separation releases contrary impulses toward nonracialism. Or, to follow a theory developed by Max Gluckman,[3] it is by virtue of this structure of South African society that conflicts in one set of relationships lead to the establishment of cohesion in a wider set of relationships. Conflict with apartheid leads to some cohesion among non-Whites in the fields of politics and sport, to greater equality among Whites and non-Whites in the English-speaking churches and other organizations, and to adjustive social relationships between the rulers and their subjects.

While it is possible to predict with some assurance the emergence in South Africa of a society integrated by other than racial criteria, the present reality is one of sharp racial conflict, and the immediate future is obscure. Much will depend on the reactions of the outside world and the flexibility of political leaders in South Africa. A great responsibility rests with the African leaders, the bourgeoisie. They must find their way among the many confusing solutions offered—multiracialism, nonracialism, African nationalism of an exclusive type or racialism, African nationalism with Africanization of non-Africans, South African nationalism, liberalism, or communism, national or racial communism. Meanwhile the policy of apartheid forges new nonracial forms of association, and new political formulations. Perhaps it is speeding up the process of nonracial integration, and the present unrest is mainly a reaction to the increased tempo of integration, or perhaps the mission of the Afrikaans-speaking people is not to preserve white civilization, but to lay the foundations of a nonracial democracy. If so, it seems doubtful whether the mission requires such great heat, such intense pressure, and release of such explosive and destructive energy.

3. *Custom and Conflict in Africa* (Oxford, Blackwell, 1955).

CHAPTER 6

Degrees of Freedom

"We've lost everything except our color" [African speaker at meeting of the Institute of Race Relations].

Col. R. Jenkins, Deputy Commissioner of Police, Port Natal Division, said today that routine raids had been carried out at Cato Manor yesterday and to-day. He told The Daily News: "We normally raid sections of Cato Manor everyday. Now that peaceful conditions have returned we are resuming this policy [*Natal Daily News,* April 13, 1960].

"To look at the law as it is, is against the interests of race relations, because all the laws are against the interests of natives. They restrict you from doing anything controlled. We often say that one day they will control us from visiting our wives. They are subtracting all the time without substituting" [Mr. A. W. G. Champion, an African leader in Durban].

Mr. Harmel and Mr. Hodgson are the first people to be placed under 24-hour house arrest . . . Mr. Harmel, Mr. Hodgson and Mr. Bernstein have been given permission to communicate with their wives, who are also banned. Mrs. Rica Hodgson's notice allows her to speak to her husband [*The Star,* Air Edition Weekly, November 10, 1962].

THE DICTATORSHIP of the Afrikaner nationalists in South Africa has not been fully achieved, nor can it be fully achieved, since Afrikaner power is too narrowly based. It rests on the control of the state, the legislature, the bureaucracy, the military and the police, and the propaganda machines of the State Information Office and the South African Broadcasting Corporation. But it is political power divorced from economic power and prestige. The industrial and commercial resources of the country are held largely by English-speaking Whites. And as for prestige, the emancipation of the Afrikaner from colonial subordination to the English—if such was indeed the historical situation—has brought rejection, not recognition, since extreme repression of non-Whites has accompanied the "liberation" of the Afrikaners. It is as if the nationalists are driven by the past humiliations of their people at the hands of the English to avenge themselves against the non-Whites, inflaming, not assuaging, their own bitterness in the process, and forfeiting their claims to prestige. And it is as if the denial of prestige drives them to further oppression in order to compel the recognition their own actions are withholding from them—a self-defeating cycle.

Deficient in prestige and economic power—though Afrikaners are beginning to advance economically and to convert political control into wealth and recognition—and representing a minority group (and even so, not all of its members), the nationalists cannot eliminate independent sources of power and monopolize the right of organization. The commercial and industrial interests of the English are organized economically in Chambers of Commerce and Industry, and politically in the opposition United Party. Roughly speaking, the United Party represents the bourgeoisie and the English, with some support and much leadership from Afrikaners, while the National Party represents the main body of Afrikaners, and draws support mainly from the proletariat, the lumpen proletariat, the farmers and petite bourgeoisie (and more recently, from its growing number of financiers and industrialists). The banning of the official opposition and the entire suspension of representative government are improbable, though the minor parliamentary parties with racially mixed membership, the Liberal Party and the Progressive Party, may perhaps be suppressed.* Nationalist power is too insecurely based to risk the estrangement of the English bourgeoisie and their possible alliance with non-Whites. Moreover, the Nationalists derive legitimacy from the parliamentary procedures of representative government. Their power was achieved by legal constitutional means, the equality and freedom of adult White suffrage being transformed into Afrikaner domination, and the Government is meticulous in the use of due legal process—even for the purpose of suspending the rule of law.

The economic and political divisions are linked with the independent organization of religion, university education, and the press. Only a minority of the population belongs to the Afrikaans-speaking churches. The English-speaking churches have a large membership of White and non-White members, and also close associations with overseas denominations and the world community of churches. They can be deprived of their schools and (under certain conditions) of their racially integrated worship, and the allocation of church sites in African areas can be controlled; priests and pastors can be attacked, vilified, and intimidated; but the churches cannot be suppressed. Religious persecution is a dangerous path for a small nation already under vigorous condem-

---

* [Added in proof.] The Liberal Party is now being suppressed.

nation, and the National Party is no doubt also restrained by intimations of religious tolerance.

The English universities and the English newspapers provide an independent channel for the dissemination of learning and ideas. They may purge and censor themselves so as not to incur the displeasure of the National Party, and they are increasingly subjected to its regulation, but they are linked with powerful interests and so enabled to resist suppression. And it seems unlikely that even the English primary and secondary schools can be fully subordinated to apartheid ideologies.

These independent sources of power—economic, religious, and educational—associated as they are with similar interests outside South Africa, counteract Afrikaner power and dictatorial control. White persons are free within certain limits to enjoy the benefits of rule over non-Whites. The limits are an acceptance of apartheid control of racial contact, and an avoidance of forbidden relationships. The non-White partner in these forbidden contacts might have been reserved for sole punishment, so that no restraint should be placed on the White man—in fact this is the case under certain conditions relating to the admission of non-Whites to White universities, or of Africans to interracial worship, when the criminal sanctions fall only on the non-Whites. The general rule, however, is that the White man is equally guilty with the non-White. There is strong disapproval of joint political activity. Inevitably, control over non-Whites means control over Whites. But a dictatorship of Afrikaner nationalists over Whites is inconceivable, given the narrow basis of Afrikaner power.

A dictatorship of Whites over non-Whites, on the other hand, is more feasible. It has indeed been imposed, particularly over Africans. This implies cooperation from the English. The extent to which the nationalists have been able to assume dictatorial powers over non-Whites indicates a substantial measure of consent by the English, or, at the very least, an unwillingness to exercise their power on behalf of the non-Whites. The conflict between the Government and the opposition, or between Afrikaner and English, is not basically a conflict about policy toward non-Whites, and it does not place non-Whites in the position of a subordinate third party, able to exploit the differences between the major powers.

Control over Africans is now approaching the limits possible in the exercise of domination over a large subordinate group by a relatively small superordinate group. The activities of Africans have been systematically analyzed and subjected to control. The draft blueprint is contained in the Bantu in European Areas Bill, which was circulated to local authorities for comment in October 1960. It includes the coordination of existing laws (many passed before the National Party took power) and their extension so as to perfect control over African freedom. It offers clear evidence of planning for total control, and of the nature of that planning in European areas, which is to say South Africa, excluding the underdeveloped African reserves.

Chapter 1 of this bill makes provision in regard to African areas for residence and other reasonable requirements, and is designed to ensure the proper accommodation of Africans. It also includes prohibition of entry into these African areas by an outside person without permit, powers to fence in the areas, to remove, curtail, or abolish them, and to summarily eject residents who commit a breach of the conditions of occupation. Chapter 2 provides powers for the residential segregation of Africans (excluding certain categories such as the few owners of immovable property of a certain ratable value, and domestic servants); the segregation of churches, schools, hospitals, places of entertainment, and other institutions mainly serving Africans; the exclusion of Africans from interracial contacts in these institutions and at meetings outside their own areas (contact within their areas being already fully controlled); curfew laws, and control over the acquisition of property. Chapter 3 is administrative, designed to improve the machinery for the centralized control of African life by the state bureaucracy.

Chapter 4 is headed quite simply "Restrictions on Bantu in Prescribed Areas," that is to say, *every* urban area, and such other areas, outside African reserves, as the Government may declare. The restrictions govern the conditions under which an African may remain in a prescribed area for more than seventy-two hours, the employment and "introduction" of Africans into prescribed areas, the status of foreign Africans, and the removal of Africans who remain unlawfully in the prescribed areas. Under Chapter 5, provision is made for the arrest without warrant of idle or undesirable Africans, and the manner in which the Bantu Affairs Commissioner is to deal with them; the removal of Africans from prescribed areas on the ground that their presence is detrimental to the maintenance of peace and order; and the removal of redundant Africans. Redundant Africans are those who are in excess of the reasonable labor requirements of the area. Proscription lists for the removal of surplus Africans are to be prepared, and these lists may include Africans born within the area, who have spent all their lives there in almost continuous employment.

Chapter 6 deals with liquor and kaffir beer, Chapter 7 with the financing of African areas. Chapter 8 contains the powers of control over African employment, including power over the right to work, determination of the nature of the employment, cancellation of existing contracts and the specifying of conditions governing the occupations of such self-employed persons as traders, independent contractors, and professionals. There is also provision for service contracts in respect of African children over the age of ten. Chapter 9 provides for Africans outside prescribed areas, and in particular regulates labor tenancy and squatting. Chapter 10 controls the recruiting of African labor and lists the powers of Government inspectors to redress grievances of African employees, but also, if so authorized, to impose summary sentences for neglect of duty, refusal to obey a lawful command by the employer, and the use of insulting or abusive language. General regulations are contained in the final chapter, as well as penal sanctions for contraventions in respect of which punishment was not already specified in the earlier chapters—an overwhelming structure of oppression.

A revised version of the Bantu in European Areas Bill was introduced in Parliament in 1963. It aroused much opposition and was withdrawn, though some of the provisions were passed in a short Act, the Bantu Laws Amendment Act No. 76 of 1963. The final blueprint, the Bantu Laws Amendment Act (1964) has now been passed.

Most of the provisions of the Bantu in European Areas Bill were already the law of the land and part of the routine administration of Africans. The denial of human freedom resulting from the detailed control of South African life has been well documented.[1] I shall add only some general comments—relating mainly to the subordination or relegation of Africans to the category of things, and to the use of terror and other extraordinary powers of repression.

The controls over Africans affect not only the elaboration of life. They are embedded at the very root of living. They govern subsistence, survival. At the gateway to employment, residence, domicile, movement, freedom, stands the Government, like St. Peter, admitting to Heaven or consigning to Hell. The analogy to Heaven is no doubt misleading. Most employment of Africans is rewarded at a level inadequate for the satisfaction of basic needs. And the saintly conduct which qualifies for paradise consists in falling within prescribed categories, giving no offence to the representatives of Government, and for the most part satisfying the labor needs of the White man.

The main instrument, and the symbol, of domination is the pass, that is to say the registration or reference book with particulars as to identity, permission to reside in the area, employment, and tax. In a very real sense, the African is subordinated to his pass, a form of what Georg Simmel classifies as subordination to a thing. In an article entitled "I am a Reference Book" in the *Golden City Post* (February 22, 1959), Lewis Nkosi, an African journalist, describes the dehumanizing quality of subordination to a thing, a pass. He is commenting on the

1. Cf. E. H. Brookes and J. B. Macaulay, *Civil Liberty in South Africa* (New York, Oxford University Press, 1958); International Commission of Jurists, *South Africa and the Rule of Law* (Geneva, 1960); Elizabeth S. Landis, "South African Apartheid Legislation," *Yale Law Journal,* vol. 71 (1961–62); and Muriel Horrell "The 'Pass Laws,'" South African Institute of Race Relations, No. 7 (1960).

death of two Africans who crept under blazing factory walls to rescue their reference books.

But it is not heroism—and certainly nothing like bravado—that can make a man go to his death in an attempt to save a Pass Book.

The motive is simply FEAR—the realisation of what his life will be worth without a reference book.

For a reference book has ceased to be a mere form of identification. It is interchangeable with the man himself.

At times one is forced to the conclusion that the man himself has less dignity, has less claim to official recognition, than the book.

For all I know, when there is need for a deputation to be sent to the Ministry of Bantu Administration, we could safely collect our reference books and mail them down to Cape Town to represent us . . .

I do not live apart from my own reference book any more. In fact I have decided I AM THE REFERENCE BOOK!

It stands for my personality. It delineates my character. It defines the extent of my freedom. Where I can live, work, and eat.

Whenever I see a police constable looking at me, the lifting of his eyes is at once adequate to make me understand that my right to walk the streets, to be about in a White area, even to confront my White fellow being with the sheer physical fact of my existence is now being called into question.

And the only answer equally adequate is the production of a reference book.

This at once assures the officer that I am a peaceful man and not a gangster or ghost.

My reference book has assumed greater importance than I can ever have. It has become my face.

What began as a system purporting to smooth my efforts to earn a living and move about with sufficient proof of my claim to the citizenship of this country, has now completely subordinated me.

My life is nothing without a pass. Without it there might even be a doubt whether I was born in this country and not in Jamaica.

As long as this is the case, obviously more of us will die in hellfires in future, groping for our reference books. Our Souls!

G. M. Pitje,[2] an African lawyer, also perceived the chattel quality of the subordination to a pass, to a reference book.

There is a rancid smell of slavery—chattel slavery—about it. Under the reference book system you are either employed or a

─────────

2. "The Effect of the Pass Laws on African Life," South African Institute of Race Relations, RR. 4/61.

vagrant or an idler or an undesirable element. The exceptions are too negligible to prove the general rule. From this there flows one element which is part of the single whole, and is in fact the central core of the whole system. The reference book is an instrument for socio-economic regimentation, dragooning and control. It creates a pattern with machine-like efficiency, and brings each and every individual throughout life under the direct eye and vigilance of the State machinery. It is an instrument for economic exploitation, social control and regimentation, forced labour and political persecution. It is more than a badge of inferiority. It is a merciless fetter strangling the life of the Black millions of South Africa. Its general effect is to deny or deprive the Blacks of their human heritage —the right of free movement; the right of choice of work; freedom of speech; freedom of thought; freedom of association; freedom of assembly and other basic rights and freedoms such as the inviolability of the human person. The African as a human is insulted in his personality. He is made a mere cipher—a cog in a huge, merciless wheel. His humanity is not recognised. The women of South Africa must also bear this mark of Cain throughout their lives. Yea, even children must wear this badge of slavery. One cannot register the birth of one's child without producing the reference book. The men of South Africa must be hunted down like wild beasts. The reference book haunts them. On a funeral march or in the church of God there is always the danger that police may break in and demand the production of reference books. This humiliation of a whole people cries out to high heaven for *vengeance*.

This reduction of the African to an object is reflected in official phraseology. To be classified as "idle" at least implies some measure of free will on the part of the item so classified. To be "undesirable" or "detrimental to the maintenance of peace and order" is also perhaps something positive, though the point of view is that of the alien ruler. But the classification of "redundant" pertains to things, not persons. The whole concept of the "canalization" of African labor is more appropriate to the harnessing of water for raw power. And this, in essence, is the approach of the South African Government toward the labor of Africans on White farms and in industry and commerce. As a servant to the needs of the White man, the African is largely reduced to the level of a commodity.

Marx conceived the status of the proletariat in capitalist society in similar terms. The worker is formally free, but compelled by lack of property to sell his labor in an insecure market at a low wage. Driven to work by his poverty, his work keeps him in poverty, so that the status of proletariat is hereditary. He is alienated from his own labor, which is detached from his personality and disposed at the will of another, as one of the factors in production. There is a commoditization of labor.

All this applies with equal force to the African worker, though no doubt many Africans derive satisfaction from employment in industry and commerce. But the compulsions go much further. An adult male tax acts as an incentive over and above poverty, driving Africans into employment. The Government pursues a deliberate policy of rendering African property "weak property," full rights of ownership to immovable property in European areas being abolished or replaced by leasehold rights. Even under a policy of granting Africans freehold rights to property in African areas, these rights would have little substance, since legal obligations rejected in the past are a poor guarantee for future security.

The African worker is in fact not even formally free. If he desires to seek work in an urban area, he must obtain a permit, which may specify the nature of the permitted work. At times, whole areas may be cut off from employment opportunities.

> You can't get permission to come into Durban as a cook in an urban area, as a waiter, as a garden boy, as a driver, as a delivery boy. There is the law. You must not cross the Tugela. Somebody came to me and asked me about it. He said he was crying with all the difficulties to try and come to Durban over a period of six months. And I said to him you will cry, my dear son, till you cry no more. They say to us that they want to *canalize* the native labor. . . . The first time I read of that expression, I can't tell you my feelings [interview with African Chairman of the Combined Advisory Boards in Durban, 1959].

Policy is directed toward the centralized control of all African employment through labor bureaus, which channel off African workers to appropriate employment. Employers notify labor bureaus of vacancies, and this provides the basis for district, regional, and central statistics, and for the requisitioning of workers. If an African loses his employment, he may become redundant and exposed to deportation. An African speaker asked where was the place of the Black man when he was dismissed. "He can't stay on earth—it's too hot. He can't go to Heaven, it's too far." And even without loss of employment, the African worker may face deportation for many reasons, including, it would seem, the more general reason that the presence of Africans conflicts with the proposed geographical pattern for the racial distribution of employment.

As additional means for canalizing or domesticating African labor, the Government has the power to reserve particular occupations for different racial groups, a power inevitably exercised to discriminate first against Africans, and then against Coloreds and Indians. African trade unions are not recognized, and their more outspoken leaders are persecuted. Instead of trade unions, a paternalist form of workers' organization has been devised. Strikes by Africans are illegal. When they protest, armed police are often called, and there are large scale arrests. Many employers appear to invoke the aid of the police in order to discipline their African workers, incorporating the police as an integral part of the organization. When all these controls are viewed as a whole, the bondage of the African worker exceeds that envisaged by Marx in his moments of greatest moral indignation over the oppression of the proletariat.

In the Government's approach to the education and political participation of Africans, there is the same denial of the African's right to self-expression, self-determination, and free will, the same relegation to the status of an object of action. Educational policy is directed toward the molding of the African, as if he were a plastic, into a form compatible with, and subservient to, the apartheid ideology of the rulers, by means of the idealization of the tribal history and the tribal soul, training in subordination to authority, and the integration of education with employment policies. Politically, Africans are relegated to the status of being administered by a central White bureaucracy. Even the concept of independent African Bantustans involves a denial of free will, since their composition and character are predetermined by the dominant group.

It is this denial of self-expression to other racial groups, this determination of their destiny, regardless of their own desires and in the interests of the rulers, this total nature of the planned regulation of the lives of subordinates, which suggests the parallel with National Socialism. And the suggestion is strengthened by the use of terror and the exercise of extraordinary and arbitrary powers to enforce submission.

Terror is reduced to routine. There is the daily terror of the routine administration of laws. No African man in the urban areas is secure from police aggression and molestation at any time, day or night. The pass laws provide the justification for confrontation in the streets and for mass midnight raids in the homes. Prima facie Africans are presumed to be criminals until they establish their possession of the necessary permits. The pass, according to a correspondent of the *Ilanga Lase Natal* (June 13, 1959),

> has this scourge about it that the father and mother and even children run away because of it. One falls into a beer pot running

away from a pass. Even when they are at table they will scatter as you see locusts and the table remains alone. This Government surprises me as to why "he" wants our corpses to be known whereas "he" does not want those of other nations to be known by passes [translated from the Zulu].

Parents are humiliated before their children, the home is violated, the security of the family destroyed.

> The pass system makes nonsense of family life. It makes nonsense of human decency, human dignity and self-respect among the African people. Like child labor during the period of the industrial revolution in England, the pass system constitutes the rape of African youth and opens the way to certain abuses and malpractices which are now and then exposed and highlighted in the daily Press, e.g. the iniquities of convict farm labor. The comfort of a home, parenthood, social stability, economic security, safety of the individual, inviolability of the human person, human dignity and peace of mind—these have lost their meaning in African life. Life has lost its sweetness. It has become one long stretch of persecution under the pass system. For some Africans there is greater safety, relative peace and security in prison. At least in the latter there is the certainty of being in prison.[3]

From time to time, the reform of the pass laws and of police persecution under the pass laws has been discussed. But an extensive system of mass routine terror is necessary to White domination, and basic changes in the pass laws seem improbable until power is redistributed in favor of Africans. Or if the pass laws are modified, then some alternative mechanism will be necessary to serve the same functions. The fact that the terror is routine does not diminish its fearsome quality. It is small comfort to know that the home will be violated at midnight rather than at noon, or that one is liable to be picked up by the police at any time or place. The values denied by the pass laws are too fundamental—the survival of the man and his family may be at stake.[4]

Routine terror is supplemented by extensive powers vested in the officials of the bureaucracy, such as the powers of the superintendent over life in the locations, of influx control officers over the right to work, and of administrators over the right to education. These powers may be expected to encourage despotism in the official, and docility in the subject. Something of this process is expressed in the nickname given to one municipal official, "Ndlovu Kayiphendulwa" (Elephant to Whom It Is Not Answered).

3. G. M. Pitje, "The Effect of the Pass Laws on African Life."
4. Enforcement of the pass laws is now being extended also to women.

Terror is conveyed more effectively, however, by the use of extraordinary, rather than routine, power. And the armory of extraordinary powers rapidly mounts. There is increasing use of force and arbitrary decree—banning of persons from membership of organizations and attendance at meetings; deportation, exile, and confinement to a restricted area; mass trials; police intimidation and violence (shown in the invasion of peaceful meetings with Sten guns, patrols of armored cars, mass criminal assaults such as those in Cape Town on April 4, 1960, and the destruction of life at Sharpeville, Langa, and Ngqusa Hill); mobilization of the military; the continuing state of emergency; massive raids for vagrancy and crime busting; secret summary trials within prison walls; and the use of arrest without trial.

These extraordinary powers also go through a process of becoming routine. The invasion of a meeting by armed police may still occasion shock, but no longer surprise. The patrol of armored cars in residential areas is taken for granted. Banning and exile evoke little comment. It is only the early use of these powers which startles, mystifies. Later they become commonplace, but still terrifying because they strike at the lives of their victims.

This process of incorporating the extraordinary into the routine may be illustrated in relation to arrest without trial, a useful—perhaps necessary—weapon for dictators. Under the Public Safety Act of 1953, the Government assumed powers to declare states of emergency, during which its political opponents might be detained without trial, though some protection, largely symbolic, was afforded by the provision that the names of those detained must be tabled in Parliament within a specified period. This is a cumbersome procedure, and the declaration of a state of emergency undermines confidence in the country and adversely affects reputation and investment. There was thus a need for a routine power which could be arbitrarily exercised without advertisement or surveillance by the courts. It was conferred by section 4 of the General Law Amendment Act (39/1961),[5] which provides that:

> Whenever any person has been arrested on a charge of having committed any offence, the Attorney-General may, if he considers it necessary in the interest of the safety of the public or the maintenance of public order, issue an order that such person shall not be released on bail or otherwise before the expiration of a period of twelve days after the date of his arrest.

There is no difficulty in making a charge; charges are often irresponsibly framed, particularly in times of crisis; the "bastard" conjunction "and/or" is a convenient device for spreading a wide net in the indictment; a charge of incitement, a somewhat nebulous and hence favored

5. For one year initially, but later extended.

charge, may be amended to an infringement of municipal by-laws; and there is apparently no obligation to even prosecute the charge. In effect, the Government assumed the power to arrest without trial for a period of twelve days. However, as this power becomes routine, there arises the need for even more extreme and extraordinary power. This is now provided, first, under the General Law Amendment Act (76/1962), which empowers the Minister of Justice to sentence persons without trial to indefinite house arrest in total isolation (apart from contact with lawyers and such other persons as a magistrate may allow), with a general prohibition throughout South Africa against the publication of any "speech, utterance, writing, or statement" made or produced "anywhere at any time" by such persons; and, second, under the General Law Amendment Act (37/1963), which gives commissioned police officers the power, without warrant, to arrest and detain for a period or periods of ninety days, with solitary confinement, persons suspected of having information relative to certain political offences.

The logical outcome of the trend toward the routine use of extraordinary powers would be a situation in which the legal norm is the suspension of the rule of law. As it is, South African political and legal institutions are profoundly changed. Superficially the forms are the same, but they are filled with quite different content. The system of government is still one of parliamentary representation for Whites, and the reconciliation of competing interests by parliamentary discussion. In practice, however, Parliament is largely a National Party ritual; only rarely are meaningful concessions made to parliamentary opposition. The situation is analogous to that of one-party government, but with the important proviso that the National Party may be voted out of power, though even this is by no means certain.

Courts still administer law, but increasingly there is a divorce between law and general principles of justice. Or to phrase the point differently, in issues affecting apartheid, the courts, often with great legal wisdom and integrity, publicly administer injustice. Injustice must not only be done, it must appear to be justly done. The mere passing of a law is regarded as its legitimation, irrespective of its nature and functions.

In the struggle for power, law is used like a maxim gun. And the non-Whites themselves perfect it as an instrument of their own oppression. The more immediately successful their campaigns, the more unsuccessful they are in the long run—at any rate from a legal point of view. The reason is that a successful campaign probes the weaknesses in the system of control, and the Government's response is to strengthen the controls precisely in those respects where they have proved inadequate. An effective legal protest against discrimination in railway waiting rooms leads to the passage of a law legitimizing discrimination in the provision of both public and private amenities. The power to declare a state of emergency, heavy penalties for defiance of laws, and arrest without trial are all responses to non-White political action.

The major target of the extraordinary powers is political opposition involving non-Whites. There are two main aspects; the control of organization and the control of ideas. Non-White leaders tend to regard the conquest of political rights as primary, though for tactical reasons they may mobilize campaigns around other issues. Their immediate goal is the organization of the masses. The struggle has as its central aspect the attempt of non-Whites to build a mass organization and the determination of the government to destroy non-White organization. The repression is exercised mainly against political organization, not against organization generally, as for example in the world of sport or religious worship, perhaps because these activities are regarded as potentially conducive to political apathy, or as substitutes for political action. In any event, the Government has not sought to suppress all non-White organization, and the powers for the proscription of organizations under the Suppression of Communism Act have as yet been exercised only in the field of politics.

For the control of ideas, the Government relies on its extraordinary powers, including bans, deportations, exile, proscription of organizations, indictment for treason, communism, and incitement, public citation by name as a communist, dismissal from employment, the banning of books and periodicals, the threat of censorship over the press, prohibition of meetings, insulation from contact and heretical ideas, house arrest, and imprisonment. Intimidating propaganda identifies interracial association with sexual immorality, the principle of "one-man-one-vote" with communism, criticism of the Government with disloyalty to country—or indeed incitement to treason—and, conversely, the enjoyment of rights with allegiance to apartheid. Somehow this propaganda managed for a time to create an illusion of the permanence of the Government and its ideology, though it would seem that apartheid being a deviation, a sport, in the contemporary world, must be highly transitory.

To the Government's strategies for the control of ideas must be added the positive, as distinct from the repressive techniques. These include the opening of some new occupational opportunities for Africans; the indoctrination of Africans through the ordinary schools, the schools for the sons of chiefs, and the universities; increased powers to the chiefs; the use of chiefs, tribal ambassadors, and educated Africans in the lumpen-bureaucracy; the inculcation of tribal sentiment and tribal pride; and rule by subdivision. From the point of view of politically sophisticated Africans, this is an attempt to use Africans as the instruments of their own oppression. For the Government, the goal is, no doubt, the withering away of force and its replacement by a self-policing, self-regulating, self-perpetuating system, with built-in psychological and institutional controls.

The task facing the African bourgeoisie, desirous of social change, is fearsome. The extraordinary powers of the Government may be routine in terms of their use, but they are not routine when applied to the individual. There is an element of caprice in their application. It may be conventional for political opponents to be arrested in the early hours after midnight, but this is no guarantee that the individual will be so arrested. He may sleep more securely at night in prison than at home, or at friends' homes, in expectation of arrest. This is what Mr. Pitje was conveying in relation to the pass laws when he commented that for some Africans there is greater safety, relative peace and security in prison: "At least in the latter there is the certainty of being in prison."

Insecurity is a major weapon of control, enlisting from many Africans a measure of cooperation, or at any rate of conformity. The life of the urban African is maintained in insecurity, like that of a foreigner in a hostile land. There is insecurity of residence, domicile, employment, freedom, and family life. Spies and informers abound. Surfaced, constitutional protest invites severe retribution and perfects the machinery of oppression, suggesting revolution as the only avenue of change. The individual may withdraw, carefully guarding an appearance of neutrality, though identifying with radical political movements. Or he may seek to extract benefits from the system of apartheid. Or he may engage in secret, underground revolutionary activity. Or he may pursue the hazardous course of promoting, with like-minded members of other racial groups, and by evolutionary means, a common society based on nonracial integration. But whatever choice he makes, the limits within which he is free to act are narrowly defined. And there are strong pressures toward racialism and revolutionary violence.

PART II

Class Perspectives

CHAPTER 7

Rise and Fall

EDUCATION was the original basis for the differentiation of what I describe as the African bourgeoisie, and it is still the most important factor. It plays much the same differentiating role as the economic factor in capitalist society. The African bourgeoisie draws fine shades of distinction in respect of education, much finer than the more highly educated Whites. Between educated, semieducated, and uneducated Africans, there is mutual awareness of difference, much the same as between social classes and, at the same time, a complex interplay of conflict and cooperation.

Formal education for Africans was linked with mission work and inextricably interwoven with Christianity, Westernization, and the repudiation of tribal traditions. As a result, the gulf between the educated and the tribesman was not merely one of learning but of an entirely different way of life. A new class arose, to some extent alienated from the tribal structure of chiefs, headmen (*abanumzana*), and commoners. The late Professor Jabavu,[1] himself an African, describes something of the estrangement between the two groups when he warns African teachers against the dangers of isolation:

> Firstly, there is loneliness, for the teacher is often the best educated, and indeed the only educated person in our Native areas and locations, surrounded by an ignorant and squalid population; secondly, the want of suitable companions, for most young men and women in our villages are not edifying companions for teachers; thirdly, beer drinking, or the alcohol demon, to which many male teachers, I regret to state, have succumbed; fourthly, impurity or immorality which, among town and town-adjoining habitations is much more rampant than is generally known.

Christianity, Westernization, and education not only tended to coincide, but they also provided the basis for further differentiation. The establishment of mission stations made possible a physical separation

1. D. D. T. Jabavu, "The Native Teacher out of School," *The Black Problem* (Lovedale, Book Department, 1920), p. 72.

between the Christian convert and the tribal heathen. Education fostered occupational diversity, and the opportunity to escape from the common fate of the peasant or laborer into the highly prized positions of minister, teacher, clerk, and interpreter. With the requisite educational and economic qualifications, an African might exercise the franchise in the Cape Colony.

In Natal, an African had the right to apply for exemption from the operation of Native Law, on proof of his ability to read and write; letters of exemption were a step toward the franchise, though this was a remote prospect, since in a period of 39 years only three Africans had been registered as voters under Law 11 of 1865.[2] According to an informant, the son of an exempted African,

> the holders of letters of exemption tended to form a separate class and were called "the exempted" by other Africans. . . . They would be treated with deference, not solely because they were exempted, but because invariably they were also educated men and Christians, and these were marks of respectability. The ordinary Zulus distinguished between *isifundiswa* (which is to say, a product of the schools, with fairly good command of English, such as school teachers, interpreters, clerks), *ikholwa,* that is the Christian convert, and *izemtiti,* that is to say, the exempted. In many cases, these three descriptions applied to one person. To be a Christian carried prestige in those days (not today, when one can get a man who is a non-Christian with a good house, motor car, wealth, and enjoying prestige because of these things).

The educated men turned toward the new world of Western civilization. They tended to reject the tribal way of life, and to place their hopes in cultural assimilation. From their ranks were drawn the clerks and interpreters who conveyed the instructions of the White administrators, and they thus became identified with the machinery of government. Inevitably, the complexity of race relations entered into the relations between educated and uneducated Africans.

The early history of the African bourgeoisie is roughly documented in *The African Yearly Register,*[3] an illustrated national biographical dictionary. Looking back over this "Black Folks' *Who's Who*" in the period of about 1850 to 1930, there were many signs of the rise of an African bourgeoisie in South Africa.

Reverend Tiyo Soga is listed as the first African in South Africa to become an ordained minister. He received his early schooling in the Cape and completed his theological studies in 1856 in Scotland, where

2. E. H. Brookes, *The History of Native Policy in South Africa* (Pretoria, Van Schaik, 1927), p. 60.

3. Edited and compiled by T. D. Mweli Skota (Johannesburg, Esson and Co., 1932).

he married a Scotswoman. He preached to many European congregations in South Africa with great acceptance, according to the biographer, and was received in audience by the Duke of Edinburgh at Cape Town. When he died, there were eulogies in the press. *The Journal* commented, "Men cannot despise the Kaffir race as they contemplate him."

Reverend Soga was followed by many other distinguished clergymen. Reverend Dr. Walter B. Rubusana, born in 1858, received an honorary degree of Doctor of Philosophy from McKinley University for his *History of South Africa from the Native Standpoint*. He was appointed Moderator of the Midland Missionary Committee under the Congregational Union of South Africa, and was the first African to be elected to the Cape Provincial Council. Others trained in England and America. The Reverend Ngidi, D.Ph., D.D., received his education in Natal and at the University of Rome. Reverend John Dube, also of Natal, was educated in America. He was the founder and principal of Ohlange High School and an ex-president and founder of the African National Congress. (In 1936 he was awarded an honorary doctorate of philosophy.) African clergymen represented their congregations in international conferences. Reverend Makiwane was in charge of European as well as African members of the Free Church of Scotland.

The legal profession had opened to Africans, initially in the form of agent-at-law, a special category of legal practitioner, licensed to practice in a defined district. Alfred Mangena was the first African "barrister-at-law" in South Africa, having qualified at Lincoln's Inn, London, where he was called to the bar. Returning to South Africa in 1910, he was admitted, after some difficulty, as a solicitor of the Supreme Court of South Africa, and pioneered the acceptance of Africans in courts where Africans had previously been admitted only as prisoners or witnesses. His life was in danger more than once, so it was said, because of his success in defending Africans against Europeans.

Dr. P. Ka. I. Seme followed Mangena. He returned to South Africa in 1910, having trained at Columbia University and Middle Temple, England, and started practice in Johannesburg. In 1916 Seme entered into partnership with Mangena. He acted as solicitor to the Swazi nation. In 1928, Columbia University conferred on him the degree of doctor of law. The third African lawyer, Montsioa, grandson of the "great and distinguished Natural Ruler of the Barolong Tribe" also trained in England, at Lincoln's Inn.

Teachers were given responsibility as supervisors of schools and as headmasters. Doctors graduated in overseas universities and commenced practice. Among them were Dr. A. B. Xuma, M.D., B.Sc., L.R.C.P., L.R.C.S., who trained in America, Hungary, and Edinburgh, and Dr. James Moroko, F.R.C.S., F.R.C.P. of Edinburgh University (they were later to become presidents of the African National Congress). One of the first nurses to qualify, in about 1912, married Advocate Mangena. Nurse Xala, daughter of a minister of religion and the third nurse to qualify in South Africa, became matron of a hospital.

Writers made their contribution to the English and vernacular literatures of South Africa. Reverend John Knox Bokwe wrote plays and composed music. Reverend Tiyo Soga translated *The Pilgrim's Progress*. Sol. T. Plaatje wrote a novel, *Mhudi,* and translated Shakespeare into Sechuana. I. Bud-Mbelle wrote *The Xosa Scholar*. There were historical studies and studies of race relations such as Dr. Molema's *The Bantu— Past and Present*. Songs and hymns were composed, and notes written on musical notation.

Meanwhile Africans also entered journalism. *The African Yearly Register* shows that they founded and edited newspapers, such as *Imvo Zabantsundu,* established by John Tengo Jabavu in 1884. Among the papers on which Africans served as editors were *The Advocate, The Bechuana Gazette* (edited by Dr. Molema's father), *Umteteli wa Bantu, Abantu Batho,* the *Native Eye, Ipepa Lo Hlange, Izwe, The Worker, Umlomo wa Bantu, Ikwezi,* the *African World,* and *Ilanga Lase Natal*. Some were ephemeral, a few are still published.

There was even some development of trade. *The Yearly Register* lists among the occupations of the celebrities the owner of the double-storey Temperance Hotel in Kingwilliamstown, a grain speculator, transport contractor, storekeeper, restaurant proprietor, insurance agent, progressive farmer, land-commission agent and township owner, owner of dance hall and bakery, bus owner.

The elite began to intermarry. The writer Sol. Plaatje married the sister of Bud-Mbelle, and the solicitor Richard Msimang married Bud-Mbelle's daughter, a nurse. The Makiwanes intermarried with the Jabavus. Z. K. Matthews, who became a professor at the University College of Fort Hare, married the daughter of Reverend John Knox Bokwe. Many of the sons of the elite studied overseas, returning with high qualifications. New bourgeois family lines were being established.

It is difficult to reconstruct with any accuracy these qualitative changes in the structure of African society. There appears to have been a rapid development of a core of African families of bourgeois substance and more than bourgeois distinction. As was also the case with the American Negro, the growth was greatest in the professional and clerical services and least in trade or business enterprise.[4] But it went beyond the training of ministers, teachers, and clerks for a segregated and subordinated society, not only in the quality of education and the

4. See G. Franklin Edwards, *The Negro Professional Class* (Glencoe, Free Press, 1959), pp. 19–20.

level of responsibility but also in the diversity of occupational opportunity, which included openings in law, medicine, and trade.

Then there seems to have been a pause, perhaps almost a retrogression, for fully a generation. Although the legal profession was opened to Africans at an early stage, and Mangena and Seme were already in practice during the first decade of the Union of South Africa, few others entered the profession until after the Second World War. The immediate causes can be identified—the reluctance of White lawyers to apprentice Africans and the barrier of a premium charged for training. And yet some African lawyers had surmounted the obstacle of training and were already established. So too, the medical profession opened early to Africans, but development has been slight and recent. Again, an immediate cause was the initial lack of training facilities within South Africa; still the pioneers had managed to train in overseas universities.

The increasing dominance of racially restrictive policies suggests a more basic reason for the check in the growth of the bourgeoisie. The early bourgeoisie flourished particularly in the Cape, where more liberal policies prevailed. After the unification of South Africa, the segregatory policies of the northern provinces began to prevail throughout the country. Jabavu's[5] comments on "The Segregation Fallacy" show this development already in the second decade of the Union. His attack on the theory that Africans "should develop along their own lines" and his arguments as to the impossibility of retribalizing Africans are entirely contemporary: they might have been written today with reference to apartheid. But the segregatory and restrictive policies in themselves cannot adequately explain the check to the African bourgeoisie, since its main growth coincides with the years after the Second World War, when the policy of apartheid was being applied most systematically and extensively.

Thus segregation and racial discrimination do not necessarily entirely frustrate the development of a bourgeoisie: they may even stimulate it. A further factor must be introduced, that of the economic base for development. Where there is tolerance toward the subordinate group, there is also the possibility of its members entering into a wide range of occupations by virtue of the opportunities in the wider society: the possession of an economic base within the subordinate group is not crucial. Where, however, segregation and discrimination are applied against the subordinate group, the economic base is obviously crucial for occupational differentiation. This does not mean that the legal profession, for example, is concerned simply with the protection of vested economic interests. The many prosecutions of Africans for

5. *The Segregation Fallacy and Other Papers* (Lovedale, Book Department, 1928).

purely statutory offences would have provided the African lawyer with
a vast clientele. Nor does it mean that disease depends on affluence.
There would have been no dearth of patients for the African doctors.
But the ability to pay for their services and their training was restricted
by the low level of economic resources. And this economic restriction
also affected the opportunity to accumulate capital for commercial and
industrial enterprise.

It seems to have been the combination of segregation, discrimination,
and poverty that barred the progress of the African bourgeoisie in
the period between the First and Second World Wars. Change occurred
not by way of diminution of discrimination and segregation but in the
economic structure of the African community. Though individual poverty persists, Africans collectively now command substantial economic
resources, sufficient to support a bourgeoisie, and to stimulate bourgeois
ambitions.

The main factors in this change have been the development of secondary industry in South Africa, increasing urban employment of
Africans, and the growth in national income. From 1921 to 1958–60,
the relative contribution of secondary industry doubled, roughly to
parity with primary industry. The net average national income increased almost sixfold, while the percentage of Africans in urban areas
more than doubled (Appendix D, Table 1). At first, during the period
1921 to 1936, the South African economy suffered a recession. Government policy gave priority to the rehabilitation of the large "poor
White" population, which was accorded preferential treatment in employment and as "civilized" labor. With the absorption of the "poor
Whites," the recovery and expansion of the South African economy
from 1933 onward, and the industrial stimulus of the Second World
War, occupational opportunities could not be withheld from Africans.
Indeed the industrial expansion rested on their increasing participation.

The share of Africans in the national income is difficult to estimate.
L. H. Samuels,[6] in a paper on "Bantu Economic Growth and Capital
Development," stressed the substantial rise in money incomes accruing
to Africans engaged in modern economic activity. He placed the aggre-
gate net annual income of Africans at £350 million in 1957–58, as
compared with £60 million in 1936, though he commented that the
estimate of £350 million might be too high. (Adjusting for the upward
trend in prices, this would still mean that total African income had
more than doubled.) In the period 1938–39 to 1959, the real earnings
of African workers in private manufacturing industries rose by 46 per
cent. J. L. Sadie,[7] in a paper on "Bantu Population Growth and Dis-

6. Delivered to the National Development Foundation of South Africa, July 1960.
7. Delivered to the same conference.

tribution of Goods," estimated that Africans received an annual per capita income (including income in the subsistence sector, but excluding "other income" of the public sector) of £13 in 1936 and £39 in 1956–57. When the effect of change in the price level was eliminated, there was still an over-all advance in the average "real income" of about 33 per cent, and of 80 per cent if the underdeveloped African areas were excluded.

These changes were accompanied by changes in the occupational structure of the African population. Most Africans still work as peasant farmers and agricultural workers, and as unskilled laborers in the towns and industries. Over the last decade, several surveys of African employment, in different areas and sectors, have shown some 66 to 90 per cent as unskilled.[8] In a tabulation of the nonagricultural occupations in 1951, of African workers in Natal aged 10 years and over almost 80 per cent of the men were general laborers, domestic servants, mine laborers, and railway laborers, and over 84 per cent of the women were domestic servants and general laborers.[9] But there are nevertheless appreciable numbers entering the more skilled occupations and an increasing recruitment in the professions and trade.

The first four categories of the occupational census include the occupations which I have counted in the bourgeoisie. In the 1951 census, these categories comprised about 59,000 persons, or almost 2 per cent of the economically active African population of 15 years and over. The comparable figures for Whites were some 436,000 persons or over 44 per cent.[10] The results of the 1960 occupational census are not yet available, and only rough estimates are possible. There were about 27,660 African teachers (compared with 17,323 in 1951), some 7,500 nurses, about 100 doctors, about 50 advocates and lawyers (with others in training), 200 laboratory assistants, 70 postmasters, 70 librarians, and an unknown number of clerks, interpreters, salesmen,

8. Ninety per cent of African workers in the Cape Peninsula in 1954, excluding professional and administrative workers (S. T. van der Horst, "A Note on Native Labour Turnover and the Structure of the Labour Force in the Cape Peninsula," *South African Journal of Economics, 25,* 1957, 282); 80% in industries subject to wage determinations, 1937–54, involving about 300,000 workers (J. A. Lombard, "The Determination of Racial Income Differentials in South Africa," Institute for Social Research, University of Natal, 1962, p. 8); 70% in two of the better African locations of Durban (O. P. F. Horwood, "Some Aspects of Urban African Employment in the Durban Area," *Race Relations Journal, 25,* 1958); and 66% in a sample of industrial undertakings near the African areas (P. S. Rautenbach, "The Impact of the Bantu on the Location of Industry and Bantu Reserves," National Development Foundation of South Africa, July, 1960).

9. J. R. Burrows, *The Population and Labour Resources of Natal,* Natal Town and Regional Planning Reports, 6 (1959), 143.

10. *Union Statistics for Fifty Years* (Pretoria, Bureau of Census and Statistics, 1960), p. A-33.

social workers, and ministers of religion. The number of African-owned retail trade outlets was estimated at 16,000, compared with 761 in 1946/47.[11]

There is thus an appreciable occupational differentiation of professionals, other white collar workers and traders. This provides the core for the elaboration of class distinctions. Entry into the prestige occupations is now relatively vigorous, but under the very different conditions of apartheid, which profoundly affects occupational expectations and prestige by redefining goals and life chances. As opportunities are opened, they are also narrowly contracted. And paradoxically, as class formation transcends tribal barriers and tribal perspectives, so apartheid seeks to confine it within the tribal boundaries, subordinating the class identity to the tribal identity.

11. Main Source, N. Mkele, "The Emergent African Middle Class," *Optima,* December 1960, pp. 217–26, supplemented by "The Progress of the Bantu Peoples towards Nationhood," No. 3 (South African Government Information Office, 1960), *Union Statistics for Fifty Years,* and F. J. de Villiers, "Financing of Bantu Education," South African Institute of Race Relations, RR. 64/61.

CHAPTER 8

Varied Perspectives: Tribal and Racial

PERSPECTIVES on social differentiation amongst Africans are greatly varied. This is to be expected where the setting is a plural society involving contact between peoples of sharply contrasted cultures and technologies and the domination of a racial minority with changing political philosophies. There are not only the perspectives of Western industrial society, with its evaluation of wealth, occupation, and education, but also those of the indigenous tribal societies and of the total racial society. From these varied perspectives, I have selected for discussion in this chapter the tribal traditional perspective, as exemplified by Zulu society, and the racial, in its most contemporary form of apartheid.

In regard to the traditional system of differentiation, Mkele[1] argues that African societies in Southern Africa were generally stratified politically but not economically, since land was available to all on a usufructuary basis, and production was for consumption not profit. I think one can accept that private ownership of the means of production was not characteristic of African societies, and that political criteria were primary in their systems of stratification, without however agreeing that this implies an absence of economic stratification. Certainly economic differences, as manifested in the ownership of cattle, the size of homestead, or the standard of hospitality, were associated with political stratification and considered to be objects of prestige.

Zulu society distinguished the chief and his kinsmen, the heads of homesteads (or *abanumzana*), and the commoners, the people who have nothing (the *abafokazana* or *abantukazana*). A commoner might rise by his own ability to the position of a chief's right-hand man. The family line was emphasized, as is no doubt customary in most small-scale societies. According to Mbata, a South African anthropologist, length of residence was also an important factor in the traditional system of stratification:

> The oldest families in any locality are the most influential—they
> get all the positions of importance, and they have a greater say in

1. "The Emergent Middle Class," p. 218.

the councils, and generally they are listened to. And their power also lies in the fact that they have a deeper lineage structure. . . . Now because of that there is the other group distinction which gives prestige to a family—it's just a matter of "whose son are you" in terms of how long have your people been here. Then people will say, "We are the tree of growth here, we grew up here." A fellow will say, "That's my father, that's my grandfather, that's my great-grandfather," pointing at the various sites and their graves. If a man can point to three or four graves of his ancestors, that man is pretty important in the area [interview, January 1959].

Bravery was highly esteemed, reflecting the military tradition of the Zulu people. A Zulu journalist thought that this was the reason that "high society" life had not developed among the Zulu people of Durban, perhaps projecting his own sentiments that social parties are effeminate.

The quality of respect was also held in great esteem, respect for one-self and for others. This quality of the self-respecting person who respects others is consistent both with an equalitarian and a highly stratified society. In the former case, it is a leveling factor, reinforcing the tendency to equality. Each individual is encouraged to think of himself as the equal of any man, with an equal right to respect. In the latter case, where respect for oneself is bound up with respect for one's superiors, it is a differentiating factor, reinforcing inequality. This was the position in the Indian caste system and also in Zulu society. To the outside observer, the behavior of the commoner or the person of low caste may seem sheer servility, a degrading denial of self respect; to the member of the society, the same behavior may be necessary for self respect.

Zulu informants are likely to regard their traditional society as democratic, since there was mobility by achievement. Observers from other African linguistic groups, on the other hand, may have a stereotype of a highly authoritarian and stratified society. Noni Jabavu conveys this stereotype in her book *Drawn in Colour*[2] in a somewhat extreme form. She is discussing the arrogance and cringing as between aristocrat and servant among the Baganda, and comments on the contrast between her own people and the Baganda and Zulu.

I was reminded of our Xhosa tradition which holds that "a man is a man, can look his superiors by blood or position straight in the eye, requires to cringe to no-one not even his Chief, since any man's 'place' is an honourable one secured by hereditary primogeniture." In that system there was no feeling of insecurity for nobody could be elevated to god-like status one day, next day dashed to that of a crab as they could under despots like the Zulu Tshaka, for ex-

2. *Drawn in Colour* (London, Murray, 1960), pp. 170–75.

ample; nobody might deal with a man as though he were less *or more* than a man. . . .

Our tradition was antipathetic to such things as had happened to the Zulu people. Politically we despise Zulus for having allowed themselves to be manipulated by a dictator, letting their "personalities as men" be extinguished. . . .

Zulus, like the Baganda, are great favourites with outsiders. Yet Southern blacks themselves generally deplore the characteristics noticeable in their social aspects: servility, fawning, degenerate effects, Xhosa in particular say, of military "discipline." These are offset by bullying tendencies. "In this you see what happens," we Xhosa declare, "when a Tshaka or Mzilikazi rises up amongst a people and institutes a despotism which cares for no man's son or daughter."

She suggests that tribes without pomp and circumstance, "ancient tradition," "fossilized clap-trap" are at an advantage, readier to take up new techniques and to respond to industrialization.

Within the traditional structures, new systems of differentiation have arisen, and many influences undermine the old values. In the tribal areas, the minister and the teacher, the educated elite, confront the aliterate or partly literate chiefs and their councillors, competing with them for leadership and prestige. Christianity and education create new lines of cleavage, introducing the values of Western society. Particularly at the old mission stations, the division into Christian and non-Christian was strong.[3] In a most interesting article,[4] A. Vilakazi, a Zulu anthropologist, distinguished also a third class of persons, those who are neither Christian nor traditionally oriented, some educated, others not. Education opens up new channels of mobility, effecting in some respects a reversal of status between the young and the aged. Then too, the traditional societies have been exporting population for many years to the urban centers as migrant laborers and as permanent settlers. Children often return for a period to the ancestral home, tribesman and townsman visit each other, men and women are deported from the urban to the rural areas. Inevitably Western and urban values enter into the knowledge and life of the tribesman.

In the cities, men of different tribes meet in new systems of relationship. They work side by side in the factories, worship together, join

3. "Chief" Albert Luthuli comments with reference to the mission station at Groutville that it was a mixed community of heathens and Christians, that he was aware as a child of the distinction between Christian and non-Christian, but that in the life of Groutville distinction did not mean discrimination or that "Christians are better." Despite great differences of education and outlook, there was no elite cut off from the ordinary life of the village (*Let My People Go*, New York, McGraw-Hill, 1962, p. 27).

4. "A Reserve from Within," *African Studies, 16* (1957), 98–99.

political associations, compete in sports, and intermarry. New criteria become significant in the evaluation of position, the criteria of Western industrial society—education, Christianity, Westernization, wealth. Traditional society and Western society stand sharply contrasted—barefoot poverty and well-shod wealth, the primitive and the modern, rural subsistence as against technological and professional specialization, the closed isolated backward-looking perspectives and the exciting vistas of an open world and of world citizenship. It is difficult for many tribal values to survive in this new milieu. There is no scope for militarism (though the situation is beginning to change); respect for bravery may be transformed into adulation for the verbally hard-hitting aggressive leader. Traditional hospitality may still be valued, but a money economy and poverty make hospitality difficult. Police raids and an oppressive system of administration are likely to undermine respect for oneself and respect for others. And such traditional criteria of evaluation as family line, relationship to the chief, possession of cattle, and ancestral graves are largely irrelevant for placing the stranger.

The educated and the politically sophisticated generally repudiate tribalism as expressed in tribal loyalties and perspectives. As one university graduate put it: "The Congress type of student has a conscious mission to overcome tribal tendency even against students from the north." This rejection of tribalism shows an ambivalence in the suggestion that "tribal tendency" between the north and the south is not altogether unreasonable.

Among the educated in particular, there is a strong repugnance for tribal society, a sense of cultural shame, a feeling that tribalism is a return to the past, to barbarism, to the primitive. The cultural shame derives from the teachings of missionaries, from formal education, and from exposure to Western civilization. And antipathy for the tribal society is now heightened by the Government's policy of retribalization. Latterly, there are signs of a revaluation of the tribal past, a searching for historical pride. But it is highly selective—qualities of personality, such as *ubuntu* (humanity), and episodes of heroic quality, such as the Zulu ruler Tshaka in the role of a black Napoleon—and not the narrow world of exclusive tribalism.

Attitudes toward chieftainship provide an index of attitudes toward tribal values, since, among the South Eastern Bantu, the chiefs are the pivot of the tribal system, and symbolize the tribal way of life. Rejection of the chief is rejection of tribal perspectives. In my first interviews with members of the bourgeoisie in Durban, there was so standardized a repudiation of the role of the chief, and so few deviations from the general pattern of response, that the problem did not seem to merit further investigation. For the bourgeoisie, the chief represents a rival system of prestige, based neither on merit nor achievement, and according neither with the values of the Western world, nor, even at times, with those of tribal society. He represents a mode of life, primitive in many respects, from which the bourgeoisie has emancipated itself. Loyalty to him is without significance for men who are removed from the reciprocal rights and obligations of tribal society and do not seek an allocation of land or a voice in the tribal councils. It is not only that the chief has no independent power but also that he has become an instrument of a policy which denies Africans the rewards of their achievements and withholds from them an equal status in the modern world.

Informants perceive the chiefs as impotent, backward, and subordinated to a hostile state. Their role is described as that of the "children who learn from their fathers and mothers," and "the police of the Native Administration Department." They are said to be "compulsorily thrust upon the people," as "a means of indoctrination," and they are called "stooges" and "hired servants of the government who must follow government without the slightest deviation." "It is as if the chief is behind a curtain and the Native Administration Department in front, and they are more important" and "The day chiefs are abolished is the day we will be liberated." There are comments on the tensions between the chiefs and the educated; most chiefs are said to be suspicious of the young and educated class, illiterate, "so how can they control people who are educated?"

> Modern times require a man who is educated, who will understand Government policy. Our present chiefs are not educated and they cannot work harmoniously with the educated class. They fear the educated because they feel the educated will take their positions. In our struggle for freedom the educated cannot meet the chiefs because the chiefs will fear they will be victimized by the Government. The person who should represent the Black man should be elected and educated. The position of the chief should be abolished completely [interview].

There also is criticism of changes in the functions of chiefs: many are elevated on the basis of unknown criteria; they transmit instructions from Government officials, instead of seeking the views of their people; and they no longer rule according to the known customary laws. They are held in contempt because of their involvement with Government policy.

> The policy of the authorities in regard to the Paramount Chief [of Zululand] is quite wrong. For every little trouble they want to call in the Paramount Chief. This is quite wrong and it is not the Zulu

way. They think the Paramount Chief has the power but in fact
he does not. The [Paramount] Chief had power in the time of
Tshaka, but after that the power was given to the chiefs, and it is
the Governor General who is the Supreme Chief. The policy is quite
wrong. If you have rainy weather then first you let your coat get
wet, perhaps that will be enough. But if not, then you let your
shirt get wet and then your vest and only after that your body.
The Paramount Chief then is our body and it is wrong to call him
in for every little thing. They made the Paramount Chief accept
Bantu Authorities and now he is regarded with contempt because
of it. By drawing him in to all these troubles, they just hold him up
to contempt [text from an interview with an open supporter of
Government policy, a defrocked clergyman, later found hanged in
strange circumstances].

But tribal perspectives are not obliterated. The intermingling of different tribes does not automatically or immediately destroy tribal sentiment. The cities do not necessarily act as a melting pot, transmuting
the dross of tribalism into the gold of Africanism. Indeed the first
effects of intertribal contact may be to sharpen the dependence on tribal
identity as a known element in an unknown and threatening world, so
that tribal affiliation becomes a basis of evaluation, and, as far as possible,
of association. There may in fact be a continuing emphasis on tribal
identity. Studies of the "pre-industrial" cities of Africa show the tenacity
of tribal particularism, while the persistence of segregatory practices in
the highly industrialized cities of the United States suggests that industrialization is not inherently a solvent of tribal exclusiveness.

Moreover, ideological rejection of tribal values and identification is by
no means equivalent to exorcism, and there is ample evidence of the
persistence of tribal divisions in intertribal situations. The following
examples from school and college life are selected by way of illustration.
A postgraduate student at the University of Natal described his experiences in a Presbyterian Mission School as follows:

Tribalism was rife there, and I had the nasty experience at first of
being rejected by all groups. The Zulus took me to be Sotho speaking and the Sothos were sure I was not. The vernacular was forbidden during the week. It was only when I had a quarrel and
people found I had been in Durban that my prestige was enhanced.
The groups Zulu and Sotho kept separate and there were violent
fights between them. There was a member of staff who encouraged
this. The predominant group was Sotho and the groups used derogatory words about each other. Zulus used the word *isilwane*, meaning
an animal, Sothos used the word *letebele* about the Zulus. The Zulus
themselves were few. The Xhosas referred to the Zulus as *in-*

kwenkwe, that is to say, one who has not been circumcised, or in other words, equivalent to a dog.

The *Natal Mercury* carried this report of disturbances at Ohlange Institute on September 25, 1959:

> Sullen groups of Native students at the Ohlange Institute at Inanda refused to return to their classrooms yesterday afternoon after being attacked by 60 of their companions.
>
> Five students have been admitted to the McCord Zulu Hospital with head and leg injuries. An uneasy quiet settled over the school late last night and no further incidents were reported.
>
> Police under Capt. T. B. Kleynhans, Senior Staff Officer, Greenwood Park, were called to the school at ten o'clock on Wednesday night after 60 students armed with sticks and stones had attacked about 120 students who were studying in the classrooms.
>
> Windows were smashed and eight students were injured before the attacking party fled into the bush. Captain Kleynhans arrived and found the students shocked and flabbergasted by the attack. Most of them were reluctant to talk.
>
> ### 58 Arrested
>
> The police switched off the school lights and waited for the attackers to return. About 6:30 A.M., the Natives returned carrying sticks, iron bars, and stones. The police disarmed them and arrested 58, who were taken to the Inanda Police Station.
>
> Students refused to disclose why they attacked their companions yesterday and the principal said that he could give no reason for the trouble.
>
> Natal and Transvaal students clashed earlier this month, when a dispute arose over a missing football boot. But the principal and staff members said yesterday that they did not think that this was the cause of the new dispute.
>
> The arrested students will probably be charged with public violence, malicious damage to property or armed assembly.

The cleavage between the students was partly an urban-rural conflict, but it was reinforced by Zulu-Sotho tribalism. Transvaal students referred to the Natal Zulu students as *amabari* (barbarians); the Natal students retaliated with the name *osiyazi* (know-alls). Local residents apparently armed the Natal students, and, on their arrest, threatened to burn down the school.

A senior lecturer at the University College of Fort Hare, himself a Zulu, commented that

> there was no racial friction [at Fort Hare] but rather surprisingly tribal friction, or perhaps it would be better to call it provincialism.

There was always an incipient provincialism arising between Transvaal and Natal and related to soccer clashes. There would be fights, sometimes stabbings, and others would gang up. This happened in my day too. Once it happened it would assume the dimensions of a Zulu-Sotho clash. That is how most incidents which had a tribal connotation took place. Tribalism was not otherwise expressed. Such phrases as *isilwane* were not used: they appreciate the context. In the dormitories, people would group together on a church basis. People mixed freely in the three men's hostels. The Students Representative Council elections were fought regularly on Congress vs. Convention lines. They were expressly political.

Tribal antagonism and identification are thus not outside the experience of educated Africans, nor indeed entirely foreign to their outlook. Hostile stereotypes sometimes emerged in the interviews with them, a Zulu image of Pondos as not clean, Xhosas as crafty, Sothos as untrustworthy, and corresponding images from other groups of the Zulus as ethnocentric, tribal, and submissive to authority.

Most of the teachers interviewed seemed to have no difficulty in rating tribal groups on such qualities as intelligence and honesty. Practice among the educated falls short of the ideal, whereas the uneducated are likely to have keener sentiments of tribal difference and less ideological commitment to universal values. Tribal identification is not necessarily expressed in formal tribal association. In Durban, for example, the African population is largely Zulu. According to a special tabulation of the population census of 1951, over 86 per cent spoke Zulu, over 7 per cent Xhosa, and under 4 per cent Sotho.[5] The remainder belonged to a variety of African tribal groups. Tribesmen are likely to come together on special occasions, such as a bereavement. The Sotho have public celebrations for their tribesmen, Moshoeshoe's Day and the ceremony of Sinyamo, but there is little in the way of formal tribal association. The Zulus themselves are a loose amalgamation of tribes. These tribes are apparently not organized in formal associations in Durban, although tribal or regional differences have some relevance in the football world. Thus the Zulu Royals are associated with Zululand, the Wanderers Football Club with the "Abaqulusi" in the Newcastle-Nqutu-Dundee area, and the Bush Bucks with the Pondo tribes[6] (often nicknamed the Pondos). Tribal rivalry enters into the competition between these clubs and sometimes results in open conflict.

It is difficult to estimate the strength of tribal sentiment in the cities.

5. Kuper, Watts, and Davies, *Durban: A Study in Racial Ecology*, p. 87.
6. B. A. Pauw mentions a similar phenomenon in the case of rugby clubs in East London: it is not an important feature of the organization of other forms of sport (*The Second Generation*, Cape Town, Oxford University Press, 1961, pp. 172–73).

The above illustrations are offered only to suggest that tribal perspectives, an awareness of tribal differences and of tribal systems of evaluation, have relevance for urban stratification. Certainly urban life encourages other perspectives. The coming together of tribesmen provides the shared experience for perception of a common national identity; so too, massed employment and a diversity of occupations and of opportunities for different styles of life provide a basis for class perspectives. The cities offer nontribal foci of cleavage and integration, and nontribal perspectives. But tribal identification, association, and perspectives persist alongside them. The tribal perspectives may be emphasized in certain contexts by a process of "situational selection," [7] so that they are dominant, for example, in the sealed-off areas of domestic life, but recessive in the economic and political spheres. Or they may become increasingly vague, or be temporarily submerged, to regain significance as the mobilization of the tribal group offers opportunities for power.

The tribal enterprise of the Government is not altogether fantastic. It calls for a restructuring of urban African relations. Occasion for acquaintance is to be primarily occasion for tribal acquaintance. Tribal ties are to replace the varied bonds of urban association. The technique is that of tribal segregation (or segregation of linguistic groups). This the Government can enforce in residence and education, over which it has effective power, but not in worship, play, or voluntary association, and probably not even in employment. Tribal segregation in the towns must remain forever incomplete. Perhaps it is not necessary for the purposes of apartheid that it should be complete. Segregation is being established at the primary levels of home and school, and these primary experiences must afford some support for tribal perspectives. They may even prove highly significant in combination with such other factors as the continuity of tribal organization in the reserves, the residues of tribal sentiment in the towns, the Government's ability to attract educated Africans into tribal service, and calculations of advantage in the promised tribal self-government. If their combined effect is to dilute the perspectives of African nationalism, and to fragment and confuse African political purpose, then the Government's strategy will have succeeded.

Class perspectives are conceived under apartheid as compatible with tribalism, the Government holding out the promise of unrestricted occupational opportunity within the tribal framework. The model is like that applied by the so-called "caste-class" school of sociologists to American society, with impermeable barriers between the castes (races), but class differentiation and mobility within each separate caste. The

---

7. Concept developed by A. L. Epstein in *Politics in an Urban African Community* (Manchester, University Press, 1958), chap. 7.

fragmentation of Africans into tribal groups requires the suppression of a class stratification, which might bind Africans together in common interests transcending tribal affiliation. Stratification among Africans must be contained within the separate tribal structures, with the chief, like a Brahmin, at the apex of the subordinate hierarchy.

Apartheid, in theory, raises vertical barriers between the racial groups while permitting within each racial group (or within the tribes) a parallel differentiation of classes. In practice, apartheid imposes an impermeable horizontal bar, subjecting Africans in many essential respects to a common subordination and restricting the full expression of class differences.

The downward gradation bears most heavily on the class which might challenge the power of the ruling group, that is, on the African bourgeoisie. In the past, this class enjoyed a special status, valued by its members, though of minor significance in the wider society. During the latter part of the nineteenth century and the early decades of the twentieth, as we have seen, the life chances of the African bourgeoisie were not altogether unfavorable. In the Cape, and to a lesser extent in Natal, Africans could reasonably hope for increasing acceptance by the dominant group as they acquired its culture, and hence for emancipation from a racially defined subordinate status. This hope receded as the policies of Afrikaner nationalism prevailed, emphasizing the primacy of race over personal achievement, undermining the special status of the African bourgeoisie, and reducing all Africans to virtually the same political and civic status.

Many circumstances would seem to explain this policy. Since the racial barriers are to be impermeable, the racial status must be rigidly defined. Any exception, a special elevated status for the African bourgeoisie, would open the way to integration. Or it would encourage the growth of a rival system of power, challenging White domination. Or it would weaken the significance of race as the determinant of status by according recognition to achievement. In any event, the interests of the lower classes of Whites, represented by the National Party, clamor for protection against African competition and for reservation of occupational opportunity. African advance must not be allowed to create independent sources of power.

Whatever the reasons, the Government has consistently contracted the rights and privileges of the African bourgeoisie. Some marks of an exempted status still remain. In certain circumstances, an African may be entitled to carry a green reference book, instead of a brown one, and secure an endorsement that he is exempt from the curfew laws. But this requires an application (hence the acknowledgment that the African belongs to an inferior stratum) and the obligation to carry his reference book with him and exhibit it on demand, in much the same way that the unexempted person carries his pass. The illusory privilege granted by the green reference book is conveyed in an editorial in *Ilanga Lase Natal* (May 23, 1959):

> When responsible men and women were deprived of their certificates of exemption, they were driven back into the irritating and discriminatory pass laws from which they had previously escaped because of their good characters and standard of education. They were forced to take Reference Books—passes. The mockery in this is that these Green Reference Books indicate that the owners once held the exemption certificates but do so no longer. Indeed the bitter, one might almost say, callous joke here is that the Green Reference Books provide the same restrictions found in Brown Reference Books.

And there is no guarantee that even leading members of the African bourgeoisie will be granted exemption from the curfew laws. A lawyer received the following reply to his application:

> I have to inform you that in view of the fact that your duties as an attorney do not ordinarily require you to be in public streets during curfew hours, your application cannot be favourably entertained. You are advised to obtain a permit on those occasions when you have to be abroad during curfew hours as provided by section 31 (1) of Act No. 25 of 1945 as amended.[8]

There are other rights for members of privileged categories (which include also chiefs and headmen), as, for example, exemption from the prohibition against remaining in an urban or proclaimed area for more than seventy-two hours without a permit and from the requirement to register contracts of employment, or to furnish fingerprints when applying for a reference book. These rights may remain, or they may be eliminated, or, as seems most likely, they may be converted into privileges granted at the arbitrary discretion of the Minister of Bantu Administration and Development. In any event, these concessions are irrelevant to political rights. The educated or wealthy African, equally with the illiterate or impoverished, is denied the parliamentary franchise that is freely available to the uneducated poor White.

This leveling process is also applied to property and prestige. The policy of eliminating African freehold ownership of land in the urban areas specifically affects the African bourgeoisie. All African ownership of immovable property is rendered weak and insecure. Although the style of houses in the urban areas provides some opportunity for con-

8. Pitje, "The Effect of the Pass Laws on African Life."

spicuous consumption, as a display of wealth and a claim to prestige, still the houses are under leasehold ownership, and mostly in the same locations as those of the workers. Conspicuous consumption can be more easily expressed in movable goods. And the consumption is all the more conspicuous because of the general poverty of Africans. It is dwarfed, however, by the display in the White community and checked by restrictive laws. Legal and customary discrimination limit the opportunity to acquire a surplus and it is only with great difficulty that Africans are moving into the occupations of the bourgeoisie in appreciable numbers. When employed in these occupations, for example, as teachers or doctors in government service, discrimination in salaries is customary. This may be justified on the ground that the standard of living of these professionals should not be elevated too far above the people they serve—again, a process of leveling. In principle, the pegging of non-White salaries at a lower rate than White for equal qualifications maintains White superiority.

Prestige may be accorded Africans within narrow circles of the wider society, but this often takes a paternalist form, through the application of a lower standard and respect for an achievement which would be regarded as commonplace among Whites. Or scarcity value may attach to an African or other non-White in interracial organization, so that he achieves recognition beyond his merits—an inverted form of racial discrimination. However, the more general tendency among Whites, particularly in the lower circles of the bureaucracy, is to withhold prestige from the African bourgeoisie. The lumpen-bureaucrats and the police often seem to make it a principle that they should treat the African bourgeoisie in the same way as the working class or the migrant laborer. If the official knows the vernacular language, he may insist on speaking it even to an African university graduate. He may ignore him for long periods of time, though patently not engaged in activity of value to man or beast: he will deny him the courtesy of a seat and may speak to him in loud and crude contempt. In this deliberate humiliation, he expresses a special antagonism, since the African has achieved, by the standards of White society, goals beyond the reach of the official.

Thus the class perspectives of apartheid are varied. Administratively the African bourgeoisie may be defined as part of that stratum of Africans who are exempt from the obligation to furnish fingerprints when applying for a reference book or who are likely to receive permission from the Government to be out at night after the curfew hour. Or it may be defined in a paternalist idiom as comprising Africans with achievements like those of a White man—a European standard of housing or a university degree, whatever its quality. Or it may be defined at the level of the lumpen-bureaucracy as the "cheeky Kaffirs," "the ones with glasses." Or it may be defined politically as the stratum from which the agitators, the "wolves," and the communists are recruited. But however defined, it represents a dangerous stratum which must be tribalized or otherwise canalized.

For Africans, the shared inequality, low status, and the low ceiling on achievements do not imply an absence of class perspectives. There is an awareness of class differences, crystallizing around the objective core of differences in occupation and education. I have already commented on this phenomenon of concern for relative prestige among deprived groups, as, for example, among the pariah castes in India. Low status, measured objectively, does not necessarily eliminate an awareness of social distinctions within the subordinate group. The distinctions may be very fine, since the range of differentiation is narrow, but they may act with all the greater force to stimulate mutual disdain. Perhaps the reduction of the members of a subordinate group to a common inequality in many aspects of life magnifies the importance of such differences as remain, and perhaps the very strength of the rejection by the dominant group intensifies the desire to differentiate.

Concern for status differences within a subordinate and rejected group must presumably be related to the values of the wider society or of the dominant group. Where hereditary stratification is accepted as part of the moral order, as in traditional Hindu caste society, and this value is absorbed by low caste groups, there is a stimulus for the latter to practice an internal, perhaps an exaggerated, differentiation. So too in a class society, the racially subordinate group may accept achieved status as a valid and valued criterion for stratification, even though the opportunity for achievement is limited. The same moral sentiments that support stratification in the wider society stimulate divisions among the lower strata.

The situation is more complex where the society offers a variety of choices. Thus South African Indians brought their own caste system into a society based on two different criteria of stratification—mainly achievement for Whites and hereditary inequality for non-Whites. It was inevitable that Indians would demand the same opportunities for achievement and the same basis for assessment in the wider society as White men. Rejecting the principle of hereditary inequality under which they suffer in the new society, they are also obliged to reject the caste system as an internal measure of worth.

Superficially, there is something strange in the reproduction by a subordinate racial group of the system of inequality which prevails within the dominant group itself. No doubt, the withholding of values renders them all the more desirable. In so far as the movement in a subordinate racial group is toward equality with the dominant group and not domination over it, the goal would be the same style of life. Equality in style of life would seem also to imply adopting the inequalities (or prejudices or discriminations) of the dominant group. Of course, there is often selective adoption, with expurgation of racial evaluations depreciating the subordinate group, or modification by the introduction of other values, such as qualities of personality (intellect, humanity) with which members of the subordinate group feel themselves highly endowed.

An alternative reaction would be the radical rejection of social inequality. Quite apart from Marxism, the open class society offers this alternative, since its ideology is composed of two strands—the equality in principle of the members of a society, reflected in adult suffrage, and the validity of personal achievement as a measure of worth. Emphasis on equality would predispose individuals toward the welfare state, socialism, or communism; emphasis on achievement would lead to the exaggeration of minor differences, since there is a low ceiling on achievement. The Negro bourgeoisie in the United States has followed the latter course of inflating its achievements, according to the evidence presented by Franklin Frazier.[9]

Within the African bourgeoisie of South Africa the radical rejection of inequality, as measured by adherence to communist doctrine, has had some appeal, though apparently not a substantial one. This I judge by the small number of communists—real, statutory, and putative—on the proscription lists of a Government highly sensitive to intimations of communism. The trend has been toward the reproduction of class differentiation. Since there is a lack of opportunity, achievement is relatively rare and enjoys an inflated value among Africans, resulting in the exaggeration of minor differences from the point of view of the outside observer. The emphasis is on rank by achievement, rather than on the concept of the basic equality of men. This trend is, however, counteracted to some extent by the fact that there is an absolute barrier to African mobility. Members of the African bourgeoisie are pushed back toward the masses by an equal subordination; if they reject the tribal perspectives then they must rely on mass support to realize the full rewards of the status they have achieved. The awareness of class distinctions is influenced by the exaggeration of minor differences in African society, the racial perspectives and discriminations in the wider society, and the perception of common life chances and a common destiny in the century of African man.

9. *Black Bourgeoisie* (Glencoe, Free Press, 1957).

CHAPTER 9

The Objective Core:
Mainly African Bourgeoisie of Durban

THE AFRICAN BOURGEOISIE, for purposes of this study, is arbitrarily defined as consisting of professionals, traders, and higher grade civil servants and municipal clerks. The use of occupational categories gives a point of departure for exploring the almost uncharted field of class differentiation among Africans in South Africa. The approach will be to examine the social correlates of occupational status, and to determine whether they cluster in distinctive patterns.

Implicit in the occupational classification is a difference in education and income. The student of law or medicine requires the matriculation certificate, equivalent to Standard X, as an entrance qualification. The poorly qualified African teacher can start with a Standard VI certificate, which is followed by three years of teacher training. For entrance to higher qualifications, the Junior Certificate (two years short of matriculation standard) or Matriculation is necessary. Nurses require at least the Junior Certificate for admission to training and since there are many applicants, the schools are able to select the more highly qualified. Social workers were at one time able to take a nonuniversity diploma: now they need university degrees or diplomas. The higher grades of clerks generally require the Junior Certificate. Entrance qualifications for the ministry in the established denominations may be either the Junior Certificate or Matriculation.

Only the traders seem able to dispense with higher education, and some are not even literate. In a sample of 75, about one-fourth had Standard II education or less, almost one half had education ranging from Standard III to Standard VII, and only a little more than a fourth held the Junior Certificate, a Teacher's Certificate or other diploma, or Matriculation and above. Still, this level of education is above that of the general African population.

Incomes for the poorly qualified may overlap with those for semiskilled workers, but for the most part there is an appreciable gulf. In Durban, the demand for legal and medical services is such that lawyers and doctors in private practice may hope to amass real wealth. Even in state, provincial, or municipal service, where there is systematic discrimination against non-White professionals in respect to salaries, the level of earning far exceeds that available to African workers. Thus in the early part of 1961, an African doctor serving as an intern in the King Edward VIII Hospital in Durban would be earning £510 per annum.[1]

Scales of pay for teachers vary with qualifications, length of service, and type of school, from a minimum, under the new scales introduced in 1963, of about £12 per month for a qualified teacher in a lower primary school to a maximum of £74.10. per month for a married male teacher, with degree and professional qualification, in a senior secondary school. Higher salaries are paid to headmasters, supervisors of schools, and subinspectors. In 1961, staff nurses in the King Edward VIII Hospital earned up to £27.10 per month, and nursing sisters from £27.10 per month to £35 per month. The range for qualified female social workers at Bantu Child Welfare was from over £29 for the lower qualification to a maximum of over £64 for a university qualification. The scales were appreciably lower in the Department of Bantu Administration in Durban, with a maximum (for a male social worker) of about £42 per month. Stipends for ministers of religion vary considerably and they may or may not receive a free house and children's and other allowances. A reasonable estimate of the range of stipends and allowances in many of the established denominations would be between £20 and £40 per month. There is now a movement for the raising of ministers' stipends in the English-speaking churches toward the same level as the stipends of White parsons. A messenger/clerk may earn only a laborer's pay, but enjoy the prospect of promotion to a clerical grade. Senior clerks can earn £65 per month. Traders are reticent about their earnings: many of the Durban traders probably earn between £250 and £500 annually, while some have substantial incomes—indeed modest fortunes.

The level of earning is low by the standards of the White community, but substantial as compared to the general poverty of Africans. Horwood[2] estimated that some two-thirds of Africans in Durban earn less than £15 per month.[3] The difference between a general wage of £15

1. In 1963 the scale for a registered doctor who had completed his period as intern was £1380–£1700 (Grade II) and £1780– £1940 (Grade I).

2. "Some Aspects of Urban African Employment in the Durban Area," p. 280.

3. In a later article, Horwood reported that 68.8% of a large sample of Africans in Durban had recorded monthly *household* incomes of less than R 36.83 (i.e. £18.9.4, "The Private Budget of the Urban Native," *Optima*, September, 1962, p. 143). A curious feature of the budgets was that mean reported expenditure (over £31 monthly) exceeded mean wage income (under £17 monthly) by almost 90%, raising doubts as to the reliability of the findings. A study from the University of South Africa of three townships in the Pretoria area gave the

per month or less and the salaries of the bourgeoisie is the difference between bare survival and some opportunity for diversion and fulfillment.

The differences extend beyond those which are implicit in the occupational classification to differences in parental background, and in occupation and education of spouses. Table 2, Appendix D, compares the occupations of the fathers of a sample population of teachers, nurses, and traders in the magisterial district of Durban with the occupational distribution of African men in the same area. There is clearly selective recruitment—a much higher percentage of professionals and related workers in the parent generation of teachers and nurses—over 25 per cent, compared with less than 1 per cent of African men gainfully employed in Durban in 1951. Even the traders are a somewhat selected population. In the first four categories of the census—the white collar occupations—the percentage of the fathers of teachers, nurses, and traders is 34, 44, and 29, respectively, that of African men in Durban less than 3.

This selective recruitment may be tested by an analysis of the occupations of the fathers of students at different levels in the educational system. The expectation would be that, as students attain higher levels of education, there would be a decline in the proportion recruited from the homes of manual workers. Table 3, Appendix D, presents this comparison for Standard V in Durban primary schools, Standard IX in the secondary schools, and medical and other students at the University of Natal in Durban. There is a considerable wastage of students at school. These standards were chosen on the assumption that most children of poor parents who were continuing school would tend to leave after passing Standard V, and that at Standard IX many students would be training for the professions. The gradation in the recruitment of students from the children of professional men is marked: 5 per cent for Standard V, 12 per cent Standard IX, 29 per cent university study in arts and allied fields, and 42 per cent at the medical school. The corresponding figures for the white collar occupations are 27, 37, 46, and 63 per cent.

average monthly *household* income as a little over £23 and the average monthly income for all earners as less than £13. Two-thirds of household heads were in unskilled employment, their average income being half that of the professionally employed ("Patterns of Income and Expenditure in the Urban Bantu Townships near Pretoria," *baNtu*, December 1961, pp. 684–85). For private manufacturing and construction industries, average monthly earnings in 1960–61 were a little over £15 per month (J. A. Lombard, "The Determination of Racial Income Differentials in South Africa," p. 3). See also W. F. J. Steenkamp, "Bantu Wages in South Africa," *South African Journal of Economics* (June 1962), pp. 93–118. The Minister of Economic Affairs gave the total estimated average annual *cash earnings* (i.e. excluding payment in kind) of Africans in mining, secondary industry, and the public sector in 1962 as R 274 (£137.—*Hansard, House of Assembly Debates*, No. 12, April 19, 1963, col. 4340). The comparable figure for Whites was R 1942.

Conversely, recruitment from children of craftsmen, laborers and service workers declines: 68, 63, 35, and 16 per cent. These occupational comparisons are crude; classification is according to the census. The category of salesmen, for example, includes newspaper boys and estate agents; the service category embraces domestic servants and policemen. Nevertheless, the trend is clear, though not precisely measured.

Associated with the higher occupational status of the fathers of the Durban bourgeoisie is a level of education well above the average. Of the 89 fathers whose education was given by a sample of teachers, 25 (about 28 per cent) held the Junior Certificate or equivalent or above. The corresponding figure in a sample population of nurses was over 30 per cent (of the 128 for whom information was available). Comparable information was not gathered for traders, but in a sample of 75, there were three fathers with a teaching qualification, one minister, one clerk, and one evangelist. By way of comparison, the South African Institute of Race Relations estimated in 1960 that about 62,000 living Africans might have passed the equivalent of Junior Certificate.[4] This would be a little over 1 per cent of the adult population.

There is some tendency toward an equivalence of occupational and educational status between spouses, both at the level of the parental generation of the African professionals in Durban and also among the professionals themselves. This reinforces the trend toward a crystallization of class differentiation, with some depth over the generations.

Thus, taking the parental generation of the sample of teachers and of nurses at McCord Zulu Hospital, there was rough educational endogamy in the categories of primary and secondary education, and appreciable occupational endogamy.[5] Similarly, the teachers themselves tended to marry teachers and nurses. In the sample, 32 of the men were married, 24 to teachers and nurses. The women teachers in the sample showed less tendency to marry professionals: five of the 17 husbands were teachers, two medical aids, four clerks, three drivers, and a policeman, factory worker, and office boy. The level of education was relatively high—10 of the husbands had passed the Junior Certificate or higher. In the total sample of 149 nurses, 53 gave information as to husbands, fiancés, and "boy friends" (a category introduced by the nurses themselves). Half the husbands, actual and prospective, were professionals or university students, one-fifth clerks, and about the same proportion were drivers, policemen, and detectives. The spouses of the 42 medical students and

4. *A Survey of Race Relations in South Africa, 1959–1960,* p. 216.

5. Complete information for parents of 82 teachers shows 29 couples with primary school education or less (i.e. up to Standard V), 36 with some secondary, and 17 mixed. Information for the parents of 72 nurses shows that in 26 of the marriages both parents had an education of Standard VI or less; in 28 marriages, over Standard VI education; and in 18, marriages were educationally mixed. In regard to occupation, the mothers of 21 teachers, and of 23 nurses, were professionals, and of these 12 and 15 respectively had married professionals.

doctors serving as interns were doctors, nurses, teachers, medical students, a physiotherapist, and two "housewives." [6]

In associational life—friendship, religious affiliation, and participation in organizations—the class tendency also emerges. Teachers in the sample population were asked to note down the names of the three people they saw most of socially, and then to give information as to occupation, education, and religious denomination. A similar question, excluding religion, was asked of the nurses at the McCord Zulu Hospital, but the form of the question was amended to three best friends (men) and three best friends (women) outside the hospital. The friends of men and women in the teaching profession are almost entirely professionals (73 and 75 per cent) or white collar, managerial, sales personnel, and students (20 and 10 per cent). There is a similar pattern for friends of nurses at McCord Zulu Hospital (52 per cent of men and 70 per cent of women are professionals, and 33 per cent and 13 per cent, other white collar categories). Education is mostly at a level associated with the professions (Tables 4a and b, 5a and b, Appendix D).

Religious affiliation of teachers, nurses, and medical students is largely to the established denominations—Anglican, Catholic, Lutheran, Methodist, and Presbyterian—not to the separatist churches and minor sects. The relevant figures for the established denominations are teachers and medical students, 76 per cent; nurses, 68 per cent; as compared with Durban Africans, 43 per cent (1951 census—special tabulation); and for separatist churches and minor sects, 20 per cent teachers, 21 per cent nurses, 15 per cent medical students, 43 per cent Durban Africans.[7] The religious affiliation of the sample of traders corresponds to that of Durban Africans (Table 6, Appendix D).

In the voluntary organizations, the location Advisory Boards, and the political parties, there is selective recruitment of leaders in terms of occupation and education. The Durban and District African Football Association was, in many ways, the major voluntary organization among Africans in Durban. Of the 103 executive members and representatives of the association over the period 1924–60, all those whose occupations could be ascertained, save four, were engaged in white-collar work, over

6. Some confirmation of parts of the argument in this chapter is given by the comments of the African psychologist, Mkele (as reported in the *Natal Daily News,* November 16, 1961): "The middle-class man made middle-class friends and married inside the middle class. Some individuals have even denied their parents rather than face the social embarrassment of having to admit to a working class parentage." He further stated that the status-giving churches were the Anglican, the Methodist, the Presbyterian, and the A.M.E.: "Not for the middle class the 1,001 Zionist churches with their throbbing drums, bundles of crosses, and flowing robes."

7. Rae Sherwood, in an unpublished study of "The Bantu Civil Servant," mainly in Johannesburg, found that the civil servants were affiliated to the separatist churches in about the same proportion as the African population of Johannesburg. This was in strong contrast to the much smaller affiliation of such professionals as social workers, nurses, and teachers.

one-third being professional men. And even the four occupations outside
the white-collar categories (a motor mechanic, a driver, a racket re-
stringer, and an orderly) represent levels of skill. In education, more
than three-fourths of those whose education was ascertained, had professional qualifications or a standard of education qualifying them for
professional training. Allowing for gaps in the tables (7a, b, and c,
Appendix D) and a measure of unreliability, and on the assumption
that many of those for whom information was not obtained would
have been of humble educational and occupational status, the tendency
toward bourgeois recruitment of the leaders is clear. Religious affiliation
is almost entirely with the established churches, and the American
Board complex of congregational churches. The large recruitment from
the American Board complex is significant, since it was the American
Board missionaries who pioneered African football in the Natal coastal
region and encouraged African initiative and leadership.

Apart from their roles within the football association, the leaders were
prominent in other voluntary organizations. Eight served on the executive of the Durban Bantu Lawn Tennis Association, 14 on the Advisory
Boards, and six as members of school boards. One member is now President-General of the African National Congress, and another was an executive member of the Unity Movement, a political organization. They
held executive positions in the Natal African Football Association, the
South African Football Association, and the South African Soccer Federation, and they contributed to the work of the Natal African Teachers
Union, the International Club, and the Joint Council of Africans and
Europeans in Durban.[8]

The African members of associations concerned with race relations are
also drawn from the bourgeoisie—inevitably so, since education is neces-
ary for participation with members of other racial groups in lectures,
debates, the joint discussion of African problems, and other intellectual
activities. Among the 49 Africans whose names were recorded in the
books of the Durban International Club as members over the period
1943–58, there was only one working-class man. Most of the members
were in the professions. (It should be noted, however, that the International Club was closed by Government action, the record of members
was not complete, and the occupations of four members could not be
traced.) In the Durban Joint Council of Africans and Europeans, 21 of
the 26 African members of the Executive during the period 1934–59
were of professional occupation (including the present Anglican Bishop
Zulu), and four are now university lecturers. There were eleven university graduates, six of them with postgraduate training.[8]

The Durban Advisory Boards, statutory bodies with both an elected
and nominated African membership, have a more varied composition.

8. Analysis by Bernard Magubane.

Nominated membership reflects the policies of the administration. One superintendent followed the practice of nominating traders, and it appears that in any event, prospective traders were attracted to membership of the Advisory Boards by the possibility of securing trading permits. Information, though neither complete nor entirely reliable, was gathered in regard to the 89 Advisory Board members who served during the period October 1948 to September 1959. By occupation (ascertained for 72 members), 23 were traders, 9 professional men, 22 white-collar workers, and the remaining 18 working class—indunas, artisans, and laborers. The educational level ascertained for 73 members is relatively high—31 had some primary education, 38 some secondary education (including 10 who were either matriculated, qualified as teachers, or studying for a degree), and 4 were university graduates. By religion, 58 belonged to the established denominations and the American Board complex as compared with 9 members of sects and 2 still maintaining traditional worship: almost 40 per cent were affiliated to American Board churches, the original and the separatist.

The major political organization throughout the period since Union was the African National Congress, and its leaders were drawn from the bourgeoisie. The distinguished men in African society—the doctors, the lawyers, the clergymen, the men with overseas training and honorary degrees, i.e. the elite mentioned in Chapter 7—occupied the major positions. *The African Yearly Register* gives the following description of the first executive, the founding fathers:

> The first president elected was the Rev. J. L. Dube, founder and principal of the Ohlange Training Institution in Natal, and also editor of the *Ilanga Lase Natal*. The first treasurer was Dr. P. Ka I. Seme, barrister-at-law, practising as attorney of the Supreme Court of South Africa in Johannesburg. The first general secretary was Mr. Sol. T. Plaatje, then editor of *Ntsala*, Kimberley, and author of a number of books. Mr. T. M. Mapikela, a building contractor, was appointed speaker. Mr. G. D. Montsioa, a barrister-at-law practising as solicitor of the Supreme Court of South Africa in Johannesburg, was appointed recording secretary. The Rev. Dr. Mqoboli was appointed chaplain-in-chief, and Rev. H. R. Ngcayiya, president of the Ethiopian Church, was appointed assistant chaplain, Vice-Presidents were Rev. Dr. W. B. Rubusana, Messrs. Pelem, Advocate A. Mangena and Mr. Makgatho.

In the initial period, the Congress faced the task of sending deputations to the British Government. The first deputation reached England shortly before the outbreak of the First World War. It consisted of Rev. J. L. Dube, leader, Rev. Dr. Rubusana, Messrs. Msane (described in the *Yearly Register* as mission-educated, a member of the choir which toured Europe, compound manager, editor, Zulu writer, local preacher, and labor agent), Mapikela (building contractor, boarding-house proprietor, member of Joint Council and of Advisory Board, and steward of Wesleyan Methodist Church), and Plaatje, the writer. Members of the second deputation to England in 1918 were Plaatje, Gumede (teacher, editor, land agent, landowner, delegate to the first and second international conferences against imperialism, and President-General of Congress in 1926), Mvabaza (managing director of a newspaper, owner of a store), Thema (writer), and the Rev. H. R. Ngcayiya (schoolmaster, court interpreter, and President of the Ethiopian Church). The *Yearly Register* gives the following account of the deputation:

> In England the deputation got busy and interviewed among others, Mr. Lloyd George, the then Prime Minister of England, Archbishop of Canterbury, Labour Members of Parliament, a number of members of the Anti-Slavery and Aboriginees Society, the Society of Friends, the Colonial Secretary, and many others. The deputation even went to Versailles. The reply it got from the Colonial Office was that the British Government could not interfere with the internal affairs of the Union of South Africa. They were advised to return to Africa and humbly submit the grievance of the black men to the Union Government. Thus the African knew for the first time, as they never knew before, that while England in 1899 fought for the liberation of its subjects, in 1914 it had no power to interfere when the God-given rights of those subjects were snatched away.
>
> In England they were advised to return to South Africa and there fight their case. This was indeed a hard blow to a subject race that had been taught to believe that the British King was always ready to defend his subjects against injustice. But the people summoned new courage. The African National Congress grew stronger every day. The leaders turned their energies towards the Courts of Law, but Parliament was busy manufacturing Acts dealing with natives, and every one of them had a sting. The Organisation had its hands full. Complaints of hardships and oppression came in from every part of the country. A few test-cases against the Government were taken to Court and each case reached the Supreme Court, where the organisation came out victorious.

This period, and the period of deputations, petitions, and reasoned argument which followed, called for leadership by the educated. The Congress leaders mentioned in the *Yearly Register* for the period from 1912 to about 1930 are mainly professional men, clerks, and interpreters, although there is an appreciable representation by traders, who seem to have been favored for the position of treasurer. Some chiefs are included, but only occasionally such humble occupations as caretaker and carpenter. This may, of course, reflect a selective bias on the part of the author. The line of Presidents-General, from the founding of the Congress to the present day, includes the most highly qualified of African intellectuals: Rev. Dube (American-trained, awarded an honorary doctorate), Mr. Makgatho (Land Commission Agent, teacher, educated in England, founder of the Transvaal Teachers' Association, local preacher and leader of the Wesleyan Methodist Church, and writer), Rev. Mahabane (a prominent member of the Methodist Church), Mr. Gumede (teacher, editor, land agent), Dr. Seme (barrister, American and English trained), Rev. Mahabane, Dr. Xuma and Dr. Moroko (both highly qualified, overseas-trained doctors), and Chief Luthuli (teacher, chief, delegate in India to the International Missionary Council, lecturer in the United States for the North American Missionary Conference, prominent in Christian councils, and now Nobel Prize winner).

In the last decade, the African National Congress has become more militant, developing as a mass movement; at the same time, the Government has become more repressive. Political trials thus provide some index of the extent to which political leadership of the Congress has maintained its bourgeois character. The Treason Trial, which started in 1956, was the most massive of the purely political trials. It arose out of a Congress of the People, at which a Freedom Charter was adopted. The accused were members of the sponsoring organizations—the Congress Alliance, consisting at that time of the African National Congress, the South African Indian Congress, the South African Coloured Peoples' Congress, and the Congress of Democrats. The occupational distribution of the Africans accused is given below in percentages. The majority of those whom the Government deemed eligible for the Treason Trial were of bourgeois occupation, but there was substantial working class participation.

Professional	13
Traders, agents, photographer	14
Clerical, office, and related workers	21
Trade union organizers	10
Students	2
Salesmen and related workers	8
Craftsmen (employed or self-employed), drivers, packers	14
Factory workers, machinists, washing, farm, and other laborers	17
Peasant farmer (Chief Luthuli)	1
Total	100

(Source: Based on information for 103 of the 105 African accused, mainly from the Treason Trial Defence Fund.)

The Pan-Africanist Congress now offers the main challenge to the African National Congress for the political allegiance of Africans. Seceding from the Congress in November 1958, founded as a separate unit in 1959, and banned by the Government in 1960, there has been little time for patterns of leadership to develop. The Executive Council for Natal consisted of 3 university graduates, 1 bookkeeper, 2 clerks, 1 self-employed commercial traveler, and 1 laborer with a Standard VII education. The background of the National Executive was as follows: 1 language assistant, Witwatersrand University; 3 school teachers; 1 law student; 1 former medical student; 2 clerks (one of whom had previously been a teacher, and also served articles in a lawyer's office); 1 university student; 1 Science graduate; and one whose occupation was not ascertained. Four of the 11 members had university degrees, 2 had been university students. Again there is a bourgeois structure of leadership.

The vacuum created by the banning of both the African National Congress and the Pan-Africanist Congress in 1960 drew a politically diverse group of Africans into a committee formed to establish a united front. All but three of the members were arrested, a total of 13. Of these, 12 were convicted by a magistrate for the offense of continuing the activities of an unlawful organization, and sentenced to 12 months' imprisonment, a conviction later set aside on appeal. The members of this committee were again largely the bourgeois elite—the only African advocate in Johannesburg; a Durban lawyer; a leading African journalist; two ministers of religion, prominent in the African Methodist Episcopal Church; a prominent Johannesburg businessman and former President of the African Chamber of Commerce; a former high school principal; a consultant on pass laws and owner of a business school; two trade union men; two political party organizers (one of them a former teacher, then businessman, and another a salesman, clerk, and later secretary), and one man who had started medicine, then switched to law. Chief Luthuli, Z. K. Matthews (formerly a professor, with an overseas education, later a lawyer, and now working at Geneva in the World Council of Churches), and Rev. Z. R. Mahabane (a minister with considerable prestige in the African community and a former President of the African National Congress) were also members of the continuation committee, but they were not charged.

There are thus indications of a trend toward class formation, as shown in the patterning of characteristics around the objective core of occupation, and in a measure of selective recruitment, over two generations, of nurses, teachers, and university students. But the class structure is far from being clearly delineated, and recruitment is relatively open. Large numbers of the bourgeoisie still derive from peasants and laborers.

High mobility through education (in the case of traders, notwithstanding limited education), restricts the crystallization of class differences into an hereditary inequality. There is such vitality of movement into fields of greater opportunity, even under apartheid, that this process of upward mobility is likely to continue. The collapse of apartheid would create a great demand for African personnel and a catapulting of Africans into command positions, inevitably transforming the structure of African society.

CHAPTER 10

Conspicuous Consumption

IN SOME MEASURE, conspicuous consumption may be an unconscious process by which occupational status is converted into the symbols of prestige, money sublimated into manifest grace. But it almost certainly expresses also some elements of deliberation, an awareness of an appropriate style of life. Conspicuous consumption is both an objective and a subjective measure of class differentiation.

The upper strata among the White people of South Africa enjoy the most rich and varied opportunities for display. Magnificent buildings along the main thoroughfares of the city testify to the commercial prowess of the men; suburban Taj Mahals in the elite residential area to the pricelessness, above rubies, of their women. Retinues of servants, both personal and field, tend their appetites, their flowering shrubs, their immaculate lawns. Exempt from labor that is of any use to man or woman, the ladies come and go, speaking of their domestic woe—the childishness, the irresponsibility, the ingratitude of Black servants in the backyard *kias*. If their hands are calloused, it is from the golf club, the tennis racquet, the race card, the steering wheel, or the reins too tightly held on horses or husbands. In sumptuous cars, traveling advertisements, they grace the banquets in aid of starving children, charity balls, country clubs, first nights, and the capitals of Europe. An assiduous press proclaims these achievements to the South African world.

By contrast, the splendor of the upper strata of the African bourgeoisie is that of the back alley. The city is virtually closed to their Rockefellers and their Oppenheimers. Their own areas lie mostly on the borders of the city or beyond. Streets are usually narrow, often primitive; sidewalks are frequently left in their raw state. Small, cheap, standardized houses on tiny plots package their family lives. Occasional public works buildings serve the more basic needs of residents. Here and there, handsome churches may proclaim the glory of God and the degradation of man.

These are the African locations, sometimes designed according to the highest standards of that special category, "African Housing." Here, for the most part, the African bourgeoisie lives cheek by jowl with the working class, an undifferentiated mass. In the past, there was some possibility of building in solid substance in freehold areas outside the locations, as, for example, in the blighted area of Sophiatown, Johannesburg. In the specifically African areas, in the territories of the Bantustans, the Government is granting freehold rights to property. But in the present cities, the main opportunity now is for leasehold ownership, within the locations, with residents building according to their own plans or to one of a number of specified plans. There is very little that would correspond to an elite residential area, even relatively speaking.

Dube village in Johannesburg, popularly described as "Parktown," after a once palatial White suburb (or, by an African journalist, as the "Sunset Boulevard" of the South Western Areas) is such an elite area. But the special status of Dube village does not appear to exempt its residents from routine police degradation. In May 1961, the residents held a meeting to complain of their humiliating treatment for being in arrear with site rentals. They were treated, they said, like "ordinary residents," fetched from their homes in the early hours of the morning, and sometimes taken away handcuffed by the Council's policemen. A leading businessman asked: "Why should they disgrace me in the presence of my customers by handcuffing me and herding me like a criminal to the superintendent's office?" (*The World*, May 27, 1961.) Perhaps the most ambitious African elite project is that described by the South African Information Service as proposed at Moroka township, Johannesburg— luxury homes on the northern slopes of a lake, with bandstands, playgrounds, and a horseshoe arena for cinema shows and tribal dances (*Digest of South African Affairs*, October 16, 1961).

Africans, in the nicknames they apply to their residential suburbs, caricature their fate with ironic humor. Some of the quality of a good location in Durban, Lamontville, may be conveyed by one informant's list and account of the baptismal names given to its subdivisions.

> *Inkawini* or *Izinkawini*, meaning "monkeys." These consist of white double-storeyed blocks, called monkeys, because being the first double-storey houses, they suggested to the people that they were being regarded as monkeys, back to the trees.

> *The Old Location*, or *Engxabano*, meaning "dispute" or "quarrel." The houses are semi-detached, barracks type. Quarrels are alleged to arise over gardens, which are semi-detached. This area is regarded as the best place to live from an economic point of view, having low rentals, lights, water, and water-borne sewerage. However, the houses are small.

> *New Look*—so called because of the new design of the house— toilets inside and each house with a distinct yard.

Izitezi—derived from the English word "stairs," referring to flats.

Nylon—refers to the houses in the ownership scheme, which came into operation at the time of the introduction of nylon clothing to Durban. According to the informant, the word "Nylon" means that "it's transparent." The house ownership scheme is one which you could just see through. Nylon is looked down upon as a dress fabric because of its transparency. The word "nylon" is in general circulation to describe a fabrication or a lie. (Another explanation is that Nylon refers to the flimsiness of the houses. One informant described Nylon as the best place to live.)

Addis Ababa, so-called because it was promised to the ex-servicemen (who had been stationed at Addis Ababa).

Gijima meaning "run." At one time it was very remote from transport and people who lived there had constantly to run to work in the morning. Because of its undesirable locality people were transferred out of other parts of Lamontville to Gijima, as a punishment —e.g. for illicit brewing. The population of Gijima is consequently quite rough. People are afraid to venture out by themselves in the night. . . . Until very recently it had no lights and no transport. It is remote from police and administration, and has a number of *tsotsis.*

Parktown, Durban North, or *Ezigwilini* ("The place of the rich"). It can also be referred to by the name of any "posh" South African suburb. It is a site and service scheme, where people build their own houses to their own design. This is the most desirable residential area, but the inhabitants of Ezigwilini are ridiculed by the others, who say they are the people who own the bricks, but not the land.

Nylon and Parktown are both "home ownership" schemes, but of different types. In the former, the selling scheme, the Corporation builds the houses, and sells them to residents under leasehold tenure: houses are stereotyped. In the latter scheme, of loans to individuals, the resident leases the site and builds to his own design. There is greater individuality in the houses, but still a good deal of stereotyping, presumably because of the low cost structure. In 1961, loans were available to a maximum of £250: if the resident received a loan, then the Corporation placed a ceiling of £450 on the cost of the house; if he financed it himself, no limit was fixed to building costs. At that time, the most expensive house in Parktown, owned by a trader, cost about £1800, the price of a working-class White home; another resident, also a trader, designed a house at an estimated cost of £2,400.

In July 1961, Africans in Durban had purchased under the selling scheme over 3,500 houses in three locations, accommodating perhaps 9 per cent of the African population of 175,000 (the final census figures, 1960). The large number of these houses is partly due to Government policy that African housing should be financed, as far as possible, on an economic basis. Housing policy may be expected to influence class structure, as for example in the distinction between areas of economic and of subeconomic housing, and in the encouragement of types of home ownership. The advantage of the selling scheme for the residents is that they are ultimately freed from the obligation to pay house rentals, though not site rentals. Thus in Lamontville, the purchase price was roughly £260 for the semidetached houses of Nylon (or £265 for each of the small number of detached houses), the repayment installments over a period of 30 years £1.5.7 per month, and the monthly site rentals in perpetuity £1.10. As housing and as a vehicle for prestige, there is little to distinguish the neighborhood or to attract the bourgeoisie, as appears from this account of Nylon by a leading member of one of the Advisory Board parties. His description is in sharp contrast to that which would be given by a White planner, working with the double standard, of housing appropriate for Europeans and housing appropriate for Africans.

> If you look at the houses you can see they are not put up for brainy people. They are put up as if they were just structures to deceive the African people. When the subeconomic houses were built for Europeans in Woodlands, no European went in without sink and water, as is the case here. The houses are never plastered, you have to plaster them yourselves. There are no gutters—the rain that falls on top digs down into the ground. We feel the Whites do not think we can think, because if they did, they would not put up structures like this, so much so that we were not supplied a garbage removal system. . . . We are just kept like the animals in the veld. All that there is, is that we must pay through the neck, and we get no services after that payment.
>
> We have to put in our bedroom doors. Really, if our authorities have to think that we earn £2.10.0 a week, and have to feed children, where do we get money for doors? When you go to the shop, no price is fixed for specially low earners—we are not considered at all. No European gets £5 per week. In industry, when they employ a new White employee, they go into the circumstances of his family—how many children and so on. These questions are asked so that they could consider giving him some advance as a result of those family circumstances. With me, even if I have ten children, I get that £2.10.0. They don't care. If ever the authorities have the welfare of the African at heart, how do you think I am going to

clothe and feed children? And send them to school. These are our complaints, because we are just thrown away like animals. No one wishes that we thrive well. If you open your eyes, you find too many children bedridden in hospital. They are not there because of accident, but because of illness. You meet fewer Europeans in hospital. What causes that? It's because of starvation. We are not properly fed. If ever the authorities would think of paying us better, there would not be big crowds like this in hospital.

Among Whites, you don't have police knocking at night—Black and White police. Other communities are not raided. If I have a visitor and he sleeps over, I'm raided, he's arrested. All this trouble, yet the house is mine. My visitor is going to be fined £1 and I £5, irrespective of whether he is my brother or not. If there is justice at all in this country, what has this poor man done? We are being robbed, because I don't know what case is being prepared against a man like that. He has not stolen—he has not harmed anyone. It would be better if these laws were not applied on a discriminatory basis. They should apply at Woodlands—raid them at night, see who is visiting there, and put them in.

I have gone through Woodlands. I often go there trying to establish the facts. Even when you get there, you find the police chase the Africans at the back, but they never interfere, knocking at the door of the houseowners. Now when they have got into the yard, why don't they knock at the door? When they visit the yards, they try to chase the sweethearts of the girls they keep, and it's against nature because these girls must have sweethearts to visit them. . . . The houseowner always has the company of his wife. Who is going to bear company of the girl who is kept at the back? . . . The question of poverty has led to immoral living—like running shebeens, selling *gavini*, in order to buy food, books, pay rent. . . . As Africans, we have a legal obligation also to look after father and mother. How can I split my £2.10.0 between two families? Do you, as Europeans, want to see us naked? We believe that Europeans would be very pleased to see us naked. If many of the shebeen dealers were not dealing in liquor, we would be naked [interview, translated from Zulu].

The elite area is a "loans to individual" scheme—Parktown. The name is ironic. It recognizes the aspirations of the bourgeoisie, the distinguishing marks of wealth, and, at the same time, deflates them by the comparison with fashionable White suburbs. Lamontville's Parktown is indeed a miserable playground for the "rich." It lies along one side of an unkempt street, Gambushe (or Parsons' Row, as it is described by some members of the city's Bantu Housing Department). At the entrance is the trader's home, designed proudly to the exact plan of houses in a neighboring estate for White exservicemen, and furnished in a sparkling new middle-class style. Beyond are a straggle of modest homes. These are single-storey, slightly larger than the homes of the common people, with some individual variations on a basic stereotype, built for the most part at a cost of between £300 and £500—the type of home one might associate with White farm laborers. And yet in this setting is the slight margin for the expansion of the bourgeoisie.

The elite structure of the population of individual homeowners appears from an analysis of applications for loans at Lamontville. In July 1961, I examined 86 such applications in the Corporation files. The information is not always complete. Some men refuse to disclose that their wives are earning. Or again, the father in whose name the application is made may be a "boss boy," the son a clerk in the Bantu Administration Department and presumably the real purchaser. In most cases, the homes were already built or in process of building. In some instances, sites had not yet been allotted. Most of the homes were in the Gambushe area.

The files disclosed that 18 wives were earning—1, a nursing sister, £28 per month, 6 between £20 and £22 (presumably nurses), 6 between £10 and £16, and 5 £8 and under. Of the men, 22 earned under £20 per month, 40 between £20 and £30, 15 between £30 and £40, and 8 salaries of £40 and over. One trader did not disclose his earnings; another, one of the most successful African traders in Durban, showed £18 per month, which must be an understatement, and a third, who had paid cash for a house of about £800–£900, gave his earnings as £28 per month, and a fourth as £30 per month. The applicants' occupations, brought up to date as far as possible, are shown below.

Ministers of religion	8	
Other professionals (including male nurses)	11	
Clerical workers	13	41
Salesmen	5	
Traders	4	
Supervisors of labor (difficult to classify—salary range is relatively high, with one exception between £20 and £30 per month).	11	
Chauffeurs, drivers, and conductors	16	
Policemen and sergeants	4	
Skilled machinists, factory operatives, caterer, tester, and compositor	8	
Gate watchman, laborers	3	
No information	3	
Total	86	

Drivers, police sergeants, and detectives earn relatively high salaries. They may move in some of the same circles as the professionals, and they are sometimes included in discussions of the African middle class.

Landed property for Africans is insecure: the rights it confers have been stripped of the sanctity associated with private property in a capitalist society, and highly discriminating segregation confines the African property owner to restricted areas in which a double standard, a specifically African standard, governs the amenities. And yet, in these "Parktowns" members of the bourgeoisie can detach themselves and find some scope for a distinctive way of life. For the rest, prestige may be displayed in motor cars, and, though less conspicuous, in household furniture on the European model. In the opinion of the Zulu anthropologist Mbata, ownership of a car is a crucial index of economic stature.

> If, for example, you are a monied man, it's no use saying you have money if you can't produce a car. A car is a very important badge of prominence. Once you have a car, people look up to you. I suppose that's in a situation where a man can't build himself a house: now in the traditional structure, to be a man, you must build yourself a large kraal, that everybody can see, have a large herd of cattle. Now in town, you can't build yourself a conspicuous kraal, or a house, so to show the world that you are worth anything, you buy a car. And if you can't buy a car, then you go in for flashy, showy clothes. And I think to a very large extent that is responsible for the African's preoccupation upon clothes. I think we Africans are very dressy.

Mkele thought that furniture was important, the more the better, and that the big American car was less of a status symbol than formerly: conspicuous reserve was bringing car owners acclaim when they bought medium-sized and small cars (*Natal Daily News,* November 16, 1961).

Clothes are an uncertain index of class, since interest in good clothes is relatively widespread among Africans. A domestic servant may be prepared to make considerable sacrifices for a good appearance. One observer suggested that men's fashions are introduced at a level below that of the bourgeoisie in an exaggerated form, and that the bourgeoisie then adopts the fashions in a restrained form. The innovators, according to this observer, are a well-defined stratum of young men who have failed to graduate into the higher occupations.

African women are becoming more fashion conscious—i.e. in terms of a sophisticated Western idiom, since there is much interest in fashions, clothes, and coiffures in tribal society. There may even be an elegant revival of tribal costume among the Westernized under the influence of political aesthetics. Papers serving the African community carry articles on fashion in dress, and advertisements of cosmetics for the straightening of hair and the bleaching of skin. These are often featured in an atmosphere of glamour and allure. There is no necessary implication of "playing for Colored" in the straightened hair styles, save in the case of men.

The beauty columnist on an African paper suggested that the fashion of hair straightening had moved upward from loose women to the middle class. This theory is not without some plausibility, since in the past, "immorality" between Whites and Africans was a crime, but not between Whites and Coloreds.

> Hair straightening used to be done by loose women, just to suit their own needs. They used to lead a double life, and pass as Coloured. Now it's taken up by the middle class. With our own hair, you can't develop head styles. When straightened it becomes pliable, and you can use hair styles. [When I suggested that Zulu women seemed to have a variety of hair styles traditionally, she said yes, that Zulu women usually have beautiful hair. She thinks the custom of hair straightening was probably influenced by Negroes.]
>
> The men object, why straighten your hair when God gave it to you that way. Even among the educated there are some who don't like it.
>
> The middle class are now also lightening their skins. There is a craze now for Archers (cream). Zulus used to admire light skins and they had special herbs for this purpose. Poor people also go in for Archers. . . . The men don't object to this [i.e. skin lightening].
>
> The middle class are inclined to use lipstick now. In Johannesburg they like it and straight hair. Men have something to say about it here [in Durban]. The women are more civilized than the men. We are quicker to take up fashions and civilization. Some women smoke but not publicly—it's looked down upon.

African nurses, in particular, set an example in glamour and elegance.

There are differences also in the style of recreation, entertainment, and celebration. Professional men would not normally go into beer halls. Some shebeens cater for the "respectable," and stock a good liquor, sold at a high price. Customers may buy a nip (a small glassful) for about 7/6d. swallowing it neat, and quickly, lest the police should come. At other shebeens, there may be a section where the higher class customer can sit separated from the common people. The pattern of shebeen life is doubtless changing, now that the Government has assumed the role of Bacchus and abolished the Black man's prohibition. But the consumption of good European liquor is likely to remain a class index, because of its high cost.

The catering tables at the markets are generally patronized by the working class. For the African bourgeoisie, there are no fashionable banquets to launch welfare programs, no civic receptions to inflate prestige. Durban has some modest African restaurants. Recently two

Indian restaurants in Durban were fully opened to Africans, and the elite patronize them. In Johannesburg, elite catering is more highly developed. The South African Railways has opened what *The World* described as a:

> posh and classy eating and meeting place if one feels like entertaining a friend or a business colleague in transit. . . . You have your meals in flashy garden setting atmosphere overlooking roof flowerbeds through large glass windows shielded by a terra cotta grille design. . . . It is a sure bet that the place is going to be the most popular rendezvous for the Reef's well-to-do young blood. First signs of the elite Romeos and Juliets showed immediately when hefty easy-Fats Tornado Maphumulo sauntered in with cute curves hanging on his arm [May 6, 1961].

The Government magazine *baNtu,* in the issue of August 1961, under the heading "They Dine First Class," described the non-White railway concourse as an "impressive fruit of one of the positive aspects of the Government's policy of separate development, namely the provision of equal facilities for both White and non-White." The publicity given to the restaurant, and to the opening of a first railway dining car for non-Whites, the Amatola, is sufficient evidence that elite catering for Africans is "news."

The glamour of the first night at theater, opera, and ballet is generally denied Africans. Opportunities for formal entertainment are very meager. The bourgeoisie is more selective, in terms of the type of entertainment and also the venue. Ballroom dancing, as distinct from jiving and jazz, is by no means the preserve of the educated. Indeed professional ballroom dancing is an avenue of mobility for working class men.[1] Ballroom dancing is a key, an invitation card, to the nurses' home. In the last few years, night life, especially in Johannesburg, has begun to offer Africans an arena for the parade of fashion, glamour, pecuniary and other prestige, in the form of occasional theater, concerts, beauty contests, an art exhibition, a sportsman-of-the-year banquet, and so on.

"Cocktail funerals" and weddings offer occasion for lavish display, and African newspapers regularly feature fashionable weddings. Photographs show men in formal dress, women in bridal gowns and veils. The following description of a wedding between a prosperous businessman and a staff nurse was given to me by the beauty columnist of the Durban African newspaper.

> An interesting feature of the occasion was, as in most African weddings, the mixture and the blending of African and Western

---

1. Pauw mentions tensions arising from the differing educational accomplishments of ballroom dancers, some of the professionals being men of lower education (*The Second Generation,* p. 175).

marriage rites. The bride wore a frothy dress of lace and tulle. It was of ballet length. Her veil was of white flimsy nylon put in place by a lovely wax tiara. She carried a bouquet made up of the lilies-of-the-valley. The bride maids wore lilac netting costumes and the whole bridal retinue the latest in Italian shoes. The bridegroom and his party wore dove grey suits.

Weddings among Africans are big and elaborate affairs. In fact small and private affairs are looked upon by friends and neighbours very suspiciously. The general opinion is that they take place because of the presence of something to hide. In these cases chastity of the female partner is always suspect.

This wedding was a grand affair and in the vernacular referred to as "a white wedding" [*umshado omhlophe*] because the bride was chaste and therefore entitled to cover herself with a veil. The expense in this wedding ran into hundreds of pounds excluding "Lobola" which was £250. The bride's father when he demanded this amount told representatives of the bridegroom that he was being very liberal with his daughter. In fact he said she was worth more than £300. Explaining how he arrived at the figure he said that besides money he spent educating and bringing his daughter up she was now a professional woman. Her leaving home means loss of revenue and £250 cannot compensate the loss her marriage had cost him.

Prior to the christian ceremony, the previous night was a busy one. A bridegroom's party visited the bride. They came singing and prancing in the traditional custom. They stood at the gate and paid a small sum of money for admission. This rite I understand is a token of showing respect of the bride's home. That done, the bridegroom's party was offered a goat which was immediately slaughtered and eaten by the party. Through the night there was dancing and singing and the bridegroom's party feted.

After the wedding ceremony in church the next day, then came the traditional part of it. All the guests got together in the big yard and speeches were made. This part of it is called "Ukuthethelela." It is a ceremony in which the parents of the wedding couple publicly declare the good and the bad points of their children. The father of the bride is the first to make a speech. The usual trend of the speech, as was the case in this one, is to tell the public how good the daughter is and that if she is found bad at her in-law's home it will be because she has acquired the bad traits there. Also it is revealed whether she is a sickly or a healthy person. One of

the main points the bride's father makes is how much the bridegroom has paid in Lobola and also mention if there is any balance
in the Lobola arrangements. The bridegroom's father replied suit-
ably and also put his son in very good light.

Then followed the public display of the woman's trousseau. A big
trunk was opened and carefully examined by the bridegroom's
party. As a rule she must come to her in-laws with certain essential
things. Items like linen, a good supply of clothes, and other things.
If after a short time during her marriage, it is found that she has
no clothes, she is sent back to her home to be clothed there. The
reason is that because the bridegroom paid Lobola her people must
buy her enough clothes to last her at least one year. At this wedding,
the bride did not only display a trunk full of clothes and other
necessary items but a bed-room suite also. After this ceremony, she
began supplying gifts to the members of the bridegroom's household. Her father-in-law was given a blanket and other members of
the family grass mats and other traditional gifts.

In the evening was a reception held at the local Hall. There was
singing and dancing until the small hours of the night. At about
noon the next day there was a wedding cake cutting party and
many people attended. Then began the sad part of the wedding.
At about three o'clock the bride said goodbye to her people and
with the bridegroom set out for the bridegroom's home, which is
her new home. There she will be called "Makoti" [young bride]
and join the household and perform all the duties given her.

When I inquired about her honeymoon I was told that such a thing
is unknown among Africans: beside the fact that when the couple begin
a new life they are so impoverished by lobola payments and other things
that they cannot afford a honeymoon, traditionally a woman after
marriage must settle down immediately at her new home and work and
breed children.

European liquor is regarded as an essential item at elite weddings. If
the families have enough money, transportation will be provided for the
guests, even over long distances. Usually wedding celebrations combine
a modern Western pattern, that of upper-class English, with traditional
elements added in deference to parents, aged relatives, and neighbors.
Some fully emancipated professionals may have a simple Western-style
wedding.

Compared with the opportunities for display and differentiation in the
White community, there is a very narrow range available to Africans,
but perhaps it is all the more significant on that account. The conspicu-

ous consumption of the bourgeoisie is set in two perspectives. It is magnified by the general poverty of Africans, and, at the same time, dwarfed by the wealth of the White man, who sets the standard of display. The tension between these perspectives seems likely to act as a spur to radical social change.

CHAPTER 11

The Awareness of Social Class

THE AWARENESS of class distinctions in complex Western societies is likely to be confused and varied in expression unless it is given direction, form, and clarity by social scientists, politicians, journalists, and other molders of social thought. Class consciousness may be implicit in the objective conditions of economic life, but its categories—the number of classes and the manner of their differentiation—require explicit formulation. It takes much discussion and dissemination of ideas before particular perceptions prevail in a population, such as class distinctions between the upper, middle, and lower, or more elaborately between upper-uppers, lower-uppers, and so on, or more radically in terms of bourgeoisie and proletariat.

In African society, the social distinction between the educated and uneducated, Western and tribal, Christian and heathen is deeply rooted. But the process of giving a specifically Western type class mold to African social consciousness seems to be recent. It is encouraged by the example of the dominant White society, as an African businessman sensed in the revealing comment that "a man who has seen other races can set Africans into classes too." And it is fostered by sections of the African intelligentsia. Nimrod Mkele, for example, speaks and writes of the African middle class. His own wedding was almost a clinical demonstration of appropriate behavior, adding, for full measure to the abundance of prestige items, a White church and a White bridesmaid. The article in *Drum* (February 1962) by his "bestman number two," headed: "When V.I.P. Weds V.I.P.," quoted the comment that, "this was bound to be a big wedding, what with Edith being a B.A. and Nimrod a well-known psychologist and M.A.," and referred to the presence at the wedding of well-known businessmen, famous writers, lawyers, doctors, and members of the diplomatic corps, and to the three university graduates in the bridal party and the attorney who served as chief bestman. The social columns of newspapers and journals circulating among non-Whites play, in the idiom of Western class concepts, on the prestige of occupation, wealth, and education, and on the activities of the "big wheels," the "upper crust," the socialites, thus helping to crystallize class self-consciousness.

The prestige accorded occupations is an important element in this awareness of class distinctions. It is often said that Africans, throughout the continent, have strong aspirations to white-collar work, and that they attach high prestige to intellectual occupations, while despising the manual. If there is a common attitude—presumably among certain strata—then it must be related to common elements in the situation, such as the values imparted at mission schools, or the system of colonial rule by officials with intellectual, administrative, and manipulative skills, or the frequent withholding of higher technical training and the employment of Africans mainly as unskilled laborers, so that experience equates manual work with rough, poorly-paid labor.

Where there are basic differences in colonial policy, school education, and occupational experience, it seems reasonable to expect differences in choice and ranking of occupations. A study by Nelly Xydias[1] in Stanleyville, Belgian Congo, of choice of occupation by primary and secondary school children, and of occupational aspirations of adults for themselves and for their sons, showed an almost exclusive concern with white-collar occupations only in the case of the secondary school children. Again in a study reported by J. Comhaire[2] of school children in Leopoldville, almost half the schoolboys who stated their choice of occupation chose salaried manual work: there was no overriding preoccupation with white-collar occupations. The findings suggest some correspondence between the occupational choices of the pupils and the Belgian policy of concentrating on primary education, discouraging the rapid growth of an elite, and emphasizing economic development with occupational advancement to a middle range of technical skills.

The choice of a career is by no means synonymous with the prestige of that career, since choice is influenced by personal inclination and may be tempered by a realistic assessment of opportunity. In any event, choice and prestige reflect different reactions to the occupational structure. The great majority of the Congolese in these studies might very well have accorded the highest prestige to white-collar occupations. This was the pattern found by Epstein and Mitchell[3] in a study of 653 African secondary school students in the Central African Federation, the rank order, with a few exceptions, being: first, white-collar occupations, second, skilled or supervisory occupations, and last, unskilled occupa-

1. With V. G. Pons and P. Clément, "Social Effects of Urbanization in Stanleyville, Belgian Congo," in *Social Implications of Industrialization and Urbanization in Africa South of the Sahara* (UNESCO, 1956), pp. 357–61.

2. "Some Aspects of Urbanization in the Belgian Congo," *American Journal of Sociology, 62* (1956), 10.

3. J. C. Mitchell, "The African Middle Classes in British Central Africa," in *Development of a Middle Class in Tropical and Sub-tropical Countries* (Brussels, INCIDI, 1956), p. 227.

tions. And this is the pattern of the prestige rankings given by 362 school children and 99 teachers in Durban during 1959–60, as shown in Table 8, Appendix D.

The primary school children rated the professions first, with pride of place to the doctor, then the clerical occupations and trading, and finally the manual occupations; the artist and the herbalist were rated at the level of the manual occupations. The pattern for the Standard IX children was about the same, though the ordering of the professions was somewhat different. They rated the lawyer second, whereas the primary school children rated the lawyer fifth; and they grouped the artist with the white-collar occupations; they accorded relatively low esteem to social work, presumably because it was a little-known profession, with relatively few practitioners, and they rejected the occupation of herbalist as not requiring formal education and being open to abuse. In their reasons for giving first rank to an occupation, the students emphasized social service, followed in the case of the younger students by education —with little mention of financial considerations—and in the case of the older students by references first to the financial rewards and then to education. There were no very appreciable differences between the responses of boys and girls. Boys gave a lower rating to the nursing profession and a higher rating to teaching.

The students were also asked what occupation they hoped to follow and what occupation they expected to follow. The hopes of the secondary school children were directed mainly to the professions (90%) and then to the occupations of independent business, clerks, and artisans (10%); the hopes of the Standard V children were also directed to the professions (78%), to the work of artisans (13%), and of clerks (9%). The expectations of the primary school children were closer to their hopes than were those of the secondary school children: 53% expected to enter the professions, 20% to become artisans, and 15% clerks, as compared with 46% of the secondary school students in the professions, 26% as clerks, and 19% artisans. The rejection of independent business, chosen only by 3% of the secondary school children and by none in the primary school, would seem to reflect ignorance of the opportunities now opening to traders. Presumably the image of the independent African businessman was that of the illiterate petty trader and curio dealer. The student population in the sample seemed to be highly optimistic about occupational prospects.

There would appear to be considerable stability in the aspirations of African children for the professions. In a union-wide survey of Standard VI children carried out a generation earlier (1935), 63% of the boys and 79% of the girls wished to enter the professions. Commerce was again largely rejected, but there was much greater interest in farming among the boys. The main professional choices for the boys were those of teacher (48%), minister of religion (over 6%), and doctor (almost 5%); and for girls, teaching (over 52%) and nursing (almost 26%).[4]

The teachers experienced some difficulty in rating the occupations, as the following comments show:

"Some people don't know some of the occupations—e.g. social workers and the few they know they consider drunkards. Artists are not respected. They would say—the African Jazz drinks is the usual remark. Others, like the herbalist, are not respected but people fear them."

"The minister of religion used to be highly respected but now he is considered as only a money maker. Most people know what a lawyer is but know nothing about the university lecturer. Many people still believe in the herbalist."

"Uncivilized people have no time for a doctor and a lecturer. Among ministers you have some who are not educated. A lecturer who is an atheist might misuse his knowledge. I don't like atheists. The lawyer is educated but he can work for your downfall even if he knows the truth."

"I hope when they refer to minister they mean recognized churches and not Zionists."

"Minister of religion—he's the most hated of all. The average African does not know these two—social worker and university lecturer."

"Minister—at present time does not earn much respect. Lots of people have tended to despise them as instruments of their suffering."

"Trader and carpenter are independent and enjoy a certain amount of respect because of their independence. There are herbalists who are respected because of their money and others who are not."

"There is no farmer in present-day African society."

"Trader—may rate above lecturer if very successful."

"I am biased against the civil servant because he is employed by the Government. They are good people."

"Civil servant—gets a lot of money, but instead of respecting them for it, hate them for it. Believe these people agents for the Government in executing laws which make us suffer."

4. *Report of the Commission on Native Education, 1949–51*, Government of South Africa, U.G. No. 53/1951, p. 43.

"Not known that a carpenter can make a good living. African carpenters so small-scale."

Nevertheless their ratings follows a well-defined pattern: the rank order given by the men and women teachers is roughly the same, and it corresponds closely to that of the school children, indicating that they share a common value system. Men rank the professions first, then the trader, civil servant, clerk, and the farmer, artist, and herbalist, followed by manual workers. Women group the trader with the artist and farmer, and the herbalist with the manual occupations. Both agree that the doctor has the highest prestige, the men rate the lawyer second, the minister of religion fifth, while the women rate the lawyer third and the minister of religion second. The men also accord higher prestige to the university lecturer than do the women.

Married teachers with children at school were asked what occupation and education they would like for their sons and daughters. In the case of sons, the preferred occupations are law, medicine, and engineering— the professions. Teaching, the ministry, and trade are virtually rejected. As for education, most of the informants desired for their sons either a university degree or the highest they could attain. For daughters, the professions are emphasized (mostly nursing, followed by medicine), and again there is little interest in teaching. Law, favored for sons, is not fully regarded as an occupation for women. Educational aspirations for daughters are lower than for sons.

Since prestige is an evaluation by members of the community, the study of the prestige of occupations among Africans in Durban would have required evaluations from, at the very least, a representative sample of the African population of over 200,000, and the evaluations of other sections of the population would also have been relevant. This was beyond the scope and resources of the present study, and inquiry was largely restricted to African bourgeois assessment of African occupational prestige. Evaluations from the teachers provide some evidence. This was supplemented by discussions with other professionals and traders. Material from these sources will be used in later sections of the study. Meanwhile, two types of supplementary evidence are now offered —first, assessments by African doctors and lawyers of their own prestige, and second, and dubiously, the etiquette followed in social introductions.

If there is any validity to the high rating of doctors and lawyers, then it should be reflected in their experience. The following extracts from interviews with doctors serving as interns in two Durban hospitals demonstrate the high prestige accorded doctors. Within their family circles, and in their villages or neighborhoods, there is great rejoicing when they qualify. Indeed, in the wider South African society, White and non-White, the attainment of a medical degree by an African is acclaimed as an achievement, often celebrated in the national press. It is not only a community achievement, but in a way, a national achievement—or perhaps more accurately, a seven-day wonder.

Since we are analyzing a subjective aspect, it seems appropriate that the doctors should speak for themselves:

> My mother and relatives were greatly excited when I passed as a doctor and so were the people around. I have not been home yet for any length of time, but when I do go, there will be a big celebration. My home is in Pietersburg and the whole village was proud of what I had done. I was the first to become a doctor in that village. . . . At wedding parties the ministers of religion have the best place and with them are the doctors, principal teacher of the area, prominent shopkeepers, and elderly respectable people. These will be given places with the bridal group. This has been happening here when I go to functions even since my student days. When one is introduced, there is first of all surprise. Is it a real doctor, like a European doctor, or an *inyanga*? You find other Africans whom you will meet in the duty room and they will ask you where is the doctor? They take it for granted that you cannot be a doctor and they have not heard of a non-European doctor. The Europeans do this too. They sometimes come here to see their maids. Sometimes when an African hears that you are a doctor, he will make a short speech and say it is good how our people are going up. We appreciate it and we are proud [He may have said, "He appreciates it, and he is proud"]. They normally talk politics, now we have our own people going up. They speak more softly and more respectfully. Many appreciate the fact that the African is going up. An African woman will clasp her hands and say, "Oh doctor," and keep on responding in this way, "Oh doctor" and so on. I often go to a health center near Port Shepstone where my wife's family live. When we went out there we sat in the bus in front. We did not know that the rule was that the more important men should sit in front and then women. When however they heard we were doctors, they felt it was all right for us to sit in front. This type of response I have been talking about one finds it more among rural women.

There is an interesting reference to the assumption by Africans that their own people cannot really be doctors in the European pattern, which indicates the rarity and grandeur of the achievement. Another doctor mentioned that African visitors, when meeting an African doctor in the corridors of the hospital, will greet him, "Hey brother," implying that they take him to be one of themselves and not a doctor:

> People were very pleased with me. They had known my ambition since completing my matriculation. In my family there was no one

who had come so far and they were pleased and impressed. My immediate community in Springs too was pleased because they had known me as a child and seen me grow up and they felt that I had brought honor to the family and the community as a person who had grown up in the township of Springs. I was the second person to qualify there as a doctor and B.Sc. The Town Council who had sponsored me were very pleased indeed. They did not give me any sort of party but I had a letter from them. The letter was from the Native Affairs Department of the city of Springs, and they did not address me by the title doctor. They simply wrote, "greetings," and then my name. I was given a party at home. I find the way they treat me quite embarrassing. They look upon me from the point of view of expecting certain standards of behavior. The doctor is looked up to as an important figure in terms of the health of the people and providing leadership. A man will come and talk about matters which have nothing to do with medicine, he will discuss financial assistance or domestic problems. He expects you to be a "know all." If you misbehave in any way, then they say, our children are disappointing us. Older people to some extent, will re-act to me in terms of my youth, that is to say, a young man and they would not expect the knowledge and experience of an older man, but they would come to me in connection with anything which involves Western civilization. The old man still seems to remain the main figure. Personal friends call me doctor, even though we grew up together. This is a matter of great embarrassment to me. I cannot say why they should. At the Medical School, we tried to discourage the formality of addressing people as Mr. My school teacher at preliminary school insisted on calling me Mr. while I was studying for medicine. I said that I looked to him as my father, he had taught me but he still insisted on calling me Mr. Even those people with whom I grew up, feel that there is a bridge, a gap, between us. I have always attempted in my own way of life to be as simple as possible, but at home they set the table rather formally when I am there, both for breakfast, lunch, and supper. I tell them that I do not expect that. In regard to diet I explained to them also that I am prepared to eat anything. They seem to have the feeling that there is certain traditional food which I will not eat. I remember the question of *amasi* which they assumed I would not eat. One day it was very hot and I asked for it. They were rather surprised. Do you eat *amasi*? We miss certain of our traditional dishes. I once went to Zululand and they laid tables for us. I wanted to sit in the same way as everyone else. They always at any function, put us at the most important table. If we were waiting for a taxi or a cab, then someone who knows you may stop and when you want to pay then he does not want to take it. You are treated something like a chief, and if you are unscrupulous, you could make a lot out of it.

The reactions to our becoming doctors among the African community are varied. People who belong to the Congress encourage our success. With some people there is the resentment that we are wanting to be better than they are but there are very many more people who encourage than resent. I came from Sophiatown in Johannesburg and my graduating as a doctor was an event. People came to congratulate my parents and when I was there, there were dinners and parties. I was only there for about ten days and there was not time to have a really big ceremony. The people there were proud of my achievement. They also called me doctor. As a doctor I have high prestige in the community. They show a great respect and they also expect you to show your position by the type of clothes you wear and the sort of car you drive. If I go to weddings or functions, I am given a place of honour. [This interview also introduces a different note, that there are some Africans who resent the achievement.]

When I qualified, they made a big splash in the papers. Oh, they made a fuss alright. I really got embarrassed. *The Star, Rand Daily Mail*. I was alone in Johannesburg, my father was here already so there were no parties. People kept telling me I must pick on the best man for a husband—somebody special. This is what the relatives say—somebody respectable, wealthy. A great fuss is made about a doctor. If you're not introduced as a doctor it's alright, you're treated as one of the masses. But if they introduce you as a doctor, my word they make such a fuss, you don't know where to turn. Perhaps it is a way of showing, now we have got people like this. Africans really appreciate people who have gone higher. . . . If you belong to the professional group and marry lower, they feel they've lost somebody down in the sea.

Similarly, comments from lawyers testify to the deference they receive and the importance of their achievement:

There is also an element of growing African consciousness, people wanting to go to their own people. They were proud of us as lawyers and I was the first [African in Durban] to go out into private practice. There is an approach that people have for their own people who have important positions.

People take it for granted that I am a leader. They engage me in the street and invite me to their homes for advice. They say I have a high prestige. . . . Only people of my class come as visitors to my house. The illiterate and the poor feel that they are of a low class. They don't show any outward sign of respect but I find it embarrassing when I find an old man giving his seat in the bus or lifting up his hat. The term *umnumzane* is used for the head of the family or for a person older than yourself or an utter stranger. People use the term *umnumzane* to me. It is not normal. You don't expect a person older than yourself saying *umnumzane*. It is not necessarily the illiterate who do that. Doctors and lawyers are on the top of the hierarchy.

Lawyers have a very high prestige and you will find that at weddings people are always anxious to please them. They will be given special positions, they are always introduced as "Mr. So-and-So, the lawyer."

The last comment, that a lawyer is always introduced as "Mr. So-and-so, the lawyer," suggests a special mode of introduction for persons in leading professions. I had formed the impression that it was common practice to mention the higher occupations, positions, and educational attainments, and I encountered many examples during the study. However, it was not confirmed by informants in the sample of teachers. Many seemed to resent the question "How does a fellow African introduce you to strangers?" as if it implied that they were not civilized, as shown for example, in the reply that a "civilized person does it like any other civilized person: 'Meet Mr. So-and-So.'" This is not surprising against a background of a special education for Africans (Bantu Education) and special forms of address in Government letters (e.g. the use of Umn. Ngubo, instead of Mr. Ngubo, and "Greetings" instead of "Dear"). Earlier there had been an instruction to Bantu Affairs Officers that they should not shake hands with Africans, but use the traditional greeting, though no one could say what it was. And when I inquired from an elderly, portly, conservative member of the Advisory Board, he lay down on his back, like a dog submitting to defeat, and suggested this was what the authorities regarded as the traditional African greeting. Of the teachers, only one in five replied that occupation was mentioned, and about half of these qualified their answers— if they are equals, or depending on whether they are educated or uneducated, or if it does not give offense. Some informants distinguished between introductions in Zulu and in English, as for example:

In Zulu ignore for a while your friend with whom you are walking. In English, introduce straightaway. He tells you who the person is and what his occupation is, if he feels you would not be offended by it. If a respected occupation, they may mention it.

If I came among other teachers, they would mention my position. But if I came among people of low educational status, they would not mention it. Mentions where more or less among equals. Mentions also when he knows that people to whom he introduces will not feel offended.

According to our tradition, have your formal greeting. First introduce stranger to your friend, then friend to stranger. "Meet Mr. So-and-So, principal of Mazenod School." Always give occupation, even if lowly: traditionally, place of birth and where you stay. Today, educated people mention occupation, not other things.

It depends—an old man will say, "This is the son of So-and-So." Otherwise they say "Mr. So-and-So" and mention my occupation.

Allowing for an unwillingness among informants to accept that the mode of introduction among educated Africans differs from the English middle class pattern, the etiquette still does not appear to be standardized. Probably there is a greater emphasis on the prestige of occupation, education, and position than informants admit.

The prestige of occupations is by no means synonymous with an awareness of class differences. The former may simply reflect a continuum, without any grouping of occupations into relatively separate categories, as the concept of class would imply. Specific questions were thus directed to probe class awareness, eliciting in the case of the teachers a seemingly chaotic array of idiosyncratic perspectives.

A preliminary question to teachers, "If you were describing the Africans of Durban to a stranger, how would you classify them?" was designed to indicate the importance attached by teachers to differences in social class. Presumably informants would select in terms of their own prevailing modes of perception from the great range of criteria available for classifying a population. The question in practice served somewhat as a projective test, eliciting concern over the hard life of Africans who were "striving for a living: haven't got the time to be sociable" and their desire to live decent lives; irritations—"African men here like jumping at and touching girls and women"; and exploratory replies, with a free association of ideas—"It would depend on their social status. They are hospitable in their homes but not so much in the streets; in the streets you can't stop them. Our people are not free; in the street they are not free: the little freedom they have remains at home. When at home, there is nobody to wrong them." Of the 97 teachers (in the sample of 99) who replied to this question, 41 mentioned class differences. The value of this evidence is however reduced by the fact that some interview schedules, contrary to instructions, were left with informants, so that their replies were no doubt influenced by the succeeding question on class differences.

The blunt question: "Do you think there are any class differences among Africans in Durban?" was likely to influence respondents toward finding class differences. Nineteen teachers thought there were no class differences, and one answered in terms of regional differences. Some of the comments in the negative answers, however, implied aspects of class structure, as for example the comment that professional people associate together but do not form a class, since they do not shut out the uneducated or keep aloof from the rank and file. This is a common theme, African sociability (humanity, hospitality), transcending social differences. Mkele mentions that while White men's etiquette was the test of respectability in the African middle class, the White man's custom of admitting guests only by invitation, especially to meals, was considered *akanabuntu,* that is, lacking in common decency (*Natal Daily News,* November 16, 1961).

The presence of class differences was affirmed by 77 teachers, though 9 qualified their answers—even if there were, there would be two; starting, not to a large degree; not sharp or pronounced; very slight, does not show much; not as in European society, a rich man can stay in the same yard as a poor and manage to talk to him without discrimination. Five responses were not classified: for example, a seemingly jocular reply—civilized, not civilized, educated, noneducated, vagrants, nonvagrants, and so on; or a reference to non-Christians attacking Christians because they teach the teaching of the White man; or an affirmative response followed by "not at the present time. The African National Congress has unified all the people: they know that they are one people and their sufferings are the same, irrespective of classes."

The actual number of classes given by respondents is as follows:

NUMBER OF CLASSES	NUMBER OF RESPONDENTS
1	1
2	16
3	34
4	14
5	7
	72

The characteristics ascribed to these classes are even more varied. The examples below have been extracted, to show the range of variation and of relevant criteria.

One-class structure
Professional people, economically in same bracket, tend to club together most of the time but not so rigid.

Two-class structure
(1) Professionals (upper class); (2) riffraff (laborers and domestic servants). The monied keep aloof, i.e. don't mix to form a class.
(1) Educated and (2) illiterate.
(1) Decent class—educated; (2) hooligans—mostly uneducated. You find that lawyers and doctors keep together and teachers also form social cliques. The nurses will then fit into all these groups. Then you have the rank and file.

Three-class structure
(1) Doctors and lawyers on top; (2) teachers and ministers; (3) unskilled laborers.
(1) Christian and well-behaved; (2) well-behaved and non-Christian; (3) interested only in liquor.
(1) Civilized and educated; (2) educated; (3) illiterate.

Four-class structure
(1) Educated and cultured. Pleasant to get along with. Mind their own business.
(2) The educated and uncultured.
(3) The uneducated and uncultured.
(4) The uneducated but cultured.

(1) The educated. They are conceited and they feel superior to the uneducated.
(2) Semieducated. They are jealous of the former but would not like to be classed with the uneducated because they feel they are too low.
(3) The uneducated. Usually the lowest paid, the unemployed, the gangsters.
(4) Ministers of religion.

(1) You find educated who are tending to make a class of their own, for instance those with university education tend to make a class of their own. They feel they are the best in social distinctions—you make a party, you invite society boys and girls.
(2) Businessmen tend to form their own class because they own cars and have money—so he can call his friends to a party. They would invite each other.
(3) Then you get those below the bread line also forming a class of

their own. With them it is mostly thinking about nothing but low wages and their poor lives. They cannot rise. They lead bitter lives. Their life is a life of misery. They can't afford to join the rest of the society.

(4) The worst class is people who live above their means. They tend to rise to meet people of society and make a mess of their lives. They pretend to be happy but they are not.

Five-class structure
(1) University educated—well-mannered and well-behaved.
(2) Educated but lead a rough life.
(3) Not educated and tend to be delinquent.
(4) Not educated but well-behaved.
(5) Not educated and still raw.

(1) Monied.
(2) Professional.
(3) White collar workers (clerks, civil servants).
(4) Factory workers.
(5) Migrant laborers.

(1) Educated class.
(2) Christians (law abiding).
(3) Uneducated (live from hand to mouth).
(4) Won't work—prey on other people.
(5) Rough element—unsociable, drink *shimiyane,* fighting, teasing, found near shebeens.

The criteria used in the structuring of the class system reveal a number of features related to change from a traditional African society to a Western industrial. Reference to African society in terms of one class—the professional people clubbing together—seems meaningless. If a society is structured on class lines, then presumably all sections are located within classes. When applied however to a society in transition, or to a plural society, there may be value in conceiving an interim situation in which a stratum emerges from an undifferentiated urban mass and becomes conscious of itself as a class by the criteria of the dominant society.

Many references are made to a dimension of mode of life, largely to an ethical criterion (morals, manners, Christianity, civilization, and culture). Such characteristics as manners, respectability, and morals also differentiate "prestige" classes in Western industrial society. The antisocial rough element, the *tsotsis,* drinking *shimiyane* and preying on other people, correspond to the amoral "Yellow Hammer" class of American studies, while a distinctive style of life and forms of etiquette characterize the leisure class and high society. The distinctions drawn by African informants are, however, of a different type; they refer generally to varied levels of adaptation to Western society. Pons[5] describes a similar phenomenon in Stanleyville, a distinction between *Kizungu* (of or with Europeans) and *Kisendji* (of or with country-men), which refers to mode of residence, but also to the contrast between the "civilized" and the "traditional, backward, savage, or primitive."

There is however no simple equation between respectability and morality on the one hand, and education and Westernization on the other. The division between Christian and non-Christian cuts across the distinction between the educated and the uneducated. Some informants carefully separate education and culture, or education and civilization, or education and respectability. Thus they refer to the morally respectable, whether Christian or heathen; to the educated who lead a rough life, the civilized and uncultured, as distinct from the civilized and cultured, the not educated but civilized; to the educated and cultured as distinct from the educated and uncultured; and to the uneducated and uncultured as distinct from the uneducated but cultured.

The category of the educated but rough or uncultured is presumably that of the young men who have failed to achieve the level of education required for the professions, or to secure professional employment though having the necessary educational qualification. I shall refer to them as the "location boys." They may be in unskilled or semiskilled occupations, or they may be unemployed, and merge with the *tsotsis,* the young delinquent elements in the location population.[6] The "location boys" use the term " 'scuse me' class" (*os'tshuzana* class) for the well-mannered bourgeoisie. This may suggest a parvenu quality in the good manners of the educated professional, or an element of effeminacy in terms of the Zulu code, or of servility to the White man, aping his ways. Whatever is implied, the phrase is used to express contempt.[7]

I have assumed that it is in the nature of subjective descriptions of class in Western society that they should vary, unless crystallized into well-defined and pervasive categories by intellectual formulation in a context of sharp economic and political conflict, or under the strong influence of sociologists upon the subjects of their study, or of Marxists on political life. Lacking to a great extent these stimuli to routine

5. V. G. Pons, "Social Effects of Urbanization in Stanleyville, Belgian Congo," in *Social Implications of Industrialization and Urbanization in Africa South of the Sahara* (Paris, UNESCO, 1956), p. 241.

6. See discussion in Appendix B.

7. Monica Wilson and Archie Mafeje discuss the hostility of the *tsotsis* for the middle class—the "ooscuse-me"—in a Cape Town location in *Langa: A Study of Social Groups in an African Township* (Cape Town, Oxford University Press, 1963), p. 149.

perceptions of class distinctions within the African community—more particularly since intellectual energy flows so abundantly into race relations—the class perceptions of the teachers are naturally most varied. Inevitably, a wide range of criteria is used, since perception must also encompass the transition from traditional society.

The perceptions are, however, not chaotic and purely individual, as they seem on first impression. There is in fact a social patterning. Informants use three main criteria, each being a familiar element in class analysis—namely, education, occupation, and morals or way of life. Only 15 informants structure the classes solely in terms of education, but 36 apply education in combination with other criteria. Occupation as a single criterion is cited by 14 informants; all told, 33 informants refer to occupation. One informant differentiates by the single criterion of morals, way of life, civilization and so on, but 22 refer to this aspect. Thus 51 informants give education alone or in combination with other criteria, including occupation, while 17 use occupation alone or in combination with some criterion other than education, a total of 68 out of 72. The main criteria are thus education and occupation, followed by the ethical aspect, with education ranking highest. The complexity and variability arise partly from the fact that the teachers use these criteria in different ways—as a continuum, such as the educated and the uneducated, in which only the extreme points are given, or as having reference to relatively discrete strata, such as the professionals. Sometimes the term "professional" may be used as a synonym for the educated, for example in a class structure composed of (1) those without high educational qualification, up to Standard I (2) those educated up to Standard VII, and (3) professionals, nurses, teachers, and clerks. Or again, the professionals may be treated as a single class, or an upper stratum may be detached, that of doctors and lawyers.

Wealth and commercial achievement are apparently of minor relevance in the class perceptions of the teachers. There is little wealth in the African community of Durban, businessmen being engaged mainly in petty trade, whereas education, relatively speaking, implies wealth; so that the teachers may be reacting realistically to the actual situation in playing down wealth and exalting education as an indicator of the upper classes. But there appears also to be a devaluation of wealth as a mark of accomplishment. When teachers were asked what qualities are most important in a man and in a woman, they chose as the most desired qualities for men, intelligence, honesty, hard work, and professional training. Intelligence and honesty were also most desired for women: thereafter the women chose for themselves professional training, followed by sociability and hard work; while the men chose for the women hard work, followed by sociability and professional training. Courage ranked fifth for men. The traditional Zulu value of generosity was as little esteemed as the Puritan virtue of thrift, while wealth, shrewdness, and good looks in men ranked lowest. Clearly this is an ideology of the intelligentsia, which these informants expressed in their structuring of the African community. They emphasize education, the value they themselves have achieved. Education has been a prime mover in the social differentiation of Africans, virtually synonymous with professional status.

From the point of view of an outside observer, generalizing the perceptions of the teachers interviewed, the following strata might be distinguished on the basis of level of adaptation: first, the educated, cultured, and civilized, those with formal education who try to maintain a White middle-class style of life within the limits of low income and under a pervasive discrimination which often withholds a deeper understanding and experience of Western values. These are mainly professional people. Below them are the mass of Africans, semieducated and illiterate, who have made their homes in the city, differentiated by their type of employment, semiskilled or unskilled, and by their moral standards, respectable or rough. Then there are the traditional tribal workers, unskilled laborers temporarily accommodated in the city. In the interstices between these strata fall the products of urban disorganization—at the higher level of the educated, the "location boys," who reject the values they cannot achieve, and at the lower level of the uneducated or semieducated, the *tsotsis,* involved in violence and crime. These latter two groups tend to merge in destructive rejection of a frustrating society.

Indications of the class perceptions of members of other strata are available mainly from interviews with university students and traders. They are offered not as generalizations about the class awareness of these strata, but merely as summarizing the views of those interviewed, in the same way as with the teachers. And they introduce some fresh qualitative aspects and suggestions as to possible relations between position and perspective.

The student population of the University of Natal, the cream of the Durban African intelligentsia, might be expected to stress education as strongly as the teachers. In fact, there is a marked difference between the responses of students in the humanities and those of students in medicine.

The humanities' section for non-Whites was virtually a training center for teachers. Teaching is the main occupation open to the educated African man, and many who were already teachers studied at the University to improve their qualifications and salary. With the provision of legal training, an escape route was opened from teaching into the more rewarding profession of law. The prospective lawyers were, however, recruited from much the same segments as the teachers. They are by no means a more privileged section of the population. They may have an intense struggle to pay their tuition fees, the necessary practical training as an articled clerk is difficult to secure, and the whole investment is somewhat speculative. Their actual employment, their level of security and financial backing, is not very different from that of the teachers. They represent, of course, the more ambitious elements.

The African medical students are a more secure student body. They enjoy bursaries, not lavish but sufficient to cover their basic expenses, and if they pass their examinations they are assured of a good income, a fine motor car, and high prestige. They come from different parts of the country, some with experience of life in the main industrial city, Johannesburg. Their class perceptions seem to reflect their more varied experience and more favorable life chances.

Of the 24 African students interviewed in the humanities section, 8 found difficulty in applying the concept of class to the African community. One perceived the African community as classless, but with class distinctions fast emerging in the form of a political class, a merchant class, professionals, and a mass of unskilled laborers. The concept of a political class is useful, since it is a class without an economic base, and since the "liberation" of Africans would immediately catapult this persecuted class to red-carpet status. Others felt that there were interest groups, not classes, a tendency for people at the same economic level to associate together, or that class formation was frustrated because the educated were drawn downward by the political struggle, or, the familiar theme, that the term "class" was inappropriate because of free association between different levels. "The best educated African still associates with a street beggar, which is not the case with Europeans. The African also does not have the sense of belonging to a class. A man might be educated, but he will still associate with the uneducated friend."

The remaining informants structure the African community by educational and economic criteria. The criteria of morals and civilization recede and the economic criteria gain in significance among the students as compared with the teachers. This difference may be related to the higher education of the students and their greater economic ambitions. They are sufficiently secure in their educational achievement to dispense with claims to prestige on the basis of emancipation from tribal values.

By contrast, the medical students show little doubt about the existence of classes and lay greater emphasis on economic factors. One student feels that the situation is confused, with neither clear-cut demarcations nor strong class feelings, another that class differences are beginning to emerge. The remainder (29) make use of class categories, stressing almost exclusively income and education, and to a much lesser extent, occupation. Wealth becomes a significant element in the class perceptions. They comment that "wealth is the factor that counts," or that "class depends on money." There are references to the "big guns," business magnates, the rich and the very rich, and an awareness of the business class. Doctors are potentially big guns financially and this prospect enters into their class perceptions.

> I think it works in three strata. There are blokes with lots of money; I might perhaps call them the elite: such people like Alexander, Xuma, and Rathebe fall in this class. The intelligentsia are only reasonably well off, but not as much as the big chaps. In this class you find teachers and other professional workers. Doctors belong to the class of big chaps by reason of their money. Then you have the numerous, illiterate, unwashed masses. I suppose *tsotsis* can be put in a class by themselves. Money and education are important factors in class differentiation. The top group got to the top through their money; they might not even have degrees. The middle group—that is professionals—has more education than money. The third group is more concerned about where their next meal will come from. They are desperately trying to keep their heads above water.

A few traders (22) were questioned about class divisions among Africans. They were not representative, their education being well above the average. Some did not conceive of a class structure among Africans, on the ground, for example, that "we ourselves do not insist on distinction. The lowest man is as free in my house as I in his house. This is the unwritten convention." Most informants (15) differentiated on the basis of the ethical criterion or way of life (respectability, good behavior, self-respect, Westernization, Christianity, urbanization), followed by education. There are different routes to Westernization or to respectability and it is this factor, analyzed by a butcher, which complicates the class perceptions of informants.

> One cannot just off-hand give a precise picture of the people of Durban because they are confronted with varying factors in the way in which they approach the Western way of life. Some people approach it through religion, others are brought nearer Western ways of life through education, and others are brought nearer through their economic standing. Then in that sense it can be said that there are classes. I can not say exactly how many classes there are. There are those people who are just religious and are called in

Zulu "Amakholwa." Then there is another class which is already
dividing itself into two classes: this is the class of the educated
Africans. There are people of a general educational standard, I.Q.
people with J.C., T.4, Standard VIII, and VII and VI. These according to my opinion form one class. Then there are people who
hold matric certificates and those who are graduates: these people
feel that they are another class. Then there are those people who
are still tribal. These are unfortunate because they are there because of force of circumstances. They no longer like to be there.

Wealth is little emphasized by these traders, though it is respected in
Zulu society, as indicated in the approving phrase "he eats well." The
above informant also stressed the economic factors.

> The people have high aims and they would like to eat good but
> because they have no money they are forced in most cases to eat
> what they do not like. A man's economic position is very important
> today: because if you are well economically you can enjoy all the
> material wealth that is enjoyed by Europeans and the people would
> have a very high esteem of you. In fact there are people with very
> little or no education but because of their success in business enjoy
> a very great esteem in our community. Education and the re-
> ligious qualities of a man are very important.

The class perspectives of these traders seem to reflect a very different
work experience from that of teachers and university students. Traders
are in regular contact with people of low occupational status, struggling
to survive, who constitute their customers. And it is to be expected
that more basic distinctions, as between roughness and respectability,
or Westernization and traditionalism, should prevail at this level.

Other occupational groups were interviewed—ministers of religion,
doctors, social workers, journalists, clerks, craftsmen, indunas, and
laborers—but not in sufficient numbers for any general picture of an
occupational perspective, and adding little in the way of qualitative
insights.

In regard to religious perspectives, there does not appear to be special
prestige attaching to any particular denominations, apart from a negative evaluation of affiliation to the Zionist sects as somewhat low class.
An Anglican minister thought it was not possible to draw a class distinction between Anglicans and Methodists. "Rev. Sikakane [Metho-
dist] once said we regard you as people who worship softly and
quietly. You whisper to God. We pray loudly, we shout to God. I
would say that the only class distinction is in regard to the sects, such
as the Zionist group, but not the separatist churches, such as the
African Congregational Church." A minister of the New Jerusalem

Church, on the contrary, said that the Zionists were "the ultimate of the middle class." This is, however, an unusual point of view. Generally, the bourgeoisie regard membership in a Zionist sect as inappropriate, though educated persons may join a sect in search of healing.

Differences in the religious affiliation of occupational strata and of leaders are related to the policies of the missionaries—the level to which they were prepared to educate Africans, the quality of the education, and the emphasis on leadership or on disciplined docility. The American Board Mission was particularly active in the Natal coastal region. It pioneered advanced education for Africans, and encouraged self-expression and leadership. The contrast with the Anglican Church in Natal (but not in other areas) was described as follows by an African Anglican minister.

> The Anglicans I think felt that Junior Certificate was good enough for a Native. It is not surprising therefore that we do not find as many Anglicans highly educated. . . . Comparing the American Board Mission with the Anglican, I would say that the American Board encouraged their people to grow as men and women. Adams [American Board] was the only place where they developed a sense of responsibility early in their training. Their discipline was not so rigid as we got at St. Chads [Anglican]. We were regarded as little school boys until we left, whereas on the other hand, because Adams had a policy of developing their people, it was disliked by the inspectors. I should mention that we also had the school of St. Augustine's in Zululand which was taken up to matriculation as the result of the influence of a young missionary. The old missionaries thought that the Junior Certificate was good enough for us.

The policy of the American missionaries no doubt explains the relatively high proportion of leading Africans in Durban who are affiliated to the American Board complex of churches, including the African Congregational Church. The evidence for this may, however, be a little misleading. The President of the African Congregational Church explained that it was the policy of his church to invite assistance from African leaders. He thought that nationally-minded people who were not members might claim affiliation to the Church as a way of achieving some prestige or of being looked upon as patriots. Apparently the African Congregational Church in Durban is a residual category for uncommitted Christians, as was the Anglican Church in England after the Second World War.

Women are more active in the membership of the churches. Of a Thursday afternoon when domestic servants have a period of release from work, they are seen on their way to church in their distinctive

uniforms, a type of regimentation which makes it difficult for the educated to join these religious associations. One Anglican minister felt that
his congregation divided into two broad strata, the educated and the
uneducated, though the ability to speak English enabled those with
little education to associate with the educated. "Economically there is
not much difference because we are all equally poor." He also suggested
a difference in the approach to leadership on the part of the uneducated
group: it "follows more directly personal leadership, because it has no
other source of information except from the person directly concerned.
If they have confidence in the person they follow him without question." The ministers of two Apostolic churches felt that there were no
classes, one on the ground that there were only individual differences,
and the other because lack of opportunity for employment and common living conditions prevent differentiation: however, the second informant proceeded to describe the educated as a better class and the
traders as exclusive and looking down on others. The minister of the
New Jerusalem Church distinguished an inferior class (not church-
going), a middle class (characterized by responsibility and respectability, church-going, and an interest in football, though little different
from the inferior class in income), and a highly educated class, a suffering class because it has to live with the lower class.

In other interviews there is confirmation of the practice of referring
to a respected occupation or position in introducing a person and of
separating out the higher classes at celebrations, feeding men and women
together at tables inside the house, while others are served outside in
the traditional way. The speaking of English appears to be a criterion
of class. It is clearly an index of education and Westernization, sometimes a substitute for education in social intercourse. One informant
suggests that the prestige of English derives from education in mission
schools, where students were forbidden to speak their tribal languages,
so that a sense of guilt attached to the use of the home language. Another informant, a dressmaker, naïvely displays the snobbish and divisive
element in English speaking:

> The people I call "excuse me" are the educated lot. People in fact
> know how to class themselves. For instance, when I have a party,
> most people, especially those who cannot express themselves in
> English, will not attend my party because they call me "excuse
> me" and they know that the majority of my friends mostly can
> speak and understand English.

At lower levels of education or of Westernization, discussion in terms
of class concepts becomes meaningless. The traditional norms for evaluating groups within the African community no longer apply in the
urban setting. They are linked to knowledge of family lines and socio-

political relationships, still relevant in the urban context when one Nyuswa meets another, but hardly relevant in the contacts between members of different tribes. The norms for group evaluation in Western society have not yet been absorbed. Consequently, the only criteria available are those of the traditional society for evaluating individuals —the self-respecting person who respects others and himself, the man who imbues his children with the quality of respect, the good man. The assessment is in terms of individual esteem rather than group status.

Westernization shapes class consciousness, not only by creating the objective conditions for new systems of differentiation through industrialization but also by providing the intellectual concepts for the structuring of group relations. Corresponding to the objective core of occupational and related differences are subjective reactions of class consciousness crystallizing in a Western idiom. There is a process of class formation. But there are also contrary processes, restraining stratification. The bourgeoisie has a shallow depth over the generations, and many of its members come, and are likely to come in the future, from the homes of peasants or laborers. The acknowledgment of obligations to the extended family binds together persons of different occupations. Professional men have sometimes served as manual workers, and such is the insecurity of African life, that with few exceptions, they may readily find themselves, at any time, in labor. Then too, Africans are for the most part equally dependent on the White man for employment and dwarfed by him in power, wealth, and prestige. There is a ceiling on individual mobility under a common subordination and an emphasis on group identity. This creates a situation for Africans in which they may be more likely to achieve advancement as individuals through the group, so that African solidarity becomes a condition for personal progress.

PART III

The Occupational Milieu: The Intellectuals

CHAPTER 12

The Intellectuals

Others have hopefully acquired education, only to find that it is Pisgah's mountain, from which they can view the Promised Land with its rivers of milk and honey, without the possibility of entering it. . . . [Education] has refined and is refining their senses and sensibilities, only that they may the more poignantly feel their present injuries, it has awakened hope and ambition only to cruelly disappoint them.[1]

THE POSITION of the African intellectual is highly ambiguous, surrounded as he is by the ambivalent reactions of others, both African and White. Even the concept of African scholar is ambiguous, and there is little in his social and academic situation to encourage scholarship.

The professional intellectual, living legitimately by his wits, is a new category in African society. Wisdom was valued traditionally, but in an instrumental role, as, for example, the wisdom of the councillor in political, judicial, or ritual decisions. This instrumental evaluation of education and of intellect persists, especially among the traditionally oriented. Intellectual achievement is assessed in terms of occupational opportunity or of its contribution to the struggle of the African people. A candidate for the doctorate degree in anthropology describes his own difficulties as follows:

A man may be very clever and they [the Zulus] admire it, but only in so far as it's an instrument to fight the other group. . . . When you say you are learning now to take an extra degree, and so on [they say], now what are you going to do with it, how will it help us? Here the Europeans have taken away our land, the Indians take all the money and are monopolizing all business, and so on, now how is your education going to help us there? And if you cannot really relate your education to the problem that must be dealt with, then they just won't understand you.

1. S. M. Molema, *The Bantu—Past and Present* (Edinburgh, Green, 1920), p. 320.

Learning for its own sake is not easily accepted, he points out. "People ask why I don't earn a living. When they ask me to attend a synod meeting and I say I can't, they ask what is it to go on learning when you are a married man?" Purely intellectual pursuits, which would establish standards of scholarship within the African community, are little encouraged.

Even when viewed in instrumental terms there is ambivalence, because the highest education does not emancipate a son from the racially subordinate status he shares with his uneducated father. And there is frustration when education does not lead to good employment, or when it creates estrangement between illiterate parents and educated children, adding to the anguish of sacrifice for children's education. An African health educator traces the conflict between educated and uneducated partly to estrangement between the generations within the family:

> There are people of the low type who have no respect for educated. They will say that some educated people misuse their gift. They say the worst drunkards are educated. This is a remark given by most people. When educated, they think they're too wise and abuse. The higher the educated become, they don't think of their illiterate community. They say they look low on them. If you look back to the background of most educated people, you will find perhaps, his father and mother are not. There are others whose parents were educated. The first group become ashamed of their parents. They will not introduce them. They don't appreciate that these old mothers had starved themselves to give education. Some will have the mother to starve in the country. If we educate our children they say, they will look down on us. They won't even come down to our level. They won't even call us father and mother. That's why there is always a line between the two groups. They despise education, because the educated don't come and work amongst them.

Suspicion of the political role of the educated, expressed, for example, in the accusation that the educated African makes money from the uneducated or sells himself to the White man, adds further ambiguity. There is both a need for the leadership of the educated, and a fear of betrayal by them. The African economist, Selby Ngcobo, feels that this suspicion is deeply rooted historically, and explains it as follows:

> Very often White officialdom of the Smuts regime looked up to the educated man as the most useful lever to work through as far as African interests were concerned. They would take you into the committee room as the sort of man they could talk to—which

created doubt and suspicion. You can talk the type of English they don't understand which also affects the relationship. In Natal the missionaries established mission stations and produced an educated type of African whom they weaned away from the tribal societies. Subsequently, he was used as a kind of interpreter, policeman, clerk, and given letters of exemption. In times of war, he was used also for spies and levies so that we have the expressions *izifundiswa* and *amazemtiti* (the educated and the exempted). They both became terms of contempt and derision. These people were regarded as betrayers or likely to betray[2] because they cast their influence with the Whites. The Nationalists have exploited this historical situation to the full. It has always been the technique of Native Commissioners to maintain their position by exercising a divisive influence against the educated. The educated are regarded by them or spoken of by them as agitators, or in Minister de Wet Nel's phrase, as wolves. Native Commissioners in the time of General Smuts would say, "we have passed a law, it is good for you. Now people will come and say it is no good. Don't listen to them. . . ." There is a tendency to accord the educated people high prestige and to want their help, but on the other hand there is fear and suspicion that they will let them down. . . . I think that we educated people are responsible for the suspicion. We were more ready to cast our lot with the White community without explaining ourselves and taking Africans into our confidence [personal interview].

An African graduate confirms these impressions of tensions between the educated and the uneducated. He comments that the attitude of the lower classes is uncertain, being in transition—in Durban though not in the rural areas—from respect to distrust. He comments on the contempt for the educated as spoilt persons removed from custom, and given to drunkenness:

They say, you have taken your child to school, you have educated him, and he is not improved. They also complain of lack of respect. They also distrust the position the educated man occupies between the European and his own people. The educated man is often the interpreter, the liaison, and is easily bribed. They associate the educated with cunning, with people who swindle in organizations, with people who know how to manipulate books. This comes from

2. Molema writes, in somewhat similar vein, of the reaction of the tribal people in the Cape to "their half-civilised and detribalised fellow-countrymen. . . . They call them Ama-Kumsha or Ma-Kgomocha; that is, literally—speakers of European languages, a word which, however, in the mind of a tribal Muntu, is always associated with something of deceit, and is almost synonymous with that meaning turn-coat, cheat, or trickster" (*The Bantu*, p. 319).

experience. They feel that we are an appendage to the Whites and would go with the Whites.

Jordan Ngubane,[3] a leading African journalist, comments on the different racial attitudes of the tribal and the educated. The tribal people, he suggests, hate the White man and would like to drive him into the sea from which he came, but they need the educated African and are uncertain how he would behave in a crisis. The educated, on the other hand, distrust the tribal man, knowing that he will be the first to betray them to the Whites. In private discussion, he said that the domestic servants, who are very close to the tribal milieu, hate the educated African above all. His portrayal of the antagonism toward the educated recalls an observation by Goldthorpe:[4]

> it is noticeable that in times of stress such as Mau Mau in Kenya or the 1949 riots in Buganda the group most consistently under attack have been the most Westernized Africans, for whom a fury has been reserved distinctly reminiscent of that against Quislings in German-occupied Europe.

And Banton refers in *West African City* to attacks made by African rioters on anyone wearing a collar and tie.[5]

Against testimonies of antagonism, disapproval, and distrust must be set observations of the extreme deference accorded the educated by the uneducated (as discussed in Chapter 11). There is often an extravagant recognition of educational achievement, of university degrees, based perhaps on the perception that the book is the source of the White man's power. The general standard of African education is too low for a critical assessment of the degree, of the university which conferred it, or of the standard attained by the candidate. Consequently the educated African is denied a test by competitive standards and encouraged to an inflated image of his achievement. Mere attendance at a university and any degree, however lacking in distinction, receive acclaim amongst the general populace, though the educated may differentiate, notably with respect to degrees by correspondence. In contrast, however, to the naïve acceptance of intellectual achievement, Africans are very critical of the behavior of the educated, setting much higher standards of proper behavior for them than for the population at large. Being relatively few in number, the educated are visible and vulnerable. This explains, to some extent, the adverse criticism, the

3. *An African Explains Apartheid* (New York, Praeger, 1963), chap. 12.
4. J. E. Goldthorpe, "Educated Africans: Some Conceptual and Terminological Problems," in *Social Change in Modern Africa,* ed. A. Southall (London, Oxford University Press, 1961), p. 156.
5. London, Oxford University Press, 1960, p. 120.

rejection on moral grounds, and the expressions of disillusionment. The great expectations of exemplary behavior, conceived as appropriate for the educated, reflect the high prestige of education.

It is in this context of ambivalence that quite contradictory observations may be equally valid. Thus, as showing hostility, one medical student comments that, "The illiterate do not like educated people. You often hear them derisively saying '*Bathini o B.A. namhlanje?*' ('What are the B.A.'s saying today?')." On the other hand, another medical student, praising the versatility of the intellectual, who is able to adjust to his own world as well as to that of the backward people, thought the uneducated tended to be content with their inferiority. "The uneducated have the great quality of respect; to them a teacher is a teacher, a minister a minister. They take you as a God. They will say nothing bad about you." These observations either relate to different segments of the population, or to different situations, or reflect ambivalence and change. Hostility for the educated is not confined to the illiterate. It may be expressed also by the educated who have failed to achieve a secure occupation or by the semi-educated who have failed to attain the educational standard required for the professions. It is only the bourgeoisie among Africans that accords a relatively unambiguous prestige to education, diminished somewhat by the growing opportunities for wealth in commerce and the changing status of the teacher under Bantu Education.

Within White society, there is again ambiguity and impediment to scholarly achievement. The missionaries detached the Africans they educated from tribal society without, however, integrating them into White society. Instead, they created a new segregated milieu. They developed the educated African as an individual because they were concerned with the salvation of the individual soul and not of the ethnic soul, and they suspended him between the two societies. He could not be integrated into the tribal group, since his education and outlook were disruptive of tribal values, and he was not accepted into the society of Whites. He had therefore to maintain his individuality and seek social participation within a new Christian-educated African community, a process which the segregated mission stations encouraged.

Education qualified Africans for the occupations of priest, teacher, and interpreter. In these occupations, Africans functioned for African society, teaching and serving their own people. Their role was not unlike that of the switches in the telephone exchange, passing the word —religious, educational, and administrative—from Whites to Africans. Working in the new segregated structure, they were again denied the higher competitive standards of the dominant society. When later some African intellectuals were appointed to the academic staff of "White" universities, the same pattern persisted. Africans were generally employed as Bantu language teachers, channeling culture from one group to another, but this time in reverse. The occupational role, like that of the social role, was intermediate between the two societies, an instrumental role shaped by others and not independent or creative.

The educational policies of the missionaries introduced a further ambiguity. These policies varied with different missionary societies and changed over the years. At first, different standards of education were often accepted either as adequate or as a matter of inevitable temporary necessity, given the starting point of an illiterate populace. Some mission schools emphasized manual skills, others a literary, humanistic education modeled on the good English schools. There was concern over character building, discipline, and obedience. In time, as educational standards were raised, the African school system drew closer to that of the Whites, and students were trained in increasing numbers for the same matriculation examination. Implicit in this educational policy was the concept that Africans would participate in the same society as Whites. Presumably there must have been some vision of ultimate integration. In other words, the schools were shaping Africans for a society which has not yet emerged in South Africa. The sheltered school environment did not prepare the student for discrimination and subordination in the outside world. He was imbued with European culture and with ideals of equality and of the sanctity of the human personality, and he was destined to live in a society which now subordinates his individuality to the group and defines the mode and level of his participation in racial and tribal terms. There was thus tension between the universal values of a humanistic education and the particular values of racial perspectives, and ambiguity because of the different definitions and expectations.

Racial perspectives impede scholarly achievements, most obviously and generally through discrimination, but with perhaps equally destructive effects through racial definitions of appropriate standards. By virtue of these racial perspectives, lettered Whites, in the same way as unlettered Africans, give exaggerated recognition to the university trained African. There is no critical assessment: it is enough that the African should move on roughly the level of the White intellectual, that his achievement should be comparable to that of a White man. The exaggerated acclaim in fact expresses sentiments of African inferiority. Much as the image of the petty African trader is established in the minds of many Whites, so too the corresponding image in the field of learning is that of the petty African intellectual, notwithstanding the high academic and professional attainments of Africans during the late nineteenth and early twentieth centuries. That an African should graduate with a university degree is in itself regarded by Whites as an achievement, irrespective of the standard attained, and there is special acclaim at the graduation ceremonies, partly, no doubt, in recognition of the obstacles which have been overcome.

The university teachers know the level of achievement, but their more critical judgment is sometimes clouded by a benevolent paternalism for the African intellectual, or it is suppressed out of anxiety not to seem racialist. Some teachers are exasperated by what they regard as indifferent application on the part of the African student, or lack of gratitude toward his teachers, or the impossibility of getting through to him, and they react with racialist rejection of the African intellect. All these circumstances again deprive the African intellectual of a balanced judgment of his achievements. If he should succeed in gaining an overseas scholarship, and thus entering a freely competitive academic world and a less ambiguous social situation, he is likely not to return to his country under present conditions. As a result, the community loses its most educated members.

Inevitably there was ambiguity in the university life of Africans, since the status of the African scholar was never fully institutionalized and is indeed somewhat anomalous in a context of extreme racial domination. The ambiguity was expressed internally in the administration of the universities and externally in the tension between university and other milieus. The effect was to cast the African student for a political rather than an academic role and to give political color to academic issues.

African intellectuals were trained mainly in the mission schools and universities of South Africa, the former segregated, the latter either racially open or racially exclusive. Some 2,200 Africans in South Africa hold university degrees (according to a report in the *Digest of South African Affairs*, February 17, 1961). The English universities of Cape Town and Witwatersrand admitted students of any race. All the Afrikaans universities (Stellenbosch, Pretoria, the Orange Free State, and Potchefstroom) limited their student bodies to members of the White group. They were not, in terms of student composition, exclusively ethnic universities, since they admitted English-speaking White students, but they were and are essentially centers of Afrikaner ethnocentrism. Rhodes University (the English university at Grahamstown) and the Pietermaritzburg section of the University of Natal were also racially exclusive though they admitted some non-White students to postgraduate courses (in the case of Pietermaritzburg, a very recent innovation). The University College of Fort Hare was open to students of all races, but since White students rarely applied, it was virtually a segregated college for non-Whites—predominantly African, as originally intended, with an admixture of Indian and Colored students. Alone of all the universities of South Africa admitting intramural students (excepting the correspondence and vacation school tuition of the University of South Africa), the Durban section of the University of Natal was racially open in its enrollment procedures, but racially exclusive in its academic education. It freely admitted non-White students, but on an internally segregated basis.

There were some ambiguities in the nonracialism of the open universities. The University of Cape Town did not accept Africans in the faculty of medicine, owing to the lack of suitable clinical facilities, and the University of the Witwatersrand excluded non-White students from its school of dental surgery on the same ground. Because of national policy, non-White medical students at the Witwatersrand University were restricted in their clinical training to wards for non-White patients and might not be present at the autopsy of a White corpse. Barriers on social intercourse were imposed at the level of intimate physical contact —sharing the same swimming bath, tennis court, ballroom, or hostel, though not the same cafeteria. Some students and members of the staff established close friendships across these barriers. At the academic level, students were selected and trained on the basis of merit. There was an implicit assumption that opportunity for achievement would also be based on merit in the larger society, and hence there was tension between the academic and other milieus.

The racial universities automatically introduced a basic status differentiation by closing the doors of their well-endowed colleges to non-Whites. For the elect, the predominantly English-speaking or Afrikaans-speaking White students, education proceeded on the basis of merit and of democratic values. There was, however, a further differentiating function in the Afrikaans universities. Here students were nurtured in Afrikaner nationalism and trained for the key positions in the Government. The racially exclusive English university can no longer serve this function for the English-speaking minority. In relation to Africans, there was little ambiguity, total exclusion from universities being quite consistent with many of the ideologies and patterns of South African life.

The University College of Fort Hare carried on the traditions of the mission school, emphasizing the Christian way of life, and envisaging presumably ultimate integration in a racially open society. Superficially it might seem that this was an environment in which internal ambiguities and tensions would be reduced to the minimum. In fact, though possibly not as a matter of inescapable necessity, internal tensions became so acute at one stage, in 1955, as to lead to the suspension of 330 students out of a total of 367, and the temporary closing of the college. The following extracts from the valuable but little known report of the Fort Hare Commission describe the politicoacademic aspects of this situation—the forms and consequences of an exaggerated paternalism; the interaction of university and other spheres in the wider society, so that university discipline is identified with political domination; and the quite political character of academic protest, which becomes the symbol, or indeed arena, of racial struggle:[6]

> A noticeable feature of student life is suspicion—suspicion of the College authorities, suspicion of many (not all) Europeans, suspicion of one another. (The last-named, a most distressing feature, would seem to be partly due to unwise encouragement of talebearing as a means of control.) The attitude towards the white man, though harmful to the students themselves, is understandable in South African conditions, and is part of the obsession with the struggle for liberation and with politics generally . . . it is difficult not to come to the conclusion that some at least of the student body are opposed to all authority as authority. We believe that this is partly due to the confusion of legitimate discipline with *baasskap*. This can be understood in view of political and racial controversies outside the College, but it is none the less harmful and dangerous. Neither Fort Hare nor any other university can exist without discipline, but it may be desirable to modernize the rules of the College, provided that such as are still necessary in present-day conditions must be enforced. Booing, catcalls, and other hostile and uncouth noises when the Principal is speaking are quite intolerable in a university institution and indeed should not be tolerated. Even worse, if possible, are the disgusting anonymous letters and lampoons that are posted up on notice-boards. The easy recourse to boycotts and other forms of direct action are also to be deprecated. Much of this sort of thing may be explained though not excused by the failure at times of the College authorities to recognise legitimate requests or their slowness in implementing those which are acceptable; and in recent weeks by errors of judgment such as the Circular asking students virtually to inform on one another. . . . The humourless correspondence between these two bodies [the Students' Representative Council and the Senate], which we have studied, reads like negotiations conducted between two "High Contracting Parties" of equal standing in an atmosphere of cold war. The exaggerated sense of self-importance of the students as indicated in this correspondence is perhaps due to the feeling that the College must be looked upon as being in the vanguard of the political and racial struggle. . . . we would urge that those in authority should not lightly turn down student requests as unreasonable, and that the habitual attitude towards student requests should be "Why not?" rather than "Why?". . . . It does seem to have happened on

6. *Report of the Fort Hare Commission* (Lovedale, Lovedale Press, 1955).

occasion that students have been reprimanded by the authorities for extreme or unwise statements made in student meetings, and that in circumstances where the only kind of evidence available was the testimony of fellow-students. We feel that no harm done by these statements can be so great as the bad feeling aroused by what seems like what unkind critics would call "snooping." It is an exaggerated paternalism, out of place with modern university conditions, which alone can explain this interference with an elementary right. . . . In student meetings those who take an unpopular line—and supporting the College authorities is often an unpopular line—tend to be shouted down; or, if they are given a hearing at the time, persecuted afterwards as "sell-outs," the most devastating term in the present-day vocabulary of Fort Hare. There is much intolerance among students, and unfortunately a considerable lack of moral courage on the part of the students generally; for many students come to Fort Hare quite ready to devote themselves to study and leave agitation alone, but they are easily swayed or intimidated by the ardent politicians who tend to lead the student body. Those who claim freedom of speech should . . . learn not to obtrude political and racial speeches into any and every kind of discussion. . . . There is a real need for encouraging self-help and student initiative. Too often students fail to take responsibility, while complaining that they cannot be trusted to manage their own affairs. This may well be a vicious circle, and more trust on the part of the authorities may gradually lead to a greater acceptance of responsibility, but there are responsibilities which students could and should have taken even in existing conditions. On the purely educational side the picture is brighter . . . We notice, however, a very strong tendency on the part of the students to place the emphasis on examinations and degrees, and what these will bring in the way of material advancement, to the exclusion of the social and cultural side of education. . . . We are given to understand that while there are few if any animosities between African and European Staff members, coolness amounting almost to ostracism exists sometimes between African members supporting different political groups . . . It may seem as if we have dealt at undue length and with unseemly frankness on the faults of the students; but we feel that the present atmosphere is not merely unpleasant but dangerous in the extreme. It struck us at times as being a spirit of evil so strong as to be almost visible and tangible—a foe to all that is normal, sane and creative, like the evil possessions recorded in the New Testament. . . . it is totally wrong that a university should come to be used as the vanguard in a party political struggle, or even to be regarded as an appropriate place in which to make propaganda for party political purposes. . . . In general the Report aims at the elimination of the relics of the Missionary High School past surviving at Fort Hare and its transformation into a modern university institution.

The conflict at the University of Natal was never as acute as at Fort Hare, and discipline was certainly not of the mission type. Nevertheless some elements of the Fort Hare situation were also present in the non-White humanities section of the University. There was paternalism, although less pervasive; there was political involvement of the students, perhaps equally intense; and there was a thorough-going penetration of the academic sphere by politics. The nature and action of these elements may be seen clearly in the final campaign waged by non-White students against segregation at the graduation ceremony. But first a distinction must be drawn between the non-White humanities section of the University of Natal (Marian Buildings) and its Medical School.

Permission for non-Whites to start courses in the humanities was given initially on the conditions that non-Whites should not use the existing buildings of the University nor be admitted to classes organized for Europeans: there was also a general understanding that they should be no financial burden on the University (memorandum by the late Dr. Mabel Palmer, the organizer, dated May 1, 1952). The establishment of the section in 1936 was a reluctant concession, not guided by any philosophy of education but reflecting the racial inequalities and the racial prejudices of the larger society. Discrimination persisted throughout, and though it was somewhat modified in later years, there was always a temporary, improvised character in the arrangements for non-White students. Discrimination was most marked in respect of the material facilities—analogous to the difference between a location dwelling and a mansion—and in the range of courses offered; commerce, social science, education, and law degrees were added to the arts degree, but training in science and engineering was withheld. The same lecturers taught at both the White and non-White centers, duplicating, triplicating, or indeed, quadruplicating lectures if necessary, and this shared resource mitigated the general discrimination. Some changes were proposed when it was too late to implement them, and, in the last period, as non-White students were being diverted to the new Government colleges, there was increasing integration of classes, not only at postgraduate levels as in the past, but also in undergraduate years, and more of the "White" facilities of the University were made available to non-White students. An Indian student has now been admitted to the course in electrical engineering by permission of the Minister of Indian Affairs, there being no facilities for training Indian electrical engineers at the University College for Indians (*Race Relations News*, April 1964).

The non-White Medical School, in contrast to Marian Buildings, is relatively free from discrimination, though problems of race relations enter into the academic and training situation, and medical students were also subject to segregatory regulation of hostels, graduation, and sporting and other social activities. The Medical School itself, established at a cost of over half a million pounds (paid mostly by the State) is a notable exception to the general rule of inferior segregated facilities for non-Whites. There is an adequate teaching staff, almost entirely White, which devotes its time to the non-White students without any competing claims by separate bodies of other students, and the facilities of the Medical School are freely available to non-Whites without racial restriction. Indeed the restrictions operate in their favor. Complaints about food in the hostels are endemic, as indeed generally among Africans at their boarding schools and at the University College of Fort Hare. But for the rest, medical students seem fairly content with the academic situation, or at any rate their dissatisfactions have not yet developed into protracted strikes and demonstrations. In the boycott movements, leadership and solidarity came from the students at Marian Buildings.

Many factors account for this difference. As we have seen, the prospects for non-White medical students are much more favorable than for their fellow students in the humanities. High prestige and relatively high rewards are assured to them—in the case of Africans, they are graduating to the peak of non-White society. Students at Marian Buildings, on the other hand, are training for the most part as teachers, often spurning the occupation for its meager rewards and opportunities, its declining prestige, but driven to it by lack of means and the hope of some security. For Africans the situation is even more frustrating, with the introduction of Bantu Education. There is often a strong feeling that teaching is no longer a noble profession, bringing enlightenment to one's people, but a political device for the withholding of education and the indoctrination of inferiority. This creates a dilemma for the students. Many are already teaching and seeking to raise their qualifications by part-time study. It is only in recent years that any number of African students have begun to find an escape into law. Marian Buildings is a prelude to limited occupational openings for students already experiencing the frustration of their ambitions. Higher education often requires half a lifetime of sacrifice. Although there is now a nucleus of African students from comfortable homes, most are struggling to pay their way, assisted by fee remissions from the University: sometimes they cannot find the tuition or examination fees and are obliged to withdraw. At the Medical School, on the other hand, African students hold substantial bursaries: these may not be adequate for their needs but they live in an affluent society compared with many of their fellow students at Marian Buildings.

Also relevant to the different reactions of students in the medical and humanities sections is the fact that Indian students are in a large majority at Marian Buildings, while African students are in a small majority at the Medical School, the respective enrollments in June 1960 being as follows:

Marian Buildings—African students 81, Indian students 558,
Coloreds 47
Medical School—African students 108, Indian students 92,
others 10

The social distance between Indians and Whites being narrower than that between Africans and Whites, Indians may be expected to react more sharply against discrimination.

The crucial factor, however, is the difference in the academic situation itself, relatively free of discrimination for medical students and highly discriminatory for other non-White students. There is a deep sense of deprivation at Marian Buildings, made all the more painful by the extensive academic and occupational opportunities and the infinitely better educational facilities for White students at the same university. Objectively considered, Marian Buildings may be less segregated than the University College of Fort Hare. Subjectively, however, the student is made more keenly aware of segregation in an internally segregated university. The discrimination is visible, part of the structure of the situation; it was imposed by the University authorities, and hence sanctioned by them; and the fact of racial separation within a single institution compels invidious comparison. It is easier to support poverty when it is the common experience of life and appears to be in the nature of things.

The rejection of discrimination at Marian Buildings, most strongly voiced by Indian students, is expressed in political movements and in the public life of the University. Active supporters of the different Congresses, Africanists, and members of the Unity Movement are all to be found at Marian Buildings. It is probably no accident that a minor political movement, the Unity Movement, should have taken effective leadership in the student body on issues of academic segregation. The ideology of the Unity Movement is based on a concept of the inevitable motivation of human behavior by material interests, and its members express a cynical view of human nature, at any rate of the human nature of their opponents. Tortured by the humiliations of the discrimination practiced against non-Whites, they voice the deep frustrations of the student body in an extreme form. Their aggressive use of vituperation, and more particularly of the epithets "quisling," "stooge," and "sell-out," give them a domination over their fellow students disproportionate to their numbers. It is primarily, though not exclusively, this group which crystallizes the public demonstrations against the University authorities, such as the boycotts of graduation ceremonies and of jubilee celebrations.

Desegregation of the graduation ceremony had advanced slowly, and under continuous pressure, through minute and delicate variations. Graduation of White and non-White students in separate blocks had given way to the sandwich method of graduation—first White students from one center, then non-White students, then White students from the second center. This in turn had given way to alphabetic graduation with racial segregation in the seating of graduands, and finally to alphabetic graduation and seating. Meanwhile racial segregation was maintained in the seating of visitors and students. This was the last citadel of segregation at the graduation ceremony (not, of course, at the University), and its defence seemed to acquire symbolic significance for the University authorities. To force the surrender of this citadel, non-White students launched their campaign, using the essentially political technique of the boycott. Again the action was symbolic, in no way affecting the basic discrimination at the University. It was rather as if the University authorities and the non-White students were engaged in a trial of strength, playing out on the academic stage the major racial and political conflicts of South African society.

The University was vulnerable. It proclaimed an academic ethic in accord with the ideals of the great universities which its own practices partly belied. It was this ambiguity that gave the non-White students and their supporters in the wider community effective opportunities for embarrassing the University authorities. Appeal was made to the higher tribunals of the academic conscience, and the moral conflict publicly exposed. Thus an editorial in an Indian weekly, *The Graphic,* on February 6, 1959, commented that

> it is pathetic and inexplicable that the University, the highest
> pedestal of learning where good sense and understanding should be
> the guiding factors, should be riddled with discrimination on
> grounds of colour. It is a negation of the very principles for which
> a University is constituted and that people of enlightenment and
> education should be party to discrimination between man and man
> is definitely preposterous.

The African National Congress and the Natal Indian Congress issued a joint statement attacking the discriminatory treatment at the graduation ceremony as

> an insult to the dignity and self-respect of non-White parents,
> friends and relatives of the successful graduates. . . . there can be
> no justification for the maintenance of racial prejudices at an insti-

tution where the main criteria is the pursuit of truth and learning [*The Leader*, February 6, 1959].

The Fifty Year Jubilee celebrations of the University of Natal in 1960 rendered the University even more vulnerable, by reason of the very public nature of its celebrations. Visitors from overseas, distinguished representatives of the highest university traditions, were invited to take part in a conference on education which was the culminating point in a great publicity program focused on the University of Natal. The spotlight for the University of Natal was also a spotlight for the grievances of non-White students. The Durban Students' Union, organ of the Unity Movement, issued a "clarion call" to students in February 1960, stressing the theme that education cannot be divorced from politics.

> The ruling class, in its mad pursuit of maintaining White Supremacy is SYSTEMATICALLY down-trodding and enslaving the oppressed both physically and mentally. Obsessed with this fascistic madness, the apostles of apartheid have chained the Non-Whites with a mountain of oppressive laws. The tentacles of apartheid reach out and entwine the Non-White in every aspect of his life.

Then follows some reference to discriminatory laws:

> Education, instead of being man's BIRTH RIGHT, is miserly extended as a privilege to the Non-Whites in South Africa. Education instead of developing the latent abilities of man, is prostituted to produce mental inferiority. These "Seats of Learning" are to produce servile automotons. These so-called Universities are converted into racial breeding grounds. These institutions, instead of allowing the individual to think freely, are converted into grave-yards for the intellectuals. . . . It is the responsibility of every student to understand that EDUCATION CANNOT BE DIVORCED FROM POLITICS. . . . STUDENTS UNITE!!! FIGHT FOR A DEMOCRATIC EDUCATION IN A DEMOCRATIC SOUTH AFRICA.

The attitude toward the University was embittered and hostile. In the issue, "The Jubilee of an Apartheid University," the Durban Students' Union called for a boycott of the celebrations.

> This Jubilee, this festivity, is not for us, the oppressed. The only people who have reason to celebrate are those who bask in the rays of happiness and contentment. That obviously excludes the oppressed. For us there is nothing but gloom, a bleak future and years of struggles. Celebrations at present are grossly premature and out of order. . . . Of course, it is undeniably true that the Non-White students have been *part* of this institution for many years and there-

fore one LOGICALLY expect the Non-Whites to participate. But to do that would amount to a superficial glance at the problem. The question to be asked is:—To what part of this institution have the Non-White students been assigned? Were they accepted as equal members in this "House of Learning?" We need not labour this question. It is common knowledge that the Non-White students were and are relegated to the backyard (Sastri College) and to the warehouse (Marian Buildings). Inferiority in facilities . . . limitations of Courses of study . . . restriction of faculties . . . the crumbs from the tables of those who NOW want to celebrate. Hence we find that the history of the Non-White students for the past so many years is dotted with complaints, attacks and boycotts. These acts constituted a condemnation of the apartheid nature of this University.

It is truly a divided house characterised by a "privileged-under-privileged" relationship. Therefore social, residential and sporting segregation have become crusted traditions of this "House of Learning." Once an attempt was made to have a cricket match between the "privileged" and "under-privileged." The very idea was an outrage and therefore evoked a stern reprimand from the patriarch of the Household.

Now, because "celebrated" guests from world over are to pour in for the Jubilee, a façade of a united household has to be presented. The public and the world must be misled into thinking that "all's well" in this University. The Non-White students and those whites who think and feel like us must have no part in the perpetration of this fraud. We must go even further in exposing the truth in all in its nakedness. It is not OUR duty to cover up the sins of the University authorities. We must show the people of South Africa and the world that the Jubilee is not an occasion of happiness for us. WE MUST DEFINE OUR POSITION and show in clear language that 50 years of Natal University is not something that we can be proud of.

The result was that students achieved an almost complete boycott of the celebrations. Guests in their finest clothes at the most fashionable event of the year—a segregated gala performance by the Royal Ballet—found themselves confronted with protest placards—"Remove Apartheid from our University," or "If gold rusts, what shall iron do?" The special graduation ceremony for the conferring of honorary degrees on distinguished visitors and the education conference were not picketed, presumably because they were not segregated. In desegregating the special graduation ceremony, the University had set a precedent which it could not readily reject in the future.

There was by no means unanimity among the students on the boycott issues. One cannot say that the opponents of the boycotts lacked moral courage, as the Fort Hare Commission suggested in the context of its inquiry into the domination of the student body by political interests. The students were all suffering under discrimination outside the University, quite apart from their experience within the University, and inevitably they reacted with sympathetic emotion to expressions of resentment. Moreover, it is difficult, at a time when educated non-Whites feel the political need for solidarity against apartheid, to face the charge of being a traitor to the cause, a "stooge," a "quisling," or a "sell-out."

The division between students on the graduation boycott was based largely on differences in opinion or principle, with an admixture of racialism. Some students felt that they were obliged to accept segregated education at the University of Natal, but that they were under no obligation to attend the graduation ceremony. Graduation was simply a formality where students paraded in gowns of different colors, "an elaborate exit out of the university, and ours is not a grand exit, because of the segregation we had experienced in our stay in this university." There was no need to expose oneself unnecessarily to humiliation. Or, more positively, the boycott of the graduation provided an appropriate occasion for a symbolic protest against segregated education. Others thought it pointless to boycott the culmination of segregated education after years of acceptance. A complicating factor was the attraction of the graduation ceremony itself. It is a brief moment of glory in which non-Whites have the rare opportunity of public recognition on a basis of equality. The student who is politically committed can derive strength from his group, and feel that he is working for something greater in boycotting the ceremony. For the uncommitted student, graduating in absentia may be a heavy sacrifice.

Inevitably, the conflict of views brought African-Indian antagonisms to the surface through the oblique issue of discrimination against Africans by Indian cinema and café proprietors. This issue became confounded with that of the graduation, and the refusal by Indian students to boycott the cinemas and cafés stimulated anti-Indian prejudice among some sections of the African student population. There were charges against Indians of opportunism, of insincerity, and of using Africans for their own ends; to some extent Indian students were held responsible for the discriminations of Indian entrepreneurs. No doubt racialism was partly a device to justify taking part in the graduation ceremony and partly an unconscious mechanism for displacing, if not resolving, tension.

The graduation boycotts were largely successful. In 1959, of the 47 non-White graduands, 40, including all the doctors, graduated in absentia, with 26 giving as their reason the racial segregation of guests. Under pressure in the year of its Jubilee celebrations, the University introduced a system of "voluntary segregation." Graduands and staff were asked to state whether they wished their guests to be seated with members of their own race or members of any race: 83.4% of the graduands and 62.5% of the staff asked for segregated seating. Most of the non-White graduands (48 of the 66) stayed away from the ceremony, 47 specifically by way of protest. In the medical faculty, 14 of the African medical graduands presented themselves, while the seven Indian doctors all graduated in absentia. There was thus a cleavage between African and Indian medical students and between the humanities section and the medical school. In 1961 the ceremony was fully desegregated—peacefully and with dignity, contrary to the predictions of those who favored the segregation of guests.

Probably more non-White students would have graduated in person in 1959 and 1960 but for the paternalism of the University authorities. This characteristic form of race relations is sustained, perhaps aggravated, in a university by the educational function of teachers for students. The role of educator is readily cast in the form of paternalism: and the paternalism is nourished by the feeling of service rendered to the students. At the University of Natal, the authorities could feel some justifiable pride in the number of degrees awarded to non-Whites (423 by March 1960). Paternalism was not entirely inconsistent with the educational function, but it could not resolve tensions arising from the desire of students for equality of treatment.

Paternalism was expressed first in the argument that students should not embarrass their friends by irresponsible action, but leave the issue in the hands of those members of the University Council and Senate who had their true interests at heart. This has the effect of stripping all initiative from the students and vesting it in the "fathers." Then, secondly, there was the threatened withdrawal of love.

> The decision of the Medical graduands to absent themselves from the Graduation Ceremony had come as a profound shock to the staff. It had completely changed the attitude of the staff towards the students of the future. Many felt that under these circumstances they might as well seek other employment as a feeling of the hopelessness of the situation had been engendered [statement by a professor at an informal meeting between representatives of the University Senate and the non-White Students' Representative Council, March 5, 1959].

The same sanction was applied by the principal in a letter to the Medical School graduates after the 1959 boycott.

> What you as a group expected to achieve thereby, I cannot imagine, but what I feel I must let you know is that you have succeeded in

alienating sympathy in the minds of many people, particularly in the medical profession, who had all along been well-disposed to the Non-Europeans and especially to you as students in our Medical School . . . Many people have said: "If that sort of conduct characterises the products of the Medical school, why bother to retain it in the University? Why not let the Government take the whole show, and then the Non-European students can have everything separate?" [April 2, 1959].

Thirdly, the issue was handled largely at the level of personal relations (almost the intimacy of the family group, with the shadow of ingratitude for the love lavished by the parents) and not entirely as an issue of principle. Paternalism involves the transmuting of ideals and moral values into personal, familial relationships, which take precedence over moral values.

You have refused to be presented for the award of your degree in person by your Dean . . . By this action you as a solid group have contrived to inflict a gratuitous insult in public on a man who had fought so hard and had sacrificed so much on your behalf. It was as if at the very culmination of the years of training lavished on you as medical students, you deliberately turned your backs on him and told him: "I won't come and get my certificate from you. You can send it by post." This is the impression your action left on the staff of the Medical School and on the public in general [principal's letter, April 2, 1959].

Apart from paternalism by the authorities, a major circumstance, which favored greater participation in the boycott, was that the manifest injustice of internal segregation and inequality encouraged dominance by the most embittered section of the student population. The Unity Movement exerted an influence out of proportion to the small number of its members not because it reflected the political views of the student body but because it crystallized in emotion and slogan the underlying resentment and intimidated the nonconformist.

The position of African university students is not such as to promote scholarly detachment. Whatever the educational environment, whether open or segregated, many do become involved in politics, and their political ideologies influence their lives as university students. Political leaders are drawn from all the universities that trained non-Whites, and it is difficult to say which environment was most conducive to political training and action or to the dominance of particular ideologies. Certainly there was intense political involvement at both of the segregated universities, Fort Hare and Natal, and this permeated student life, giving it some of the qualities of a political struggle. Presumably the open universities, with their large numbers of politically uncommitted White students, provided contact with more varied perspectives and a counterbalance to the obsessive intrusion of political ideologies into the academic milieu. At the same time, the greater freedom within the open universities may have stimulated a more intense resentment of discrimination outside.

In an internally segregated institution with unequal facilities the academic environment takes on a political color. The imposition of segregated inequality is a political decision, not in the sense that it has been taken by a political party, but rather that it expresses the political attitudes which have shaped racial discrimination in the wider society. Conversely, educated Africans were committed to a universal system of values—assessment of the individual on merit, and equality regardless of race. This was largely the ideology of African intellectuals, reflecting their material and ideal interests (but now undergoing change as a result of increasing racialism and the possibility, or probability, of African majority rule). Consequently, academic discrimination was interpreted not as an isolated element in the separate context of education but as a violation of universal norms affecting political, economic, and social life. Even the "purely academic" issues tended therefore to become political issues.

In the detached type of segregated unit such as the University College of Fort Hare, students are insulated from effective contact in a hothouse of embittered resentment. Political involvement is fostered by bringing together, in isolation, a population of students aggrieved by their deprivations in the wider society. The medical school of the University of Natal is also a detached, segregated, non-White unit. But it is not isolated: students are freely in contact with the outside world, and the nature of their studies, the intense concentration demanded, and the potentially high rewards and fulfillment on graduation all help to detach them from political preoccupation. The medical students seem less politically committed than their fellow students, although they respond to much the same appeals and reflect in their attitudes the same ideologies.

Location of the university has an influence on political ideology and participation. In Durban there was easy access to political leaders and political headquarters, and a strong Congress tradition. University students in Cape Town were exposed to the intellectuals of the Unity Movement, which was well-established in the Cape Western area. The Cape Eastern area had a long tradition of political struggle, and many students entering Fort Hare were already committed to the policies of the African National Congress or of the All-African Convention. The traditions of the universities are also relevant: the kind of student political groups established in them, and their fluctuating fortunes. And the racial composition of the student body exerts an influence—whether it is racially exclusive or provides the interracial contact and experience from which a more inclusive concept of the political struggle can be based. But the role of the universities in the political involvement of non-White students is probably subsidiary, affecting the content of their political ideologies and the manner of their participation rather than the fact of their involvement itself. This situation derives at the present time from the application of apartheid and the struggle for liberation in the wider society. National emergencies and protests have their immediate repercussions in the university community, particularly at the segregated universities, where sympathetic demonstrations by students have sometimes totally suspended academic activity. And the culling of political leaders by imprisonment, bans, and exile places responsibility on the university students, who become the second echelon leaders, so that there is a continuous preoccupation with politics, and the political perspective dominates the academic.

Anthony Ngubo, in an unpublished study of African intellectuals, argues that the opportunities are too restricted for Africans to establish themselves as members of an intellectual elite and that for them, education is purely an instrument for better employment opportunities and higher status. He suggests that scholarly detached academic intellectualism is a luxury which only a free people can attain and enjoy and that African intellectuals are in no position to engage in this luxury when they have not achieved demonstrable necessities. This seems a doubtful proposition in view of the intellectual preoccupations of the Jewish people in the ghettoes of Europe. Subordination and deprivation may even stimulate scholarly detachment. The lack of an intellectual tradition in the African community is obviously a significant factor in this connection, but so also is the acute stage of racial conflict in which the political leaders are the potential saviors. They constitute the prestige group, both for the urban masses and also for the students, and the latter attach or subordinate themselves to the political elite. Ngubo comments that very few Africans have made any contribution to the store of knowledge in academic fields available to them, their mental energy being spent in political thinking. He argues that the lack of a true intellectual elite seems to leave a vacuum in the African community. The intellectual elites of eastern and western Europe, plus a few West Africans make up the wise men. Non-African intellectuals fashion thinking, and hand it to the African educated elites, who in turn disseminate it among their people. He concludes that educated Africans form a potential educated political elite: scholarship will be a future development.

Political involvement has the effect of pushing many educated Africans back to the masses. In the past, the structure of African society might have been conceived crudely in terms of a great body of tribes-men and a small "class" or "community" of the educated, bound to-gether by Westernization, civil privileges, and an opportunity for personal advancement. Today the Government seeks to return the intel-lectual to his tribal group. Increasing use is made of the chiefs as the channel for communication with the masses, bypassing the intellectuals. Definition of life chances by the authorities is essentially in group terms: individual mobility must be confined within the tribal or linguistic group. The intellectuals are too vulnerable to resist these pressures un-aided. Most educated Africans must seek employment in organizations which are under White control: even the independent professionals—doctors and lawyers—can readily be deprived of a livelihood. Hence individual salvation for the intellectual is not readily achieved by per-sonal advancement nor by the collective effort of the intellectuals, and the situation thus turns the intellectual toward the masses.

Changes in the structure of the African community assist identifica-tion with the masses. The large urban proletariat has been exposed to Westernization and shares in some measure the ideas and preoccupations of the educated. There has been an infusion of educated Africans into the ranks of the uneducated. In consequence of Bantu Education, some teachers have been obliged to seek manual employment. The schools have trained more young students than could be absorbed into the white-collar occupations, and many of these are also occupied manually. Sharing the aspirations of the educated elite, but denied the opportunities and material rewards, they form a middle group between the bourgeoisie and the stable urban proletariat. Embittered, frustrated, aggressive, non-conformist, suggestible, and prone to violence, they reject the polished behavior of the educated elite, the os'tshuzana ("excuse me") class. They are an important element in the growth of a mass movement, exerting pressure on the educated and providing a link with the masses.[7]

The Government has now taken the final step in segregation at the university level by establishing the racial or ethnic university as the only model. Ethnic exclusiveness is represented in the tribal university colleges for Africans—the University College of Zululand at Ngoye for Zulu and Swazi students, the University College of the North at Turfloop for Sotho-, Tsonga-, and Venda-speaking peoples, and the University Col-lege of Fort Hare for Xhosa—and in the ethnic University College of

7. Based on an analysis by Ngubo. Gordon Wilson, in an article on "Mombasa—A Modern Colonial Municipality," in Social Change in Modern Africa, ed. A. Southall (London, Oxford University Press, 1961), p. 104, reports a somewhat similar development. For the first time in the history of East Africa, he writes, educated Africans, at least educated to the point where they can read and write in English and Swahili, are unable to secure employment in white-collar jobs. They are forced to work as laborers, and they are able to communicate with the illiterate group by reading to them political speeches and manifestos reported in the press.

the Western Cape at Bellville for Coloreds and the University College at Durban for Indians. At the same time, the racial exclusiveness of the Afrikaans universities is now being imposed on the English universities, which can only admit new non-White students by special Government permission.

The ethnic colleges offer Africans opportunities for employment in academic fields, not limited to Bantu languages. They could, therefore, provide the occasion for scholarship. But they are essentially political institutions, part of the program for harnessing education to apartheid, and seem unlikely to attain university standards. Control is authoritarian. Members of the staff hold either State posts (that is to say they are civil servants), or Council posts, which are also controlled by the Minister, whose approval is required for appointment, promotion, or discharge. The incumbents of State posts are guilty of misconduct if they do, or cause or permit to be done, or connive at any act which is prejudicial to the administration discipline or efficiency of any department, office, or institution of the Government; or if they display insubordination by word or conduct, publicly comment upon the administration of any department, become a member of any political organization, take active part in political matters, or become pecuniarily embarrassed. In the case of a Council post, the Minister may instruct the Council of the University to institute an inquiry into the conduct of the staff member and direct the Council to take such steps against him as fall within the competence of the Council. The conscience clause, affording protection against exclusion on religious grounds, was deliberately omitted. The composition of the Council and Senate is controlled by the Minister, and Africans are relegated to subordinate roles in advisory councils and advisory senates. Academic salaries are also discriminatory.

The activities of students are carefully regulated. The Rector has power to control meetings, student organizations, the circulation of any publication for which students are responsible, the release of any statement to the press, and, indeed, all student contact with the outside world. Sanctions are heavy, since expulsion from his university college may have the effect of totally excluding the student from full-time university study in the Republic. This has not prevented African students from coming together across tribal and university bounds. In December 1961, at a conference of students drawn from the African ethnic universities, Natal, Roma, and many senior schools, the African Students' Association of South Africa was formed to unite African students, to promote close contact with other students at home and abroad, and to stimulate interest in educational and cultural advancement. The conference declared its opposition to all forms of discrimination in education and to the use of education to further party political ends, as in Bantu Education, and pledged itself to strive for free, compulsory, and universal education (but not divorced from the demand for a democratic society). Because African students suffer disabilities peculiar to their group, the conference decided that the association should be composed of African students (*The Graphic*, December 22, 1961).

At the University College of Fort Hare there has been continuous friction. The new system was received with hostility, as reflected in the poster displayed during a demonstration in October 1959: "Maree, Verwoerd and Co., University Funeral Undertakers, Afrikanerdom Embalmers, Specialists in Cheap Intellectual Coffins." The demonstrations have continued, with expressions of extreme hostility against the Rector, the expulsion of the Secretary of the Students' Representative Council, the building up of police forces at a neighboring police station in September 1960, and the temporary closing of the college in June 1961, following a demonstration in which the buildings of the college were painted with slogans—"To hell with Verwoerd and his Republic," "Democracy not Boerocracy," and "Solidarity with our Masses." At the University College of the North, there have been reports of occasional hostility: only the University College of Zululand, among the African universities, seems peaceful.

In the circumstances, it seems unlikely that the ethnic colleges will provide either the academic skills or the environment for the training of African scholars. And as for experience relevant to political outlook, the colleges offer only the alternatives of tribal revivalism or exclusive nationalism.

CHAPTER 13

Teachers

EDUCATION in the traditional societies of South Africa was embedded in other institutions. Teaching was not a specialized role, but widely diffused in the society. At some stage or another, almost every member of the society functioned as a teacher. There was little in the way of formal instruction and little differentiation in education. Education was related to status in the society; since the societies themselves were relatively undifferentiated, with limited specialization, education tended to be more or less uniform within each sex. The concept of education as an instrument of directed social change could hardly be present in a society where education was not a separate institution.

The missionaries introduced education as an institution of White society, not of African society. It was hardly possible for them to use the approach followed in community organization of stimulating the community to provide the new services until sufficient numbers of Africans had been educated. In effect, as we have seen, the missionaries tended to detach their converts from the traditional society, and, more particularly in the mission stations, to create new societies of Christian, educated, Westernized Africans. From the missionary point of view, education was an essential part of the process of directed culture change, that of evangelization and civilization. However, in time the objectives of missionary education became somewhat ambiguous in relation to trends within the wider society. Africans were receiving a type of education which qualified them and raised their aspirations to participate as equals. This ambiguity became more marked with the rise to power of the Afrikaner nationalists and with their rejection of even the ultimate equality in a common society implicit in earlier doctrines of trusteeship.

Present Government policy seeks to resolve the ambiguity in African education by means of Bantu Education. This is a key element in the program of directed change toward apartheid society. African education is being embedded in tribal society as a separate institution. At the same time, it remains an institution of White society. In fact, education is one of the major points of articulation between the dominant White and the subordinate African groups. It is part of a system of intercalary institutions which include the Bantu Affairs Department and the Bantu Authorities, and it is designed to secure such ideological changes within African society as will harmonize with the apartheid policies of White society.

Apartheid is essentially a system of total control based on the model of social segments, integrated by interdependence and common values. The analogy with the caste system is not inappropriate. Traditional caste society rested on segmentation and the maintenance of social distance between the castes through institutional separation and caste loyalty, while Hinduism provided a broad framework regulating and rationalizing the relations between the castes. The policy of apartheid aims at achieving segmentation by means of separate institutional structures for each racial group (or ethnic or linguistic group among Africans) and the inculcation of racial or ethnic pride (which presumably implies disdain for other groups) so that separation will be self-maintaining. Integration is to be achieved through institutional controls by the dominant group, the location of the different racial or ethnic groups in their predetermined positions in the overall structure, and the inculcation of appropriate ideologies. Within the dominant society, Bantu Education is a part of the centralized state administration of all African affairs: within African society, it is a separate institution for the fostering of group exclusiveness and other attitudes in support of apartheid.

Afrikaner nationalism was itself promoted by separate institutional structures—in churches and schools, in welfare, commercial, industrial, and political organizations. This meant reducing the contacts with other groups and the cross-pressures of varying loyalties and affiliations that might have promoted a less exclusive outlook. In consequence, the sentiments of nationalism were continually heightened by experience within an integrated set of institutions regulating life from birth to death. Superficially it might seem that the Afrikaner nationalists are extending to the African those dispensations they themselves most highly value. But there is the crucial difference that the Afrikaners offer their own people the world—domination over South Africa—whereas the use of the same techniques offers Africans only subordination, in terms of the realities, not the promises, of apartheid. And Africans themselves are to be the instruments of this subordination, though the Afrikaner nationalists and their fellow travelers occupy the command posts in the system. In particular, a most important role in the system of control is assigned to African teachers, that of training children for their racial status in a well-defined hierarchical structure and of shaping the attitudes appropriate to that status. There is the further crucial difference that Bantu Education is linked with tribalism, not nationalism. African nationalism is the main challenge to Afrikaner nationalism, and the tribal fragmentation of Africans is a condition for the maintenance of Afrikaner power. The system of education and of cleavage is thus based on the tribal or linguistic group.

Bantu Education effects a radical change from an educational system emphasizing individual development, conceived in some ways as an end in itself, to a system which subordinates the individual to the group and deploys education as a means to the political ends of alien rulers. Where the missionaries showed concern for the cultivation of the individual and his religious growth, there is now conversion to the tribal identity. Where the mission high schools assembled African students of varied tribal background, extending perspectives and loyalties beyond the traditional societies, the Bantu Education Schools seek their return to the tribal milieu. Where the missions cultivated English as the medium of education after the elementary standards—it was mostly the English-speaking missionaries who devoted themselves to the education of Africans—Bantu Education cultivates tribal sentiment through tribal vernaculars.

The new policy seeks to locate the schools and universities within the confines of the traditional societies, geographically, administratively, and intellectually. When introducing Bantu Education, the Prime Minister (then Minister of Bantu Affairs) rejected the current practice because it ignored the segregation or apartheid policy, whereas education should stand with both feet in the reserves and have its roots in the spirit and being of Bantu society: the Bantu must be guided to serve his own community in all respects (in his Speech to the Senate, June 7, 1954, Debates 1954 II, cols. 2595–2620). Clearly it is necessary to provide elementary school training where students live, including the urban areas, but policy aims at locating higher primary education (i.e. the second four years of education) and especially post-primary education within the reserves. With the continued increasing urbanization of Africans under apartheid, it seems unlikely that a tribal location of higher education can in fact be realized.

Administratively, Bantu Education centralizes state bureaucratic control and at the same time extends the influence of traditional authority. The types of school are: Bantu Community Schools, Farm Schools, State Schools, Mine, Factory, and Scheduled Schools, and Un-aided Schools (these are mainly Roman Catholic, and likely to diminish rapidly). In 1960, 70 per cent of the State and State-aided schools were graded as community schools, and these are ostensibly controlled by Africans under a system of school committees for each community school and school boards for a cluster of schools, although a committee board may be established in certain circumstances.

The school committee in tribal areas consists of: three members nominated by the chief or headman or tribal authority from among the parents of students after consultation with the parents and the Secretary for Bantu Education, two members nominated by the tribal authority in areas where there is a constituted tribal authority, two members nominated by the Secretary to represent religious or other interests, and a chairman and vice-chairman nominated from the members by the chief or tribal authority after consultation with the Secretary. Similarly, the school boards are the nominees of the White bureaucracy and the tribal authorities. For purposes of organization, the Bantu community schools in the tribal areas are firmly located within a revised form of tribal authority, in a framework of central state bureaucracy.

In the urban areas, the State controls the membership of the committees and boards, but there is a measure of democratic participation. The committee consists of: two or more members nominated by the Bantu Affairs Commissioner after consultation with the Advisory Board and the manager of the Bantu Administration Department, two members nominated by the Secretary for Bantu Education to represent religious or other interests, four parents elected by a meeting of parents of students, and a chairman and vice-chairman nominated by the Secretary. The four members elected by parents must be approved by the Secretary; hence no category of membership is exempt from the seal of official recognition. Moreover, the Secretary may at any time dissolve a school committee on grounds of incompetence, and terminate the tenure of any member. So too in the school boards, all members must have official approval, and most are nominees. It is the absence of the traditional authorities which distinguishes the urban from the tribal organization of education. But the urban school system may be assimilated in some measure to the tribal pattern, under the policy of extending tribal authority to African life in the urban areas. The Minister of Bantu Education announced plans for ethnic advisory committees on education and for a general advisory council (*South African Digest,* October 1, 1962). Presumably the ethnic committees will be the agency for communicating the tribal ethos, and the council the agency for centralized coordination. (The Advisory Board for Bantu Education has now been established: see *Bantu Education Journal,* May 1964, pp. 204–07).

The intellectual linking to the traditional societies is to be achieved partly through tribally homogeneous schools fostering exclusiveness by isolation from intimate contact with out-groups, but mainly through the school curriculum. Bantu Education rests on the concept of a special type of education regarded as appropriate to the ethnic qualities of the Bantu peoples and represents a radical departure from the previous system of giving basically the same education to all racial groups—that is, in terms of content though not in terms of facilities and opportunities. The Government rapidly assumed a virtual monopoly of teacher training (excluding some training in the Roman Catholic school system, which is not recognized by the State as qualification). Since the instruments of Bantu Education are the African teachers themselves, it is essential that they should have the appropriate training and attitudes. In the schools, an important medium for conveying these attitudes is the subject of social studies.

Social studies is a composite course, including history, geography, citizenship, and good conduct. In geography, the pupil moves from his province to South Africa in Standard IV, to Africa in Standard V, and only in Standard VI (in his eighth year of schooling) to the geography of the world—that is to say, most school children will be left with the limited local perspective, since only a small percentage goes as far as Standard VI. History is largely confined to South Africa until Standard V, when a few facts are introduced about inventions, discoveries, and medical progress. The syllabus in Standard VI is divided into two sections: South African history and general history, the latter offering a series of topics from classical history, Charlemagne, Mohammed, the mode of life in the Middle Ages, the invention of printing, and a journey by ship in the time of Jan Van Riebeeck.

Citizenship and good conduct offer in Standard III the child's duties, privileges, and responsibilities in the home, village or town, school, and family; in Standard IV they show how a child is bound to the people of his home (conceived in terms of the tribal family), and emphasize respect for age, authority, and his fellow man, the need for the services of a variety of Government or Government-approved officials, including the headman, chief, policeman, and location superintendent (categories largely rejected by the educated African), and also the need for doctors and ministers of religion, and how to assist these officials and professional men in their work. Standard V offers material on tribal organization and government, inculcation of good habits (neatness, thrift, obedience, self-reliance, temperance), government constituted Bantu bodies, and apartheid measures of control, with only city and town councils and some welfare benefits falling outside the limited scope of the official pattern for Bantu development and control. In Standard VI, the school child is offered a glimpse of how the country is ruled, the real centers of power: members of Parliament "without detailed reference to party politics," the Cabinet, Government departments (with special reference to the work of the Departments of Bantu Affairs, Justice, Health, and Agriculture and with emphasis on officers who deal directly with the Bantu people), provincial government (noting the services rendered to the Bantu people), the Bantu authorities, and the chiefs. It is with this background knowledge of the world that children leave the primary school and that the lower grade of teachers, who still carry most of the responsibility for African elementary education, commence their three years of teacher training.[1]

The missions not only extended education broadly to Africans but also founded schools for an elite education, "Black Etons." Bantu Education, by contrast, aims at mass education (initially four years of schooling) and careful regulation of elite education. As numbers have increased, so per capita expenditure has decreased. The number of pupils in State and State-aided schools rose from 938,211 at an annual cost of £8.10.10 per pupil at school in 1954 to 1,411,157 at a cost of £6.18s. per pupil in 1960.[2] Since about one-third of African children of the ages 7–14 are not at school, the per capita expenditure would be about £4.60 per child of school-going age (7–14) as compared with about £67 per White child, for whom there is free and compulsory education to the age of 16. Education is neither free nor compulsory for African children. Most of the increase in school enrollment is at the primary school level, and indeed in the elementary classes. Enrollment in the secondary schools rose only by some 16,000, from 32,907 in 1954 to 48,994 in 1960.[3]

The threat to standards, associated with rapidly rising numbers and falling per capita expenditure, is aggravated by the consequences of Bantu Education for quality of staff. Many able teachers who opposed Bantu Education have either left the profession or been dismissed. Policy is directed to the extensive employment of female teachers.

> I wish to close my remarks in regard to teachers by pointing to a serious lack of proportion between the number of male and female teachers. As a woman is by nature so much better fitted for handling young children and as the great majority of Bantu students

1. According to figures supplied by the Minister of Bantu Education in regard to teachers employed by his department in 1961, there were 15,149 teachers with the lower grade teacher's qualification out of a total of 28,103. Teachers with a university degree numbered 896 (*Hansard, House of Assembly Debates*, No. 8, March 12, 1963, col. 2567). The approach to history, geography, and South African government becomes broader at High School level (see "Teaching of Social Studies in the Secondary School" by the staff of the Amanzimtoti Training School, *Bantu Education Journal*, October and November 1963).

2. The comparable figures on March 31, 1962, were 1,562,843 pupils, with a per capita expenditure for the preceeding years of R 12.3, i.e. £6.3s. (*Hansard, House of Assembly Debates*, No. 7, March 5, 1963, col. 2129).

3. Sources—papers from The South African Institute of Race Relations: J. W. MacQuarrie, "The Bantu Education Act and its Implementation," NCR. 84/58, and "The African in the City: His Education," NR. 130/1960; F. J. de Villiers, Secretary for Bantu Education, "Financing of Bantu Education," January 18, 1961. E. Hellman, in "Some Comments on Bantu Education," *Race Relations Journal*, vol. 28 (1961), gives different statistics but a similar general picture. The most recent figures for enrollment of African students are 1,710,857 in primary schools, 53,683 in secondary schools, 5,720 in vocational and technical schools, and 630 at university colleges (*South African Digest*, February 20, 1964, p. 6).

are to be found in the lower classes of the primary school, it follows that there should be far more female than male teachers in the service . . . As long as the number of primary students is so overwhelmingly great, the department will concentrate mainly on the training of female teachers. To-day about 70 per cent of the teaching force is male, while that should rather be the percentage of female teachers [Prime Minister's Speech in the Senate, June 7, 1954, cols. 2614–15].

Increasingly, young girls with a Standard VI education and three years of teachers' training (i.e. the Lower Primary Certificate) have been taking over the education of primary school children; there is the possibility however that this lower primary teachers' training may shortly be withdrawn in favor of higher qualifications. With the passing of time, all the teachers will have been trained in government centers, and their role will be that of herd girls shepherding the new generations into the Bantustan kraals.

At the same time, there is control of elite education. This is necessary for reasons of state. The concept of the intellectual development of the individual to his fullest capacity is subordinated to the basic principle that African education must be integrated with the sphere of life to which Africans are assigned under apartheid. Of the earlier system, the Prime Minister complained that it drew the African away from his own community and misled him by showing him the green pastures of European society in which he was not allowed to graze, that it prepared him for life outside the community and for posts which did not exist, and that it created a class which had learned to believe that it was above its own people, and felt that its spiritual, economic, and political home was among the civilized community of South Africa (that is the Europeans)—a frustrated class because its wishes had not been realized (Prime Minister's Speech, June 7, 1954, col. 2619). Bantu Education defines the boundaries of aspiration for Africans. The pastures in which they may graze are the ethnic heartlands. The role of higher education is that of conservative adaptation, not the cultivation of personality as a creative agent in social change. It is still selective, in the sense of preparing a small number of students for the professions, but it has ceased to offer an elite education. As a result of the subordination of African education to political objectives, there was a steep decline in the number of students who qualified for university education, and when the 1960 results were announced it seemed as though the flow of new entrants from the schools to the universities would shortly cease. Since 1960, however, there has been a considerable increase in the numbers qualifying for university education. The next step is almost certain to be the establishment of a spe-

cial and inferior Bantu matriculation examination. As the higher grade
of language qualification becomes increasingly an African language,
the knowledge of English, the one universal language offered Africans,
will hardly prove adequate for access to the world of learning.

In the process of implementing Bantu Education, the status of the
African teacher has been graded downward. Previously he was a member of the new elite, leading his people outward into the world. Today
he is forced back within the group and subordinated to it. The official
reference group is the tribal or ethnic unit, distinct and inferior, not
the dominant White group. The rationale for discrimination in salary,
as given in the Prime Minister's speech quoted above, shows this principle of evaluation relative to the group:

> That at once brings me to the matter in which the Native teachers'
> organizations have always taken the greatest interest, namely the
> basic principles in regard to their remuneration. The slogan ac-
> cepted fairly generally by them, is "equal pay for equal work,"
> by which is meant equal payment with the European and further-
> more "payment in accordance with qualifications irrespective of
> race or colour." I therefore want to make it very clear that their
> starting-point, where they make this demand, is completely in-
> correct. The salaries which European teachers enjoy are not at all
> a usable or a permissible criterion for the Bantu teachers. The
> European teacher is in the service of the European community
> and his salary is fixed on a basis of comparison, with the income
> of the average parent whose children he teaches. The salaries of
> teachers in the European community are not at all regarded as
> very attractive.
>   In precisely the same way the Bantu teacher is in the service
> of the Bantu community and his salary must be fixed accordingly.
> In contrast with what I have said about the European, teachers'
> posts are very much sought after amongst the Natives. There is
> definitely no shortage of people who apply for vacant posts, and
> it is therefore very clear that the Bantu teacher within his com-
> munity already occupies a very favourable financial position.
>   Measured by this standard, and I have no doubt that it is the
> correct standard to apply, it seems to me that the present teachers'
> salaries are quite sufficient and there can be no question of an
> increase because teachers will then be even more favoured in com-
> parison with the parents of the children under their care and it
> will favour them at the expense of those who must help to bear
> the burden of the education [Prime Minister's Speech, June 7,
> 1954, cols. 2613–14].

At the same time the prestige of the African teacher is being debased by the increasing recruitment of young, poorly qualified girls as teachers. It is debased also by the teacher's political role, which many Africans find repugnant, and by its pure instrumentality in the hands of alien rulers. And it is debased, finally, by the insecurity built into the position of teacher as a means of control, rendering him vulnerable to White officials and to African school committees and boards. Under the appearance of delegated authority, the Government's powers of control are as complete as regulation and bureaucratic organization can make them, while the involvement of Africans behind the democratic façade of school committees and boards adds further hazards to the career of the teacher.

The regulations governing the African teacher in Bantu community schools specify a long list of acts which constitute misconduct. These include encouraging through his acts or behavior disobedience or resistance to the laws of the state, active identification with a political party or active participation in political affairs, publication of a letter or article criticizing any Government department or any Government official, or behaving, acting, or neglecting to act in a manner which in the opinion of the school board is deleterious to his position as a teacher, regardless of whether such behavior, act, or negligence has been defined in the regulations or not (*Bantu Education Journal*, October 1962, pp. 435–36). No legal representation is permitted at the inquiry into charges of misconduct or of inefficiency.

Control in the Bantu community schools is exercised through the school committees and school boards. The school committees bring to the notice of the school boards matters affecting the welfare or efficiency of the schools; for this purpose they have access to any school or class (but without interfering with the teacher's conduct of his duties) and they can compel a teacher to attend any meeting for purposes of supplying information; they have power to inquire into any complaint affecting the school or teaching staff, to recommend an inquiry on grounds of lack of qualifications, incapacity in the teaching medium or any other incapacity, to consider inspection reports and make recommendations to the school board, and to advise the school board in all matters connected with the appointment of teachers. Other powers include the institution of a school fund, consideration of reports on income and expenditure, maintenance of buildings and grounds, and the erection of buildings after consultation with the Department and the school board.

The school boards have power to maintain and control community schools subject to approval of the Minister, to plan and promote building of schools, to employ teachers and investigate complaints submitted by the school committee, to hear appeals from certain decisions of the committee, consider reports referred by any inspector of schools, and to

supervise finances. Prior approval of the appointment of a school teacher
to a subsidized post must be obtained from the Secretary for Bantu
Education. The effect then is the appearance of powers of appointment
to subsidized posts being vested in the board, but not the reality (Government Notice R. 1177, dated August 5, 1960, deals with school committees, committee boards, and school boards). The White Inspector of
the Durban South Circuit stated in an interview (November 29, 1960)
that the school boards appoint teachers to the primary schools, apart
from head teachers (the Inspector has a veto, but normally these appointments go through), that the appointment of head teachers is referred to him, and that he controls secondary school appointments.

Powers of dismissal, transfer, reduction of emoluments, and reprimand
vest in the school board, which acts as a board of inquiry in regard to
charges of misconduct or inefficiency. The decision of the school board
is final. When the Federal Council of African Teachers' Associations
asked that there be a board of appeal from the decisions of the school
board, that the teacher should be entitled to legal representation, and
that in all cases of dismissal full reasons should be given, the official
reply from the Minister and Secretary for Bantu Education (September
2, 1960) was as follows:

> (a) Teachers in community schools are employed by the School
> Boards, and it is therefore only right that the Board should have
> the final say regarding the teachers in its service. It is customary
> for the employer to engage or to dismiss his employees, and this
> must therefore also be the privilege of the School Board where
> teachers are concerned.
> (b) There is no justification for an Appeal Board to be constituted
> as this will interfere with the authority of the School Board. When
> Bantu Authorities take over they may wish to consider such a step.
> (c) Even when Bantu Education was administered by the Provin-
> cial Authorities legal representation was not permitted at an en-
> quiry.
> (d) There are valid reasons why the Board should not give full
> details when it decides to terminate the services of a teacher.
> Teachers who are dismissed for misconduct are always aware of the
> reasons for such action. It may also not be in the interests of the
> teacher himself that the reasons for his dismissal be disclosed.*

The Department in fact controls both the appointment of teachers by
the school boards and their dismissal. In the latter case, it can use the
simple device of refusing to subsidize the post. In theory, the school
board may continue to employ the teacher, provided it manages to raise
the funds for his salary. In practice, withdrawal of the subsidy means

* Asterisk indicates that quoted item has not been rechecked.

dismissal, and there is no obligation to give reasons. As Mr. MacQuarrie observes,[4] teachers have to eat, and stopping their subsidies is an effective way of getting rid of them.

> Thou shalt not kill but needst not strive
> Unnecessary to keep alive.

When the Federal Council of African Teachers applied for clarification of this power, the Minister and Secretary replied (September 2, 1960):

> The Department is naturally interested in the standard of work of a teacher, and should it become evident that the teacher is not fit for his post or that he is disloyal in the execution of the task for which he was appointed, then the Department cannot continue to pay subsidy for a post which would enable the Board to continue employing such a teacher. The Boards may however decide to pay the salaries of such teachers themselves as they are the legal employers. There were occasions when certain teachers neglected their duty in the school and were more interested in political activities. The Department cannot subsidise posts for such teachers but the School Boards concerned may pay the salaries of these teachers themselves. There is nothing new in this attitude, as teachers in European and Coloured schools are likewise forbidden to participate in politics.*

The Government does not hesitate to use its powers. In the process of reorganization, posts were abolished by withdrawal of subsidies. Teachers were dismissed for opposing Bantu Education or for political activities: opposition to Bantu Education is defined as political activity. If a dismissed teacher is persona non grata with the Government, then he may be denied the opportunity of teaching anywhere in South Africa and indeed of moving to other territories: he may also lose his domicile. It has been made abundantly clear to the African teacher that for teachers who are not "faithful" there is no place in Bantu Education. And to be a faithful servitor of the South African Government is by no means conducive to prestige within the African community.

Bantu Education involves African teachers in a basic dilemma. If they are dedicated to the ideal of leading their people into the modern world as the equals of any group, then their very idealism is subverted. They become the agents of an alien policy which they reject: the noble role of the leader in enlightenment is transformed into the ignominious status of the instrument for a modernized tribalism. There is a curious paradox here. Elsewhere on the continent, Africans strive for Africanization in the sense both of Africans occupying the main positions in the society and of selected revivals of traditional culture; whereas in South Africa

---

4. "The African in the City: His Education."

* Source could not be rechecked.

the process of Africanization is enforced by the enemy group, which itself monopolizes the command posts. The deification of the native language is certainly less meaningful when forced on reluctant educators by foreign rulers. The very imposition of Africanization from the outside is a denial of Africanization, since its essence lies in the free interpretation and expression of the African personality. Africanization as the creative role of a more basic humanity, as the destiny of a third force in world affairs, becomes the recrudescence of the noble, if modernized, savage in tribal insulation from the world.

Explicitly or implicitly, teachers must have some concept of the relationship between the school system and other institutions, some image of the society for which they are training their students. In the past, the image of the future society was perhaps vague—a common society with ultimate equality for Africans. Now the future character of African society and its relationship to Bantu Education have been made explicit, so that teachers, in their routine duties, are inevitably confronted with the political issues of the day.

Our study of African teachers in Durban gives some impression of the resultant dilemma. Toward the end of the interviews, they were asked a series of questions to clarify their reactions to the policy of apartheid and its application to Bantu Education. These dealt with the franchise, separate development or integration, the tribal way of life, solution to the South African race problem, and intermarriage. Interviews were held during and immediately after the state of emergency in 1960, so that great significance attaches to the rejections of Government policy. At a time when men and women were being imprisoned without trial and without preferment of charges, only deep conviction would permit a questioning of apartheid.

Informants were asked to check the choice that came closest to their opinion on the franchise:

> Franchise [vote] should be:
> (a) limited to the Whites;
> (b) limited to matriculants regardless of race;
> (c) limited to persons having completed Standard VI, regardless of race;
> (d) universal on the principle of one man–one vote.

There was no information from one of the 99 informants. All the others rejected the present position (virtually limited to Whites): 51 were in favor of a qualified franchise, regardless of race (10 chose matriculation as the qualification, 41 Standard VI), the remainder (47) favored universal franchise. This is a surprising result. The African political organizations stand firmly for universal adult franchise, and Africans favoring qualified franchise are often regarded as "sell-outs". Undoubtedly the educated tend to favor an educational qualification, and there might possibly have been more choice of this alternative but for the knowledge of the racial manipulation of franchise qualifications in plural societies. As between the sexes, men were more inclined to favor universal adult franchise, and there was a slightly greater tendency for those favoring universal suffrage to stand for African control.

The next question raised the issue of separate development or integration.

> The future of South Africa should take the line of:
> (a) separate development along ethnic lines;
> (b) economic integration with a social colour bar;
> (c) a non-racial society with equal opportunities to all and no colour bar;
> (d) control by Africans as the majority group.

Separate development is ostensibly the National Party policy. The social color bar with economic integration is somewhat like the United Party policy in one of its many phases. Only three informants, all women, chose these alternatives. The major choice was the integrated society, the nonracial society with equal opportunities (69 choices), while 27 respondents favored control by the African majority. Men were more inclined to select African control.

Informants were hostile to the revival of the tribal way of life, as indicated by their choices of alternatives.

> In South Africa one should:
> (a) keep and revive the tribal way of life;
> (b) let the tribal way of life alone, without either encouraging or discouraging it;
> (c) spread education, soil conservation, health services, etc. without trying to destroy the tribal way of life as a whole;
> (d) destroy the tribal way of life and introduce the Western way of life as fast as possible.

Only one informant favored the revival of tribal life, and five a laissez faire policy: 74 chose the elimination of tribal life through education, and 19 the more radical policy of destruction.

An open-ended question asked: "If everything happened as you would like to see it happen, what would your solution be to the South African race problem over the next twenty years?" Most answers (about 3 in 5) were in terms of the sharing of power, cooperation and equality, and division along lines of interest rather than race. About 1 in 5 submitted specific recommendations—redistribution of land, compulsory education, integration at school, raising of wages, and doing away with apartheid. A slightly smaller number of responses proposed African control, Black freedom, the repatriation of non-Africans.

> There would be no race problem because only Africans will be in this country. All the foreigners would have been expelled.

> All nations should go where they belong and leave us in our own country.

> Well, if it happened according to my wish there would be no race problem, as the African would be regarded as the rightful owner of the place and other races will be required to do as Rome does.

> Firstly, I'd grant equal rights to all races. Secondly, Africans as it being their birthright to rule South Africa, should be given more benefit as it is the case in other countries.

> We should all believe and call ourselves Africans. Training of young men overseas. Whites can stay, provided they accept that African interests are paramount. Promote education. Study Russia, China—technological development, but keep free enterprise provided human lives are more important than material. Grander African federation.

At the end of the interview, informants were asked their views on intermarriage. Of the 97 who expressed definite views, 45 accepted intermarriage, 52 disapproved. The main category of acceptance was that marriage was a personal matter for the individuals themselves to decide (28): the informant might not care for intermarriage, but respected the rights of others. Ten informants were positively approving, as for example:

> I think it could help to do away with the so-called "White Supremacy." The Whites would learn to treat their spouses with equal respect and not like animals. At this time of crisis intermarriage could actually solve the racial problem which is the core of all disturbances.

> I believe that in the ultimate end miscegenation will be the solution toward a common world society of one nation where there will be no international or racial friction.

> I would like it because as years go by the nation would die naturally.

Other comments were that it should be "left to providence and time" and "no objection." One informant felt that "we" were not sufficiently educated for it, and two that they would approve, but for the children. There was the same type of qualified answer among those who rejected intermarriage—that the children suffer, that there is dual loyalty, that the children are never comfortable, and that no racial group can as yet accommodate Coloreds (given by nine informants). The main ground of rejection was for the sake of racial purity (22). Some said simply that they were not in favor of intermarriage.

There was thus among this sample of teachers considerable rejection of the basic tenets of apartheid—virtual unanimity in the rejection of separate development, racially restricted franchise, and the revival of the tribal way of life. Solutions to the racial problem elicited from most informants a democratic ideology, or—the very antithesis of apartheid —African control; while intermarriage, the crucial taboo under apartheid and similar systems of racial domination, was acceptable to nearly half the sample. And yet the duty of inculcating apartheid falls on these teachers. Their reactions to the teaching profession, as they expressed them in the interviews, are affected by this basic dilemma.

As their main reason for entering the profession, the teachers gave a positive evaluation of teaching—a love for teaching, service to the community, the role of light-bearer to the nation. A second category of reasons was negative—lack of opportunity, force of circumstances, a stepping stone to other occupations. Conditions of service—security, respect, prestige, holidays, and better living standards—were apparently not a dominant motivation. In general, women were more inclined to stress service, men lack of opportunity. Comments on the three things informants like most about teaching mentioned first service to the community, and then conditions of employment (mainly holidays, weekends, and railway concessions, with only 11 references to security and better pay—though teaching is more highly paid than most other occupations open to Africans). These replies must be related to the occupations teachers would have preferred to enter. Only 12 answered that there were no other occupations they would have liked better. Medicine and law were the preferred occupations for men, nursing for women. This does not necessarily imply rejection of teaching, since law and medicine are more highly rewarded and honored occupations, and nursing offers a career to married women, which is denied them as teachers.

The remaining questions elicited a great volume of reaction against Bantu Education. Of the 232 items informants mentioned as the most disliked aspects of teaching, 121 related to Bantu Education, 66 to conditions of service (unequal pay for women, transfer from one school to another, favoritism in promotion, low salaries, clerical duties), and 45 to items intrinsic to the work—such as daily preparation, repetition of lessons, routine—or dissatisfaction with colleagues, principals, inspectors, or supervisors. One woman complained, "It is a strenuous job on the brains"; and another stated, "I like to enjoy with the little ones asking funny questions to me. I dislike to have homework after school."

In reply to the question whether their attitude to teaching had changed, 73 informants said their views had changed, 56 referring specifically to aspects of Bantu Education. The question whether African education had improved or worsened over the last 20 years caused some difficulty. The period of 20 years was chosen so as not to direct attention specifically to Bantu Education, which was only introduced in 1954. Informants again reacted against Bantu Education: 51 said African education had worsened as a result of Bantu Education, 25 that it had improved until Bantu Education, then worsened; 21 said it had improved, or improved for a time, on a variety of grounds—more Africans at school, more graduates, greater parent interest, and, in approval of the new curriculum, that more subjects and the official languages are taught (4 of the 21). Analyzing other replies of these 21 respondents, 15 refer adversely to aspects of Bantu Education. Presumably under any system of education, there would be adverse criticism by teachers, but not of the volume and nature reflected in these questionnaires.

The specific complaints against Bantu Education may be classified in terms of conditions of service, decline in standards, change in status, the subordination of education to political goals, and the dilemma of the teacher.

Women teachers in particular complained of overwork and large classes. These dissatisfactions flow from the administration of Bantu Education, with its emphasis on mass literacy (or at any rate, mass education for four years). The increased enrollment, but lower cost per pupil, is achieved partly by a larger ratio of pupils to teachers and a double session system in the substandards, that is to say, the most elementary standards, where the same teacher takes two successive waves of pupils, each for two and three-quarter hours daily, sufficient justification for the complaint of overwork—"the heavy burden of teaching 100 children a day." Teachers complained of a student load per teacher of 50, 55, and 60: "We have about 20 per cent more in each class. Classes vary from 50–55 in high school: worse still in lower classes."

Other grievances related to the retrenchment of experienced married women and their replacement by inexperienced girls, the red tape of the centralized bureaucracy, stagnant salaries, lack of pension, expulsion without reason, and insecurity. One headmaster commented: "I think with teaching your mind is curbed towards certain grooves. There are things you are afraid to say and speak out. You do what you are told to do—you have no way of coming to the creation of your own thing."

A decline in standards is ascribed to a variety of factors: the deliberate reduction of standards, the discouragement of Latin and sciences (but, conversely, better instruction in sciences though poor in languages), double sessions, emphasis on manual education, and a scanty syllabus. The qualifications of the teaching staff were said to be lower as a result of the dismissal of bright teachers and the appointment of "females fresh from college whose salary is low." It was said that "the recent crop of teachers know absolutely nothing, they can't even utter a single correct sentence in English." Above all, a main target of attack was the teaching in the vernacular and the introduction of one official language immediately in the first substandard and the second after six months, so that the child has to cope with three languages.

The vernacular was rejected as inadequate equipment for the modern world and as shuttering off the windows to the outside; it did not fit pupils for life, it had impaired their knowledge of English. "The bread language is not given preference," and "pupils are limited to their own sphere and factory work; the vernacular is a bar to employment." One teacher made the interesting comment that he did not like teaching sums in the vernacular: it was so unreal. The rejection of the new system of language teaching was almost universal: 66 teachers favored the old system of vernacular teaching for the first four years of schooling, and thereafter a European language, while 28 favored a European language throughout. Only one teacher thought the vernacular should be used throughout, and four thought it should be used in the primary schools. In regard to the relative emphasis on English and Afrikaans, none felt that Afrikaans should be given more emphasis, 13 wished that only English be taught, 53 favored a stress on English, and 33 (mostly women) an equal emphasis.

The revival of the vernacular (ethnic language is perhaps a more accurate term) is often associated with nationalist movements, as in the case of the Afrikaners. For Africans it poses a problem, since there are many languages, and their revival might stimulate tribalism rather than nationalism. Moreover, the revival of the African languages has not arisen from among Africans themselves, but is imposed on them from without, presumably to foster tribal divisions. In this policy, there is apparently a confusion of cause and effect. Strongly growing tribal or national sentiment may stimulate interest in the tribal ethnic language. The reverse is unlikely, that a compelled study of the language would revive a dying tribal sentiment. In any event, the policy may be self-defeating, since the very imposition of the tribal language stimulates resistance and rejection.

The prestige of the teacher had declined, according to informants, as a result of the devaluation of the profession and of education generally. Factors mentioned were loss of security ("now it is even more repulsive since the change: strictly speaking it is no longer a profession: it is organized on *togt*—daily laborer—basis"), too many teachers ("furthermore the teaching profession among our people is no longer a noble profession as it is with other races: there has been overproduction of teachers—teaching has been the only profession all along and that has tended to cheapen it"), and lack of opportunity for the educated, so that people have begun to despise education ("some people think it is even better to be a policeman than a teacher").

The system of school boards and school committees in particular was conceived as a degradation of the status of African teachers. It has indeed effected a change in the relations between the educated and the uneducated. In the rural areas, the teacher represented a different system of prestige, based on education, in contrast to the chief, who was usually uneducated but drew his authority from tradition and the support of the uneducated and pagan. At present, although some chiefs are educated and the Government has established chiefs' schools for the education of the sons of chiefs in conformity with the principles of apartheid, the basic conflict between the two systems of prestige, the modern and the traditional, remains. Indeed it has been sharpened by the Government's policy of placing the chiefs at the apex both of African society and of the school boards and school committees in the rural areas. In the towns, teachers complain of the indignity of being subordinated to the uneducated members of the committees and boards. In Durban, the school boards are largely recruited from professional and white-collar groups, with standards of education higher than those of the community as a whole. The Inspector of the Durban South Circuit explained that it was more difficult to find suitable members for the school committees than for the school boards. In any event "their jobs do not call for much education, provided they have wisdom and are ready to serve." And it is of course the members of the school committees who are in closer contact with the teachers.

The teachers complained of corruption (which the Inspector felt was not justified), appointments through bribery or other nonacademic considerations, petty jealousy, the dismissal of teachers on political grounds or because of personal hatred, insecurity, and the spurious nature of African "control" of education, the fact that the "school boards can only do what is put down in regulations—only strait-jacket ideas." They complained that "Bantu Education is said to be where Bantus administer their own education. In fact we have no say in the curricula. It is brought to us cut and dried." And they were especially concerned about the change in the relations between the educated and uneducated, always in some tension, as the following extracts illustrate:

> You can imagine an educated man to be directed by an illiterate person! . . . The schools should be above—something ideal.

> A lamentable fact about it is that the Government is trying to create enmity between the Africans by placing these people in a

position who know nothing and tend to bully teachers because they think teachers look down upon them.

A teacher in my very young days was held in great esteem. Today through pronouncements of Ministers, they have lowered that esteem by saying teachers are employed by the parents through the school boards, and can be dismissed by them. These illiterate people misconstrue this.

The whole thing is just there to throw the teachers against the community.

The interviews reflected perception of the political role of Bantu Education, and feelings of bitterness and frustration. Bantu Education was described variously as:

An instrument of oppression:

It prepares us for servitude.

The whole process of teaching has been turned into a political tool. We are made tools to inculcate inferiority complex into the children.

I am being used as an instrument to suppress the aspirations of my people. I am not free to say what I want.

The sort of education which streamlines the people into being hewers of wood and drawers of water falls far from the ideal in education.

Its objects are quite immoral because it aims at permanently stunting the child to fill a lower status in society.

This is to drive us back to the Dark Ages—Tribalism.

Content of the syllabus being whittled down to conform to political ideologies to which we don't subscribe.

Training to be only of use to their people.

An instrument of indoctrination, and against one's convictions:

In teaching the syllabus, you may even be led to condemn your own people and work against your convictions. You may be forced to say Dingaan was a bad man, when you know in your heart of hearts he was a good soldier.

Some of the things one has to teach are quite revolting—one knows the right thing but cannot teach that. One has to teach the good of

Bantu Authorities and the school boards and the advantage of paying higher taxes because it is said it is for our education—even when one knows that people don't have the money. On Monday people were asked to pay these higher taxes through the radio— exactly what we are asked to teach.

We are no longer teaching, but we are poisoning the children.

The enforcement of mother tongue instruction is intended to shut out ideas which are considered bad for the African. Bantu Education is intended to produce people who will profess a particular ideology and would have no independent judgment on certain issues confronting the African; and, worst of all, it encourages tribal parochialism. The Minister of Native Affairs stated that our station in life is that of servants. It becomes difficult faced with the syllabus that the children should pass, and finding in subjects like history people regarded as our heroes being duped savages.

Also contents of subjects. The syllabus is compiled by people holding a distorted point of view. That distortion is passed on to the African teacher to pass on to the African child. Distorted in the sense that in the 20th century we lay too much stress on tribalism and dividing the children, which are dying a natural death.

Under Bantu Education syllabuses definitely stress that the child must be prepared and fitted for life in the reserves. A very narrow aim. Girls doing homecraft are supposed to learn how to use cowdung to smear rondavels, cook grain vegetables of indigenous type. They learn this at home. It is a waste of time. Should be trained to do whatever everyone else would do. Most of them leave in Standard VI or VII and become domestic servants.

Unnecessary topics in social studies. Why do we need services of a chief, a headman? Object is merely to support Bantu Education. Also in aims, handwork emphasized, return to tradition. Importance of police, agricultural officer, stock inspector, location superintendent. Impress necessity of work done by Government. Respect of age, authority, fellow man.

A special Bantu education, not a universal education:

Being prepared for a particular life as against universal education.

I didn't like the idea of the adjective to qualify education. There is only education.

Our young children are going to be crippled. Universal education is better because one can fit in anywhere.

In the past the syllabus was the same. We even had other races at the same school.

I hate this Bantu Education because we are being singled out among other races and given a special type of education.

Since introduction of Bantu Education there were quite a number of changes I didn't like. Bantu Education is based on a philosophy that an African is inferior to the White race. Therefore he must receive a special education—to mold him to fit an inferior position in life, which is not true.

This then is the dilemma for many African teachers in the sample: the feeling that they are debasing their people, not uplifting them— "a noble profession: now . . . a poisonous drug"—uncertainty about aims, and guilt about their role. "I feel the future for the child is dark and I am contributing to it." Publicly, there is little that an individual teacher can do to solve his dilemma. The teachers are too vulnerable. Work opportunities are limited for those who reject the official policies. For the sake of security, they must be guarded, particularly in a school system informed with spies. The Federal Council of African Teachers' Associations provides some means for tactful representation and action, as do the provincial and local associations, but even at this level it is dangerous for the individual teacher to expose himself. Sharp punishment has been administered to the teachers' associations, including the Durban Branch of the Natal African Teachers' Union.

Prior to Bantu Education, the Durban Branch was somewhat moribund, with a small and inactive membership. Even at a stage when Bantu Education was being vigorously debated throughout the country, the Durban members of the association appear, from the minutes of their meetings, quite uninformed. In August 1953, the Executive, according to the minutes, felt "that we should have a talk about the transfer of Native Education to the Native Affairs by an official of the Education Department, but this was a busy meeting and a talk could not be arranged though the time is most suitable for such a talk."* In September 1953, the minutes record an argument in favor of the teaching of citizenship, as Africans do want to become citizens of South Africa. Members were obviously afraid to comment on official statements and policies. Thus in the October 1953 meeting, the matter of selecting important articles from the *Natal Teachers' Journal* "was asked with fear that, as such articles are official, the Education Department on discovering such, would take action against teachers."*

During 1954 and 1955, the members began to be informed about Bantu Education. There was a talk by the White Inspector of Education. "You may receive an inferior article," he said, "but you must not be worried but wait and see." And the minutes record that he tried to straighten the backbone of this red herring by saying that in Pretoria "he was one of the members of the Syllabuses Committee."* A prominent African teacher spoke on "The Role of an African Teacher," stating:

> I am now of age and I can no longer be wailing to a White man. . . . The African is just as important a human being as anyone else. . . . We are responsible for the destinies of this country. The first thing is to do away with that complex feeling of inferiority which has been inherited from parent to children, that unquestionable obedience to orders. Ladies and Gentlemen, we are a Wonderful Race.*

Criticism was offered of the new type of education "for Africans only:" the Child Education Fund was established to counteract some of the evil effects of Bantu Education; and the meeting in September 1955 concluded with the singing of the African national anthem.

Then the teachers moved into a more militant phase. The Presidential address in May 1956 was delivered "with such vigour and caution that it attracted the serious attention of the teachers."* The Vice-President in September 1956 related Calvinism to Bantu Education. The Boers looked upon the Africans

> as the condemned lot of whom the God of Calvin spoke. With this firm conviction Boers have absolutely no humane regard for an African. According to them, if Africans are predestined for hell it would serve no purpose being sympathetic to them while here on earth. Education, therefore, which would tend to loosen the bonds of slavery is viewed with great concern by the Boers; thus the implementation of Bantu Education serves to perpetuate the religious belief they hold and maintains the African in his proper position.*

At the next meeting, November 1956, a prominent member of the African National Congress spoke on the "Outline of Development of Resistance to Oppression by African People." This was a review starting with the Bambata Resistance and ending with the African National Congress program of action and the Freedom Charter.

> In conclusion [the speaker] requestingly said:
> 1) The educationist can help to acquaint the young children with real facts about their own leaders. In this way questionable information could not be passed from generation to generation.

* Source could not be rechecked.

2) Consequently it is necessary that South African history should be rewritten and more correctly.*

The meeting closed with the singing of the national anthem. At the next meeting the Chairman announced "that teachers should teach school children the proper meaning and singing of the African National Anthem. The meeting closed with the singing of the National Anthem with dignity and feeling."*

At this point (1956) Bantu Education was beginning to stimulate national sentiment among the teachers. At the close of the next meeting, over 100 teachers were present and the two national anthems were sung. (When the meeting started, an hour and a half late, only 28 teachers were present.) In September 1957, there was a discussion of the stand teachers might take in defeating Bantu Education. In February 1958, we read that three members have been visited by the Criminal Investigation Department, actually the Special Branch, the President and Vice-President being among them. In May 1958, the quarterly meeting decided that the Special Branch visit be not pursued further, as the visit was not linked with the Teachers' Union. (In fact, it was linked with the Teachers' Union.) About 80 teachers were present at the close of the meeting and the national anthems were sung. Teachers were disturbed by the fact that a call for help to the Treason Fund, at an Executive meeting, was immediately known to the White Inspector of Education.

At the meeting in September 1958, the President announced that he, the Vice-President, and the Secretary had been served with notices of the termination of their duties to take effect from September 30, 1958. The President spoke on "The African Parent, Teacher, and Child under the Bantu Education System." The new system would be such as to manufacture out of the African child "a docile servant who will accept his backward slavery conditions as a creation of God."* It is not enough for the African child to know about the reserves and locations he lives in: like all children he must know the world at large. Some Africans thought it was their duty to take positions under the system in order to rescue the education of their children. But school boards and committees do not appoint or dismiss teachers, they merely recommend. They can do nothing about the syllabuses, "in fact they are merely there to administer the poison that Pretoria manufactures. We cannot be deceived therefore about the part played by these people —they cannot be otherwise than 'yes men' to the N.A.D." (Native Administration Department). And as for the African teacher, his status and salary are responsible for his failure to interpret into practical action his condemnation of Bantu Education. He concluded that "the

* Source could not be rechecked.

struggle for the democratisation of the education of the African child must go on." *

At the next meeting, the new President paid tribute to the three dismissed teachers: "Our hearts are dripping with blood." The meeting closed with the singing of the two national anthems, and the militant period is over.

The teachers' associations continue to raise, in a discreet way, issues affecting the profession, but with little impact, and the individual African teacher is left to resolve the dilemma for himself. He may try to introduce his own perspective, balancing, for example, the official picture of the Zulu warrior Tshaka by comparisons with Napoleon, and leaving the children to draw their own conclusions. One teacher professed the following ingenious reinterpretation of the White man's civilizing mission:

> I overcome the problem of being used as an instrument by telling them that the Jews suffered in Egypt for many years, but they had a hope for a deliverer who will come one day to free them from slavery. I always tell my children that God created four continents—Asia for the Asiatics, Europe for the Europeans, and Africa for the Africans. He separated these people by seas, which is apartheid. Afterwards God decreed the boundaries and allowed those races to come to Africa to teach us Christian religion and civilization, and now those people have done their work, their mission is over. My feeling now is that freedom is at hand although we are still being dominated by these foreigners. In other words, the Messiah has come to lead us out of bondage, and that is why there is a scramble out of Africa.

The Government has introduced politics into African education and inevitably transformed many African teachers into politicians. Since they cannot express themselves directly, their political role is somewhat incalculable, as is that of the new generation of African students whom they educate.

* Source could not be rechecked.

CHAPTER 14

Clergy

THERE HAS BEEN so little research into the sociology of religion in South Africa—though much prayer and lament—that I offer with hesitation these tentative suggestions relevant to the occupational milieu of African clergymen in "White" churches.

For many Africans conversion to Christianity was seemingly a serious commitment, and not merely a matter of expedience. For the sake of Christianity, they were prepared to abandon their traditional societies, and even to identify with the White colonizers. Dr. A. C. Jordan[1] comments that "with the spreading of 'the Word' went the widening of the gulf between Christian and Pagan. The chiefs and their pagan followers were still fighting with determination to retain their independence; the 'Believers' [Christian Africans] were either 'neutral' or actively supporting the coloniser." And he refers to an essay written in 1863 by Tiyo Soga, "The Believers and the Red-ochred," in which Soga shows that the gulf between the two groups had become so wide as to affect their personal relations. "The converted African has lost *ubuntu* [generosity, respect for human life irrespective of position]: and the pagan can no longer expect hospitality amongst the Christians. He gives an instance of a pagan traveller whom he found sleeping in the open veld on a cold winter night because none of the Christians in the village would admit him into their homes."

Noni Jabavu,[2] granddaughter of John Tengo Jabavu, a Fingo and first editor of IMVO, describes the religious zeal of her forebears. She writes:

> We young people in the forties and fifties of this century listen and shudder to think how unbearable life must have been in such a hive of puritanism, of perpetual endeavour. We catch glimpses of the earnestness that must have accompanied it when, nowadays, our elders associate to "fight Demon Alcohol" under the

1. In a seminar paper on "The Political and Cultural Aspirations of the Southern Africans as Reflected in Xhosa Literature," given to students at the University of California, Los Angeles.
2. *Drawn in Colour,* p. 130.

banners and badges of "The International Order of True Temp-lars," for example.

And she asks, comparing the situation with Uganda: "Where in this part of Africa were the equivalent of our Southern frenzied or earnest, 'pierced' people, *amagqoboka*, who, in our language, were pierced with something of the urge to triumph over the slough caused by the former way of African life being broken and made invalid in the present era?"

In the context of Zulu society, Chief Albert Luthuli[3] bears witness to the profound revolution which Christianity brought into the lives of converts:

> Conversion meant an entirely new way of life, a new outlook, a new set of beliefs—the creation, almost, of a new kind of people. They were still Zulus to the backbone—that remained unchanged except for a few irrelevant externals. But they were Christian Zulus, not heathen Zulus, and conversion affected their lives to the core [though without discrimination toward non-Christians in Luthuli's home at Groutville].

It would be a simple matter to multiply examples of the deep com-mitment to Christianity, and also to gather contrary examples of super-ficial and expedient conversion.[4] The balanced perspective awaits de-tailed historical research and the collection and analysis of life histories. Meanwhile only general impressions are available. At this level I would select as a measure of the significance of Christianity for Africans the immense proliferation of separatist churches. Although the 2,201 un-registered churches and the 4,500,000 members claimed by the Federa-tion of Bantu Churches in South Africa (*Drum*, May 1961, p. 35) were greatly exaggerated, there can be no doubt that the separatist churches, registered and unregistered, serve millions of Africans. The 1951 census gave the membership as over one and a half million. Granted that the separatist churches provide avenues of leadership and self-expression, that the motivation may not be purely religious, and that to some extent religious separatism is an alternative for political action, nevertheless the presence of a Christian idiom in these churches seems ample testimony of the significance of Christianity for Africans. To this I would also add the evidence of bitter denunciation by Africans and rejection of Christian practice, and indeed of Christianity, which is meaningful only against a background of deep religious commit-ment.

3. *Let My People Go*, p. 20.

4. Dr. A. C. Jordan mentioned to me the acceptance of missionaries by some Xhosa chief-tains for the sake of rainmaking, and the expulsion of one missionary group from a site specially allocated in a drought-ridden area on failure of prayers for rain.

Ambivalent reactions are associated with Christianity in at least two main respects—"Churchianity" as it is sometimes called, referring to the many antagonistic denominations, and the conflict between the "Word" and the deed. Dr. Jordan, in the paper mentioned above, uncovers this ambivalence in the very early period of conversion to Christianity. He writes:

> The people begin to see the divisions among the church bodies as a disrupting force, making political unity among the Africans impossible. They begin to recall that the first African convert, Ntsikana, warned them to be *imbumba yamanyama* "hard, solid sinew," that is, an inseparable group. To counteract the threatening disunity, they form a political organisation called *Imbumba Yamanyama*. Poems are written in memory of Ntsikana, who, though accepting "the Word," foresaw the damage it might do to national unity.

Writing from Peddie in December 1883, S. N. Mvambo says, in part:

> Anyone looking at things as they are, could even go so far as to say it was a great mistake to bring so many church denominations to the Black people. For the Black man makes the fatal mistake of thinking that if he is an Anglican, he has nothing to do with anything suggested by a Wesleyan, and the Wesleyan also thinks so, and so does the Presbyterian. *Imbumba* must make sure that all these three are represented at the conference, for we must be united on political matters. In fighting for national rights, we must fight together. Although they look as if they belong to various churches, the White people are solidly united when it comes to matters of this nature. We Blacks think that these churches are hostile to one another, and in that way we lose our political rights.

Here the fragmentation into exclusive denominations is seen as a divisive factor, like tribalism. But the criticism of denominationalism goes deeper. Jordan quotes the comments of one writer, in 1875, on the quarrels between the churches: "We thought they had brought one Saviour, one God, because they carry one and the same Book of Scriptures, which will save anyone who accepts it, no matter to what church he belongs." And another, in a poem written in 1884, contrasted the messages of peace with the endless warring among the churches who "hold one another's throat not with the embrace and caress of the peaceful dove, but with the savage grip of the fierce wild-dog," and added that the whole world lies agape for the smiling message of the Gospel while the "armies of Jesus" shed human blood "like any of the children of Satan." This raises an even more fundamental question, that of the conqueror lurking behind the missionary.

Today, almost one hundred years later, denominationalism is still an acute issue, though there are councils and conferences for the religious of different denominations, and an ecumenical movement. Reverend Mokitimi[5] lays some responsibility for African separatist sectarianism on missionary denominationalism.

> In 1850 there were 11 different European missionary bodies at work in South Africa. In 1938 the number had risen to 44. When one remembers the mutual criticism and, sometimes, vilification which used to take place among these agencies one can appreciate the confusion wrought in the African mind. This denominationalism suggested a new form of tribalism and contributed towards the ease with which secession took place and new "tribes" were formed.

Reverend Zaccheus Richard Mahabane (in 1924 President of the African National Congress), in his presidential address to the 1959 Conference of the Interdenominational African Ministers' Federation on the theme of "Evangelisation of Africa South of the Sahara," questioned whether the Christian Church could face the challenge, "being lamentably and roughly split into two big camps, Roman Catholicism on the one hand and Protestantism on the other, while the latter is again torn asunder into a string of Sectarianism of bewildering dimensions." He described Africa as having emerged from ignorance, superstition, vice, degradation, barbarism, savagism, psychic unconsciousness, intellectual insensibility, and mental unawareness—a series of descriptive phrases which powerfully convey the repulsion of an educated Christian of an earlier generation for the traditional way of life and presumably reflect mission teaching. Now, he said, the Hour of Renaissance has come, and Africa is calling for Guidance and Leadership, for the unloosening of the bonds of spiritual enslavement. If the Christian Church is to meet this challenge, then there must be a spiritual rebirth, a joint mission front, indeed a reunion of the Church, and also a breaking down of the middle wall of partition between White and Black, a Christian community in which racial discrimination is eliminated and the policy of apartheid is taboo.

It is natural that doubts as to the role of Christianity should have been aroused in the early days of conversion. Evangelization proceeded at the same time as the conquest of the tribes in a series of bloody wars. And the division between the tribesmen themselves, between those who utterly rejected the White man and his religion and those who became devout Christians, as well as the division between Chris-

5. "African Religion," in *Handbook on Race Relations in South Africa,* ed. H. Hellman (Cape Town, Oxford University Press, 1949), p. 570.

tians of different denominations, would have posed sharply the issue of the relationship of Christianity to foreign domination. And the issue is posed as sharply today, when the Government claims, and the Dutch Reformed Churches dispense, spiritual sanction for the secular policies of apartheid. The effect for many Africans is that of clothing naked oppression in Christian vestments. This makes it difficult to separate White oppression from the Christian doctrine, the fruit from the tree, the deed from the "Word" (their deeds speak so loudly that their voices cannot be heard). It is the issue of the political functions of Christianity and that of the divergence between Christian doctrine and Christian practice, rather than denominationalism, that is the main source of disillusionment and resentment today.

The antagonistic reaction of Africans to the involvement of Christianity in apartheid is a matter of common observation. Mphahlele[6] describes his own personal conflict and spiritual disenchantment as follows:

> Just now, I don't think it's fair for anybody to tell me to expect a change of heart among a bunch of madmen who are determined not to cede an inch, or to listen to reason. It is unfair to ask me to subsist on mission school sermons about Christian conduct and passive resistance in circumstances where it is considered a crime to be decent; where a policeman will run me out of my house at the point of a sten gun when I try to withhold my labour. For years I have been told by white and Black preachers to love my neighbour; love him when there's a bunch of whites who reckon they are Israelites come out of Egypt in obedience to God's order to come and civilize heathens; a bunch of whites who feed on symbolism of God's race venturing into the desert among the ungodly. For years now I have been thinking it was all right for me to feel spiritually strong after a church service. And now I find it is not the kind of strength that answers the demand of suffering humanity around me. It doesn't even seem to answer the longings of my own heart.

White pastors are aware of the problem posed by the identification of the policies of the State with the Church. I select an example from the Cape synod meeting of the Nederduitse Gereformeerde Kerk, where the actuary of the Bantu (daughter) Church said that most people could not differentiate between the Church and the State; that ministers of the Church were branded, and the word "Dutch" had become simultaneously with the word "White man," a swear word; and that on meeting somebody in the street a normal conversation could take

6. *Down Second Avenue* (London, Faber and Faber, 1959), p. 178.

place until the minister was asked to what church he belonged but that immediately the word "Dutch" was mentioned a wall was built up dividing the minister from the other person (as reported in the *Natal Daily News,* November 1, 1961).

African pastors may find their Christian witness affected. A leading African Anglican minister in Durban commented in an interview as follows:

> I feel that the members of the congregation are affected by what the Government is doing. Their action confuses people on the point of religion. It becomes difficult for the people to understand us, because the Afrikaner Nationalists always say that what they do, they do in the name of Christianity. However, our interpretation of religion is different from them and it is difficult to know where we stand. However this does not affect the attendance, though it is difficult to say exactly . . . We Anglicans are fortunate in that our Bishops have been outspoken against any form of discrimination. This makes the people happy in that the Church condemns apartheid.

But, conversely, an African minister of the Reformed Church, with a congregation of thirty, mostly illiterate, experienced no difficulty:

> Our Church supports the Government's apartheid policy and we are expected by our White churchmen to run our own churches when we are able to do so . . . Our Church is prepared to help African people attain all what they want. I am in full agreement with what Congress asks for, but I disagree with their methods. If the Congress people could be converted to our church, the Government would be prepared to listen to them. Most of the Government [Cabinet] Ministers are members of one of the three branches of the Reformed Church. I am very keen to meet some of the Congress people and to discuss with them and advise them of how to go about if they want to be successful.

The Christian sanctification of apartheid sharpens the resentment over the political role of the Church, but the resentment itself is deeply rooted in the past. Today, this resentment is so crystallized as to be almost stereotyped in its expression. I think immediately of such statements as that first the White man had the Bible and we had the Land, now the White man has the Land and we have the Bible; or to quote Chief Luthuli:[7] " 'You close your eyes obediently to pray.' " goes the saying, " 'and when you open them the whites have taken your land and interfered with your women.' " Antagonism is directed against

7. *Let My People Go,* p. 131.

the instrumental role of Christianity in White domination and not specifically against the Dutch Reformed Churches.

The burning of churches is some evidence of a diffuse antagonism. One cannot argue that the burning of a church of a particular denomination necessarily indicates antagonism toward that denomination, since there appears to be a haphazard element in the selection. In two accounts given me of church burnings in different areas, the mob was easily diverted from one church or the other by participants in the mob action, who appealed on such grounds as the fact that their mothers worshipped in the church or that a father preached there. This suggests an ambivalence, a recognition of the claims of churches on the loyalties of Africans, perhaps even the recognition of a right to these loyalties, and at the same time a general hostility toward all churches, of which the quite catholic selection of churches for burning is further evidence.

Chief Luthuli argues against seeing a significance in the burning of churches which is not really there. He writes that a rioting crowd seeks a symbol on which to vent its anger, and that, lacking any symbols in the African locations except the buildings erected by Europeans, such as beer halls, schools, and churches, its destructiveness turns indiscriminately against these buildings. In other words, the building, not Christianity, is the symbol of the White man. And yet almost immediately Chief Luthuli acknowledges his understanding of church burning as a reaction against the failure of the churches.[8]

> It must be remembered, too, that some such buildings *appear* to serve the community, while in fact they do not. I have already shown that this is true of beer halls. Schools come into the same category, not because they are schools, but because they are Dr. Verwoerd's Bantu Education schools, not loved but bitterly resented. I cannot rid my mind of the fear that something similar may apply to the destruction of churches . . . how far is it not tragically true that these churches have become distorted symbols? How far do they stand for an ethic which the whites have brought, preached, and refused to practice? . . . White paternalist Christianity—as though the whites had invented the Christian Faith— estranges my people from Christ. Hypocrisy, double standards, and the identification of white skins with Christianity, do the same . . . The burning of churches I condemn and deplore. I deplore it utterly. Reluctantly, I must confess that I partly understand it. The churches above all were to have brought us not apartheid but

8. Ibid., pp. 131–32. Wilson and Mafeje write that the opposition among *tsotsis* to Christianity and to "decent people" explains why church buildings are so often set afire in a riot (*Langa*, p. 102).

fellowship one with another. Have they? Some measure of human failure is inevitable. Even so, have not many of the churches simply submitted to a secular state which opposes expressions of fellowship and our membership one of another? Have not some even gone so far as to *support* the outlook of the secular state?

Resentment of the political role of the Christian churches is specially intense since there is the tendency or the desire to conceive of religion as nonpolitical and as transcending the worldly and self-seeking. The disillusionment is all the more extreme and cynical, because of the initial worldly innocence as to the relations between religion and society. An equally deep disillusionment is evoked by the practices of the Church within its own religious community, that is to say, by the routine discrimination which many churches impose or permit in their own internal organization. And the disillusionment draws its intensity precisely from the contrast between these practices and the noble and exalted character of the Christian message. Again this sentiment of disenchantment is deeply rooted in African experience, and has acquired its characteristic and stereotyped forms of expression.

Racial discrimination within the Church is not a specifically South African dilemma. Indeed it would appear to be almost characteristic of the Protestant divisions of Christianity. The authority of the Church may be undermined by its own witness, as acknowledged in the report of the International Ecumenical Study Conference in 1959.[9]

> The fact is that we so often say the right things and yet our deeds undermine the authority of our words. Consider, for instance, the question of racial discrimination. St. Paul could speak with authority about reconciliation, for in the Church of the first century it was obvious to all that the middle walls of partition were being broken down. Bitterly hostile and mutually scornful Jews and Gentiles were in fact being reconciled within the Church. We declare the Christian word that condemns social discrimination, but behind our declaration looms the shadow of the middle walls of partition being built up within the Church by fear and prejudice.

And the failure to regulate the internal organization of the Church by the principles of its religious ethic inevitably suggests hypocrisy, a fault the Methodist Church of South Africa frankly confessed.[10]

> To assert a 'spiritual unity' among Christians while denying its expression in corporate liturgical and sacramental worship savours

9. *Dilemmas and Opportunities* (Geneva, World Council of Churches, 1959), p. 43.

10. *Christian Convictions about Multi-Racial Society,* Methodist Church of South Africa, as revised after the 1960 Conference, p. 15.

of hypocrisy. We confess with shame that our Church has been and is guilty of this hypocrisy, and we call upon our members to repent and to put into practice what we believe and assert.

While the questioning of Christianity among Africans is a subject of general comment, its nature and extent are difficult to determine. Logically a distinction can be drawn between the practices of devout Christians, such as ministers or elders, and Christianity itself, or between the role of Christianity in a given society and the doctrines of the Christian religion, in the same way, for example, that a distinction can be drawn between the theory of communism, and communist practices in a given society. Understandably, however, there is a tendency for these two aspects to become confounded, and for Christianity to be rejected because of its exemplars, or its functions for White domination.

In an attempt to gain more understanding of some of the qualitative aspects of the reaction to Christianity I asked teachers in the Durban sample a number of open questions:

> What is your feeling about religion?
> And the contribution of the missionaries?
> And the role of the church in South Africa today?

Also, so as to gain an impression of the distribution of favorable and antagonistic reactions among these teachers, I somewhat arbitrarily classified replies as positive (or approving), negative (or rejecting), and mixed, and extracted a crude quantification. Since the number in the sample was 99 (53 women and 46 men), the figures which follow can be treated as percentages.

The contribution of missionaries elicited most approval—67 positive responses. Comments ranged from enthusiasm for the wonderful work of the missionaries in education, medicine, and spiritual guidance, to mild patronage—"good work in a way." The evaluation of religion was almost equally positive—62 responses—mainly in terms of spiritual goals, but also of religion as a social institution. When, however, inquiry turned to the role of the Church in South Africa today, the positive responses declined sharply to 32, and some of these were in fact normative, discussing what the Church should do, and thus implying criticism of current practice.

There were few negative reactions to the role of the missionary (7 in all), but an appreciable number of mixed reactions (24—one teacher did not reply to this question). The main rejecting themes were as follows:

(1) excessive monetary demands; (2) variability in motives, some having come for service, others for selfish ends, with a distinction drawn between the dedication of the early missionaries and the materialism of their followers, as for example:

What I think is that Livingstone and pioneers of religion were probably honest men. Their followers decreased in honesty as they became more materialistic. The building of church schools I admire but the failure to apply the Christian religion to the very converts and inmates of these schools cancels out the purpose of these schools. And I take religion as practiced now as a betrayal of real Christian principles. To my mind it makes this betrayal from people who know true Christianity a double betrayal against us as people and against Christ himself. Furthermore it is known where that Christian religion started—with a poor man—it is thus a value if it tries to relieve a poor man of spiritual enslavement, so that to change the [teaching?] of Christ for the embellishment of the Church now is wrong—so that the spiritual values have been supplanted by material values. And the worst indictment is the bolstering up of temporary Government by the same religion—e.g. justification of apartheid and all its evils by quotations from scriptures. So that my quarrel with religion is not with principles but the way the principles were brought to me—*and I fail to divorce the principle from the man who practises it.*

(3) the indiscriminate destruction of custom, both good and bad: "We are now a confused race . . . if civilization were brought by traders, it would be better. I consider our customs very good."
(4) a questioning of sincerity, as in the comment that missionaries brought civilization, schools, hospitals, and slavery; or such comments as: "They have not taught us the real gist," and "Not the cream given to us."

In regard to their feelings about religion, the negative responses (12) and mixed responses (24—one response could not be classified) traversed much the same ground as in their evaluation of the missionaries. There were complaints of too many financial demands; dissatisfaction with church administration, the attitudes of ministers, and sectarianism; a variety of personal reactions; and an antagonism toward Christianity as an instrument for racial oppression.

It was brought here to tame the Africans. The people who brought religion are the worst hypocrites. They don't uphold Christianity as preached by Christ.

In the South African set-up, I feel that it has done more harm to the African people—created unnecessary divisions in our ranks, diverted interests of people on false hopes. Africans are made to believe suffering on earth is worthwhile, so long as they are to see the kingdom of God. Except for a few ministers like Father

Huddlestone and Archbishop Joost de Blank, the rest don't care about the political sufferings of the African.

It appears religion was used to inculcate inferiority complex in Africans: e.g. whenever we have—if we decide—on nonviolent means of struggling, some of the ministers come out to say it is un-Christian which means they are supporting the Government. They also tell Africans not to struggle—they must suffer in this world in order to be happy in heaven.

Political factors hinder people from participating in Church affairs. Generally, by the mere look of things, the White man has made other races believe it's something belonging to Whites. Practice apartheid in Church. Feel more a political affair, than a religious affair.

In my church they are there to indoctrinate people into servility.

The main volume of hostile reaction came in the assessment of the role of the Church in South Africa today, with 33 negative reactions and 30 mixed (three informants said that they would not know, and one did not answer). The main theme was in terms of race and political relations (47 comments). There was first a radical rejection. I classified only four responses under this heading. The function of the Church was described as that of subduing people: "That's why the Dutch Reformed Church is interested in evangelization." The churches should be scrapped: they have become the mouthpiece of political parties. They soften people so that they can be ruled easily. They convert the heathen and keep him occupied, while at the same time they make an alliance with the civil powers.

The religious and political implications of sectarianism attracted more attention (9 comments). There was comment on the confusion created by sectarianism, the difficulty in appraising the work of the Church when it speaks in so many voices. And there was discussion of the divisive aspects, the separation of Africans into different denominations. This is a crucial point. Christianity might have provided a basis for the integration of the tribes. Since the majority of Africans are professing Christians, about 60 per cent according to the 1951 census,[11] the integrative power of a membership of some five million Africans in a few churches would have been a major political factor. As it is, because of sectarianism, their political perceptions are subjected to a great variety of cross pressures resulting from religious fragmentation. Moreover, sectarianism operates to the advantage of the Government in still another respect. An informant makes the point that by

11. *Union Statistics for Fifty Years*, p. A-29.

reason of the fact that the Nationalists belong to one church they are more unified than the opposition parties who belong to each and every other church. Though the informant wrongly regards the "Dutch Reformed Church" as one church, there can be little doubt of the greater politico-religious unity of the Dutch Reformed Churches as compared with the denominations to which the opposition belongs.

Most of the remaining comments (23) dealt with related aspects of the failure of the Church, tested pragmatically. Informants declared that the Church had failed in its witness to the brotherhood of man, since there was conflict between race and race: "The tide of racial strife is ever-mounting as the Black people are unable to reconcile its [the Church's] teachings with the political and economic structure ordained by the ruling White Christians." They commented on the failure of the churches to oppose racial oppression, with some favorable mention, however, of the opposition shown by the Anglican and Catholic Churches. They attacked discrimination within the churches, claiming that the churches which opposed apartheid, themselves practiced apartheid: the Church had failed to convince the African of the unity in Christ because it had treated its African clergy in a different way and had failed to uphold the human dignity of the African as expressed in politics, economics, etc. They commented that: "Even in church we are made to ride the third-class coaches," and that "Africans are very religious. They have been trusting Europeans as more religious, but [are] now losing faith because they don't practice what they preach." And there was repugnance for the fact that it was in the Church itself that discrimination was practiced: "Where we think we'll meet on an equal basis as Christians, that is where we find worse apartheid." For the rest, informants commented that religion had lost most of its influence, politics having become the religion of South Africa. The Church was advised to interest itself in politics, but also condemned for doing so. And there was some perception of the changing role of the Church, confronted with a problem hitherto not experienced, the political consciousness of Africans.

The major point emerging from this analysis is that the disillusionment is more particularly with the churches, and not with Christianity itself. The doctrines of Christianity are distinguished from the practices of Christians, the early missionary role from the later pastoral role. There is some contagion from the deed to the word, but it is quite remote from that embittered disillusionment in which anything savoring of religion is indiscriminately rejected. No doubt there are other strata which express to a far greater extent the radical rejection of Christianity than does this sample of relatively conservative opinion in a conservative province. But even though the reactions of these teachers may be relatively restrained, their criticisms of a religious discrimination which mirrors the discrimination in the wider society, and their suspicions of the political role of the churches today, point to the contemporary crisis of race relations within the Christian denominations.[12]

The analysis of the political role of the churches is beyond the scope of this study, save as it contributes to an understanding of the position of African clergy, and I propose only to suggest some general approaches to the problem. I will link the discussion to two quotations.

In *Delayed Action*, by Professor A. S. Geyser and others,[13] Dr. A. van Selms writes about "The Communion of the Saints and the Colour Problem" as follows:

> If there is no longer any difference between that which is valid in the Church and that which is valid in the state, then one of two things has come to pass: Either the millenium has dawned or we are living in Revelations 13. If we can explain the Bible and the articles of faith in such a way that they cause us no difficulties in our lives and do not bring us into conflict with state and society, then there is every reason to ask ourselves whether we are really giving it the correct interpretation. For the Bible is holy and the articles of faith interpret Holy Scripture, but the world we live in is sinful. It is unthinkable that the Bible could speak without coming into conflict with the world. If they wanted to cast the Master from the precipice at Nazareth, will they leave the servant peacefully in the pulpit or academic chair? The peace in which the advocates of apartheid in the Church spend their days ought to make them uneasy—we are not talking here of apartheid in the state and in society; precisely the fact that they encounter assent everywhere, that they are praised and applauded, that the newspapers quote them and members of the state speak of them with appreciation, is a warning to them from God. For it is written: "Woe unto thee when all men shall speak well of thee, for your fathers acted likewise towards the false prophets."

Dr. van Selms is concerned with the Communion of the Saints and apartheid within the Church, but the issue is the broad one of the traditional tension between the world and the religious ethic. This tension may be used as a basis for analyzing the political role of South

12. It seems probable that there is an increasing rejection of Christianity among Africans. This is, however, purely a matter of speculation. A generation earlier, Ray E. Phillips gathered somewhat comparable information from fifty-four educated African Christians, in which much the same themes were announced by informants as recorded above (*The Bantu in the City*, Lovedale, Lovedale Press, 1938, chap. 6).

13. Pretoria, N. G. Kerkboekhandel, 1960, pp. 45–46.

African churches in terms of the religious reactions to apartheid and other forms of racial discrimination. The extremes are clear—complete absence of tension (or more positively, the sanctification of apartheid) and total tension (or absolute rejection).

The Dutch Reformed Churches approach the extreme of the sanctification of apartheid, the elimination of tension between Church and Afrikaner State, and the identification of the political and religious spheres of Afrikaner nationalism. The description of the Dutch Reformed Churches as the National Party at prayer is exaggerated. Many members of these churches support the opposition United Party, not the National Party, though this does not imply, of course, that they reject apartheid or other forms of systematic racial discrimination. Moreover, there is tension between the Dutch Reformed Churches and the National Party Government, as shown in occasional expressions of concern over injustices contingent on the implementing of apartheid, or in declarations of dissident religious opinion, or in the trial of Professor A. S. Geyser on charges of heresy, presumably the religious counterpart of the political treason trial. But the tension is greatly reduced. The Dutch Reformed Churches have served to promote Afrikaner nationalism. They have given that impulse to social action which has made possible the self-righteous imposition of extreme racial discrimination. And they have helped to create, to proclaim, and to sanctify apartheid. To an appreciable extent the political philosophy of the State is the revelation of the Dutch Reformed Churches.

However, the identification of apartheid with Christianity cannot be complete. At any rate, that is how it seems to me, writing as a layman on an issue which divides theologians in South Africa. The basic conflict is between a religion which offers individual salvation and a political philosophy which offers group salvation. In July 1960 a newsletter of the Dutch Reformed Church quoted from an editorial in *Die Kerkbode,* official journal of the Nederduitse Gereformeerde Kerk, which gave promise of a reconciliation of this conflict: "We are in a special position to show the world how the Christian message can enter into the life of the various population groups, satisfying the national characteristics and bringing people from various groups to a joint confession of Christ." The statement emphasizes both the ethnic distinctiveness and the joint confession. In fact, the actual practice is that of a separate confession. The reconciliation would seem designed to effect at most a joint and several ethnic confession of Christ, which is a highly ambiguous concept calling for reinterpretation of Christian teaching in the direction of an Afrikaner nativistic revivalism, i.e. the blending of the Christian ethic with traditional Afrikaner racial beliefs.

Some of the African separatist churches no doubt fall into the same category of belief as that of the Dutch Reformed Churches, namely that of sanctifying racial separation in the service of racial politics. But the separatist churches as such are not necessarily anti-White, nor necessarily concerned with African political goals, though it is difficult to assess their position since they are obliged to proceed with great caution. They are dependent on the Government for recognition and they work in a milieu informed with spies. If they have acquired property—and in the separatist church movement, property represents the quest for a secure haven, a recognized status, a new Jerusalem— then they have made themselves even more vulnerable to control by the State. Thus the African Congregational Church—a church with appreciable property holdings, founded in 1917 by way of separation from the American Board Mission and originally aspiring to be a national church—appears to have exorcised politics. During the Passive Resistance Campaign in 1952, members of the special branch of the police appeared in church to note down sermons, and the Church Council resolved that members engaged in politics should withdraw, for the time being, from an active role in church affairs. Articles about the Church in *Ilanga Lase Natal* were discontinued so as to avoid exposing the Church to State criticism (information from a former General Secretary of the Church). The Government has extensive powers of control over the building of churches on location land: according to the President of the African Congregational Church, rights of occupation are conferred as long as a church behaves. But the church buildings represent a large investment. By reason of this and other considerations relating to the interests of his church, the President declared his resolve to avoid politics absolutely.

There is thus a declaration and an appearance of detachment from the political milieu.[14] Or there may be an appearance of direct support for apartheid. For example, the journal *Drum* reported that Bishop Walter Dimba, President of the Federation of Bantu Churches in South Africa, had compared the spirit of forgiveness shown by Christ on the Cross with the spirit of forgiveness shown by Verwoerd at the time of the attempt on his life: "Verwoerd is the man I know and that is my Jesus Christ" (*Drum*, May 1961, p. 37). But what significance should the observer attach either to the apparent political neutrality, or to the seeming political subservience? Is it not more probable that many of the separatist churches will move into the spiritual service of African liberation movements?

At some levels, there may be a political convergence of African

14. B. M. G. Sundkler quotes the following statement by the President of the African Congregational Church. "Of course, the Group Areas Act affects me. Think of all the property we own! But I like this Nationalist government. And I tell my people, don't take any interest in this colour bar. Forget about it, forget about politics!" *Bantu Prophets in South Africa* (London, Oxford University Press, 1961), p. 304.

theology with Afrikaner theology, as, for example, in the case of the Zionist and Messianic churches. The African prophets, recreating Christianity in harmony with traditional beliefs, may find the Promised Land for their religious communities within the Bantustans. Sundkler writes[15] that "all the evidence goes to show that prophet and chief tend to agree over the essential issue—a Bantustan *apart*, a Church *apart*." Here there is a meeting of purposes at the level of the traditional milieu, and the policy of apartheid may indeed be fostering a nativistic revivalism, both in the African and Afrikaner churches.

A meeting of purposes between Afrikaner and African political aspirations, at any rate in their consequences for religious separation, may also be found in the concept of the religious expression of the African genius, a concept analogous to the apartheid maxim of "development along their own lines." This concept was outlined to me by an African Methodist minister. He was reflecting on the racial segregation, discrimination, and European dominance within the Methodist Church, and on a suggestion he had previously made that the separation might therefore be carried further to the stage of separate synods, Africans to have their own chairmen. "I feel that the African must be placed in the position in which he can bring his own genius into the interpretation of Christianity. His ways of understanding would help to add up to the whole treasury of the Church." There would seem to be a gradation of steps, from resentment against the identification of Christianity with the West, to desire that more scope be given for African religious virtuosity (the separatist churches appear to be achieving this), to the final stage of a racial syncretism between Christianity and negritude, or a political syncretism between Christianity and Pan-Africanism. This final stage, in no way suggested by the African Methodist minister, would cast African theological conceptions in the mold of contemporary Afrikaner national theology, but in the service of African nationalism. There would thus be a state of acute tension with apartheid, not in principle—this would be the same—but in terms of rival political demands.

The extreme of the principled rejection of racial separation is represented by many of the English-speaking churches in South Africa. Doctrinal tension with apartheid is at its maximum. These churches have denounced apartheid as un-Christian, and they have suffered the destruction of their educational mission. The doctrinal tension arises from the perception of the infinite worth of the individual, since God's image resides in all men, and the dedication to the ideal of individual salvation. Emphasis on the individual as the unit of value, and hence emphasis on nonracialism, confronts the idealization of the racial or ethnic group.

15. Ibid., p. 312.

Mphahlele[16] questions the ability of the Church in terms of its values to oppose racial oppression, arguing that the high evaluation of the individual personality stands in the way of effective action:

> The Church, with its emphasis on the value of the individual personality, has continued stubbornly to bring outmoded standards to the situation; a situation where a powerful *herrenvolk* has for three centuries done everything in the interests of the *volk*.
>
> Where persons have been oppressed as a race group, the Church has sought safeguards and concessions for the individual, evading the necessity and the responsibility of group action. And while it fixed its gaze on Calvary or kept up an aloofness from political realities, the road has been slipping back under its feet. It never seems to have occurred to the Church that right under its nose has been growing a calculating white barbarism, among those it considered as hereditary custodians of Christianity, custodians who need mission stations in their very midst. I cannot but reaffirm what I said in a B.B.C. talk in 1955 on the African intellectual; that to us, the Church has become a symbol of the dishonesty of the West. I'm still suspending belief and disbelief as far as the necessity or uselessness of organised religion goes. All I know is that I found no use for it in South Africa; that since 1947 when I stopped going to church, I have become progressively weary of all the trappings of mystical formalism that go together with South African "Churchianity."

The issue Mphahlele raises is analogous to the controversy as to whether reduction of racial tension is best achieved by strategies directed against prejudice or against discrimination. And it is understandable that an African who is suffering acutely under extensive racial discrimination should reject the suggestion that relief must wait upon individual changes of heart.

Between the extremes of religious affirmation of apartheid and of absolute tension with apartheid are a variety of ethics, some of which, although neutral, serve in the context of South African society to give tacit support to racial discrimination. Even where there is doctrinal tension, there may be subsidiary doctrines or psychological approaches which serve in practice to reduce or even to eliminate tension. The possibilities seem almost infinite, because the sacred writings provide so great a store of texts, and the argument is often so remote from simple logic.

One major category of doctrines or approaches for the reduction of tension is based on the insulation of religion from the secular world. Religion is detached from the rest of society, becoming a segregated

16. *Down Second Avenue,* pp. 221–22.

formal periodic observance rather than a way of life. To some extent this has been the solution for many South African English-speaking Whites. Or the solution may be on the basis that to Caesar must be rendered the things that are Caesar's. The Bible may be accepted as the work of God, as normative for all the political, social, cultural, and religious activities in which man indulges, but the Church acknowledges the basic rights of the State as a particular divine institution to regulate the lives and actions of its citizens. Or again the concept of unity in Christ may be regarded as a spiritual, not a secular, conception, which carries no practical implications for this world. Or the emphasis may be that the Church is concerned with the hereafter, and not with this sinful world, and that the Church's leaders must therefore abstain from secular involvement.

A second category involves the transmuting of social issues to problems for the individual conscience. The resolution of tension may be in terms of an emphasis on help for the suffering in a private Christian way, individual charity rather than social justice: the solution lies in love. There may be such Christian charity and love that deep commitment to a specific point of view is dissolved in tolerance. It is said that one cannot read the word of God like a book elucidating every possible situation: we are all sincere and should not stand in judgment.

The quotation from Dr. van Selms and the argument thus far concern tension between religion and the world. A second quotation, from Reverend W. A. Visser't Hooft,[17] stresses rather the adjustment between religious and other spheres of action:

> History as well as present experience prove that the Churches are social institutions whose life is largely determined by the general habits, convictions, or prejudices of the nations in which they are planted. We must even go farther and admit that, in view of the all-too-human tendency to confuse a merely social tradition with a sacred religious tradition, they are often slower than other social institutions to respond to changing social patterns. But that is by no means the full truth about the Churches. Within these often conservative institutions there operates another force which Christians believe to be the Holy Spirit and which others may explain as a re-emergence of the basic and original Christian convictions. When this force of renewal takes hold of the Church the entangling alliance between the Church and the society around it is broken, the Church re-affirms its freedom to follow its own inner laws and manifests its own distinctive characteristics.

17. *The Ecumenical Movement and the Racial Problem* (Paris, UNESCO, 1954), p. 61.

There are two lines of analysis involved here—religion as a social institution related to the other institutions of the society and religion as a revelation, a force of renewal transcending the social bonds. I shall confine myself to the former aspect, though mentioning also certain social changes which may stimulate the Christian conscience, without, however, suggesting any materialistic determination of the latter. And since Dr. Sundkler has analyzed the social context of the African separatist movement (or movement of religious independence), I shall restrict my own discussion to the multiracial churches.

The multiracial churches tend to be White settler churches, that is to say, they reflect or reproduce White settler policies. This is a description which cannot be applied to the Catholic Church, though even the Catholic Church is not exempt from the influences of settler society. Perhaps the sharpest contrast to the settler church, outside of the African separatist movement, is provided by the development within the American Board Mission. Due possibly to the very small migration of Americans, the missionaries of the American Board did not serve White congregations (apart from a period during which the Reverend Lindley ministered to Afrikaners), and it seems that the interests of Africans were paramount, there being no competing interests. The policy was to establish an indigenous church; and a number of steps, as well as the Congregational form of worship, encouraged growth toward "self-sufficient, self-propagating, and self-supporting" churches (as an American Board missionary described the contemporary Board churches). Thus independence was fostered by the fact that the Church established its own rules at an early stage, and by the changing role of the White missionaries who were removed first from direct pastoral work, later from the position of superintendents, and who now serve as advisers. The pioneering work of the American Board in education, hospital services, and religious organization, the encouragement to Africans "to grow as men and women" (a phrase used by an African Anglican pastor, contrasting American Board policy with Anglican, presumably in Natal), and the independence of the Bantu Congregational Church are testimony of dedication to African interests. This has not saved the American Board Mission from African separatism, the most notable secession being that of the African Congregational Church. Yet the President of the latter church, time and again in discussion, referred to the American Board as "the Mother Church," presumably indicating a measure of continued identification.

The main distinction between the American Board churches and the White settler churches is that the former did not develop a multiracial membership, only multiracial guidance and administration. The direct influence of a membership of White settlers is obviously crucial, but there is also an important indirect influence, affecting the ethics and perspectives of the ministers themselves. This emerged in the interviews. An American Board missionary, for example, thought that where a missionary was also a parson to a White congregation, this placed him in an entirely different category, and he sought, in this difference, some explanation of the distinctive contribution of the American Board. Or again, an African minister in Durban described his dilemma over the threatened removal of his church in consequence of new road planning proposals. If he were to approach the minister of one of the European churches, asking that his congregation be received, he might very well be told that he could have the hall—meaning quite specifically the hall and not the church—and even then only at such times as the hall was not being used by the White congregants. He phrased the problem hypothetically, but I understood him to be recounting an actual incident, which he then interpreted in terms of the context within which the White minister works:

> The minister has to administer to the spiritual and material needs of his people. Among these material needs are the idea that some Europeans have that it would not be proper for them to mix with non-Europeans. What is the minister to do about it? It will require a great deal of time in order to educate the Europeans and he does not have the time. This separation is, of course, not in accordance with the ideals of the Church. On the other hand I can understand the difficulties of the ministers who are confronted with these practical problems. At the same time it does in effect mean that apartheid is being practiced in the Church, though the policy specifically denies this.

And finally, an African Methodist minister commented as follows on the way in which the pastor's witness is influenced by his charge:

> The White ministers share the fears of the people they serve. They see everything through the eyes of the White man. They are mostly South African born, but even if they are not, it doesn't seem to make any difference. They live all the time with the White people.

The White settler churches reproduce many of the discriminations in the wider society. The details vary, but, generally speaking, discrimination is expressed in stipends and benefits to ministers of different races. Thus, in the Anglican Church in Natal [18] the basic stipend, as laid down by the Diocesan Synod in 1959, was £500 per annum for White clergy, £335 for Indian and, £225 for African. This was later raised for White clergy to £550, Indian £375, and African £275. A White clergyman

18. The correct name is the Church of the Province of South Africa. The South African census combines this church and the Church of England in South Africa under the heading "Anglican Churches."

performing the same duties as an African clergyman, for example as a priest-in-charge of an African Mission, would be paid at the higher rate. Marriage and children's allowances were also at a carefully differentiated racial rate, though the extent of the discrimination was somewhat reduced by the provision of residences. (Policy varies in the Anglican dioceses: in Cape Town for example, there is no discrimination in stipend.) Discrimination in the Methodist Church of South Africa and in the Presbyterian Church of Southern Africa followed roughly the same pattern as in the Anglican Church in Natal.

Segregated worship is customary in the White settler churches, but not always obligatory. It is in fact contrary to the declared policy of many English-speaking churches, though the welcome to non-Whites depends on the love and wisdom of the members, officials, and clergy. While church buildings tend to reflect the general discrimination, there are now some handsome churches in the African locations, and perhaps the days of the daub-and-wattle church are coming to an end.

Many of the mission churches do not have full status. To the extent that African members are served within this framework, there is the familiar subordinate role. Constitutional advancement may be through graded steps. Thus the Presbyterian Church of Southern Africa in 1960 resolved that the African Missions Committee should be renamed the Church Extension Committee (African): this was public recognition that over the years, the Church had grown in strength and stability by the addition of many African members, and that the relationship within the Church was no longer that of missionary to convert, but that of fellow members in equal standing: the next step, but a long way to go before that day dawns, would be the declaration of a Church Extension Committee without any bracketed adjectives.

The highest offices tend to be reserved for Whites, though not as an inflexible principle. In the Natal Diocese of the Anglican Church, only White clergymen were members of the Chapter in 1959: there were no non-White capitular canons, although three non-White clergymen held positions as honorary canons. An African Anglican minister in Durban expressed his opinion that appointments to the Chapter were based on merit: he did not think there was discrimination, but he added that: "No doubt, there is also an element of conservatism." He explained that practice in the Anglican Church varied: there were two African members of the Chapter in Zululand, and one in Bloemfontein, who subsequently became an archdeacon in Basutoland. An African priest became Chairman of the Durban Anglican Church Council, and was later raised to the position of Suffragan Bishop in the Diocese of St. John's, that is to say, the principle of African advancement was accepted in an area predominantly African, though with a substantial White membership. In the Presbyterian Church there was at one time an

African moderator of one of the districts, and in the Methodist Church an African now holds the position of President-Elect of the Methodist Conference for 1964–65. These examples show some opportunity for African advancement in the Church, but the general pattern, in this as in other aspects, is the conventional one of racial discrimination. Many of the arguments justifying the discrimination are the same as would be offered in the secular world: that the calls of an African minister are not the same as those of a White minister; that an African minister is among the most highly paid in his community whereas the White minister is among the most lowly paid; that it would not be right to elevate the African minister financially too far above his fellows; that African parishes are poor and should not be called on for additional contributions, nor should White congregations be asked to subsidize the ministerial stipends of Africans. These arguments would be quite irrelevant if the middle wall of partition were broken down. They reflect the stereotyped thinking of racial segregation. The changes toward greater responsibility, and also toward reduction of discrimination, are recent. To some extent they are the result of pressure within the Church community and of conflict outside it. They reflect the growing political consciousness of Africans and the end of the discriminations of paternalism.

A number of factors seem relevant to this process of change in the White settler churches. In suggesting these factors, I do not wish to imply that the religious conscience is not an independent factor in its own right. However I do not know what significance to attach to it, nor how, for example, one might compare the significance of the religious conscience with that of, say, the sporting conscience. I am concerned rather with some of the broad social factors within the Church which may be expected to activate the individual conscience—I am not asserting that the individual cannot transcend his environment.

The racial composition of the churches is an important variable in the process of change. The Methodist Church has the largest African membership of any of the churches. In the 1951 census over a million Africans are shown as Methodist. (The actual figures of Church membership are lower.) The corresponding figure for Whites was under 220,000, and for Coloreds and Indians about 103,000. The Church is overwhelmingly African in composition. By contrast, the Nederduitse Gereformeerde Kerk, which may be regarded as the pure type of White settler church, had at the time of the 1951 census a declared affiliation of over one million Whites, while Coloreds and Africans each numbered less than 300,000: a ratio of almost two Whites to one non-White. The ratio of non-Whites to Whites in the "Anglican Churches," as reflected in the 1951 census, was quite the reverse, almost two non-Whites to each White (about 580,000 Africans, 230,000 Coloreds, and 5,000 Asiatics, as compared with some 417,000 Whites). While the "Anglican Churches" are thus predominantly non-White, they have a larger White following than the Methodist Church, both absolutely and relatively.

It may be supposed that the strongest pressure for change would be exerted in the Methodist Church. And it is in fact in the Methodist Church that the nomination of an African for the highest office, that of Chairman, has come to symbolize the assertion of equality. In 1957 the African candidate, Rev. Seth Mokitimi, received relatively few votes, but his continued nomination in the annual elections seemed to promise final success. In 1962 he was defeated by only one vote. The Church appears to be adjusting to the inevitable changes. It instituted the position of deputy-chairman for each district, and seven African deputy-chairmen were appointed in 1961. This was a solution somewhat analogous to partnership (like a proposal in the Presbyterian Church for dual moderators). At a more significant level, the Methodist Church is conducting among its members an educational campaign against racial discrimination, based on a clear and uncompromising statement of religious principles; and it is seeking to reform its own church community and its own discriminatory practices. These are all indications of a resolute attempt to transcend the racial prejudices of South African society. In 1963 Rev. Seth Mokitimi became President-Elect of the Methodist Church of South Africa. Similar processes are to be observed in other English-speaking churches—proposals to narrow the discrimination in stipends, to promote interracial contact, and to foster common worship. A substantial African membership inevitably exerts cross pressures, and there is no reason to suppose that even the Dutch Reformed Churches will be exempt from these pressures.

A second variable in the process of change relates to the organization of the Church itself, whether hierarchical or democratic. Pronouncements by the leaders in a hierarchical church may not in the least reflect the attitudes and reactions of the members. It may well be that the decisions of the more democratically organized Methodist Church, though taken with great difficulty, have far more significance for race relations than the clear and inspiring calls of the Anglican Archbishop, or the lead of such Anglicans as Bishop Reeves, Father Huddlestone, and Reverend Scott. There are differences too between the hierarchical churches. Pronouncements of the Catholic hierarchy seem to penetrate more deeply than those of the Anglican. In the Anglican Church, the dioceses have a considerable measure of autonomy and the structure is perhaps not unlike that of a feudal society, though there is an accountability on the part of the bishops to the clergy and the laity. Because of this structure, the politico-religious attitudes of the Anglican Church are perhaps the least predictable, and may include the whole range from radicalism to extreme conservatism on racial issues. The distinction between hierarchical and democratic churches also carries other connotations. Churches seem to have their characteristic ethos, spirit of discipline, and quality of expression. The greater militancy of Africans in the Methodist Church may perhaps be related to the practice of leadership within the Church, and a conception that Christianity trains people not to submission, but to fight their battles in a cool Christian spirit.

A third variable in the White settler church is the ethnic and class composition of the White members, as, for example, the contrast between the English-speaking churches, representing a White minority, in opposition to the Government, and the Afrikaans-speaking churches, representing an entrenched majority. It may be that change in the status of the English in South Africa has created greater understanding for African deprivation. The more middle-class structure of English-speaking White churches no doubt acts as a barrier to common worship with Africans, though perhaps not to the same degree as does the more working-class structure of the Dutch Reformed Churches. In the former case, the wider class differences impede ease of association—in the latter case, the narrower class difference is threatening to status.

The extent of effective provision for constitutional change is a further factor in the reform of the churches. If constitutional channels are lacking, then African separatist movements are likely to follow. Presumably separatist tendencies among Africans in the Methodist Church are restrained by the fact that they do have the constitutional opportunities to assert their rights within the Church. If they should succeed in establishing themselves, however, there may well be defection by White members, either in the direction of religious withdrawal, or through membership in a racially more compatible church, such as the Dutch Reformed Church or a White separatist church. When an Anglican church in the diocese of George was desegregated, it was reported that all but three White parishioners left their church.[19]

It is in this milieu that African clergymen find their vocations. They are encased in ambivalence. There is ambivalence toward Christianity among Africans—the deep spiritual devotion of some and the disillusioned cynicism or, indeed, bitter hostility of others. There is ambivalence within the White settler church itself—the ideal of spiritual brotherhood and the practice of material discrimination. There is ambivalence in the role of the clergyman—the duty to sublimate personal self-interest in spiritual and selfless service and, at the same time, the insistent call for justice and recognition. Perhaps it is by not sublimating their personal

19. E. S. Munger, *African Field Reports, 1952–1961* (Cape Town, Struik, 1961), p. 738.

dilemma that African clergymen will make their most significant contribution. Perhaps it is by militant assertion that they may stimulate a more thoroughgoing penetration of everyday life by the Christian ethic, leading their fellow White Christians from mere profession to a Christian way of life. Perhaps the new evangelists, bringing a renewal of Christianity to South Africa, will be the African clergymen.

CHAPTER 15

Nurses

by Hilda Kuper

OVER THE PAST EIGHTY YEARS nursing has become one of the most highly rated professions open to African women. It carries more prestige in the community, more power in the adult world, and greater personal security than teaching, which was formerly the main ambition of the educated.

In traditional African society, care of the sick was a nonspecialized function of a kinship circle, and nursing required no special qualification and received no specific reward. It was the duty of a mother to look after her young, a wife to care for her husband, and all older women qualified by personal experience to act as midwives. Intimate treatments, such as the popular custom of giving enemas, were performed by relatives of the same sex as the patient. Occasionally patients were brought for treatment to the homestead of a specialist, but there was no separate institution for the sick. A person was taken into the home of a family whose friendly interests were assured. A sickly child might be sent away from a home where the mother suspected the jealousy of co-wives as cause, to stay with her own kin where there was greater security. The obligation to care for the sick was part of a network of kinship obligation toward a particular person. The isolated stranger had no place. Illness and other misfortunes were projected onto evildoers or attributed to breach of taboo or the anger of ancestors, and traditional specialists were consulted to discover the cause and prescribe the treatment. But responsibility for the cure was never placed directly on the quality of the nursing.

In sharp contrast are the status and role of the Western-trained African nurse, who functions primarily in an alien institution, the hospital, and whose relationship with her patient is structurally depersonalized. Yet the treatment required from the nurse may be both more intensive and physically more intimate than that involved in fulfillment of most kinship obligations. Moreover, the position of profesfessional nurse confers in itself an authority that overrides formalities imposed outside the hospital by differences in age and sex. The contrast between traditional and professional nursing is crudely illustrated in the inevitable situation of death (the most crucial attack on the solidarity of a close kin group). Traditionally, the corpse, the focus of elaborate mortuary ritual, could only be handled by special relatives. In the hospital, death is part of the daily routine and the body is handled by the nurse as a neutral functionary. Hospitals and clinics, the institutionalized milieu for professional employment, are part of a Western folk system of medicine. The scientific element, symbolized in microscope and laboratory, underlies the rationalization that health and life itself depend on such qualities as accuracy and hygiene. Each hospital activity is fitted into a time routine and pattern of authority, and efficiency demands strict discipline and a readiness of subordinates to obey orders. In this Western system, nursing is regarded essentially as a woman's occupation.

The ambivalence inherent in the nursing position is obvious. There is a contradiction between the traditional system in which nursing is part of the network of reciprocal rights and obligations that constitute kinship, and the Western system in which illness, not relationship, is a factor which determines institutional care.

Nursing bestows on African women new opportunities for freedom of individual development, but carries the burden of added responsibilities. It brings them past the threshold of Western knowledge, but shuts the door of equality in their faces. Among traditionalists in South Africa, a woman's activities are restricted to care of home and children, and the cultivation of subsistence crops. Status is conferred by marriage, validated by bride price. Polygyny is the ideal for men, and motherhood the highest fulfillment of women. Routine domestic and economic obligations bring neither the public power nor the prestige that is attached to the military, pastoral, and governmental roles monopolized by males. Technology is simple, trade and specialization limited. The main specialists are smiths, herbalists, and diviners. Smiths are always men; herbalists are usually men; and it is only as diviners that women are freely acceptable. Herbalists, who are functionally involved in the intimate affairs of outsiders, acquire their knowledge deliberately and voluntarily, and hence women can be excluded because the role is incompatible with that permitted them by their society. The power of divination, however, is bestowed through involuntary possession by ancestral spirits and it is considered dangerous to try and thwart their manifestation in man or woman. Training for the nursing profession is similar to that of the herbalist in its emphasis on deliberate choice, and the recognition of the right of a modern girl to enter the nursing profession indicates major changes in traditional structure and values.

Training of African nurses was pioneered by missionaries who had to overcome both African traditionalism and Government apathy. Dedicated to the combat of practices and beliefs regarded as obstacles to conversion and as inimical to health, missionaries in the mid-nineteenth century began to bring doctors into tribal areas, dispense Western remedies, and open hospitals. African women were employed initially as domestics and given duties as nurses' aides. The first deliberate instruction dates from 1871, when an Irish woman was appointed as both matron and tutor to a mission hospital in the Cape. A succession of African women learned from her the rudiments of Western hygiene and the reading and writing of English together with the catechism. In 1902, Lovedale Mission Hospital inaugurated a three-year training course leading to a hospital certificate. Two exschoolteachers were enrolled, one of whom, Cecilia Makiwane, was subsequently sent to a professional school for further instruction. In 1907, having passed the professional examination of the Cape Colony Medical Council, she was recognized as a trained nurse. But initial progress in professional qualifications was slow, and by the time of Union, 1910, when there were already 3,446 qualified African teachers, Cecilia Makiwane was still the only fully qualified African nurse.[1]

Training increased after the First World War, with Government and provincial hospitals following the lead given by missionaries, and by 1961 there were 22 general nursing, 11 midwifery, and 7 mental nursing schools. A limited number of supervisory posts were opened to African nurses, and specialist training was introduced. Great as this advance in professional training and opportunity has been, however, the African nursing profession is still contained within a framework of racial differentiation, and is subject to political control.

Health services provided by the central Government, provincial administrations, and missions are coordinated and finally sanctioned by the Department of Health under a Cabinet Minister. Racial segregation of White and non-White patients in wards is traditional, and since 1948 policy has been directed to the spatial separation of White and non-White institutions. In every hospital, the staff is stratified by both professional qualification and by race. At the top are the superintendent and the matron. As yet no hospital has an African superintendent, and there are few African matrons. The nursing staff ranks from sisters in charge of wards to the newest trainees, visibly distinguished by such insignia as caps and epaulets. By law no African may exercise authority over a White—it is in fact a punishable crime to place an African nurse in authority over a White nurse, save in an emergency—and if two nurses of equal professional status are in the same ward, the White is

1. "Nursing Services for 15 Million People," Fact Paper 89, South African Information Service, Pretoria, 1961.

automatically the superior. A White nurse has a better chance of quick promotion if she is prepared to work in a non-White hospital. One senior White nurse stated that "many White nurses prefer non-European hospitals where chargeship positions are a certainty." The hierarchy that exists in Government and provincial hospitals thus reinforces the racial patterns of the plural society.

Despite the conspicuous cleavage between Whites and non-Whites that characterizes South African life in general, and despite the deliberate policy of separation, close interaction between the different groups is inevitable in the health services. The slogan of the South African National War Memorial Health Foundation that "disease knows no colour bar" contains a kernel of truth. The health of Whites depends on a certain minimum of control over disease among non-Whites. With the growing interdependence of the races, the numbers of non-White hospitals and personnel increase, extending the points of contact.

The history of the nursing profession also indicates a fundamental ambivalence, a desire on the one hand to help Africans acquire selected items of Western civilization, and an unwillingness to allow them to compete on an equal basis. As early as 1914, qualified White nurses organized into an association to promote the interests of the profession. The pioneers were of English background, and many were dedicated women, deeply philanthropic, either through religious conviction or social idealism. But theirs was the philanthropy of maternalism. They encouraged the extension of African training and helped persuade State authorities to provide financial assistance to mission nursing schools, but they did not admit Africans as members of their association.

The anomaly of exclusion from a professional group in which persons of different race not only hold similar qualifications but interact in the same institution was constitutionally embedded in the White settler way of life. During the War years, pressure by liberals was directed against these racial exclusions, and in 1944, the Government of General Smuts passed the Nursing Act, which made compulsory the registration of practicing nurses and midwives of all races, and also membership of the statutory professional association. However, no non-Whites held or attempted to hold any official position, and their status as full members was barely effective before the Nationalist Government assumed control in 1948.

The effect on the nursing profession itself was not immediately manifest. Nursing was not seen as a major issue in the Afrikaners' struggle for power. African nurses had too dependent a relationship on White administrative as well as professional staff, and, like all civil servants, were debarred from politics. With the increasing entry of Afrikaans-speaking girls into nursing, a crusade for apartheid was inevitable. The ideology of superiority could hardly escape challenge by African achievement. African nurses received their preliminary education in mission schools, some with relatively high educational standards, while numbers of Afrikaner candidates emerged from less competent and more narrowly oriented Calvinist institutions in the platteland (backwoods). In competitive state examinations, Africans publicly disproved the assumptions of racial inferiority, and in the hospitals, African nurses began to express resentment against perpetual tutelage by less qualified Whites.

Inherent in apartheid were the obvious solutions—the Bantu Education Act and a new Nursing Act. The Bantu Education Act was passed in 1953. By 1960 and 1961, at the time of our interviews, sister tutors complained that the level of entrants had fallen, as for example:

> Many of the girls can scarcely write or understand the language of instruction. I predict that if this trend continues we will have to lower our entrance qualification and either debase our standards or keep the girls for a much longer period of training. Already Africans have six months more than Whites to enable those from the more isolated areas to become familiar with Western medicine and hygiene, and make up some of the cultural difference.

The new Nursing Act, passed in 1957, provided for the registration of nurses by race and for separate representation of Africans and Coloreds on purely advisory committees of the Nursing Association, with executive control vested in the White members of the Board and Nursing Council. The explanation offered by Nationalist supporters was that separate registration provided an accurate assessment of nursing resources in each racial group and that separate advisory boards allowed for free expression of special racial needs. An initial proposal that Africans form a separate but autonomous association was rejected by the South African Nursing Association on the ground, according to one informant, that it would end up as a "communistic body." For many White nurses, the familiar technique of sealing off African discontent in "advisory boards" was an acceptable substitute.

Opposition by a small liberal minority inside and outside the nursing association was ineffectual. In Durban and Johannesburg, African nurses demonstrated in protest. A few of their leaders, in consultation with politically active Whites and non-Whites, formed an unofficial, nonracial association, the South African Federation of Nurses. Its membership is small; not only has it no recognized authority but nurses fear they will be penalized by matrons "who are on the watch for people who have complaints against the administration." In provincial and Government hospitals, the matron is expected to exercise her authority in accordance with Government policy. Thus African nurses in some hospitals complained that the matron was compelling them indirectly to take out registration (pass) books.

Looked at from the outside, the nurses form a select legally-defined association in the wide society. Admission into the association is based on fixed principles of education, age, and sex; membership, demonstrated by a uniform, is validated by certificate and registration. Breach of set standards results in disciplinary action and ultimately expulsion from the group. Looked at from within, from the viewpoint of the nurses, the association has no single loyalty but is composed of two major color groups, each subdivided into several levels. Even in a professional situation racial loyalties may run counter to professional identity. Non-White nurses, irrespective of qualification, are treated as a subordinate group within a White-controlled statutory association. Superior achievement by non-White individuals accentuates rather than reduces intergroup tension. Such techniques as separate registration, differentiation of uniform, and educational isolation eliminate comparison and reduce the possibility of contact on the basis of equal status.

Many African nurses have their first experience of close interracial contacts in the hospital. Indians and Coloreds as well as Whites are on the staff of some non-European hospitals. Cooperation with White doctors starts and stops at the work level, and social distance is enforced by legislation. With Indian doctors there is the possibility of greater intimacy and of love affairs leading to marriage. Nurses said that Indian men in general were more courteous and polite than Africans.

> They get up for a nurse in a bus, causing less polite African men to threaten to beat them, accusing them of wanting to take us.

> Indians talk more politely to nurses but nurses are afraid to go with them because they are afraid of trouble from Africans.

However, most nurses were opposed to Indian-African intimacy, largely because Indian men appeared ashamed to carry on open relationships with African girls and seldom contemplated marriage. I quote two of many comments:

> African girls are despised for going to Indian men. If they loved these Indians, I would not say it is bad, but they don't go with them during the day. There is a tendency for nurses who have affairs with Indians to stick together, probably because they feel the rest are against them.

> If my sister fell in love with an Indian, I would try to stop her. As Africans, we should not fall in love with anybody of any other race. It is not likely at all that the man takes it seriously enough to marry her. I don't say that Africans are always serious, but at least you have better grounds for hoping.

African nurses expressed strong preference for the company of African doctors, both inside and outside the hospital. Not only is there easy communication but African doctors are said to show greater sympathy and understanding for the African patient. "After all," as a nurse explained, "African customs are part of the background of the African doctors."

The relationship between the nurses themselves is also racially regulated. Indian nurses are relatively few but are distinguished by culture and often religion from Africans, and the attitude toward them depends in part on the regulations of the hospital. Africans recognize that the general behavior of the Indian girls is more subdued and inhibited, that they do not touch alcohol, nor dance or mix freely with men, and that their appetites are culturally more restricted. Some hospitals make no official concessions to such differences; in others Indians receive special food and various privileges, such as permission to visit their families more frequently. Though the Indian nurses said that they had not asked for special consideration, African nurses resented it as favoritism. Preferential treatment restricts association on the basis of equality. In times of crisis, these concessions are made positive grievances, both against the authorities and Indians in general. But in hospitals where Indian nurses "stay with us, eat with us, sleep with us, and treat us as equal human beings, we regard them as such too, and accept them." There is however little doubt that the difficult Indian-African interaction outside the hospital impinges on interaction within the ward.

Between White and African nurses of the same status, there is often a mild joking relationship, but seldom real intimacy, and the joking is primarily from White to African, and not vice versa. African nurses are afraid to answer back lest they be accused of being "cheeky," and they said that when complaints were made to the authorities, the word of the White nurse carried more weight. But African nurses very carefully pointed out that their relationship with specific White nurses was often very good and based on mutual respect. What they resented was the automatic assumption of superiority and the delegation of power on the basis of color alone. The older nurses in particular resented being ordered about by a young White sister with less experience and competence than they had themselves. One informant commented that these White nurses impeded the effective running of the wards because they lacked experience and stood around or sat in the duty room: they were theoretical, whereas African Sisters had to get down to the job. African nurses are aware that their salaries are far less than the salaries of White nurses with the same professional qualification and that unemployment and pensions are also racialistically calculated.

Between African nurses there is a consciousness of identity. Hospitals do not recruit on a tribal basis, and large hospitals with high reputations bring together girls from many different tribes and even different provinces. Thus girls came to McCord Zulu Hospital not only from Natal but from the Cape, Transvaal, and the three High Commission Territories, and, in addition to Zulu, they represented six different mother tongues. Isolated from kin and in strange surroundings, new bonds are formed through shared experiences and mutual interests. The following quotation indicates a widely expressed reaction: "Friendship is not decided by the place from which you come, but you will always mix with people you feel free with. Friendship in general follows provincial lines simply because you know those people from the same place as yourself."

Nurses recognize that differences in cultural background may restrict the development of friendship, and some out-group stereotyping is inevitable. Cape nurses pride themselves on a longer educational tradition and greater Westernization, and also consider the town girls more friendly and compatible than the country girls. It appears that tribalism becomes subordinate to professional interests and wider loyalties, but remains a potential source of conflict. When nurses of different groups quarrel, insults may take a tribal twist. But overtly, tribalism, unlike racialism, is not a clearly divisive element in the hospital.

The dominant position of the White nurse is culturally rationalized. The main allegations are that African nurses cannot carry responsibility, that they lack the quality of kindness to their patients, are often neglectful and sometimes even cruel, and that they are careless with equipment. Comparisons between African and White nurses reflect unfavorably on the African in general, though recognition is given to outstanding individuals. For example, a senior nursing official said:

> There is a considerable difference on the whole in African and European nurses. The odd African nurse can be found who, when trained, has fully adopted Western ways, but that is only one in a few thousand. We have a sister at King Edward, for example, who is in charge of a hostel of 400. She is highly respected and the hostel is beautifully run. In the majority of cases, if you put Africans in charge of a ward, the equipment and discipline deteriorate.

A sister tutor at a nursing conference said that nursing as Europeans know it did not come naturally to non-Europeans, that they seemed unsympathetic, and that their attitude to male patients was often cruel, because they were suddenly in a position to give orders to their men.

In opposition to these adverse criticisms is the evaluation by some White doctors that when African nurses are given responsibility and respect they respond well, but that when duties are arbitrarily imposed and there is persistent supervision, the self-reliance of the nurses is undermined. Generalizations of cruelty or neglect of patients have not been substantiated, and undue publicity has been given to isolated incidents. The many different qualities of both patients and nurses are bound to produce some conflict, and the nurse as a public servant bears the brunt of blame. When the nurse is African, any failure on her part is racialistically interpreted. African nurses themselves point out that in many non-European hospitals wards are overcrowded and there are too few African nurses to give adequate, let alone praiseworthy, service. Their load of patients is much higher than in European hospitals. Criticism, they say, should be directed against the hospital administration, and not against the African nurse.

Viewed objectively, it is clear that in addition to racial prejudice, differences in cultural values and administrative organization underlie most of these contradictory assessments. African women are accustomed to the authority of men and older women. Respect is shown by social distance, and enterprise is primarily between peers. In the cooperative enterprise of the hospital, by reason of its bureaucratic structure, differences in rank are expressed in the power to enforce orders. Senior nurses, irrespective of age, must assume command, and junior nurses must obey. White nurses, associated with the over-all power of a pigmentocracy, assume the right to exact obedience. African nurses have no such recognized claim.

The nurses' relationships to patients are affected by reciprocal status positions, and vary with factors of age, sex, and education. Many said that they preferred to work with children, both because of their love of children and because they could exercise their authority without challenge. They have difficulties with uneducated women and with uneducated or semieducated townsmen, as the following comments illustrate:

> Women patients are spiteful and sensitive to orders by other women.

> Uneducated women are the worst patients. If they are older than we are, they don't like us for telling them what to do, and if they are our age, they are jealous of our position.

> It is easiest to deal with educated patients. The uneducated men from the country are also all right. They know what respect means. The greatest trouble comes from the *tsotsis,* who respect nobody.

Behavior toward the sick is further complicated by the traditional attitude to pain in many southern African societies. African men and women are trained to control their expression of suffering, and initiation rites, where still practiced, stress bravery and demand fortitude. Men brought into the casualty wards with terrible injuries behave with self-control often commented upon by Westerners, but expected of them by their own people. Similarly, African women in difficult birth seldom cry aloud, not because they are insensitive to the pain but because it is contrary to the mores. Sympathy may be felt, but the sick must not be encouraged to indulge in their symptoms; to submit to illness is believed to provide witches and sorcerers with the opportunity to be fatally effective. Many African nurses have little understanding of the Indian attitude toward illness, and express impatience at the unashamed weeping of Indian women and the relatively weak physique of Indian men. African nurses who retain this type of traditional outlook are committed to standards described and condemned by Whites as hard, cruel, and unsympathetic. And even nurses who accept the tenets of Christianity do not consider that kindness, which is very highly rated in African society, should be expressed in indulgence and a permissive attitude to weakness.

Technological differences give rise to special problems of adjustment. Country girls with the necessary academic qualifications may have little knowledge of the Western way of life, and African conditions in urban slums are no introduction to hospital standards. Some of the nurses come from Western-type homes, others from a traditional background. Nurses themselves are very conscious of the cultural differences which may appear trivial but are heavily charged with emotion. A girl from the country recalled:

> When I came from school into the hospital, I was quite lost. What was written in the books I had been taught, was not what I found in the hospital. I had never been inside a White man's house before. I had washed my clothes in the river and ironed on a stone. I think one of the hardest things for me was to squeeze my feet into the shoes they gave at this hospital.

In an animated group discussion, third-year trainees laughingly but strongly criticized a matron who had written to their parents inviting their opinion on a matter of hospital discipline. They pointed out that many of the parents were quite illiterate, that they had never been inside a hospital or any other White man's institution, that they were afraid to displease the matron in case it affected their daughter's career, and that they would therefore try to answer in a way pleasing to the matron. And all agreed that the matron should first have discussed the matter with them, in order to know the extent to which she could rely on the replies of the parents.

The Florence Nightingale tradition is obviously not part of traditional African culture, but the handing over of a lighted lamp has acquired a meaningful symbolism in the graduation ceremonies of African nurses in various hospitals. In essays written by all newcomers at the largest training school in Durban, on the subject of "Why I Took Up Nursing," the reasons varied from the utilitarian to the philanthropic; the majority of students said they wanted "to help the sick" and "help mankind." Motives are always difficult to assess, and the overtly expressed may not be the real reason behind action, but there is ample evidence that Africans have come to recognize nursing as a noble profession, and that the nurses themselves are aware of the ideal. In response to questionnaires, the quality mentioned most frequently as desirable was kindness, and the one most undesirable, laziness. It was also clear that the image which the nurses had of the profession involved a strong element of compliance; independence appeared relatively unimportant.

Behavior toward colleagues and patients is part of the broader institutional context. In mission hospitals, the staff is more carefully selected for moral qualities, and Africans receive more courteous consideration. The matron of a large mission hospital stated: "We insist on the use of the word African, and patient and staff must be treated as human beings." In some mission hospitals all facilities are shared by the staff; in others there is segregation of living quarters. At provincial hospitals, even if the superintendent and matron are sympathetic, White doctors may treat Africans as inferiors, and refer to them as "natives." The general pattern is one of racial segregation outside of professional duties and intimate personal relations across the color bar are difficult.

African nurses relate both moral and material factors in their assessment of hospitals. The respect for human dignity in the mission hospital is linked with a more severe discipline and lower rates of pay during the long period of training. Nurses complained that at McCord's they were not allowed male visitors except in the public lounge, nor might they walk with a man in the street when in uniform, nor were they allowed to visit their families even on their days off. One informant concluded: "They are afraid that if we sleep at home we will become pregnant. They treat us like children here; life is too short for such strictness." At the same time the nurses appreciated the ethical content of their training and the high reputation of McCord nurses for devotion and discipline.

The relative value attached to particular conditions varies with individual attitudes. A mission-trained Sister who later moved to a provincial hospital stated:

> The Christian atmosphere at McCord's never gave one a chance to complain. I felt guilty if I wanted to complain. It was also an odious thing to do because my parents were supporting me. When I came to King Edward's, they knew nothing about prayers for patients and nurses, which we had enjoyed. You need to have something to help you feel for a patient, to help you feel what he is suffering—his agony. A nurse must heal not by medicines alone, but also by personality. We who have trained at McCord's felt

rather superior to the other nurses, but stayed on because of the pay.

Another informant, also at King Edward, thought that the treatment of nurses depended on the character of the matron and superintendent, and instanced the improvements introduced by a new matron:

> She has only been here two months, but has already arranged for meetings with staff, and is willing to listen to us, and not just order us about. She is even wanting to build a chapel. She sees you can have religion even in a provincial hospital.

It seems more likely that institutional arrangements limit the role of matron and superintendent, and that the granting of greater responsibility and the recognition of individual worth at a mission hospital such as McCord's encourage nurses to dedicate themselves to the ideals of the profession.

The nurse is identified with Westernization and modernization. At social gatherings she is introduced as "Miss or Mrs. X, Staff Nurse at such-and-such a hospital," and is seated with other educated guests. Nurses see themselves as educated, Christian, civilized, and sophisticated, and formulate for themselves norms selected somewhat at random from observations of "decent" White middle-class and mission school behavior. Many nurses dress smartly, wear high heels, straighten their hair, and glamorize their appearance. It is considered not becoming for a nurse to drink excessively, smoke in public, use obscene language, fight or shout in the street. Her recreational activities include tennis, ballroom dancing, parties, cinemas, and the reading of women's magazines. The training in nursing is also a training in urban sophistication.

African nurses are conscious of their identity as an elite group. They discussed very articulately several categories of their own people whom they considered different from themselves. The first basic distinction was between the educated and the uneducated; the dividing line was not altogether rigid, but most agreed on Standard VIII, the minimum qualification for entry into the nursing profession itself. The educated were further subdivided into the "very educated," which included all people with postmatriculation training, not necessarily university degrees. The uneducated were subdivided into those who were able to read and write a European language, English or Afrikaans, and those who knew only the vernacular.

These distinctions were correlated with religion and morality. There were "Christians" who were "educated and civilized, true believers." And there were "traditionalists," who were also "civilized but not educated." In between were the "no-goods," variously labeled *"ulova"* (from loafer), *ihuzu, umhumushi, tsotsi,* children of Mkumbane (a local slum), and women described as *onontorotyi* (rubbish). In group discussions nurses referred to these people as "the enemy" and viewed them as both physical and social dangers.

> The *tsotsis* want us and they also despise us because they know we despise them.

> If a nurse is in uniform or not, they stand in front of her and say in Zulu, "Hi, stop there," and try to date her. If she says no they abuse her and may even hit her. She must keep a pleasant face. If they ask her name she should give a false name and if her address, the wrong address.

> Perhaps the men behave like this toward us because they are jealous, knowing that we won't marry them. As patients they have to listen to us.

> They hate us and insult us. If they hear us speaking English they shout and swear at us and say we are trying to attract other nations because we straighten our hair and wear lipstick and nail polish. They call us "cheap line." The latest term was "two and one half cent piece."

Tsotsis have no respect for the person, and nurses have considerable justification for their attitude. A recent report describes how African women wearing lipstick or jeans or straight hair were grabbed and pinned to the ground. They were told that their mouths had "gone rusty," and sandpaper was used in several instances to remove the lipstick. Their hair was forcibly cut off. The women appear to have organized in self-protection, and two assailants were put out of action with shots from pest sprayers filled with ammonia. A nurse, speaking on behalf of her colleagues, said: "Let them come with their scissors; we'll eliminate them like flies, as the vermin they are" (*The Star,* Overseas Edition, August 3, 1963). The nurses distinguish themselves very sharply from the *onontorotyi* women, who are described as wearing "tight skirts, hair in bangs, much cream to lighten the skin, high heels, and big earrings." They are much more "flashy" than the well-dressed nurse. "*Onontorotyi* are very jealous because we have decent, well-paid jobs and they haven't, and they know the men are after us and not them."

The loafers and loose people are clearly distinguished from the traditionalists. "We feel at home with traditional people because they have respect. Nurses don't frequent shebeens and drunkenness is only common among low class nurses who are also prepared to talk quite freely about their adventures and experiences."

Though nurses are relatively wealthy, very few mentioned wealth as an index of superiority. Poverty does not yet identify an African with lack of civilization. Thus the group described as "children of the slum [Mkumbane]" included some who were "very rich and smart crooks." One informant put it neatly: "Class difference does not lie in education or wealth but in moral behavior. There are 'high bugs' who work for higher ethical ideals, the middle who try to imitate the high bugs, but fail in one way or another, and the low group that doesn't even try. They are satisfied with what they are."

In South Africa, stratification is primarily along racial lines, and occupations coincide less closely with social class. An African household can bring together persons occupying roles far apart in prestige, because other identifications, identifications of kinship and shared activities are more important. Many nurses have close relatives who are illiterate manual laborers—a brother who is a road worker or a domestic servant or an unskilled factory hand. The mother of one nurse is employed as a cleaner in the same hospital. Though most of the nurses listed professionals among their closest friends, others included laborers and domestic servants. Social snobbery is not crystallized, and nurses acknowledge the sacrifices required for their education and do not reject their less educated kin.

In densely populated urban centers, the educated are less formally distinguished from the uneducated than in the smaller townships or rural areas where personal relationships are more intensive and strangers cannot easily be fitted into the established pattern. At the same time, the nurse or teacher in the country has a smaller group of people with whom to associate on the basis of special interest, and may be brought into more frequent contact with the uneducated.

Religion becomes an important factor in identification. Christians, educated or uneducated, distinguish themselves from non-Christians, who may style themselves as "the people" or be pejoratively labeled as "heathens." In the early days, Western dress, set by missionary standards, divided Christian and civilized from pagan and savage. For nurses, the uniform, which identified them with White colleagues, was a prized mark of acceptance as well as of achievement.

The acceptance of nursing as a profession requires at least superficially the adoption of a Western way of life. The norms of hygiene and diet imposed on behavior in the hospital conflict with those which operate in the more traditional homes, but spatial separation mitigates open opposition. Conservative parents are often proud of a daughter who has become a nurse, but they may not change their own way of life to conform to the standards to which she has grown accustomed. It appears that it is easier for the nurse when with her family to accept their standards than to attempt to reform them. However, nurses cannot openly be traditionalists, especially in urban centers. They are prevented by the most potent factor, the sanction of ridicule, from identifying with "the illiterate and the primitive."

Nursing brings high economic rewards and there is a great demand for training. It is one career open to women even after marriage and the birth of children. The preliminary years of education are treated as an investment. Sometimes relatives other than the parents are prepared to pay for the schooling of a bright child, on the understanding that after she has qualified, she will not only return the full amount, but help support her benefactor. The bride price of nurses is as high "as for the daughters of kings." They are the princesses of the modern community. Lobola is accepted as part of Christian marriage whether or not the husband is a professional, and nurses attach sufficient importance to this old custom to be willing to contribute toward it themselves if necessary.

Nurses are not allowed to marry during their training, and should an unmarried trainee become pregnant she is immediately dismissed. Traditionally, marriage follows a period of sexual experimentation which usually starts soon after puberty. Marriage is considered the normal relationship of adults, and nurses considered that 21 to 25 was the best age for a woman to marry. Education and professional training have often postponed marriage, and increased the risk of premarital pregnancy. Childbearing is considered the main biological function of adult women and some parents object to restrictions placed on the girls during the long training period. An educated African man argued: "This is the time that a woman should bear, she is full grown and strong, and should not have to wait. A woman who does not bear wastes herself." On the other hand, the promise of a future economic security makes other parents support a regime of strict supervision during training. Nurses also point out that the traditional techniques of preventing conception are no longer acceptable to urban men, and unless they are prepared to follow the mores, they will lose their potential husbands.

A conservative mother tried to dissuade her daughter from taking up nursing, arguing that: "Seeing so many men you will lose respect for them. What sort of wife will you be? You will know too much." And a conservative father stated: "You will expect too much and men will be reluctant to marry you."

A nurse's relatives, as well as the nurse herself, are eager that she marry well. She is constantly told that she must pick "the best man for her husband, someone special, someone respectable and wealthy. You get married because you want to be protected, not to support your husband." But it may be difficult for nurses to find husbands as educated as themselves. Marriage to men of lower status is considered preferable to spinsterhood. Some nurses have deliberately remained single, a situation unacceptable in traditional society and incompatible with the traditional socioeconomic structure. The Christian ideal of monogamy is generally advocated by nurses, but many thought it so foreign to the nature of African men that it could not really be enforced. They also pointed out that monogamy was one of the reasons why boy friends were afraid to commit themselves, and sexual rivalry was a frequent source of tension between nurses. The acquisition by women of education and Christianity appeared to militate against the security of marriage.

The laws of the country reflect the marginal position of the African woman, whose legal status was described by a group of experts as being "in a state of confusion, not to say chaos." On many questions that commonly arise, it is hard for lawyers, let alone laymen, to understand precisely what a woman's rights are.[2] Custody of children, rights of inheritance, and other socioeconomic claims vary in detail from tribe to tribe, but generally speaking under traditional law a woman is subordinate all her life to males, to the father before marriage, to the husband and his kin after marriage. The principle that African women are "perpetual minors" is codified in Natal and, subject to numerous modifications, is the basis of law in the other provinces. Inconsistent attempts have at times been made to differentiate between educated and uneducated, and exemption from "customary law" was occasionally granted individual women who could produce the necessary character and educational references from Whites in support of their application. The system of exemption, which removed many of the disabilities in African customary law, has been abolished, but under specific circumstances women may still obtain emancipation from the control of a male.

Emancipation rests ultimately in the discretion of a native commissioner, and government policy is largely directed at gaining the support of rural men who benefit from their present legal domination. The procedure for emancipation is not widely known. Many nurses are eager to retain their earnings and invest in property or in savings, or in other ways be independent, but their legal status is as subordinate as that of the least educated of African women, except in those instances where they have found channels for obtaining emancipation. African nurses labor under the double disadvantage of being educated women in a male-dominated society and of being Africans in a White-dominated society.

Several of the more articulate African nurses said that they themselves accept the legal inferiority of women in African society as cus-

2. Julius Lewin, "The Legal Status of African Women," *Race Relations Journal,* 26 (1959), p. 152.

tomary, and only deplore it when relations with husbands or guardians become tense. Then they find themselves caught in a web of anachronistic laws from which there is little escape. Similarly, many African nurses born into a plural society accept their role as subordinate to Whites and are only beginning to voice demands for equality and freedom. This growing consciousness among African nurses is part of broader movements operating at two levels—first, the emancipation of the African woman, and second, the emancipation of the African people. The emancipation of African women derives much of its force from economic pressures on traditional society—the necessity for women to obtain money to supplement cultivation in impoverished rural areas, the long absence of the men as migrant laborers, and the responsibility which often falls entirely on the women at the present time to raise and educate the children. Psychologically as well, the women are liberated by the realization that the male occupations of traditional society do not carry prestige in the modern world, and that their own economic contribution is as important. At the national level, poverty, bad housing, absence of proper health facilities, restrictions on movement and occupation, summary destruction of illegal shacks, and the raids and assaults by police affect even the most educated nurse through her network of relations in the community. And nurses are not immune from the discriminatory legislation of apartheid.

Nurses as a group have taken very limited action on broad political issues. Educated men frequently commented that the nurses were mainly interested in marriage and were politically unaware. "They are only concerned with nail polish and status," and "They come into contact with a certain amount of misery and want to help it but don't realize the political causes. They just go out with their boy friends and come back to the same protected life. Their boy friends don't speak politics with them, as it would just be a lecture. Their ambitions are shaped by the fashion and beauty columns which constitute their main literature. Smartness in appearance is what they desire above all." The nurses agreed that they have little political involvement. Some spoke vaguely of the need for unity, equality, and cooperation. Others were not prepared to risk their positions by taking part in political action, or they were satisfied with the status quo. Some were cynical: "Where will action take us?" Many were apathetic. Only when they felt their own positions directly threatened did nurses take positive action. It might perhaps be logical to expect that African nurses would be strongly anti-White. But this is not altogether the case. On the contrary, there appears to be a general tolerance of other racial groups, especially Whites. The replies to the questionnaires by the nurses at McCord's expressed little racialism. On the question of intermarriage, a recognized touchstone of prejudice, over 50 per cent were against intermarriage, but mainly on the grounds of discriminatory classification of children and differences in cultural background: very few argued for "racial purity." Nearly 50 per cent of the nurses stated that they had "no problems" working with "other races," interpreted almost exclusively as Whites, some of them mentioning that it was an advantage to work with people of different cultures and learn their customs. Those who replied that they had specific race difficulties mentioned "the color bar" and the inferior status of Africans in education and standard of living.

Sociologically, there are many circumstances which might mitigate racialism among African nurses. First, African nurses are recognized by Whites as an elite among the African people, and, within the limits of discrimination, they receive preferential treatment. Second, the professional world of the nurses is created by skills introduced by Whites, who set the standard of competence, and whose approval is desired and required for prestige and promotion. Third, in a plural society, people relate themselves primarily to their own defined in-group, and African nurses see themselves as part of the African population. Many of their personal problems arise from their contacts with the uneducated in their own race. Hence they express stronger antagonism and aggression against "the rubbish" amongst their own people than against White outsiders. Fourth, the color cleavage is part of an historical cultural context into which Africans and White South Africans are born. People accept fundamental status relationships as given. Only when these relationships are challenged do people take action in particular situations. Fifth, it follows that new groups and alliances are constantly being formed as part of social development. With the political awakening of Africans, nurses are beginning to identify with specific patterns of political behavior which may or may not link with wider movements. As long as the nurse is professionally contained within the present medical structure operating through racially regulated institutions, her political action is neutralized. She must either accept her protected position or move into a political, nonprofessional milieu. Finally, the nurse is in a unique position in the particular type of plural society characteristic of South Africa. She is trained to provide a basic social service for her people in an institution which brings her into direct intimate contact with Whites trained in the same profession. Even African teachers on mixed staffs in mission boarding schools are not bound together in such intimate physical and emotional contact. The patient is not a pupil, and the ward is not a classroom. Emphasis on idealism and service to the community are part of the indoctrination of the nursing profession, and this helps to maintain peaceful association even in times of intense antagonism. The functioning of a Red Cross in times of war illustrates this principle on a wider field.

CHAPTER 16

Mainly Residual Professions

THIS CHAPTER gathers together many of the remaining occupations of the bourgeoisie—the lawyers and doctors, journalists and writers, the social workers, and the senior civil servants (both Government and municipal). They are relatively few in number, and many of the professions are not represented. Architecture, dentistry, and accountancy have not been opened to Africans. For a short period, the University of Witwatersrand offered Africans training as engineers; one African qualified in 1961, and one is still in training, but this avenue was closed by the Government. The Government is, however, now opening the profession of pharmacist to Africans.

The cavalier grouping of residual occupations in a single chapter carries no suggestion that they lack significance. On the contrary, they all represent important public roles. African lawyers and doctors, by their achievements, demonstrate the prowess of the African race. If they are in private practice, they enjoy some freedom from the built-in controls over African occupations, and a source of substantial income —not derived from the White man—which gives them a slight measure of independence: they are not entirely without defenses against racial discrimination. And by reason of their education and prestige, they are the potential leaders of the political movements.

It is sometimes said, with reference to the now sovereign African states, that during the struggle for independence men in the liberal professions formed the militant elite, not being haltered, like the moderate elites, by employment as civil servants. Clearly there are also factors involved other than the intrinsic quality of an independent occupation and a humanistic tradition, and these other factors may be decisive. Thus the professions of lawyer and doctor in South Africa have changed far less than their political role. Lawyers and doctors were active leaders of the African National Congress, not only during the many years of conciliation but also during the last decade of militant action and incipient revolution. Hence, the interpretation of the changing political ideology of Congress is to be sought in the changing social situation and not in the inherent qualities of the liberal professions. Moreover the political reactions of lawyers and doctors are varied. Some withdrew as the Congress became more radical in its demands. Others helped to shape these demands and the militant programs to achieve them, apparently indifferent to the personal hazards: neither their education, their prestige, nor a modicum of independence has protected them from the full range of repression—trials as Communists or traitors and bans against membership in organizations, attendance at meetings, and movement outside narrowly defined areas. Two lawyers, leaders of the African National Congress, are now political refugees, while a third is a political prisoner, after a period in which—unlike the Scarlet Pimpernel with whom he was compared—he moved underground in his own country and surfaced outside of it.

Journalists and writers have also been active in the African political movements, and again there is a long tradition of political involvement. Quite apart from any specifically political role, they are potentially leaders of opinion, but restricted by low standards of education among Africans, racial barriers, lack of an independent African press, limited opportunities for publication, and a dependent status, for the most part, as employees in White organizations, including the propaganda departments of the Government. African civil servants are part of the structure of power and at the same time its objects: they wield power, though on the periphery, and they wield it against themselves. At the same time, they are acquiring the skills of government, looking toward the higher posts in the administration, and preparing, perhaps, for a future role as ruling bureaucrats. In any event, they provide the cadres of trained African administrators.

Social workers, like ministers of religion in the White controlled denominations, have contact with varied layers of the African population, bridging the gap between the uneducated, the semieducated, and the educated. They have a public role, but as yet little political significance, differing in this respect from ministers of religion. Whatever the status of ministers, whether employees or spiritual entrepreneurs in charge of their own enterprises, and whatever the spiritual content of their services, they perform a political role. And this is equally true whether they direct attention to individual salvation and compensation in a paradise of hereafters, or whether they offer Messianic hope for the future on this earth, selecting their texts from Exodus and likening their people to the Israelites under the oppression of Egypt, or whether they identify with the political aspirations of Africans here and now, and invest with deep spiritual meaning their desire for freedom. By contrast, social workers seem politically irrelevant. But they are in touch with the populace, and at the same time, they move easily in the elite of African society. The importance of these occupations merits more extended discussion than is given here.

During the main period of my research, there were five African lawyers practicing in Durban at one time or another: two come from Natal, two from the Cape, and one from Basutoland. Four are of middle-class background, and one is the son of a laborer. Their educational qualifications are higher than those of many White lawyers: three have both an arts and a law degree, one an arts degree with a postgraduate diploma in education and the law certificate, while the fifth was content with the minimum requirement of a law certificate. None has ventured to practice as an advocate, presumably because there would not be sufficient African lawyers to support him, and briefs are expected to flow in racial channels.

It was only in 1950 that the first African clerk was articled in Durban. Payment of premiums was an obstacle until the Natal Law Society forbade the practice in 1942. According to one African lawyer, Africans in Natal tended to regard law as a European preserve; it did not occur to them that the law was permissive, allowing Africans to serve articles of apprenticeship, and when they realized this, they had difficulty in becoming articled. They were dependent for articles on sympathetic White lawyers, of whom there were not very many in Durban—at least not many who were sympathetic enough to admit African clerks to their own offices. Several White firms, however, opened their doors, as did Indian lawyers, who had broken earlier into the White preserve, and in 1961 there were about ten Africans serving articles in the Durban area, and several others studying law—over twenty all told, including the practicing lawyers.

The many statutory offences which apply to Africans, the systematic repression of African political activity, and the troubled times generally ensure a large and regular flow of work, so that there is little or no competitive strain with White firms specializing in African legal work, or with Indian firms. The first African lawyer to start private practice ascribed his success not so much to ability as to favorable circumstances: he was well known, having served his articles in a popular office with a large African practice, and there was an element of growing African consciousness, people wanting to go to their own people —they were proud of African lawyers. The second lawyer to qualify expected that his practice would be confined to Africans, but finds that he also has Indian and some European clients: "people are interested in quality."

The lawyers in Durban complain little of discrimination and this is surprising. There is incongruity of status—White petty officials in the law courts, many of them Afrikaners, working with and serving African lawyers. In some courts in other areas, African lawyers have been subjected to the indignity of separation, so as to avoid the contamination of equality in pleading from the same bar with White prosecutors. An African lawyer in Cape Town was deprived of his practice by the simple device of requiring him to vacate his office in the urban area. Toward the end of 1961, two African lawyers in Johannesburg received similar notices to leave their offices under the Group Areas Act. In a memorandum, African lawyers and articled clerks complained that the policy was apparently designed ultimately to make it impossible for Africans to appear in the ordinary courts of the land, and to restrict them to tribal tribunals under Bantu Authorities. They pointed out that it was implicit in the notices (received from the Johannesburg City Council) that Africans must be restricted to practice exclusively among their own people, and more particularly of their own village or location; and they drew attention to the insuperable difficulties in conducting practice from an African township. The notices were withdrawn, but the moral was clear. The Government seems at pains to instruct African lawyers in private practice that their independence is spurious, merely by grace of their White masters, and that real independence can only be achieved by revolutionary change. Some of the African lawyers have clearly mastered this lesson.

Many factors would seem to account for the relative freedom from discrimination in Durban. The presence of established Indian areas in the urban center of Durban, from which Africans conduct their practices, would seem to make confinement to the locations under the Group Areas Act somewhat outrageous. In the courts, Indian lawyers, some very able, charming, and tactful men, pioneered the frontiers of discrimination, so that the entry of Africans as lawyers, and not as criminals, would have occasioned less shock. The ethics of practice and the framework of legal principles control to some extent the open expression of prejudice. And the antagonisms between Afrikaans- and English-speaking Whites may have some relevance, as indicated by the comments of two African lawyers:

> The average civil servant here who is Afrikaans feels oppressed by the English. He is anxious to show how anti-English he is by attending to me before an English attorney. This happens also in the Police Force, and they tend to give you better treatment. Also, they like to tell you that I am not well treated by the English. I speak to them in Afrikaans.

> I speak Afrikaans and I think this is very important in dealing with them. They feel that I come from some other part of the country and they will sometimes make remarks about the English people in Natal.

Apparently some of the Afrikaner officials feel less revulsion for the Africans than for the English, and this lesser degree of revulsion becomes a bond of relative cordiality in certain contexts.

Whatever the reasons, African lawyers in Durban seem well pleased with their reception. They comment that there is no discrimination even in the country courts; that magistrates try to be extra careful, so as to prove that they are not racial; that the staff, the magistrates, the police, and the White lawyers are very courteous, that they do not distinguish at all; that when magistrates meet you out of court, they will speak to you; that the reception by judicial officers has been very gratifying and contrary to expectations. Only one complained of the public prosecutors, that most of them suffered from complexes because their knowledge of law was inferior, and that relationships were mostly official, perhaps "because of the invisible curtain."

If there is little or no discrimination attaching to the practice of their professions, the African lawyers in Durban are nevertheless subject to the general discrimination. Two have managed to avoid criminal courts, in other than their official capacities, and they also seem to have avoided political involvement, one being detached from public affairs and the second committed to sports administration. The remainder bear the stigmata of race. One was a school teacher before he became a lawyer. According to his account, he opposed Bantu Education, was charged with public violence, and spent a week in prison before his acquittal on that charge; failing to find employment as a teacher in South Africa, he taught in Swaziland at a mission school for a period of eighteen months, losing that post as a result of erroneous representations in regard to his political views made by the South African Government. The second, a leading member of the African National Congress, was among the innocent men arraigned in the mass treason trial; he was arrested without charge at the beginning of the emergency in 1960, secured an almost immediate release through the courts, escaped into exile, and now practices in Basutoland. The third, an active member of the Liberal Party, was arrested by the police under the curfew laws while he was returning to his home after a meeting of the Institute of Race Relations. Later, in a complicated incident, in which the police interfered with a young White man who had called for members of an African concert party, he was not only assaulted but charged —a conventional police technique. And in 1962, he was acquitted, on appeal, of a charge of continuing the activities of an illegal organization (when as a member of a committee of leading Africans he had sought to build an African united front), and his sentence of twelve months imprisonment was set aside.

There were only two African doctors in private practice in Durban during the period of research. Most of the doctors were serving as interns in either the King Edward VIII Hospital, a large and over-crowded provincial hospital for Africans and Indians, with teaching

ILLUSTRATIONS

Plate 1. Sports officials lead their football teams onto the playing fields.

Plate 2. Elite of the African bourgeoisie caged in the Treason Trial.

Plate 3. Honoring a graduate.

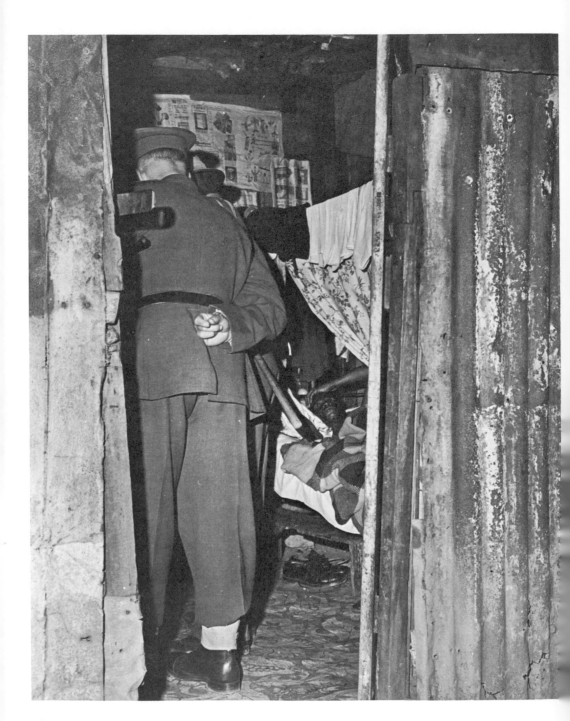

Plate 4. Routine police raid.

Plate 5. Experiments in Africanization: The Minister of Bantu Administration and Development fosters African idiom.

Plate 6. Experiments in Africanization: Revival of traditional costume by wives of African political leaders.

wards for the University of Natal, or in the McCord Zulu Hospital, a small missionary hospital for non-Whites. They contrasted the good personal relations, the respect accorded the doctor, the devotion to the patient, the discipline of the nurses, and the freedom from any form of racial discrimination in the missionary hospital with the impersonal relations, the lax discipline of the nurses, the lack of appreciation for non-European doctors, and the racial discrimination and segregation in the provincial hospital.

It seems likely that most will enter private practice. Of the thirty-six African graduates during the period 1957–60, as shown in a list furnished by the assistant registrar of the Natal Medical School in March 1961, ten doctors were already in private practice, and twenty-one were still at McCord, King Edward VIII, or other hospitals. There was no information for four doctors, and one had died. The main openings, outside of private practice, are in government and provincial hospitals, where African doctors are subject to discrimination and White overlordship. Those who were assisted in their studies at the University of Natal by Government bursaries are under an obligation to repay half the sum advanced, to confine their practice to non-Europeans, and to practice in areas approved by the State until the loan is repaid. The salaries of African doctors in government service are, of course, discriminatory. Quite apart from the special situation of bursars, opportunities for specialization and for permanent posts in government service are only now being opened, and presumably they will be restricted. African doctors are beginning to be appointed as registrars, and in 1961 an African doctor, who had practiced for some years outside Durban, became Bantu District Surgeon for the district of Mapumulo. An official announcement of his appointment mentioned also that in the local churchyard of Mapumulo there is a tombstone to the African Doctor Nembula, who died in 1880 (*baNtu*, November 1961, p. 574). It has been a long journey, and the road is still steep.

Viewed from the outside, the discrimination against African doctors in King Edward VIII Hospital is not extreme, and certainly no more marked than the discrimination against most African ministers in the Anglican Church of South Africa (Church of the Province), which proclaims a liberal policy in race relations. In 1959, a report on behalf of a subcommittee of the South African Society of Medical Women (Natal) disclosed the following items of differentiation: salary, one sixteenth less (actually the discrepancy was higher, the non-White ratio at that time being about four-fifths in the case of interns, and a little over three-fifths for Grade I medical officers); provision of tea room facilities and of beds for White doctors on duty in the casualty ward, but not for non-Whites (one ward, maternity, was fully desegregated, however), some slight difference in the food provided; and white coats, of equal quality, marked with blue tabs for non-Whites and red for Whites —perhaps simply a laundry arrangement, since the doctors live in segregated quarters.

Viewed from the inside, the discrimination is not simply a source of minor irritation. The extent of the discrimination is perhaps less important than the fact of the discrimination. Indeed the more trivial the discrimination, objectively considered, the more obvious is its symbolic character. The saving in salary as a result of discrimination against non-White doctors has obviously no financial significance in the hospital budget nor any other direct significance. The rationale and the significance of the discrimination lie in the fact that it is a symbol of racial domination. An all-pervasive racial philosophy is thus asserted in the irrelevant context of medical care, and deep resentment is evoked precisely because the reaction is against the racialism, rather than any of its specific manifestations. That is to say, the discrimination has symbolic significance on both sides, for Whites and for non-Whites, and any incident of discrimination, however trivial in itself, may suddenly become weighted with all the connotations of racial strife in the wider society.

Race relations within the hospital have apparently improved over the last few years. At the time of my inquiries, in 1959 and 1960, resentment was directed more particularly against the administration. Other aspects of the training and work situation appeared to be satisfying. Initially, non-Whites had been suspicious of the proposed medical school: only inferior standards could explain the segregation. But good facilities and teaching, and skillful direction by the Dean, have fostered some pride in the Natal Medical School. Relations between African and White doctors were cordial, according to informants' accounts, and senior African students in the clinical years confirmed this impression of good relations with White doctors. Resentment might arise indirectly because of the discriminatory situation, rather than the work relationship, as indicated in the complaint by one doctor against the difference in salaries. "These Dutch boys get more than we, but do less work. Their mistakes are condoned." And there were two other complaints of greater latitude shown toward White doctors.

Friction might be expected in the relationship between African doctor and White nursing sister, an African man in a position of authority over a White woman. This would be in addition to the normal clash between the authority of the Sister, often with many years of experience, and the authority of the newly-fledged doctor. I had understood from a senior official in the nursing services that matters were so arranged that the African doctor did not give the White Sister instructions. But when I put the question to an African doctor—do you have any difficulty in giving instructions to White Sisters—he appeared puzzled. "You give instructions to them in the same way as to others or rather you don't give any of them instructions. You say: 'Sister, will you kindly see to it that the patient has . . .' " In general, the doctors found the relationship satisfactory. One African woman doctor complained bitterly:

> You feel Sisters [White] are specially looking for something to report against Africans, not Whites. Perhaps because before we came, and it was not a teaching hospital, they were in control. White Sisters don't take instructions from us. You have an African Sister or staff nurse in the ward, and you give her instructions. Then the White Sister comes to the African staff. She may take no notice of you, behave as if you were not there. Some take it willingly. If they work with you, you give them instructions. If not, you avoid them.

In this case, the additional factor of rivalry between women undoubtedly entered into the relationship. At one time, the relationship between White Sisters and African doctors was strained, but there has been a selective process, with White Sisters who were not prepared to work with non-White doctors moving to other hospitals.

Senior students still had many complaints about White Sisters: they think students are to be tolerated because they cannot do anything about it; relations between students and Sisters (apparently all, White and non-White) are not good; White Sisters are definitely intolerable, and this applies to most African Sisters; if you approach a Sister to go into a ward, she will give you the cold shoulder or tell you that you are a bother; Sisters on the whole, and particularly White Sisters, are bossy; most African Sisters think students will take advantage of them, and White Sisters regard you as a potential danger because soon you will be their senior, they want to show you that you are right down there (this from a woman student). There was the inevitable traumatic experience.

> I remember at one time when I had broken a knee in a soccer game, I couldn't walk. I went to the hospital and reported in one of the Sisters' offices. She was not in. I decided to sit down and wait for her. When she came in she had so much to say about my sitting on a chair meant for Europeans, that I had to answer back. She immediately 'phoned the Superintendent and told him I was insolent and that I had sat on a chair reserved for Europeans.

One student commented that there was a European Sister who did not show any unpleasant reactions to the students: he had never expected to find a European who had no irritating habits.

There was no doubt some racial prejudice at work, and it could be directed more freely against students than doctors; but it seems probable, from the relative absence of complaints by the doctors, and the fact that students also complained about the African staff, that it was not so much racialism which the White Sisters expressed, as resentment of the nuisance students represented in the carrying out of heavy and demanding duties. Perhaps they were also compensating for the impending inequality of status, as the students qualified. Generally, the work relationship appeared to be relatively free from racialism. In the case of White Sisters—and they would provide a crucial test—official policy had helped to reduce racial tensions. For the rest, staff are working in a situation of high responsibility and under great pressure. The focus is the patient. In the tension of emergency work, of a struggle which may mean life or death, the professional duties are dominant. The relationships are between professionals rather than between members of different racial groups. The situation seems to be much the same as that in which people of the most varied backgrounds are drawn together in the face of a common danger. And the training of the doctor would be in the direction of rejecting racial considerations in the work situation, whether in connection with patients or colleagues. The fact, too, that many of the White doctors were trained in the open Universities of Cape Town and Witwatersrand probably eased the situation.

Resentment would tend to be expressed against the hospital administrators, since they are not directly involved in the work situation, and since most discriminations are imposed administratively. Impersonal relations are no doubt inevitable in so large a hospital, but resentment went beyond complaints of impersonality to expressions of antagonism and charges of racial prejudice. The following episodes were recounted in interviews, and are repeated, not as evidence of the facts stated, nor as evidence of the attitudes of any of the administrators, but rather as indicating some of the conflicts inherent in the situation:

> Then one early morning in Casualty a European woman and her husband brought in a servant. She called to the houseman: "Hey, Jim." She picked the wrong man. "I'm not Jim," he said, waving his finger at her. She thought him impertinent, the husband came along, there was an argument, the sister arrived, she called X. And then there was trouble. We were told we are civil servants, and however the public behaves, we must be courteous. How would a European civil servant in the magistrate's court react, if we said to him: "Hey John." We were told if we couldn't behave like that, then next time it happened we would have to leave. We were also told that Natives are called "John" and "Jim" in South Africa— we should be used to it.

Attitudes of people here [McCord's] are as between person and person with the patient being the center of activity. Down there [King Edward's] it is that between seniors and a junior who has to be driven to do his work and, of course, his race counts a great deal, e.g. something happened and Dr. Y blamed it on non-White doctors and medical students. It turned out to have been done by his White workmen. Workmen had been working near the doctors' quarters, using oxygen cylinders to close the road to motor traffic so that they could use step ladders without the danger of being knocked down by cars. As I said, they forgot to remove the cylinders when they knocked off at 5 P.M. In the morning Dr. Y came driving along this driveway. He found it obstructed at this point. Without asking anybody about it, he said it had been done by non-White doctors and medical students. He stopped nearly everyone who passed that area to tell him what education does to non-Europeans and how little it changes them. Later he learned that it was his workmen and not non-White doctors who had done it. He had to apologize to doctors and students.

The whole situation is charged with tension. There is first the tension which arises from the symbolic character of the discrimination, which I have already discussed. This symbolism has a further aspect. South African society is saturated in racialism, and almost any element can thus become a symbol of race and of racial conflict. Race relations in the hospital represent in microcosm the racial struggles in the wider society. And the African doctor is regarded as a representative of his people. At any moment, he becomes the prototype of the African race. It is thus difficult for the African doctor to emerge from the invidious racial matrix. An error is not a human error, an individual error, but evidence of the genetic inferiority of the African. And the African doctor may feel that he is on trial before a prejudiced judge and a loaded jury.

The attitude of the superintendent at King Edward is different from McCord's. At McCord's if you make an error in treatment and something happens to the patient, the Superintendent stands on your side, and acknowledges that everyone is subject to error. Here they ask "Why did you do that?" and you are made to feel that it is because you are a non-European. When we are on duty we never dream of leaving the grounds. White doctors do so and they may go off to the beach. Something may happen when they are away, but nothing is done, but if you do it then it is always said non-Europeans are this and that. We try to show them that we are responsible and we go to extremes to prove it. The non-

European houseman takes his duty seriously. If anything happens, Dr. Y takes the view that you are a non-European, that you are negligent, hopeless.

A second source of tension arises from sharp contrasts between the different perspectives, and from sharp contrasts between social environments. African doctors are at the very peak of African society. The achievement of medical status is such that many Africans have barely adjusted to this possibility for their own people. An African doctor is beyond the range of their normal expectations, and Africans accord their doctors the highest prestige. In the context of this perspective, any suggestion of inferiority in the wider society is all the more deeply wounding. And the discrimination in the hospital has no rationale, no moral justification: it cannot be dressed up. It is as if the two perspectives, the inflating perspective of an exaggerated prestige and the deflating perspective of racial inferiority, meet in the person of the African doctor.

The contrast in social environment has somewhat the same consequences. However discriminatory the hospital situation, and however much the hospital may reproduce characteristics of race relations in the outer society, the hospital represents a relatively idyllic multiracial environment. But the doctor lives in the outer society as well as in the hospital, and the racial conflicts of this society affect relationships in his professional world. Moreover, the doctor is obliged to adjust to these contrasting worlds. He moves rapidly to and fro between a situation of near equality and one of humiliating inferiority. It is like moving from light into darkness.

> As a medical you are a person enjoying life and the next moment you are looked down on. You go 'round the wards acting intelligent with other doctors, with European doctors. Then you go away, each separately. Now you are just a non-European. Then you meet them again shortly and you act intelligent and then you are back again. In a short space of time you are subjected to different phases. When you started to become a doctor you felt that on your own effort you could free yourself from a lowly station of life and you would be a free-thinking, independent person. For some, the situation in which the non-European doctor finds himself creates a feeling of frustration, a frank hatred. For others, there is the hope that things will sort out and one goes on hoping for the best.

The African doctor, of all professionals, is probably in the best position to avoid political involvement. He enjoys high prestige in his own community, and can derive a sense of social service, and the simultaneous gratification of profit, from private practice. Since his patients are Africans, generally speaking, there is less likelihood of interference through the tribal policies of the Government, though the doctor may be obliged to conduct his practice from a location. Perhaps he can even harden himself to the realization that many of the diseases he treats are social diseases, consequent upon poverty and discrimination. Inevitably, however, some doctors are drawn to militant action, more particularly since there is the respected tradition of African doctors serving in the African National Congress. And they bear the scars of the judicial process, whether arraigned as leader of a deputation which failed to disperse, or for the destruction of a reference book, or for high treason.

The occupation of social worker is not well-known in the African community although social workers are often featured in the social columns of the non-White press, and seem to be well-established among the social elite. This may be due to the fact that only small numbers are in practice. In 1959, according to official sources, there were ninety-nine African social workers employed in South Africa (*Bantu Education Journal*, October 1960, p. 468). Their occupational status is that of employees under White control, but their role is relatively unambiguous. They serve the welfare of the African community, with little suggestion of instrumental use in the political aims of the Government.

It is essentially in the field of social welfare that there has been an outpouring of good will, more particularly by English-speaking Whites. This is the reverse side of discrimination, the reaction of benevolence flowing directly into service for Africans. The provision of welfare services is by no means inconsistent with White privilege and domination, quite the reverse in fact, since largess and charity are the marks of a ruling estate. There is paternalism, but not of a punitive type. Government benefits and allowances are gravely discriminatory, and the welfare organizations themselves reflect the prevailing discrimination in the society at large, both in terms of salary scales and executive responsibility. But the field of social welfare is distinguished by the devotion and idealism of many of the voluntary workers.

The Durban Bantu Child Welfare Society may serve as an example of the social work environment of African social workers. It was established in 1935 by a combined committee of Africans and Europeans. One of the African foundation members, Mrs. I. Sililo, became the first secretary of the Society, and was in charge of the welfare work. Africans often regarded her as the "Child Welfare," and referred to "Mrs. Sililo's Society." The parent body is a major welfare agency, the South African National Council for Child Welfare. It is a federal body, consisting largely of autonomous affiliated Child Welfare societies, the European societies having direct representation, while the non-European societies have indirect representation in a Standing Committee on Non-European Child Welfare Work.

The Durban Bantu Child Welfare Society is largely controlled by a White voluntary committee, and by White supervisors, but with African participation. An African clergyman, Bishop Zulu, had been vice-chairman of the society, and he occasionally took the chair at meetings. At the end of 1960, the administrative and case work staff numbered seventeen (thirteen Africans and four Europeans), eight posts being qualified social workers' posts. The salary scale for a university qualified African woman social worker was in the range of £400 to £750 per annum, as compared with a scale, for similarly qualified Europeans, of £540 to £1040. The supervisory positions in the office were held by White women, but a non-European had previously been employed as a senior social worker at a salary of £45–£50 per month, and in 1961 an African woman was being trained for the position of case supervisor, at an expected annual salary of £575 rising to £750, the policy being to hand over responsibility to Africans. The prospective African supervisor felt challenged to prove that Africans were as capable as Whites, and to open up White posts for Africans, but she was finally attracted to welfare work in Swaziland. An African was Matron of the Infants' Home, and three crèches were also under African supervision.

The Government's policy of cleavage is now being applied to the field of social work. The basic principles were set out in the report of a Government committee inquiring into the financing of voluntary welfare organizations. It recommended that the social welfare care of families and persons be given within their national, cultural, and religious groups; that preference be accorded separate voluntary welfare organizations for the different non-European groups: that non-Europeans be encouraged to accept increasing responsibility for social work among their own people, and that in cases where Europeans were doing such work, this must be considered a temporary transitional phase.[1] Present policy is directed toward the realization of these principles, effective sanctions for the detachment of non-Whites from joint endeavor being provided by the withdrawal of subsidies, the provisions of the Group Areas Act and the Native Laws Amendment Act, and to some extent by the apprehensions of the White workers themselves.

The training of African social workers is now controlled by the Government. The Jan H. Hofmeyr School of Social Work was obliged to close as a result of the withdrawal of its subsidy, and the former interracial universities can no longer accept African students, save by special Government permit. At the same time, separation is being extended into the field of social work practice and into the professional

1. *A Survey of Race Relations in South Africa, 1953–1954*, pp. 141–42.

organization of social workers. In 1957, the Bantu Affairs Department informed welfare organizations that it could not approve of the control of social services for Africans by voluntary White bodies or by mixed committees. Interested White persons could serve on separate advisory or fund-raising committees, but the activities must be conducted by committees consisting only of Africans. Sites or buildings in African townships needed for these activities must be leased only to all-African committees.[2] Further restrictions affect African projects (sited) in areas zoned for other racial groups; these projects must be moved to African areas, and resident White members of the staff must be excluded from projects in African areas. At the level of the professional associations, there are now separate European and non-European associations. In Durban there is an inactive interracial association of social workers.

The consequences of the new policies are mixed. On the one hand, Africans gain access to positions formerly often monopolized by Whites. On the other hand, these new opportunities are subordinated to the Government's apartheid policy, and barriers are raised against interracial cooperation in a field of traditional joint enterprise. Moreover, horizons contract, with increasing racial disparity in the range of services and in the level of grants and social pensions provided by the State.[3]

The writing of books, the editing of periodicals, and the craft of journalism have a long history among Africans in South Africa. They were an early reaction to culture contact. Texts in the vernaculars were required for church and school: there was interest in the traditional societies, in proverbs and folktales, and there was the stimulus of contact between people of different race and culture. Africans contributed to this new literature of culture contact, mostly in the vernaculars but also in English. A sensitive account of the early beginnings of African literature is given by Dr. A. C. Jordan in a series of articles contributed to the journal *Africa South* in 1957–59. In a review of some of the writings, Mphahlele[4] comments that in the 1870s the South African Negro in the Cape Province was already writing creatively—protesting, but at the same time trying to reconcile the White man's violence with the Christianity he was preaching. Professor D. Ziervogel[5] regards serious creative writing among Africans as a more recent development:

> Although the first novels appeared about fifty years ago, it has been only in the last two decades that the Bantu have seriously proceeded to write. Approximately 300 books which merit the term

2. *A Survey of Race Relations in South Africa, 1959–1960*, pp. 250–51.
3. Ibid., p. 16.
4. *The African Image* (London, Faber and Faber, 1962), chap. 8.
5. "The Development of the Literature of the South African Bantu," in *Bantu Language and Literature* (Bloemfontein, Union Festival Committee, 1960), p. 8.

"modern" or "serious" literature have been published. Of these, about one-fifth are collections of poems, one-seventh plays, and the rest novels, short stories and the like. Other publications, such as school literature, are, of course, much more numerous.

C. L. S. Nyembezi,[6] a former Professor of Bantu Languages at the University College of Fort Hare, sees the achievement as one of small beginnings. And Lewis Nkosi[7] seems to look to the future rather than the past for the creative writing of fiction by Africans. He dismisses the vernacular literature as more or less moribund, comments that apart from Peter Abrahams, Black writers in South Africa have not produced novels of any competent execution, and sees indications of a new burst of literary "activity" in the 1960s.

Literary Africanization is fostered by the Government and its supporters. Again, there is some meeting of sentiment between African Nationalists and Afrikaner Nationalists, and there is the strange paradox of aliens offering Africans the opportunity to grow as writers, in their vernaculars. In July 1959, the Continuation Committee and the Literature Commission of South African Churches convened a meeting of African writers, of whom eighty-seven attended, coming from South Africa, South West Africa, the High Commission Territories, and the Central African Federation. According to an official report, the authors, 23 of them university trained, had written 245 books including 37 volumes of poetry, 28 plays, 20 grammar books, 10 biographies, and 10 translations, some of which were of Shakespeare (*Bantu Education Journal*, November 1959, p. 511). Though English was the language used throughout, the stress was on writing in the vernacular (according to a correspondent at the conference, in *Race Relations News*, July 1959, p. 121). The chairman of the conference, Moderator of the Southern Transvaal Regional Synod of the Dutch Reformed Church, exhorted the authors to write in their own languages:

> Unless the peoples of Africa are trained and assisted to convey to paper their noblest thoughts, their highest ideals and the most profound truths that fill their hearts, their development must eventually be arrested or become distorted. An illiterate group of people, with no literature to convey the truth as it is apprehended by them, may advance in knowledge and culture up to the point, but they will always be haunted by a sense of immaturity and underdevelopment and by the fear of slipping again into the abyssmal depths and folly of ignorance and unenlightenment. The peoples of Africa should realise this and they can only be brought to this realisation

6. *A Review of Zulu Literature* (Pietermanitzburg, Natal University Press, 1961).
7. "African Fiction," *Africa Report*, October 1962.

by their own speakers and writers addressing them in their own language.

Let no man be so foolish as to say that all that can be said and ought to be said, has already been expressed in the many languages of Europe and other countries, and that it is all to be had for the asking. The ability to read and write in a foreign language should not be scorned by any man. But the nations that have made their full contribution to the development of thought in all fields of human endeavour, have done so in their own language. Africa should breathe and speak in the language of the children of Africa. Unless that happens, its best achievement will be no more than a weak imitation of what others have said and done [*Bantu Education Journal*, November 1959, p. 511].

The professional adviser to the Bantu Education Department phrased the ideology as follows:

If . . . a talented person with an aptitude for writing, chooses to write in a foreign language, it is a loss to his own language which rightfully has a claim on his talents. [Only his mother tongue] enables a person to give form to his innermost experiences and firmest convictions spontaneously and without effort [*Race Relations News*, July 1959, p. 121].

This attitude, so incongruous at a conference where circumstances compelled the use of English as a lingua franca, was challenged on the grounds of the limited public for books in an African language, and the wisdom of mastering the languages of the country and using any of them. One speaker said: "We do not want to lay stress on the things that divide." Others warned against the tendency toward an excessive and irrational veneration of one's own language which inevitably leads to exclusiveness.[8] However, a proposal for the establishment of a Bantu Academy was accepted by the conference.

The small potential reading public in an African language (in South Africa) is further reduced by low standards of education. A speaker at the authors' conference quoted figures to show that of the one and a quarter million Africans at school, 65 per cent might be expected to leave between the second and fourth years of the primary school classes, and only 40,000 to reach secondary schools. In consequence of the small number of readers in an African dialect, publishers were reluctant to publish a book unless it had been accepted for the schools. Authors at the conference felt that this "cramped their style": for fear that books would not be prescribed for schools, they did not feel free to correct the

8. *Race Relations News*, July 1959, p. 122.

African stereotypes created by English and Afrikaans authors, to portray an African triumphing over a White man, or generally to express the struggles and aspirations of their people.[9] An African writer who had gone to prison as a resister during the 1952 campaign commented in an interview that the only way to avoid restrictions was to cut up the book into serial form for magazines, or, if the theme was politically oriented, to publish it overseas in English under a pseudonym. Another writer complained that under Bantu Education there was a dislike of controversial books, and an editorial in *Ilanga Lase Natal* (August 22, 1959), in supporting a plea that the Zulu Language Committee, which scrutinizes Zulu books for suitability in the schools, should not include Education officers, asked: "Are our children to be given milk-and-water books to read in schools so that they shall grow up with no sound literary judgment and perception?" and added: "Our writers must be allowed to write from their own angle not from the European angle."

Standards of writing in one of the African languages of South Africa, as also in Afrikaans, need not be high. There is a small reading public, little competition as compared with writing in more universal languages, and the satisfaction of ethnic pride presumably substitutes for aesthetic appreciation. Moreover, critical appraisal can savor of a lack of patriotism if made by a member of the group, or of racialism if made by a stranger. Circumstances thus tend to discourage creativity in these languages. The African author can emancipate himself from the restriction to schoolboy vacuity in the vernacular by writing in English, if he can meet the intense competition. Two Africans have recently established themselves as English writers, Noni Jabavu and Ezekiel Mphahlele—both, incidentally, live outside of South Africa.

Most African creative writing in English takes the form of short sketches and short stories. Mphahlele[10] ascribes the prevalence of the short story form to the paralyzing effect on non-Whites of the political and social climate of South Africa: the organization of mental and emotional faculties required for a poem or a novel or a play is all but impossible. Nkosi[11] questions this interpretation, and finds contributory factors in sheer sloth and in the low standards set by some magazines, which thus encourage a detour from the long labor of good writing. But he does not minimize the serious problems facing the Black South African writer: physical rootlessness, emotional instability, lack of contact with the outside world, and disbarment from such local cultural activities as theater, serious film exhibition, and musical concerts.

There does not appear to be any distinctive quality about African writing in English which would set it apart from writing by Whites.

9. Ibid.
10. *The African Image,* p. 186.
11. "African Fiction," p. 6.

Some of the more idiosyncratic writing is highly mannered in the idiom of such writers as Damon Runyan. Content reflects the social milieu of African life. White characters tend to be denatured, in much the same way as African characters portrayed by English writers—a consequence of the many social barriers to intimate understanding. There is brutal violence and tough, indeed grotesque, realism in African stories, as there is in their daily lives. African writers are themselves not exempt from this violence. The outstanding journalist Henry Nxumalo, who reported in *Drum* on the forced labor conditions in the farming community of Bethal, and on the dehumanized treatment of convicts in a Johannesburg prison, died of stab wounds in an Orlando township gutter. Lewis Nkosi, who won a Niemann Fellowship at Harvard University, was handed over by an Afrikaner police sergeant to a chief and a mob of tribesmen for a savage beating when he went to investigate disturbances at Zeerust on behalf of his paper (according to evidence reported in the *Golden City Post*, November 23, 1958). Three months later another reporter was murdered at Alexandra township. The leader of the Msomi gang sent his gunmen through the *World* building to intimidate the staff, and guards had to be posted at the door of the boxing reporter when he offended "King Kong" (*The World*, October 5, 1962).

T. Hopkinson,[12] former editor of *Drum*, contrasts, in an interesting passage, the partly creative sublimation of violence in Elizabethan life with the frustrated inward brooding of African life.

> The urban African, like the Elizabethan, knows mortal life as bloody, superstitious, violent, exuberant and tender—and, much as they envy the whites our high standard of living, our freedom from arbitrary arrest and imprisonment, and our power over the material world, few of them, I think, would exchange their fierce experience of life for our tame one—few, that is, of the men.
>
> Like the Elizabethan, too, the African looks out on a mysterious world. Because he knows comparatively little about it, yet feels in his bones that he will one day inherit all it has to offer, he is eager for progress and enlightenment. He wants to expand, develop and to learn. In this he is constantly thwarted, partly by the urgent demands of his own physical nature, and partly by obstruction arising from the political and social organisation of the country. The Elizabethan took to learning, to literature; he took to the seas, feeling the world was his; he expanded out of his inner violence, he also acted his violence out upon the world through war, discovery and adventure.
>
> The African, confined in each direction, turns his thoughts in

12. "Deaths and Entrances: The Emergence of African Writing," *Twentieth Century* (April, 1959), pp. 332–42.

and broods the deeper. Those thoughts, expressed in his writings, are like the lightning I see from my balcony, running every night of the year along the horizons of the Reef, continually signalling an unheeded menace.

But I do not see anything characteristically African in this literature of violence.

A growing non-White press provides greater opportunity for creative writing, at any rate in tabloid form, and for professional journalism. The term "non-White press" is somewhat of a misnomer as far as Africans are concerned, however. The independent African newspapers have disappeared, or have been absorbed by White owners. There is now a rapidly expanding White press specifically catering for Africans. The growth of this press reflects awareness of a changing distribution of power, more favorable to Africans. At a more immediate level, it expresses, among other interests, the interests of manufacturers in African purchasing power, and of the Government in propaganda; and it is encouraged by a rise in literacy among Africans and by developing techniques of pictorial presentation. Also Africans are apparently tolerant of the large volume of advertising matter which makes it possible to sell the papers at a low price. Most of the control over the national press, White and non-White, is in the hands of English-speaking Whites. This is an obstacle to totalitarian control by the National Party, which makes the English press a special target of attack, and seeks to emasculate it by intimidation and censorship, and by direct competition. Especially in the African field, the Government and its supporters have rapidly extended Afrikaner interests.

The non-White papers do not compete with the White press, but deal largely with news and articles of special interest to Africans. *Zonk* is a remarkably innocuous monthly journal. *Bona,* also a monthly, conveys Government propaganda to a partly captive public. *Ilanga Lase Natal* and *The World* are newspapers, the former a weekly, appearing largely in the vernacular with items in English addressed to the middle class, the latter mainly in English and with daily and weekly editions. *Post* (formerly the *Golden City Post*) brings together sensational news for an interracial public, avidly gathers in reports of immorality trials, and offers political, sporting, and social comment. *Drum,* circulating in South, East, and West Africa, and now appearing also in a Zulu edition, gives some scope for creative writing: in the past, it often expressed a strong crusading zeal. *Elethu* (now the *Mirror*), a new weekly, seems to combine safety-valve functions with Government propaganda, although this has not saved its reporters from arrest under the pass laws (*Elethu,* December 22, 1962). There are a number of smaller publications, and a few periodicals for children and for the religious.

New opportunities have thus opened in the non-White press, and there are also new openings in the White press. The English national press, in its White newspapers, begins to cater more and more for African readers. Africans are photographed, and not only in the role of faithful servants or amusing primitives: the term African is gaining currency, and also the use of courtesy titles. In the past, the *Natal Daily News*, for example, in quoting verbatim from a speaker, would deliberately substitute the word "Native" for African: today African is the accepted term. In consequence of the growing interest in African readers, Africans are finding openings as "stringers," occasional contributors, or in more stable employment as staff members. The overseas press is also providing opportunity, and some African journalists serve as correspondents for overseas syndicates. In the non-White papers, all positions are open to Africans, including that of editor. Sometimes the role of the African journalist is merely that of translating official handouts. In other cases, particularly in the journal *Drum*, Africans have been encouraged to develop as journalists.

Opportunities expand, but under close restraint. White journalists who oppose the Government's policies are also under restraint. The many repressive laws, the grave penalties under them, and the persistent attacks and threats by the Government discourage free expression. For the African journalist, the restraints go much deeper. Salary is naturally discriminatory, though some editors and reporters earn well. And always there is the White man in control, who lays down policy. There may even be a White "ratifier" to scrutinize reports in the vernacular, lest they be phrased satirically, a characteristic technique of passive resistance. A leading African editor told me that "in regard to freedom to write, what I want you must know [is] that in relation to White people, the White person feels that he must always have the last say. If there is any disagreement of policy then I have to give way. Apart from the manager, we also have a White man who comes in to advise on the editing." This is an explosive combination—of opportunity and restraint. The opportunities grow, but the Africans are still haltered: and it is easy to sense their deepening resentment as they move nearer the green pastures in which they are forbidden to graze by alien fiat.

The role of African clerks in municipal and government service is beset with ambiguity. These are the traditional occupations of the educated, and enjoyed high prestige, presumably because of the access they gave to new skills and their association with the power of government. Many apply for the vacancies in the Durban Bantu Administration Department. To take some extreme examples, in 1955, the Department received 179 applications for two posts of Senior Clerks and two of Grade I Clerks, and, in May 1960, 14 applications for Senior Clerk,

20 for Grade I Clerk, and 46 for Grade II Clerk. At the same time, more senior posts are now becoming available. Apartheid explicitly promises Africanization of service posts within the African community, and Africans themselves exert pressure for the fulfillment of this promise. In fact, apartheid is extending the range of opportunity within the civil service, and Africans are beginning to occupy such positions as Postmaster, Assistant Magistrate, or Assistant Location Superintendent. But the new opportunities are tied to apartheid; as responsibility is extended, it is denuded of content, and segregated and circumscribed within tribal or ethnic boundaries. The African civil servant is thus placed in the position where he can only attain real power and responsibility by overthrowing the bureaucracy to which he owes loyalty.

There is ambiguity also in the relation of the African public servant to the community he serves. The bureaucracy demands unconditional loyalty from its African civil servants, while Africans expect such educated persons as civil servants to lead their people, to challenge the very laws they are expected to administer. The office requires that the rules be carried out to the letter: Africans expect their own people to circumvent the rules under which they suffer. The White bureaucrats demand that their African underlings identify with them, the White rulers: Africans feel that these underlings are their own flesh and blood, and often fail to understand their apparently hostile administration of rules. As one municipal official commented, in discussing this dilemma, he would introduce change "toward making the office understood to be only an agent or a cat's paw."

If the Bantu Affairs Department and the Bantu Administration Department only provided services, the problem of the African public servant would not be acute. The position of sports officer in a municipal welfare section is not too ambiguous. But many of the activities of the departments include control—the administration of Africans and alien rule over them. Even then, an African civil servant, such as an interpreter in a court, may help his people in many ways and gain a reputation for sympathy and understanding. When involved with the bureaucracies, Africans generally seek out their own people, in the expectation of help and human kindness. Where the role of the African civil servant is to administer harsh laws, however, and he is given no discretion, as in the case of influx control, then his dilemma cannot be resolved.

Influx control screens African workers, determining whether they are entitled to seek work in the area. When I visited the Durban section in June 1961, the following procedure was followed. The applicants gathered in a courtyard, where they were herded somewhat crudely by African municipal police. They then presented themselves at a window of a room where African clerks were in attendance. If the applicant was clearly entitled to a work permit, the African clerk authorized its issue.

The clerks exercised no discretion whatsoever: the applicant's right to a permit had to be absolutely clear. If not, the clerks referred him to the White men sitting inside the room at a row of tables. Though I was not seeking a work permit, I found the spectacle of the four White men frightening, and I could well imagine the fearful anxiety of African applicants, since it was these foreigners who would determine their fates, whether they should be given the opportunity to seek work, or be endorsed out of the area to rural poverty and despair. And it was the African clerk who played the part of the executioner's assistant. As one clerk explained:

> If you refer him inside, they know you have made a decision, other-wise you would give him a permit . . . We are very unpopular. At all times from morning to sunset you have to control yourself, to keep your temper, to make the man understand it's the law. He comes. He thinks you will understand. You are his own people. And then you go and send him inside to the White man. "How can you do it to me?"

The unpopularity carries over into daily life: "Wherever you go, you never know what can happen . . . When they introduce you, a neigh-bor will say *'Olapha Kwa Zinti'* [he is at influx control]. He says it with emphasis. As soon as he does that you know what it means."

Within the office itself, in relation to White civil servants, there is further ambiguity. The work situation of the African public servant varies. Some of the White officials, more particularly among the seniors, are courteous and considerate, and conduct themselves with decorum in relation to African subordinates. They may seek to ensure that their offices are free from the grosser forms of discourtesy. For the most part, however, the contacts of the African clerk are with the lower echelons of the White bureaucracy. For him, the post is a valued one in terms of African occupational opportunities, whereas the position of minor bu-reaucrat in a Bantu Department ranks low in the hierarchy of White occupations. Relatively high educational qualifications are required of the African clerk, while the White official may be poorly educated, with little other intellectual qualification than the ability to speak an African language: and he is paid at a preferential rate, highly discriminatory against Africans. This level of the White bureaucracy tends to attract crude men, or perhaps they are brutalized by their duties in the Bantu Departments. They often handle African "clients" with rudeness, bel-lowing, swearing, and obscenity, so that African clerks are caught in a conflict of loyalty. Some behave in the same way, perhaps attracted by abuse of power, or resolving the conflict of loyalty by an overidentifica-tion with the White official: others suffer vicariously, and seek to control their resentment and help their people as best they can. Moreover, the

African clerks are themselves exposed to coarse, domineering behavior by men whose relative lack of qualifications should place them in subordinate positions.

It is this situation which would seem to explain the results of a study by R. Sherwood,[13] in which African professional and clerical workers placed greater emphasis than comparable American workers on pleasant human relations at work as a source of job satisfaction and unpleasant relations with authority as a source of job dissatisfaction. In general, Sherwood found a striking similarity in the range and content of satisfactions sought by each group in the work situation. Among Africans there was a higher degree of uniformity in job motivation "indicative of a cohesive, middle class of Africans, sharing common goals and aspirations, and firmly motivated by Western values in so far as job attitudes can be said to reveal these." And the ideal of service was overwhelmingly more important to Africans than any other work motivation, and strikingly more potent among Africans than among Americans.

There is one further aspect of ambiguity, and that is in the relationship of African clerks to the class of educated Africans from which they are recruited. Sherwood,[14] in the preliminary draft of an unpublished study of the Bantu Civil Servant, carried out mainly in Johannesburg, reports that "21.8% of male professional workers in the sample see the civil servant clerk as 'a traitor, etc.'" This is not a high proportion since most of the male professional workers were teachers and the research was carried out in 1955–56, when the Bantu Education Act was being implemented. In discussions with educated Africans in Durban, I found an unexpected tolerance for the African civil servant. They tended to judge him not so much by his position and its duties, as by his attitude to the work and his identification with his own people, though there were some departments in which they themselves would not serve. Commenting on Africans within the more notorious sections of the administration, to whom the charge of "sell-out" might seem reasonably applied, they mentioned help received in difficult situations. Also, African civil servants are acquiring the skills that will be needed on "liberation" and the civil service has for a long time been a traditional field of employment for the educated. Still there is much ambivalence, and grave danger for the African civil servant who gains the reputation of being a "spy," "informer," or "stooge."

Of all the positions open to the African bourgeoisie, that of the civil servant is the most ambiguous and the most highly charged with conflict. In law, medicine, social work, nursing, and even in teaching under

13. "Motivation Analysis: A Comparison of Job Attitudes among African and American Professional and Clerical Workers," *Proceedings of the South African Psychological Association* (1956–57), No. 7/8, pp. 27–28.

14. "The Bantu Civil Servant," p. 122.

Bantu Education, service to the community is largely inherent in the occupation. This is less true for the civil servant, since his contribution depends on the political objectives of the Government. And the present official role of many African civil servants is to implement and administer apartheid. Thus, these African civil servants serve the interests of Afrikaner nationalism under a political ideology which extols the virtues of service to one's own people, and which exhorts Africans to dedicate their lives to the service of their own African groups.

The Occupational Milieu:
The Traders

CHAPTER 17

African Traders: Dilemma for Apartheid

In the most isolated corners of the Bantu areas and in the recently completed Bantu urban townships, the Bantu shopkeeper stands behind the counter of his own business. In the building industry the Bantu handles the trowel; in the South African Police he upholds law and order in the dwelling quarters of his own people; in the Post Office and everywhere that Bantu live and move and have their being, the opportunity for rendering service to their own community has been amply afforded them and shall be built out actively [Christmas message by the Minister of Bantu Administration and Development, *baNtu*, December 1958, pp. 5–6].

Tremendous opportunities exist for enterprising Bantu in the commercial sphere. It is the Government's policy to encourage Bantu to serve their own people in all spheres of life. The spending power of the Bantu has increased rapidly in the last ten years. Experts have fixed the total spending power of the Bantu at £365 million per year at the present time, and according to the Government's policy of separate development, Bantu traders can tap the spending power of their own people to a large extent. Bantu spend about 98% of their income ["Trading as a Career," *Bantu Education Journal*, September 1959, p. 384].

IT IS DIFFICULT to know what the Government hoped to achieve by its promise that Africans would be given the monopoly of trade with their own people in their own areas. Certainly, in terms of the moral professions of apartheid ideology, the promised monopoly is elementary justice. But it conflicts with the political objectives and the practical realities of apartheid. To promote a potentially powerful African trading class is hardly consistent with the restoration of the traditional societies, in however modernized a form, since trading was not a recognized occupation in traditional society, and since its introduction would create new bases of power undermining the authority of the chief, and stimulate wide interests transcending the tribal boundaries. Nor is it consistent with the structure of National Party Government, which represents the

Afrikaner petty bourgeoisie; the Government cannot realistically deprive its own supporters of substantial opportunities for profit and give them to the despised Bantu, or build a class which might one day challenge its own domination. Probably, the Government planned no more than a limited and controlled development of African trade in African areas, which would offer Africans the seductions of a petty traders' paradise as an inducement to accept apartheid. But it seems to have misjudged the situation, by failing to realize the economic potential of a monopoly of trade in African areas, or to appreciate that many Africans would be fired with a crusading zeal for the material rewards of a capitalist society. And its policies have had the effect of encouraging the rapid growth of African petty trade, and of unleashing forces which will finally challenge rather than support apartheid.

The Government has in fact created for itself an insoluble dilemma. If it seeks to withdraw the promised monopoly, it will expose the "positive aspects" of racial separation as a rationalization of Afrikaner domination, a transparent device, and at the same time provoke the enmity of a class of persons who may be expected to pursue their interests with the same ruthless determination as the rising bourgeoisie in other countries and other periods, or indeed as the Afrikaners themselves in South Africa. If, on the other hand, the Government abides by its undertaking, it will antagonize some of its own supporters; and it will encourage the accumulation of wealth by African traders and stimulate them to seek greater rewards than can be found within the confines of their own tribal or linguistic communities, thus recruiting their support for African nationalism.

Neither the trader nor the industrialist was part of the traditional structure of South African Bantu societies. The buying and reselling of commodities for profit was alien to them. There were links to the professions in the medicine man and the herbalist, and to crafts, in such specialized occupations as that of the smith, the wood carver, and the potter, and in such household skills as the preparation of skins and weaving of mats. But the crafts were carried on in conjunction with subsistence agriculture and cattle rearing, and not as independent occupations. The concept of the independent businessman, as of the wage earner, was a product of culture contact. And in the contact situation, there were many obstacles to the establishment of African trade. The origin of African urban employment in migrant labor had left its stamp on wage scales. There was the assumption that the wage need provide only for the worker himself: earnings would be supplemented by subsistence agriculture in the reserves. The rights to tribal property thus served to depress the wage level, providing a subsidy for the White employer rather than a measure of independence and surplus for the urban African workers. It was therefore difficult for Africans to accumulate capital where the general wage level was one of bare subsistence or less. Moreover, Africans were dependent on other groups for apprenticeships in trade, and on Europeans for the opportunity to trade. At the entrance to the world of trade stood the European gatekeeper, the urban local authority, granting or withholding licenses; and the image of an African trading bourgeoisie was as remote from European policy as from traditional tribal life.

In the Province of the Orange Free State the opportunity to trade in urban locations was denied Africans,

> on the grounds, so far as can be learned—
> (a) that the Free State has traditionally disapproved of urban trading by Natives;
> (b) that the holders of trading licenses would acquire a permanent stake in the town;
> (c) that Natives are in the European area purely to serve the requirements of the Europeans;
> (d) that the interests of European traders would suffer;
> (e) that Natives might be or become the tools of unscrupulous persons with superior financial resources.[1]

The Journal *The African Trader* (January 1958, p. 21) commented that Africans were only allowed to have cafés for the sale of such bare essentials as sugar, tea, coffee, and tinned meat, and that a limited number of peddlers and hawkers were given licenses. The elimination of competition, no matter how small, was not confined to towns of the Free State. D. D. T. Jabavu[2] complained of the unreasonable trade jealousy of the Englishmen of the "Fighting Port" of East London (Cape Province), which had constantly refused trading to Africans in their own urban settlement.

In some areas, trading appears to have been in the nature of a protected occupation for the disabled. The city of Durban had such protected trades as the sale of snuff and *mahewu*, tailoring, and handlaundering: for the rest, the policy was to grant Africans small trading facilities. This hardly exposed Europeans to competition. A. W. G. Champion, in providing a list of Durban African businessmen in 1929, commented that he had "only discussed the bigger people, that is to say, those who use scales and weights." This expresses graphically the petty quality of African trade in Durban.

The position appears to have been the same in the country as a whole.

---

1. *Report of the Interdepartmental Committee on the Social, Health and Economic Conditions of Urban Natives* (Pretoria, Government Printer, 1942), para. 313, p. 25.

2. "Bantu Grievances," in *Western Civilization and the Natives of South Africa,* ed. I. Schapera (London, Routledge, 1934), p. 295.

The Native Economic Commission of 1930–32 reported that in the rural areas there were few instances of Africans successfully carrying on trade for themselves: in the Transkei, Europeans had a monopoly of trade, and in other areas a virtual monopoly. In the urban areas of the Cape, Natal, and Transvaal, a number of Africans had established businesses on a small scale, and the Commission commented that the length of time these businesses had been in existence showed that the owners could make a living from them. With reference to developments in the main commercial and industrial center of the country, the Witwatersrand (or Reef), the Commission quoted testimony from Major H. S. Cooke that there were some five hundred shops in the locations, and that the average trader seemed to do reasonably well and few seemed to fail to make a living: he knew of none who could be regarded as prosperous (U.G. 22 —1932, pp. 137–38). Phillips[3] found the situation more precarious. He commented that in 1936, wholesalers estimated that there were between five and six hundred African retail traders on the Reef, at least four hundred of whom were in the grocery business. Knowing how inadequately their background had prepared them for business, he was not surprised to discover that only two or three retailers were keeping adequate books, taking inventories of stock, and keeping track of their businesses. Wholesalers estimated that not more than 10 to 15 per cent of these men were "making a living" out of their shops: business mortality was high.

There was little development of an African trading class before the Second World War. Since then industrialization and economic growth have provided such opportunities for Whites that there was less reason to restrict petty African trade. At the same time, conditions became more favorable for African enterprise. Their purchasing power was increasing. Their influx into the towns and their segregation in the locations offered an immediate and populous market. Because of these changes, and because of acculturation and growing militancy, Africans were ready to force their way into trade, as shown by the growth of illegal African trading in some of the African slums of Johannesburg during and after the War and in the African areas of Durban when the African-Indian riots of 1949 disrupted the normal routines.

Some indication of the state of African retail trade at the end of the war is given in *The Report of the Commission for the Socio-Economic Development of the Bantu Areas in the Union of South Africa, 1954–1956.*[4] Of a total of 33,065 retail businesses in 1945–46, 891 were in African hands, i.e. 2.7%. Almost all the African businesses were one-man businesses. In contrast to the other racial groups, partnerships did

3. *The Bantu in the City,* p. 20.
4. A summary of the report was published by the Union Government, No. U.G. 61/1955.

not attract Africans, and there was not one African retail business registered as a company. The businesses themselves were small and limited in scope—hawkers, peddlers, butchers, grocers, and "Native Trading Stores" formed 89% of the African retail businesses. "Native Trading Stores" (that is, general dealers trading mainly with Africans and situated in African areas, including the locations) constituted 42.5% of retail stores owned by Africans in 1945–46, yet only 9.9% of all "Native Trading Stores" were in African hands. African stores carried less stock and yielded appreciably lower profits, about one-third of European profits per business, in 1946–47.[5]

African trading was still negligible, but it was growing, as shown in the following statistics for the Bantu Areas outside the towns.[6]

NUMBER OF GENERAL DEALERS IN BANTU AREAS (RURAL)

1-1-36	European	1117	Bantu	119	Colored and Asiatic	65
1-1-46	European	1268	Bantu	433	Colored and Asiatic	104
1-1-52	European	1319	Bantu	1199	Colored and Asiatic	115

The African percentage of general dealers' stores had thus increased from 9.1% in 1936 to 24% in 1946 and to 45.5% in 1952. The Commission estimated conservatively that African stores accounted for 10% of the total turnover of stores in these Bantu Areas during 1951–52. The divergence between the African percentage of stores and of trade showed, however, the extent to which African trade had remained on a small scale, and the Commission sought the reasons for it "in lack of capital, business acumen, experience and business training, location of store and purchasing power of the population served and last, but by no means least, the personality and integrity of the storekeeper." [7]

Government policy continued to stimulate the further growth of African trade both in the Reserves (or Bantu Areas) and in the urban locations. In the Reserves in 1959, there were 2,373 African general dealers as compared with 1,199 in 1952, and 4,104 in other independent commercial activities (many being hawkers and peddlers), as compared with 3,881 in 1952,[8] while in the African townships of Johannesburg alone, 1,683 licenses were issued to African traders up to June 1958 (*Bantu Education Journal*, September 1959, pp. 385–6).[9] At the same time, Africans were showing more enterprise, particularly in Johannes-

5. *Commission Report*, vol. 3, chap. 9, pp. 52–55.
6. Ibid., vol. 9, chap. 22, pp. 13ff.
7. Ibid., vol. 9, chap. 22, p. 37.
8. *A Survey of Race Relations in South Africa, 1958–1959*, p. 98.
9. According to the Minister of Information, in 1962 there were 4,576 Bantu businesses in Bantu homelands and 7,850 Bantu businesses in urban Bantu townships situated in White areas (*Hansard, House of Assembly Debates*, No. 13, April 23, 1963, col. 4536).

burg, where they were beginning to organize for the promotion of their commercial interests, and to venture into finance and large-scale enterprise.

The founding of the African Chamber of Commerce in Johannesburg in 1955, stormy though its brief history has been, marks progress in African commercial organization. Its objects are to foster commercial and industrial development among Africans, to resist unfair competition in African townships from other non-African groups, to secure more favorable conditions for trade, and to assist the trader in his difficulties. Educated men are active in a field which has largely been the preserve of the relatively uneducated. The first executive of the African Chamber included among its eleven officers six former school teachers, two of whom were university graduates and one a law student (*The African Trader*, July 1958, p. 18). Professors, teachers, and doctors are entering commerce, or acquiring commercial interests.

Finance corporations are being established. The Ikaheng Finance Corporation, Limited, was registered in December 1958, with a share capital of £100,000, to provide loans, guarantees, trained personnel, business advice, encouragement of new enterprises, and general assistance in the economic development and well-being of the African community. The Bantoe Winkelierse Helpmekaar Vereeniging, with a membership of 2,000, ingeniously uses the cession of life insurance policies to the bank as security for overdrafts in favor of its members: traders are thus assisted to raise capital, and help is extended if a member's business falls into difficulties. Lawrence Reyburn[10] mentions also the Johannesburg and District Traders' Association, which was formed in about 1959 to advance cash loans to traders and to represent their interests.

In addition, there are ventures into large enterprises, such as the Itekeng (Put Yourself to the Test) Syndicate (Pty) Ltd., wood and coal wholesale distributors; and the Orlando African Cartage Association. Some successful traders are diversifying their interests: the January 1959 issue of *The African Trader* carries a picture of a trader who is the owner of a dry cleaning business, an executive member of the African Chamber, Managing Director of Itekeng, and Deputy Chairman of Ikaheng (Zakheni) Finance Corporation. These are the heralds of the new capitalism. New avenues are being opened, and new opportunities seized. Much of this proceeds under the aegis of apartheid policy. *By devious routes, the ethic of Afrikaner Calvinism appears to be fostering the spirit of African capitalism.*

African success stories receive much publicity, partly from Government propagandists and partly from newspapermen for whom African

10. *African Traders, Their Position and Problems in Johannesburg's South-Western Townships* (South African Institute of Race Relations, No. 6, 1960).

business success is news. There is Ephraim Tshabalala, who started out as a butcher twelve years ago and now owns three butcheries, a trading store, a café, a hairdressing salon, and a garage with one of the biggest individual petrol sales in the Union. He plans to build a £60,000 bioscope: his daily takings are said to exceed £1,000. Then there is J. M. Lutoto, who owns an expensive car and a fleet of passenger buses; and there is a flourishing all-Bantu wholesale firm, the Vendaland Trading Company, at Sibasa. "These successful Bantu traders set a fine example to prospective Bantu business men or enterprising Bantu youths with a flair for commercial subjects" (*Bantu Education Journal*, September 1959, p. 386).

The Government publication, *Digest of South African Affairs*, May 9, 1958, in an article entitled "Successful Undertakings Abound in Reserves," ascribes these to an " 'apartheid tariff wall' which has excluded all non-Bantu initiative from the Bantu areas." In a box in the same article, under the heading "Bantu Become Millionaires" is an account of "three Bantu 'millionaires' in South Africa" who pay a total of more than £30,000 a year in income tax. One was reported to have paid £7,000 income tax in £1 and £5 notes, which he brought to the office of the Receiver of Revenue in a battered suitcase. "The second 'millionaire' is 'Dr.' Alexander of Durban. He resides in a big house with plush furniture, owns a big American car and rents a suite of rooms in a city office building where he employs 40 Bantu typists to attend to his huge mail order herb cure business." To the humble establishment of the third "millionaire," roll "luxurious limousines containing his patients, or clients, as he prefers to call them." All three are herbalists. There is a good deal of patronage in these accounts—the word "millionaire" in quotes (implying the very different standard for Africans), the references to the plush furniture, the big American car, and the luxurious limousines.

This patronage is present also in the press reports. There is the element of a nine-day wonder in African trading success and middle-class comfort, but also appreciation of the self-made man, who has overcome many obstacles. Mr. Tshabalala becomes "the herdboy with a Midas touch" who cannot sign a check, and now takes his money to the bank in an armored car with an escort of four Europeans armed with guns, though he started with only £17 capital. He is reported to have bought his wife a £1,500 car. One of the herbalists is described as having an Oriental-style palace, many houses and farms, and a fleet of American cars. When he offered a reward of £8,000 for the return of some drums washed away in a flood, it was sensational news. Mr. Alexander, the second millionaire in the Government account quoted above, was reported to have rebuilt his trade empire after sequestration of his estate, when creditors demanded £150,000 which he could not pay (though his properties and businesses were worth more than £250,000). "He wanted to prove that in spite of every handicap an African could conduct an intricate business and build up a financial empire equal to that of anybody else. He realised that he had become a symbol to his people" (*Post*, June 7, 1959). He has, in fact, not yet succeeded in establishing his empire ("Millionaire Alexander Goes Free" and "The Amazing Rise and Fall of Alexander the Great," *Post*, January 13, 1963).

The Johannesburg *Star* carried a series of three articles on "Wealth in the Townships." It described African traders as self-made men: starting with few readymade advantages and minute capital, they had risen to become the new aristocrats of an emergent society (June 29, 1959). There is reference to "the money elite—Natives not only well-to-do but in the super-tax class, men with strings of properties and with luxurious homes that many Europeans would envy." Many of the traders are described as well-educated, but one or two of them can scarcely sign their names to the four-figure checks they can command. The success stories include a man with a group of stores who started with 11/6d in his pocket and a job as delivery "boy" for a bottle store. Mr. Tshabalala appears again, and also the then President of the African Chamber of Commerce, a man who started from humble beginnings— his father was a laborer, his mother a washerwoman—took his B.A. degree, left teaching for commerce, and recently added to his businesses the first specialized shoe shop in the townships. The second article (June 30, 1959) refers to the homes of these "location Lower Houghton-ites:"—the doctor with a £6,000 house, the printer with a £7,000 home "complete with luxuries like a cinema projector." Two more success stories are offered, one of a hotel proprietor, and the other about one of the first Africans to start a limited liability company, now head of a family business employing about 70 people, with a block of shops, virtually a department store, a garage, and a trucking business. The third article places these success stories in perspective. "Municipal officials and others in a good position to know will tell you that about £40,000 or £50,000 is probably the limit of any individual Native fortune on the Rand. Which is, of course, 'peanuts' by the upper-income business standards of White Johannesburg, but nevertheless a comfortable sum of money for anybody to have put together" (July 1, 1959).

Interwoven with the success stories is another strand—realization and appreciation of African purchasing power. By the magic of statistical computation, the obvious poverty of the individual African becomes the wealth of Africans collectively. The old stereotypes are replaced by globular and fluctuating estimates of the African share in the national income. This purchasing power is offered to Africans in the form of the monopoly of trading with their own people in their own areas, and, as such, provides a major selling point for apartheid. But it is also offered to Whites. Thus, the Minister of Bantu Administration and

Development, in a speech to the Afrikaans Chamber of Commerce, Durban, on October 9, 1958, displayed the golden fleece of an African purchasing power amounting to £365 millions per year. What made this purchasing power even more attractive was that Africans spent most of it (98%), that African acquisition of goods was rising more steeply than European, and that Africans were buying larger items and not merely small quantities of basic necessities: among urban African families, 10.9% had radios, 17.7% gramophones, 41.7% sewing machines, and 84.7% stoves. Yet the same speech was reported in *baNtu*, the official publication addressed to the African people (December 1958, p. 23).

The intention cannot be to incite Whites and Africans to compete for African purchasing power, since the Government's consistent policy has been to protect Whites against non-White competition. It is rather to invite them both to partake of this purchasing power in the traditional discriminatory South African manner. There is no implication, that is to say, of setting the groups in competition with each other, if the concept of the African trader is that of the very small shopkeeper. The large profits and the big business in stoves, radios, and wholesale trade would be mainly monopolized by Whites. But Africans would also participate, though at the different level of petty trade. And indeed it might well be necessary to accord the occasional African trader some opportunity for substantial success, so as to encourage African acceptance of separate development in much the same way as the possibility of rising from mill hand to millionaire might be expected to encourage the acceptance of private enterprise.

Simultaneous with the statistical computations of African purchasing power are success stories of the individual monied consumer. These may take a different turn when told by Whites and Africans. Thus, the Minister of Bantu Administration described how he had met a "blanketed native" carrying a roll of £1,000 worth of notes. He was concerned to show that the potential for mobilizing Bantu capital was greater than people realized; it must be used, he said, to help the Bantu build up his own people: Europeans must not be parasites on this Bantu capital (*Natal Daily News*, February 4, 1959). In African hands, these stories may show the folly or arrogance of the White man, and build self-confidence.

> An African friend of mine walked into a car-dealer store to look around. The proprietor of the store took offence at the "Native" for going round the show-room inspecting the various models. He definitely fancied one of the cars. But before he could speak to the salesman he was told to get out of the shop—"this is not a place for loafers." Half-an-hour later, three blocks away, the

African was signing papers for a £1,500 car. The first man lost not
only a customer, but goodwill, for the African has never stopped
to advertise the arrogance and stupidity of that first car-dealer
[*The African Trader*, June 1958, p. 5].

Or again, the African psychologist Mkele, in his address to the Second
South African Advertising Convention in September 1959, told a story
of an African who wanted to buy an expensive sportscoat. The White
salesman suggested a cheaper one. The African bought two of the more
expensive coats, three pairs of flannels, wrote a cheque, and said "de-
liver."

The consumption of luxuries by Africans is regarded as newsworthy,
indicative of change from the traditional image of Africans as consumers of basic necessities and cast-off clothes. Reports in the press
reveal that Africans are not only a substantial part of the market for
the more routine goods, but that they buy luxuries and quality goods,
such as expensive hats and clothes, beauty preparations, and manu-
factured liquor. White merchants begin to respond to the new situation.
Africans are being generally accepted as customers, save in service estab-
lishments: separate hatches are disappearing; there is a greater tendency
in the towns to apply the principle of first come, first served; the
fitting of shoes and dresses is becoming common; and some shops cater
specially for Africans, and employ African salesmen.

In a word, the African is money. He has, of course, always been
money for the White man—as exploitable labor. And the systematic
exploitation of African labor is now being perfected by the Government through influx control, labor bureaus, job reservation, restrictions
on ownership of property in freehold, low wages, industries on the
borders of the reserves, the traditional methods of migrant labor and
taxation, and the increasing compulsion on the African to pay for his
own services. There has also long been interest in African purchasing
power: the concession stores on the gold mines were often, in themselves,
little gold mines. But the interest was limited and haphazard. Now,
with a substantial African purchasing power and expanding needs, the
problem arises of the systematic exploitation of this wealth.

There are three possibilities. The first is in terms of free competition.
It requires studying African needs and canalizing, developing, modify-
ing, and satisfying them by advertisement, salesmanship, industrial production, and efficient distribution. This approach is more likely to appeal
to the established industrialist and merchant, largely English-speaking.
It also allows scope for the African retail trader, and for the African
wholesale merchant or manufacturer, if he can successfully compete
with Whites. The second approach is to reserve the purchasing power
of Africans for Africans. Seemingly this is what the ideology of apart-

heid promises. In universities, churches, and other fields not involved in competition with Africans, there may perhaps be verbal supporters of this policy, as a moral obligation under separate development. It is less likely to appeal to those who must sacrifice their prospective profits. The third approach is to use the power of the State to secure, by repressive measures, this purchasing power, or a lion's share of it, for the White group. This is certainly in accordance with the practice of apartheid. As a policy, it may be expected to have the strongest appeal for the new class of merchants and industrialists, largely Afrikaner, struggling to gain an increasing share of the wealth of the country, more particularly since the Government expresses the interests of Afrikaner nationalism. Between the second and third approaches, between the promise to Africans of the monopoly of trade in their own areas, and the realities of an Afrikaner conquest of political power and an Afrikaner struggle for economic power, there is an irreconcilable conflict.

The following arguments against a policy of African monopoly over African trade are given in an editorial in the official journal of the Afrikaans Chamber of Commerce (*Volkshandel,* October 1959). While the Afrikaners were opening up the country and making it safe for White civilization, other groups were taking the opportunity to entrench themselves in commerce and industry. All the Afrikaners received by way of thanks was a backlog in commercial and industrial enterprise. Now that the Afrikaner is trying to catch up, the Government puts forward a policy of monopoly for Africans over African trade, thus again placing the Afrikaner at a disadvantage. This policy could be justified to some extent if it succeeded in winning the good will and loyalty of the African toward his White guardians. But, on the contrary, as the policy of separate development is applied, antipathy and agitation against the Whites rapidly increases. The purchasing power of the African, according to this source, can be placed at £500 millions, most of which is earned in the big cities. The well-intentioned plan of the Department of Bantu Administration and Development to give the Africans the opportunity to acquire capital and experience in the locations, after which they would transfer their businesses to the tribal areas, is a pretty ideal, but with little hope of realization in practice. A good businessman with the opportunity of dealing in hundreds of millions of pounds of purchasing power is not going to give it up for the sake of a purchasing power of several millions in the Bantustans. There are already indications that this new class of African capitalists finds its best investment in the financing of agitators and agitations with a view to a trade boycott, so as to conquer this great purchasing potential for their own location trade.

It is an admirable argument of the Department that in the past differ-ent exploiting elements were allowed to gain control over trade in the location and might serve as a channel to spread subversive propaganda, and that therefore the trade should be reserved for Africans. The real danger, however, is that the new class of African capitalists may itself, for economic reasons, play the same subversive role. Far-reaching conse-quences may flow from the small beginnings which have been made, and which have already reached considerable dimensions, as, for ex-ample, in the meat trade. The ratio of Africans to Whites is 3 to 1, and will be 4 to 1 by the end of the century. Non-White wages more than doubled in ten years, from £56 per annum in 1938–39 to £129 per annum in 1948–49. In the same period, the number of non-Whites working in private industry doubled from 190,000 to 405,000. Their incomes thus multiplied more than four times over ten years. These are the sober economic facts and tendencies.

The arguments are thus that the Afrikaner is being penalized for his contribution in opening up the country, that there is great potential wealth in the African market, and that the economic interests of the African will lead him to action against the Whites, to economic boy-cotts and to subversion. To these arguments should be added two more, which are implicit. First, Afrikaners well know how effectively na-tionalist and racial sentiment can be organized for domination by a group and used for the advancement of its own entrepreneurs, since these are the techniques they themselves applied. And second—an argu-ment based on sophistry but appealing all the same—the urban locations are in White areas, the cities are White, industry and commerce are White, and the money Africans earn by employment in the cities is White. It therefore belongs to White people and must come back to them. This White money paid to Africans by White industrialists should be sufficient for them to buy the basic necessities from the White traders, who, after deducting their profits, will return it to the White economy. The White pool of White money must remain intact. "If the Whites cannot control trade in the locations, then the money that the Bantu earn from the Whites will not come back to the Whites" (*New Age*, October 1, 1959, quoting a report in *Die Burger* of a statement by the President of the Afrikaans Chamber of Commerce).

Control of the distributive trade in White areas must therefore be vested in White people. And this was in fact the recommendation of the Afrikaans Chamber of Commerce at its 1958 conference. It op-posed the granting of trading licenses in the locations, and favored the establishment of White trading areas outside the location. Clearly the Minister of Bantu Administration and Development could not accept a proposal which would have meant the reversal of apartheid policy, and the withering away of African urban trade; and he was obliged to seek a compromise between the conflicting interests of the groups, one with the vote and the other voteless.

In October 1959, the Minister acknowledged to the Afrikaans Chamber of Commerce that he appreciated that a permanent African trading class might be built up in the locations under the protection of his Department, and that this trade might in the future offer a threat to White traders. Although at the moment location trade was mainly in consumer goods, as the "native" traders built up capital, they would also deal in radios, clothes, stoves, and so on, which could be a threat to White trade in the neighboring areas. These possible difficulties could be overcome by policy in two directions. The first was that the licenses for "native" dealers in the locations should be limited to the daily living necessities, such as bread, meat, meal, tinned food, groceries, sweets, and so on. This side of the matter was being thoroughly investigated, so that the necessary steps could be taken. It would be a violation of the policy of separate development to allow the development of large, well-established "native" businesses in the locations. The second direction was that the African "native" trader must realize that he could only transact business temporarily in the locations. The Minister was weighing the practical application of a policy which would make it clear to the leading traders in the locations that their trade facilities were temporary; that they must go and promote their businesses in their homelands; and that the conditions of their trading in the locations were that they were there only to gain experience and accumulate capital, for which the opportunities in their home areas were extremely slight (*Die Transvaler,* October 24, 1959).

The Minister thus sought to allay White opposition by the suggested restriction of the African trader in the locations to temporary petty trade. At the same meeting, he made another suggestion in which was also implicit the idea of petty African trade and large Afrikaner trade. He pointed out that the small share of the Afrikaner in the wholesale trade impeded his thinking about "native" trade in White areas. According to figures a few years back, Afrikaners owned only 1% of the country's wholesale businesses, as against 20% of the retail. He invited them seriously to consider entering wholesale trade, which could also serve the Bantu trade and promote "our" economic development. The effect would be to reward both sections, through opportunities for large wholesale trade to Whites, and for petty retail trade to Africans.

The Minister was pressed from two sides on his statement of policy. The Afrikaans Chamber of Commerce, as we have seen, thought it unrealistic to believe that African businessmen would abandon their established businesses in the urban areas, and move to the tribal homelands. The Chamber was not reacting to the threat against African trade, but to the fact that the threat did not go far enough. Opponents of the Government's ideology, on the other hand, reacted to what they regarded as the cynical abandonment of the policy of separate development immediately it conflicted with the interests of the Whites. When the opposition press gave prominence to the Minister's statement of policy, he explained:

> that the basic principle was to give adequate protection to White businesses in White areas and to encourage and help Bantu traders to develop in their own areas. Concerning Bantu businesses in the large locations near the White towns, I made these three points:
>
> 1. White traders will not be allowed in locations. The Bantu there will have to be served by their own Bantu traders.
>
> 2. I cannot countenance any suggestion that Bantu traders should be shut out of locations by White traders on the borders of the locations who would then provide the necessities for the Bantu in the locations. This, to me, is unethical.
>
> 3. I added that it was against established policy to build up large and established Bantu businesses in locations. These should be built up in the Bantu's own areas.
>
> When a Bantu trader in a location has sufficient capital to establish a large business, he must move his business to his Bantu area, where the necessary facilities exist, among them the establishment of Bantu towns. Another Bantu trader must then replace him. In this way these Bantu traders will make a contribution to a diverse economy in their own areas. White trade in White areas will be most effectively protected and Bantu trade in Bantu areas will be best encouraged and developed. This is the only just and fair principle for the traders of both sections of the population.
>
> Only when a Native business-man comes to me and says, "I want to turn my store into a luxury business or a big departmental undertaking like a bazaar, and employ a number of people," will I say to him, "The place for that is in the Bantu areas" . . . I shall not ask any Native enterprise to go to the reserves until there are comparable towns, markets and opportunities for him there. It would be inhuman to send him out into the country where there was no business to do. It goes without saying there will be no significant movement in the near future. But I am pressing ahead with the formation of towns in the Bantu areas. . . .[11]

11. Quotations in Reyburn, *African Traders,* pp. 18–19, and from *The Star,* October 26 and 28, 1959.

The effect of these policy statements is that the urban locations are White areas, that only the small African trader is acceptable, and that the growth of African trade must be controlled in the interests of White competitors. The Chairman of the African Chamber of Commerce protested that this robbed apartheid of one of its much vaunted features: it had been understood to impose a vertical bar, now there was to be a horizontal bar as well—a Black area becomes a White area when it suits the Ministers, and African traders are simply told, "You're too successful. You had better move. . . . An African can make and sell *vetkoekies* but he cannot start a bakery" (*New Age*, November 5, 1959). And in 1962, when he applied for additional trading sites, the Department of Bantu Administration and Development replied that in future trading rights in urban areas would be restricted to Africans qualified to reside in the area concerned, that Africans could not establish more than one business each in their home towns, and that it was not the intention to create capitalistic Bantu enterprises in White areas. Africans were given trading rights in urban areas as a "privilege" only. Moneyed Bantu ought to be directed to the Bantu homelands, where they may invest their capital on a permanent basis.[12]

In 1963, the Department issued a circular to local authorities informing them that trading by Bantu in White areas (i.e. the urban locations) is not an inherent primary opportunity for them, and that the establishment of Bantu businesses which do not confine themselves to the provision of the daily essential domestic necessities of the Bantu, which must be easily obtainable, must not be allowed (*Natal Daily News*, April 23, 1963). According to *The Star* (Overseas Edition, April 20, 1963) the circular instructs municipalities to be very sparing with licenses for African businessmen, to prevent existing African businesses from expanding or putting up their own buildings, and even to discourage Africans from acquiring such enterprises as dry cleaners, garages, and petrol stations. The Minister explained in Parliament that no new principle had been introduced. In this he spoke perhaps more truly than he realized. It was apparent from the tenor of his reply that he regarded African urban locations as falling within the White areas, and permission to trade there as somewhat of a concession. Where Bantu could obtain their requirements without undue inconvenience from traders in a White area, he said, there was obviously no need to permit any further Bantu-owned business undertakings within urban Bantu residential areas.[13]

In the Bantu homelands, immediate conflicts of interest arise at the level of retail trade. In such tribal areas as the Transkei, White traders

---

12. *A Survey of Race Relations in South Africa, 1962*, p. 167.
13. *Hansard, House of Assembly Debates*, No. 13, April 23, 1963, col. 4544.

have been long established and demand the protection of their interests, while Africans exert pressure both against White traders and the Government, for fulfillment of the promises of separate development. Official statements fluctuate in an attempt to satisfy the opposing interests, sometimes offering Whites the assurance that Africans were insufficiently developed in business acumen and technique to be a threat, and that it would be generations before they possessed that knowledge and experience; and sometimes offering Africans the assurance of the paramountcy of their interests in their homelands. It would seem that the present direction of Government policy is toward securing for Africans most of the retail trading rights in these areas (apart perhaps from reserved "White spots"). Indeed it is difficult to see what other policy could be pursued without totally discrediting apartheid, or exposing White traders to grave danger.

In the sphere of industry there appears to be no immediate open conflict of interest. The industrial development of the Bantu homelands is an integral part of the Government's ideology, and one of the inducements offered to Africans to accept apartheid. In practice, however, it reserves for Whites most of the major opportunities. Policy is directed toward the establishment, on the borders of the tribal areas, of industries owned by Whites and served by the cheap labor of tribesmen. Maximum advantage is thus given to the White entrepreneur in the exploitation of African labor within the framework of Government ideology. Some opportunities for industrial enterprise in the tribal areas are extended to Africans through the Bantu Investment Corporation of South Africa, Ltd. This was founded in 1959 with a White board of directors appointed by the Minister of Bantu Administration and Development, and a share capital of £500,000 held and subscribed by the South African Native Trust. It appears from the small amount of share capital, now increased to £1,000,000, that only a minor program of industrial development is contemplated. Moreover, according to a statement of the Secretary for Bantu Administration and Development, the policy would not be to encourage the establishment of large Bantu industrial undertakings, but to assist financially or otherwise smaller undertakings which could easily be managed and controlled by the Bantu (letter dated March 17, 1959, quoted in *The African Trader,* March/April 1959, p. 18). And development would be under the paternal sponsorship of the Investment Corporation, which would thus control African initiative and enterprise.

The policy of reserving the lion's share in the industrial exploitation of the African areas for Whites, while offering Africans quite minor inducements, must give rise to a sharp conflict of interest between the two groups in the future. It is only because few Africans are as yet engaged in industry that there is no immediate conflict. But Africans will soon reach out for the rewards of industry, and the struggle for industrial opportunity will merge with the struggle for trade. Apartheid stimulates both the spirit of capitalism and the spirit of racialism, and the fusion of capitalism and racialism is likely to prove as powerful a force among Africans as it is already among Afrikaners.

CHAPTER 18

African Traders: Problems and Perspectives

THE IMAGE of the African trader which emerges from statistics of their growth in numbers and from the play of propaganda is misleading. The present reality is that of petty traders, severely restricted by official policies and by their own limitations. They have built a bridgehead into the world of commerce, but they have still to capture the prize.

We can find perspective in the consideration that the press proclaims roughly the same handful of success stories, and that these would be of no interest if achieved by White men, their news value lying solely in the fact that it is Africans who are directors, or run a dairy, or own a neatly kept general dealer's store, a substantial home, or a good motor car. Or we can find perspective in the issues of *The African Trader,* published in Johannesburg to promote the African Chamber of Commerce and the Association of African Commercial Travellers, and addressed primarily to the traders in Johannesburg. Though this is the area of greatest opportunity for urban Africans, the milieu which emerges is that of petty trade conducted by amateurs. There is advice to traders to gear their shops for Christmas sales, and comment on the extent to which wrong change is given, with the suggestion that traders consult the Cash Register Company. Africans, it is said, show an inability to handle money properly: thousands of pounds are dissipated fruitlessly through negligence, dishonesty, and ignorance. A trader must know what to buy and when to buy. Overcoats only sell in winter time, and raincoats only sell during the rainy season. Competitive prices are a more effective means of attracting customers than the magic of medicine men.

The African Trader of July 1958, in an article on "Economic Squeeze," comments on the way in which the African shopkeeper squanders his initial credit with the wholesaler. Soon he forgets that he is living on borrowed goods and that only about 15% of his sales price represents profit. He cannot pay his accounts, credit is curtailed, he begins to fall into debt, he runs away from his shop to avoid creditors, summonses are served, and judgment taken. The shopkeeper complains that the wholesaler (who would be non-African) had never given him a square deal, while the wholesalers complain that: "these African boys have a golden opportunity to make money. We give them our money to carry on business and all they do is mess around—they have many suitors, they gamble on the race course, they drink during business hours, they use our money to buy cars and are never to be found at their place of business." And the writer asks whether so much capital from the financiers, manufacturers, and wholesalers must be wasted in the sands of African trading. "Must the African trader allow the vast purchasing power running into millions of pounds each month to pass from him as if through a diamond mesh wire netting back into the circuit of European commercial life without the African taking his due share of that wealth and enriching energy?"

In the same issue, there is reference to a survey of African trading throughout Southern Africa, which reports a great lack in understanding of business management and deplorable bookkeeping, most bookkeepers being unable to present a proper and correct statement of the affairs of their clients. There is said to be a tendency for African storekeepers to buy goods where the best terms of payment are offered, rather than the most competitive prices. They thus drive away customers sensitive to price levels. Banks, building societies, and other suppliers of capital are reluctant to operate in the African townships because of the present way of conducting business. According to the survey, a large percentage of storekeepers in the African townships are on the verge of bankruptcy.

Reyburn,[1] in his study of African traders in Johannesburg's South Western Townships, also paints a picture of inadequacy. Almost half the traders interviewed in a sample of 47 had no education or only primary school education (up to and including Standard V). Although 35 of the traders kept books of some sort and records of their transactions, their systems were often haphazard and incomplete. He thought it probable that African traders in general overpaid for their purchases from merchants: the 2½% discount, given fairly freely outside the townships on many items, was seldom, if at all, given to African traders. Half the traders had suffered at least one burglary or robbery. His report showed that facilities were modest: less than a third had telephones or access to telephones, less than a quarter were provided with electricity. It was almost solely the general dealers who earned high profits, and then only if they carried the optimum amount of stock and bought in the best markets. Competition in most areas was keen and even an efficient general dealer could find himself worked out of business. In the other categories of trade, although a few large-scale undertakings in specialized fields were apparently prospering, the pov-

1. *African Traders.*

erty of customers and the high capital costs and overhead made it more the exception than the rule for traders to thrive. The precarious finances of many shops rendered it difficult or even impossible for their owners to pay moderate membership dues to organizations of traders.

A final corrective to the propaganda perspectives is provided by an analysis of assessed income in the Report of the Commissioner for Inland Revenue for the year 1958–59 (U.G. 71/1960). A total of 2,448 Africans received assessments, representing a net assessed income of £1,307,000, as compared with 920,743 Whites with a net assessed income of £887,067,000. The number of Africans with assessed incomes of £1,000 and over was 236, of Whites, 339,059, a ratio of 1,432 Whites to 1 African. In the range of £8,000 to £10,000 there were 3 Africans, while 2,421 Whites received assessments in respect of net assessed incomes of £8,000 and over. Assessments to Africans engaged in trade, property dealing, industry, construction, and transport numbered 377, with net assessed profits of £295,000, an average of £782, while 10 Africans sustained losses of £7,000. In retail trade alone, excluding liquor, there were 29,487 Whites with a balance of net assessed profits totaling £27,526,000. In the liquor trade, there were 1,466 assessments to Whites, with a balance of net assessed profits totaling £2,256,000. For the tax year 1961–62, 556 Africans were liable for tax amounting to about £22,272 as compared with 887,150 Whites liable for £77,897,-809 tax.[2]

The difficulties of the African trader arise partly from his own deficiencies, such as the lack of a commercial tradition, but more generally from the discrimination which restricts opportunity to acquire education, experience, and capital, and which enshrouds him in controls.

In addition to controls specific to trade, African traders are governed by the same system of controls as Africans in general. They are regarded as foreigners in the cities, and need permission to remain in an urban area. In the past, only a few categories had an automatic right to urban residence, and this right was restricted to a single town, as, for example, the town in which an African had resided continuously since birth, or, among other conditions, in which he had worked continuously for one employer for not less than ten years. In 1964, even this limited right was withdrawn. In any event, the value of the right was much diminished by extensive powers for the arbitrary termination of urban domicile. Discretionary powers of banishment, without trial, are conferred on the Minister of Justice under the Suppression of Communism Act, No. 44, of 1950; on the Governor-General, in effect the Minister of Bantu Administration and Development, under the Native Laws Amendment Act No. 54 of 1952, if he deems it expedient in the general

2. *Hansard, House of Assembly Debates*, No. 12, April 19, 1963, cols. 4351–52.

public interest; on an urban local authority under the Natives (Urban Areas) Amendment Act No. 69 of 1956, if in its opinion the presence of the African is detrimental to the maintenance of peace and good order; and on the Minister of Justice, if he is satisfied that a person is promoting feelings of hostility between Europeans and any other section, under the Riotous Assemblies Act No. 17 of 1956.

These controls provide for the political domestication of the trader. He dare not be openly militant, save within the framework of apartheid policy. This no doubt partly accounts for the conflicts and fissions within African commercial organizations such as the African Chamber of Commerce—the frustrations being expressed inward—and also for the detachment of many African traders from involvement in community affairs, a matter of common complaint by educated Africans.[3] It is as difficult to draw out a trader in political discussion as to extract from him information about his earnings. The controls enable the authorities, through their powers over domicile, to dispose arbitrarily of the opportunity for urban trade, while the African trader, in contrast to the White trader, is deprived of the right to move freely between towns in search of more attractive opportunities. Indeed, trading location is virtually determined for him, and he may be restricted to the limited area set aside for his linguistic group.

Under Section 9 of the Natives (Urban Areas) Consolidation Act No. 25 of 1945, policy is directed toward confining Africans in segregated locations, villages, and hostels within the towns. In the past, there were a few areas outside the municipal locations where Africans had acquired property in freehold or were engaged in trade, but even these small pockets are being eliminated. The effect of this policy of segregation is to deny Africans choice of trading site, and to some extent, choice of trade. The Bantu Administration Department of the city plans the siting, nature, and quota of the businesses in its locations and hostels. The plans may or may not be efficient, since business acumen is not one of the qualifications required for administrators of African affairs. All that the trader can do is to apply for a particular type of business on a particular site, when applications are invited. He

---

3. An African informant gave the following very different explanation for the detachment of the African traders:

The traders are people who keep to themselves and do not take any interest in community matters. There are two reasons for this I would put forth: in the first place it is that the African trader feels that his people are economically very poor and mixing up with them would invite him to sympathize with their difficulties and in this way be tempted to help them and as such he feels his financial position would be drained, hence he must keep away from them. Another reason is that the African trader is suffering from old superstitions of bewitching. He feels suspicious of the movements of his people towards him and he is always under the impression that they might do him a lot more harm than good; added to this is an inferiority complex because most of them lack education.

can, of course, draw the attention of the administrators to the need for a business and his desire to conduct it, but he is dependent on the decision of this stratum of officials who control African life in the cities. He is thus largely denied the opportunity a White businessman has of looking around for premises with a good location in which he can launch the trade he desires and sell the commodities in demand. In consequence, the energies of the prospective African trader may be directed toward trade in general—a grocery or a catering table or whatever else is available—rather than a particular trade. And the possibility of business success may be largely predetermined by the quality of the administrative decisions taken by White officials.

Within the locations or hostels, the African trader, both as a resident and in his occupation, is subject to the supervision and under the powers of the White Superintendent and of the Director of the Bantu Administration Department. Recent regulations promulgated for Durban, under Provincial Notice No. 383 of 1960, illustrate the range of available powers.

For residential purposes, an African may enter a Durban location as a tenant of municipal accommodation, or as the purchaser of rights of occupation to municipally-owned premises, or as the holder of a permit to a site on which he builds his own premises. He must first of all satisfy the Superintendent that he is a "fit and proper person," which is to say that from the point of view of character, behavior, disposition, health, or habits he is not likely to be an unsuitable or undesirable resident or occupant. In the case of tenancy, the Superintendent may terminate the contract on grounds which include—subject to certain safeguards—unemployment and employment outside the urban area, leaving the premises for more than one month without the written permission of the Superintendent, ceasing to be a fit and proper person, and failing to discharge any liability within fourteen days. The purchase of the right of occupation to municipally-owned premises confers tenure for a specified period, not exceeding thirty years: the Superintendent may however cancel a certificate on one month's notice in writing, on roughly the same grounds as those for tenancy. In the case where an African builds a home at his own cost on a site allotted to him, but owned by the municipality, no period of tenure is specified: the effect is to confer indefinite tenure, until termination by the Superintendent in the same way as for a certificate of occupation. Control by the Superintendent is thus built into the rights accorded Africans, and these rights never confer the security of full ownership. Even when an African has purchased rights of occupation or built at his own cost, he still requires official authority to sublet, or to sell, cede, assign, make over, alienate, pledge, hypothecate, or encumber his interest in the premises.

The regulations in regard to trading distinguish between premises provided by the Council and premises built by the trader. In the former case, the Superintendent has the right of termination on one month's notice if the trader is convicted of certain offenses—including two convictions for contraventions of the regulations within a period of three years—or if he dies, or is declared of unsound mind, or if his estate is sequestrated, or if he is thirty days in arrears with payment of his rent, or absent from his business for a period longer than that specified by the Superintendent on application to him. Though this latter provision was no doubt designed to control unauthorized dealings in trading rights, or neglect of business, it is perhaps the clearest symbol of the subordination of the African trader in the locations. Where the trader builds his own premises to approved plans, no fixed tenure is provided, unless a specific agreement as to tenure is contracted. The trader does not become the owner of the property: the Superintendent, with the approval of the Director, may cancel the trading rights on one month's notice on the same grounds as for a trading tenancy.

In consequence of these limitations on property rights, African traders in the locations cannot readily raise capital on their investments. They have no immovable property to offer as security: bonds over their movable assets are not attractive to the White investor, since he cannot exercise rights of occupation on default of payment, and few Africans have the means to invest money in loans to traders.

Some of the controls operate through the process of screening applicants for trading rights. In Durban, for example, application is made to the Superintendent on a prescribed form, giving particulars of identity—registration number, tax identity number, name of Chief, district of domicile—and of qualifications and eligibility—experience in the trade, educational standard, literacy in either official language, capital and how kept, other assets, criminal convictions, state of health, and presence of partners. A woman may only apply for trading rights on a tenancy basis, provided she has Letters of Emancipation from Perpetual Minority: she may not apply to build on a trading site. The form of application provides for four reports: the Superintendent's/Supervising Overseer's, the Senior Superintendent's/Supervising Overseer's, the Registering Officer's, and the Director's report and decision. The reports may be very cursory:—"I cannot recommend a female" from the Supervisor, and "Female, not recommended" from the Senior Supervisor, or they may even be based on rumor—"Rumored that this man is working in conjunction with Indian traders at . . ." from the Supervisor, and "It is said that this man is in the hands of Indian traders and in any case he does not appear to be a good type" from the Senior Supervisor. The Registering Officer checks on the right of the applicant to be in an urban area, the Superintendent that he is a fit and proper person to carry on trade in the location and legally entitled to be and remain in the urban area, and the Director makes the final decision.

The decisions are taken entirely within the bureaucracy. There is no open hearing, as in a licensing court, to which application must still be made for a license. And there is no opportunity to meet the objections raised, a system which invites abuse. Some corrective is provided by the Corporation's policy of asking the Advisory Board in the area to make a recommendation—though this may simply substitute one abuse for another—and by a general right of appeal against decisions of the Superintendent and other officials to the Native Commissioner, and from him to the Chief Native Commissioner.

When permission to trade has been granted, additional controls begin to operate. In the locations of Durban, the number of assistants and each assistant individually must be approved by the Superintendent. The trader must personally carry on his business and supervise the work of his assistants, permission from the Superintendent being required, as we have seen, for absence from business. The Superintendent may at any time require proof from a trader or his assistant of compliance with the regulations relating to residence in the city. The trader is required to keep proper books in respect of his business transactions in one of the official languages, and the Director has the right to call for an audited balance sheet and auditor's report. And the Director may summarily cancel trading rights in the locations, even if the trader has built the premises himself, on the grounds of "gross misconduct of any kind which, in the opinion of the Director, makes it undesirable for the trader to continue to carry on business in any location, Native village or hostel."

Some of these powers over residents and traders are exercised to enforce influx control; others to eliminate what the Superintendent would regard as subversive elements; others in terms of health regulations and to control nuisance; others out of paternalism, and no doubt a desire to foster some African trade. The combined effect is of a massive weight of oppressive rules, as can be seen in the concluding sections of the regulations, which list numerous *criminal* offences, such as failure to pay rent or electricity charges, failure to maintain a site number in a clear and legible condition, failure to report a leakage in homes to the Superintendent, failure to report that a lodger has ceased to reside in his premises, and failure "to obey any lawful order by the Superintendent or person authorised by him."

Inevitably, the African trader must seek liberation from restrictive controls, and choose, in terms of his interests, between the main political parties and philosophies in South Africa. A purely democratic policy would have the advantage of freeing the African trader from racial discrimination, but the disadvantage of obliging him to compete on the same terms as traders of other groups. This is a major difficulty, since most African traders lack a commercial background, capital, and training, and come late into a field which has been appropriated by others: they need a privileged or protected position, not bare equality. Certainly in terms of the current situation, where poor and inexperienced African traders are virtually limited to their own group and must share this custom with traders of other racial groups, racial monopolies and racial exclusiveness would provide the needed support, and these are explicitly offered by apartheid.

In respect of the promise of opportunity to serve their own people and the exclusion of other racial groups, there is then an immediate convergence between the interests of African traders and the ideology of apartheid, notwithstanding the many restrictions and controls. The Chairman of the Durban Combined Location Advisory Boards commented that:

> The present Government has grasped this opportunity to boost up their apartheid policy with all its implications. It may prove to be a blessing in disguise to us . . . Apartheid is no doubt to the advantage of the African business man. I say this as a man who hates segregation. In this one respect, it is a blessing in disguise.

The President of the Durban and District African Football Association expressed the same point of view.

> The Nationalist Government was a God-send to the traders. The traders are well disposed to the Government in this respect [that Africans should trade with their own people] . . . The one thing the traders feel the Government has done is to give them an opportunity to get shops.

Inevitably traders seek to exploit the promises of apartheid. "An ox is held by its horns, whereas a man by his word. We should catch the Government by their words, if we want the truth about their efforts" (translated from the Zulu, *Ilanga Lase Natal*, February 28, 1959). Few African traders seem too unsophisticated to exploit the policy of separate development, as shown for example, in this simple letter to the Secretary, Native Affairs Department, Durban, by two women, who give all the appropriate cues—they use the word Bantu, their cakes are sold only to the Bantu race, they refer to Government policy for Bantu trade, and there is even an appeal to anti-Indian sentiment. They write that they sell:

> home made cakes, called the fat cakes, we have been arrested more than 30 times by the South African Police, for not having the

licenses of that kind. Have applied for licenses without success.
Told to get out of the office . . . this home-made cakes are very
health for bantu people, we are only selling this kind of cakes to
the bantu race . . . at 1d. each. They are made of oil, baking
powder, flour, sugar, salt, clean water, only, but still we are not
given a license for such food . . . lots of Indian shops in Durban
selling this home-made cakes . . . And yet, you have allowed
the bantu people to trade among themselves.

The letter was taken up by the Bantu Affairs Department, but without success, since the peddling of food conflicted with health laws.

At a more sophisticated level, there was the vigorous campaign of a
trader against the refusal of a general dealer's license in his own tribal
area, as a result of opposition by a few White men.

I felt that if the Europeans were true, they would allow me to
develop my shop in the country because that is government policy
. . . I then wrote a letter to the Minister of Bantu Development,
the duplicate I sent to the Chief Bantu Affairs Commissioner, the
triplicate to the Bantu Commissioner in ———— and kept one for
myself . . . The matter is still under consideration. I wrote with
the full hope that they would look into the matter because we
have been told to look back to our homelands . . . I wrote to
Mr. X a personal letter. I told him that he came to preach Bantu
Authorities and then I am refused a license. Is it the way it should
work that when it is going to injure the European it must not
apply, but must apply in the case of an African? This man took
my letter and sent it to Pietermaritzburg. I am glad he did that.
They must make us see the glaring picture of Bantu self government. Seeing is believing . . . Afrikaners are bad and we like
them for that. They tell us we are boys and we must develop
in the mountains, but they still keep the Europeans in those mountains. We did not say Europeans must leave our areas, we still want
to live with them, but they should not kick us out in what is called
our homelands. If I came to town they will kick me out and where
will I go. That is why I say the African is not satisfied, he is baffled
by this official and that official. The African has nowhere to live
. . . When I had a discussion with Mr. X, I told him that most
of our Chiefs are not educated, that they come to us by night like
Nicodemus to seek advice and if we are treated badly, we will tell
them not to accept anything because they will be stoned to death
by the people. I feel the sword must cut both ways. We should
not be excluded from trading in our own areas. If that happens
we will tell the people not to take the word of a White man and
then we will be called agitators. There is a Zulu saying which

goes:—*"Akukho soka elingenasici."*[4] X is bad, but he has got a ray of light. If he tells me to go and develop in my homeland I agree with him.

Further evidence can be found in *The African Trader* of this exploitation of Government policy, and also of the manner in which the racial monopoly of trading opportunities encourages racialism. The declared policy of the African Chamber of Commerce was to resist "unfair competition" in African townships from other non-African groups: it would especially oppose State trading and similar practices (*The African Trader*, June 1958, p. 17). And the Chamber concerned itself with such "unfair competition" as non-African traders operating on the *fringes* of African townships; non-African coal agencies in direct competition with African coal distributors in predominantly African areas; and Christmas hampers being organized by non-African persons without trading licenses in African townships (March/April 1959, p. 10). In a letter in the same issue of the journal (pp. 19–21), the secretary of an African firm of coal distributors complains, in effect, that White coal distributors are offering more competitive terms, and continues in racially antagonistic language to protest against Chinese trade in the townships, contrary to the policy of apartheid.

> We have the most disgusting element in this coal trade, namely the Chinese Coal Merchants in Kliptown. You find them in Orlando, in Meadowlands in Moroka, in almost every part of the African townships. These have penetrated into these townships and dispose of their coal just as they please, to the detriment of the African coal dealers. Strange enough, these menacing lot do not seem to be subjected to trading permits in African Townships. But the Municipality of Johannesburg is very enthusiastic about the ejectment of our fellow businessmen in town. It is time now that African Chamber of Commerce must protest in most vigorous terms against this monstrosity and fallacious policy of the Nats [i.e. Nationalists] masquerading in the name of Apartheid.

The convergence between the promises of apartheid and the interests of African traders is, however, only superficial and temporary. Afrikaner and African trading classes are in direct competition, as we have seen. The steps are easily taken from separate development and service for one's own group to nationalism (and boycotting of non-African traders in a "Buy African Only" campaign) and to racialism (and the driving out of other groups, or rule by the African majority). Only the first stage is compatible with the ideology of apartheid, and even then not with its practice. Apartheid would lay but a modest founda-

4. Meaning: "No one is without a blemish."

tion for African enterprise, while withholding the rich prizes, and would subordinate African commercial development to Afrikaner interests.

A rising commercial class appears to develop a great voracity. Perhaps the explanation is that its members are recruited from strata of the population with low and regular expectations of income. Trading breaks these norms of near-subsistence living and offers endless vistas of rising standards. There are now no limits to the ambitions of the trader and, the making of money being defined as a morally praiseworthy enterprise, he acts with a ruthless disregard for the interests of others. It is to be expected that many of the African traders will not scruple to exploit racial antagonism, first for the rewards offered by apartheid, and then, as they gain the strength to set aside the burdensome restraints, for the rewards of the wider society. If the Afrikaans Chamber of Commerce, with almost unlimited opportunities in the country as a whole, was not prepared to forego the opportunity for profit in the impoverished urban African areas, why should the African trader and industrialist forego the opportunity of profit in the rich and highly developed areas of South Africa, particularly since the African has numerical superiority? Why should he crouch beneath a racial ceiling on his endeavors, fixed in the interests of another group? Why should he not use his numbers for the conquest of power and the enrichment of his own race by means of state power, according to the precept and example of the Afrikaner nationalists? It would seem that the political philosophy of the Pan-Africanist Congress most closely corresponds to the interests of the African traders.

CHAPTER 19

The Durban African Trader: A Case Study in African–Indian Relations

FEARS OF INDIAN COMPETITION among the English-speaking Whites of Durban stimulated anti-Indian prejudice and anti-Indian discrimination. These fears were already voiced in the 1880s, some twenty years after the arrival of the first indentured Indians in South Africa, and the present pattern of Indian trade, its segregation and high concentration in petty retail enterprise, has been shaped by prejudice and discrimination. Today Indian traders are well-established in retail trade. They cater to the African market, and their prices are highly competitive. If the English, occupying the command posts in Natal, were not prepared to meet Indian competition on equal terms, how much more compelling must be the desire for discriminatory supports by an African trading class still struggling for a place in the sun, still sheltered and swaddled by the paternalism of the Durban city fathers.

African trade in Durban was deliberately fostered by the City Council, but at the level of petty trade. The following account of its history was given by the Senior Supervisor of locations, who was associated for many years with African trade.

> In the early days . . . the policy was to give as many small trading facilities as possible with the object of enabling as many Bantu as possible to make a living. The policy was really forced on us at that time, which was about the real beginning of Native trading in 1918. Natives had no idea how to trade, nor capital, and they could not really tackle a business which needed stock. We had to beg them almost to open grocery shops. They were not interested in the sort of business where you made a farthing or a halfpenny on a particular article. Instead they went for things which had a quick turnover, such as the serving of meals and butcher shops . . . Subsequently we followed a mid-way policy . . . [the manager] took coercion to get them to trade on a bigger scale as grocers and greengrocers. At first we made little progress but in time they came

forward. We soon found out, however, that in almost all cases the traders were nominees of the Indians. This did not apply only to the Indians but sometimes the Native trader was a mask for Europeans . . . This was in the late 20s and the middle 30s.

Gradually the Natives became more business-minded. The department was exceptionally slow in realizing this and we fell behind in the provision of premises. Not until the . . . [1940s] did the Department begin to give them better facilities. Now we have a wave of overtrading. There were too many who went into it with the idea that everything was a profit. They made no arrangements for depreciation and so on. Any number could not meet their dues and were turned out by the municipality. Today we have people coming forward with capital and in some cases they are good traders. The policy of the Department was nailed to two principles. First of all, one man, one business. Secondly, that there should be daily tenancies[1] with no good will and no inheritance. (I have never understood the reason for it but I think it is because it avoids complications. These people were on municipal property and we had to be sure that the people were suitable. The heir might not be suitable or he might not qualify in terms of current regulations and apart from anything else, there was a long waiting list.) Seven or eight months ago a subcommittee sat to relieve the position. They put forward new principles, first of all that the panel must give priority to a suitable heir in reallocating the site of a deceased person. Then the panel recommended the relaxation of the rule of one man, one business, and also recommended that companies should be encouraged . . . There is now a solid core of steady, middle-class people with here and there some outstanding traders . . . The prospects of trading in their own areas, especially with the entrenched idea of serving their own people, are particularly bright. Added to this is the increase in earning capacity. There is one drawback and that is that in the past the great majority of our trading schemes were subeconomic. Now they are economic, which means that they pay higher rents . . . There are still considerable numbers of traders whom we have to protect from themselves. An important principle we have introduced is that we will not build shops for letting to Natives in the future. We will allow them to build for themselves. The drawback, however, is that they can only have a lease of the property. Alexander made the mistake of putting up a building worth £52,000 and they can't borrow money on these leased premises. We did all that we could to assist Alexander by, for example, giving him permission to sublet.

---

1. There are daily tenancies in the eating houses and beer halls, not in the ordinary location businesses.

The number of African licenses increased from 75, or 1.46 per cent, of all licenses in 1930, to 776, or 3.99 per cent in 1962. Most of these licenses fall into a few trades dealing with foods—catering tables and tearooms, general dealers, retail butchers, fresh produce dealers, and hawking and peddling. Though some trades are not represented, such as those of plumber, electrical contractor, baker, apothecary, garage keeper, public entertainment, dyer and cleaner, there is a wide spread of enterprise. The licensing figures do not give a complete picture, and for 1959, the year in which this study of African traders was made, I estimated their number as about 650, or about 800, including hawkers and peddlers. To this should be added illegal traders, and a variety of craftsmen, plying independent trades, without licenses, such as painters and motor repairers, giving a total somewhere between 900 and 1,000. And then there are the roadside vendors of offal, and the itinerant vendors bringing in home produce and artifacts. (See Table 9, Appendix D, for the racial distribution of licenses and estimates of African traders in 1959.)

Some of the traders have been carrying on business for over twenty years. In 1959, in two of the locations with a longer history of trading, the average number of years during which the present occupants had traded, was about nine and fourteen respectively. African traders in the locations have a virtual monopoly inside their areas, but they labor under many difficulties, and most of them are petty traders in food. Stalls at the beer halls, eating houses, and markets provide fairly stable opportunities for a livelihood, though sometimes the allocation of stalls is such as to create too intense competition, or the trading center is sited off the beaten track or exposed to outside competition. The business of butcher is generally a successful business for Africans, and most of the butchers at a meat market do reasonably well, selling to all racial groups, including Whites.

It is difficult to estimate the profits of the trader, and the traders themselves are secretive. The Chairman of the Combined Location Advisory Boards estimated the annual profits of the successful African trader at between £200 and £500, while the Durban Junior Chamber of Commerce gave an estimate of about £250 to £1,000. There are certainly some African traders who do better, and it is possible to build up an extensive trading interest even from a small stall. Taken as a whole, African trade is of little significance in the economy of the city. The Durban Junior Chamber of Commerce, which conducted a brief survey, thought that there was no likelihood of any substantial increase in African trade unless some means were found of capitalizing the traders, and that the Government's policy of encouraging internal trade among the African people had not the remotest possibility of bearing fruit unless the Government took definite steps to provide facilities for the loan of capital to traders. The efforts of the African traders were described as excellent, considering the severe handicaps under which they exist in Durban.

The handicaps, as we have seen, arise partly from official policy—though it was also this policy which promoted African trade in Durban—and partly from the circumstances and background of the trader himself.

The position of the African trader remains deeply insecure, even after he has surmounted the initial obstacle of acquiring trading rights and licenses. The right to occupy trading premises under municipal control may be readily forfeited for certain offences, and trading tenancies can be terminated on one month's notice in the locations and even on twenty-four hours' notice in the eating houses and beer halls, where tenancy is on a daily basis. Building one's own shop may be an attractive opportunity, though hardly where the land is held in lease for a relatively short period or for no guaranteed period. The establishment by Alexander of the big departmental Ebony Store in Lamont Township on land held under lease for a period of twenty-five years, at a cost of over £50,000, may have been justified. Perhaps the money could have been recovered and handsome profits earned over the period: but it is a heavy risk to take, and the business failed.

Even assuming that the trader remains in occupation, he works for an uncertain future. He has no assurance that his son will be able to inherit his business, and he cannot dispose of the good will in open market, as can a White trader. Traders complain of "the insecurity of the whole business. We request the N.A.D. [i.e. Native Administration Department] to devise ways and means whereby our next of kin may derive benefits after the death of the father. We see no reason why this privilege should be denied us." "They say they own the place and they are free to give the stall to anyone they like." "The municipality is against the idea of giving the shops to our children when we retire." It can be no inducement for a son to train in his father's business when he does not know whether he will be permitted to inherit. And the father is denied a major incentive when he cannot pass on his business to his son as of right, but has to depend on the discretion of White officials. The Director of the Durban Bantu Administration Department said that it was policy to advertise the trading rights on the death of the trader, but that if the heir had assisted in the conduct of his father's business, he would have a strong claim: he still does not have a right.

Added to these basic insecurities are the inadequate facilities for trade. Shops are generally small; the trader cannot select a site; insurance companies are reluctant to insure, because Africans trade in areas where there are many burglaries—and traders often fail to keep proper records of stock; there is a lack of postal deliveries, telephones, and storage space.

Handicapped by these inadequate facilities, the trader must still meet the keen competition of established traders in town for the purchasing power of impoverished Africans. Residents are obliged to leave the locations and hostels for their daily work, and find it convenient to buy from the well-stocked shops in town selling at competitive prices. Most of the African traders in the locations seem reduced to carrying the basic necessities, often parceled in minute quantities. The Chairman of the Combined Location Advisory Boards commented:

> We can't really make much profit. Only Natives buy from us and they don't buy big things. They buy groceries and groceries are controlled. We make a penny or a halfpenny. On sugar you don't make more than 2/6d. per 100 lb. bag . . . I don't think the difficulty is that African traders don't stock the goods. The buyer buys what he is going to eat today and tomorrow. It's only the very quick turnover that gives us profit. Africans pay by installments. We can hardly afford to give them credit because we have hardly an extended account ourselves for credit. I pay cash . . . We cannot really compete by stocking clothes and furniture. We simply don't have the capital.

African ability to compete is further affected by the racial prejudices of the consumers and the established patterns of trade. Whites generally patronize their own shops, save where prices are so competitive as to make racial prejudice a luxury. Indians deal with their own people and also with Whites. Africans buy from all groups, but mostly from Indians. It is only African traders who are mostly limited to their own group. In service trades, requiring physical contact, such as hairdressing, their custom is exclusively African, and they must meet competition from Indians. Some craftsmen and traders draw non-African patronage, a tribute to their skill or low prices or both, but in general, the African trader must be satisfied with African custom only, and this custom he shares with other groups. An African tea-room proprietor expressed his resentment that while Africans trade with Indians, Indians will not buy from Africans:

> The next door tea room is Indian-owned. It's always changing hands. Every year it's changing hands [he is emphasizing his ability to meet competition]. I didn't want to go there and meet all that competition. But I couldn't go anywhere else. Africans are supposed to deal with Africans, but Africans go into the shop next door. I can't complain because I have an Indian landlord. So I share the Africans with him. But Indians only buy with him. They are so particular that they won't even buy a box of matches from me. They are very particular to buy only from their own people. If they can't get anything there, then they might come in to me.

The trader's own limitations also seriously affect his commercial potential. There is first the mode of recruitment into trade. Until Africans began to develop as independent traders and craftsmen and professional men, they could only enter the new world of industry and commerce by working for the White man. Today working for a White man becomes a distinct occupational category. An informant will say, with some pride, "I have never been employed by a White man," or "my father never worked for a European." For the sons, there is the possibility of employment in the shop or in a profession or by a European. "No child of ours helps here. Most of them are in the professions. We tried one of our sons but he was very unreliable and so we decided that he goes to work for a European." The hardships suffered under a White master may be regarded as a desirable apprenticeship for the shopkeeper's son.

> A young man must first of all work for a European in order to experience hardships because if he starts too early on his own he will not be aware of what difficulties we experience outside. My son, before he comes here to assist me, will have to go and work for a White man and when he comes here he will appreciate what struggles I had and he will not misuse the money as most children of well-to-do Africans do.
>
> A young man must work first for a White man. He must experience hardship because if he starts too soon on his own he might be careless and think life is easy.

Training is generally acquired on the job, either from fellow Africans or from Whites. It is often meager. In some cases, a traditional craft is passed on from father to son, as for example spear and shield making, or producing African curios for the tourist market. Or a man may have acquired skill in carpentry at school, and now make simple furniture or wooden trunks. Rarely, an African may have been trained to a high level of skill by a White employer, as for example in the making of saddles. In most cases he must acquire the skills for himself. He borrows clippers, practices illegally over weekends on residents in the location and finally sets himself up as a barber. Or he becomes friendly with an African watchmaker and learns the trade from him, establishing himself independently with such efficiency that he achieves the final mark of success, patronage by Whites. Or he may have worked for a White or Indian shopkeeper, possibly as a messenger. A bookseller, for example, was inspired to sell books to his people by the sight of thousands of schoolchildren coming to buy books in the shop where he was employed.

Of the 60 traders who gave information in regard to previous work experience, 31 were employees in a variety of occupations not related to their trade, including 5 schoolteachers and two agricultural demonstrators; 20 were employed in businesses related to their present trade, 7 of them by a father or brother; and the remainder had previous experience of independent trade, or came in directly or through hawking. Many of the traders were thus complete amateurs. And they commenced trade under the most varied circumstances.

Sometimes the entry into trade has called for a fanatical devotion to the Puritan ethic.

> When I was a boy I worked for Bakers, Ltd. During that time I bought offal, cooked it, and sold it to the people at the hostel, especially those who were lazy to cook. When I was working for Bakers I was still a small boy and I was earning only £2. a month; but from the offal I made more money, which gave me £3.–£4. a month profit. I used to put this money aside until I bought a motorcycle.
>
> When I left Bakers, Ltd. I was employed by the Railways, where I worked for one year and got my yearly leave. I used my leave to sell sour milk. I went to buy milk cans at Malvern, put them in my house until it got sour, then sold it. From this I made money and bought a side car for my motorcycle. The motorcycle cost me £150. I put the milk cans in the side car, so that I was able to buy more gallons of milk in this way. After some time I bought a small van which I used for the same purpose.
>
> I used to make quite good profits, but now that they introduced this artificial sour milk, I decided to apply for a table here. Sour milk was paying me more because I visited people in their homes when selling it, and now I must wait for people to come here. In my sour milk business I had no competition whatsoever.

Or again, the trader acts under the sheer drive of necessity.

> I came to Durban in 1945. I worked in a butchery. I was earning £1.10.0. a week. Realizing that this money was insufficient to support me and my family, I started buying meat and selling it at a profit. To do this I employed the services of two boys and I paid them 15/- a week. I did this for one and one-half years. I then left my European employer and continued selling meat. I had no license and when found I would be arrested. Then came a time when there was the shortage of soap, especially the blue soap. I would buy cases of this soap and go to Pondoland where I sold a bar for 2/6d. With this money I bought fowls which I carted to Durban to resell again. After that I bought cows and slaughtered them and sold the meat. All this was illegal and I ran the risk of being charged. Then came the riots in 1949 and the burning down of Indian shops. I took a chance and sold groceries in my shack until I got these

premises. When I began this business I had never been to school. I only did night school a few years back.

Or he is inspired by the dislocation of Indian trade after the 1949 riots, and the enticement of profit.

> You want me to tell you about how we began our business, well as a Christian I think I must tell the truth. We started selling things after the 1949 riots because the people here had nowhere to buy groceries. At the time there was only one small shop in front of the office which had practically no stalls. We used to see Indians from Isipingo coming with lorries full of these groceries and we felt that they were doing a lot of money and we turned one of our rooms into a shop where we could sell to the people some of the things they required.
>
> After a time we had a table where we sold vegetables and fruits. At that time because our house was next to the "X" Secondary School I decided to make fat cakes for the children and also sell sweets. The children used to flood to our house and buy these. It was these cakes which brought in a lot of profit. At that time I also joined the stock fair and this enabled me to save a lot. Every month I was able to save about £50 a month. At the time my husband was working at the railways as a police and he was earning £20 and his money from that time on was never used to maintain the family but I maintained the family from the proceeds of the groceries and fat cakes. After we had invested enough money my husband left the railways to personally manage our shop and from the proceeds of that small shop we were able to pay cash for this house . . . We are now building a better shop. [Account by the wife of one of the most successful traders in Durban. Superficially she enacts the role of the subordinate African woman, standing against or partly behind a pillar, with eyes cast down, when speaking to me, or sitting on a straight chair at the edge of the room, while I sit in a comfortable lounge chair.]

The selection procedures applied by the Corporation in areas under its control give preference to applicants with higher qualifications, but education is still low (though above average), and capital is generally inadequate, though some applicants have substantial resources. In applications for the trading stores at Chesterville Location, capital ranged from £25 to over £300 plus the ownership of five properties. The effect of inadequate capital is to favor the marginal trader. In the slums of Cato Manor, where many traders moved from illegal into licensed trade, that is, in the relatively uncontrolled situation of the open community, the circumstances more strongly favored the recruitment of the marginal traders. They were marginal as residents in an area of urban disorganization, some of them not eligible to remain and seek employment in the city, and they were marginal as lacking the facilities for trade, so that they resorted to dealing, even in food, from their unhygienic shack homes. The whole development took place in the interstices of Durban society, in terms of area, legality, and mode of operation, like that of shebeen queens or gangs.

Religious organizations and buying clubs may provide an umbrella from which the marginal traders can come into the open. In the following application[2] there is a strange interweaving of religion and commerce.

PARLIAMENTARY SOVEREIGNTY.
(TSHAKA THE KING)
I HAWU LAMA AFRIKA.
INVUSELELO YAMA SIKO KA ZULU:

Prayer Meetings and Provincial Board. Organisation of the Bantu United Service in Africa. Nehemia 9.2.3.1. Exodus 20.5 Mateu 5.18.17. Luke 9.62.
Bank. For Dismemberments of Ethiopia (Addis Ababa) Under No. D.1/3. No.N.1/14/3.

I.H.L.A. Bantu Sovereignty.
x for the Union of Africans x
Duduza, Natal.

This organisation is supporting an application by N. Mbhalla for a temporary permit for a Grocery Shop.

The Organisation has asked him what does he want with a store. He said he wants it for the purpose of helping him to support his family as he does not get enough support; and he does not intend to supplement his income by stealing.

That is why the Congregation is supporting his application for a temporary permit for a Store. This application has been reported to 12 members of the Executive Committee.

It has been supported under the Conferences of Delegates of this meeting.

President, Chairman, Organiser, Treasurer and Bookkeeper, Inspector, Secretary.

I.H.L.A. Bantu Sovereignty
For the Union of Africans,
DUDUZA, Natal

---

2. Translation of a letter written in Zulu.

Or again, the founder of the Aborigines Brotherhood Community, which is still in the making, notifies his intention to set up a large business venture, and seeks guidance on the draft constitution. The constitution encompasses almost the whole of life. The general aim is "to guide the Bantu Community in the natural way by men and women of gravity and wisdom of its own race, to a best standard of living; and do so in an orderly way; by teaching them the art of self-control within small community units and thereby preparing them for shouldering efficiently the corresponding responsibility in respect of a wider area." The specific aims are:

1. To improve our national character.
2. To create heart-cleanliness within ourselves [read Mat. 5:8].
3. To create systematic, psychological, and logical directions leading to the nearest attainable mitigations and the solutions of problems of poverty which ruins life and labour, health and happiness of tens of millions of us [Bantu Community].
4. To create a vast network of united firms for the benefit of the Bantu Community.
5. To create a shield of protection of the welfare of the community, we intend to elect some of us for the formation of a protective body of special constables.
6. Any member of this community who becomes dangerous or snake-like or even suspected to be contradicting with rules and regulations of this community will be dealt with by the management.
7. All members of the A.B.C. acknowledge whole-heartedly their loyalty to the Government, not of South Africa alone but of Africa as a whole.
8. People who believe in shebeen-richness or dagga-wisdom should not consolidate themselves with the A.B.C. at all.
9. No one allowed to ask the public for funds without the consent or permit bearing the signature of the General Overseer of the A.B.C. . . .*

The general effects of marginal recruitment, modest standards of education, lack of capital and of experience were to be observed in a course conducted by the Durban Junior Chamber of Commerce for African traders on seven Sunday mornings in 1959. The total enrollment was about eighty-five, mostly traders in Durban, a few quite substantial; very minor traders had not been approached to attend the course. The selection and handling of topics were based on a preliminary survey, and adapted to problems raised during the course. Contributions from the traders ranged from the most elementary questions to shrewd, critical comments. About half took notes, some were illiterate. At the request of the traders, the lectures were interpreted from English into Zulu. And in order to meet the needs of some of the traders, the final examination was an oral one, with an interpreter and examiner at each table. As a measure of the poor equipment of some traders, there were questions on how to check goods ordered or how to take stock when the trader cannot read or write, and a complaint that traders lose money when they ask wholesalers at what price they should sell and then sell at that price. A section of the traders must have been working with little knowledge of costing, stocktaking, and profit making. The Junior Chamber found it necessary to conduct the course and the examination at a most elementary level, as shown for example in the following questions:

> Question 1. Do you need ready money to start a business—why?
> Answer . . . Yes, to buy stocks, pay rent, fit out shop, etc.
> Question 3. Why should a shopkeeper stay in his shop during business hours?
> Answer . . . Because no one will take as good care of his shop and he can best guard against theft.
> Question 7. What are Cost Price—Gross Profit—Net Profit?
> Question 8. How often and why must you take stock?
> Question 11. If you do not have a bank account where or how should you keep your money?
> Question 12. What is a cash book—why should you keep one?
> Question 15. Why should you buy goods at the lowest prices?

The examinations were taken by fifty-three traders, and certificates were presented with much ceremony at a graduation attended by the Native Commissioner, the Director of the Bantu Administration Department, and the ex-President of the Junior Chamber of Commerce. The traders seemed to attach importance to the occasion. They came well dressed, giving a strong impression of the sober lesser bourgeoisie, and seemed to value their certificates. A leading trader proposed a vote of thanks. The traders, he said, owe profound gratitude to the Junior Chamber of Commerce for having taken the initiative to train them. June 14th (the day of the graduation) will be remembered as the writing of White history for African traders by the Junior Chamber of Commerce. African traders had won the theoretical battle. It was now left to see whether they would do likewise practically.

There are some African traders in Durban who compete successfully, and whose interests might be served by open competition. Most, however, need the protection they receive, such as the racial reservation of trading opportunities in the locations, and the right to keep extended shop hours. Protection may perhaps impede the emergence of a strong class of traders in the long run, but it seems to be a condition of immediate survival under conditions in which Africans are poorly equipped to trade, while their competitors are highly experienced and long established. This was the opinion of a number of informants. The Superintendent of Locations, when asked whether the system of protection might not encourage inefficiency, replied that Africans could not compete with Indians. The Senior Supervisor of Locations in Durban thought that Africans had succeeded as butchers in the market because the Indians there dealt only in mutton. Mr. R. Cope, Supervising Overseer, reported in 1955 that at the Victoria Street Eating House, Africans avoided the grocery business "as if it was contaminated with leprosy," the reason being the "formidable number" of Indian traders in the adjoining market. On the African side, a well-established location trader, prominent in public affairs, commented that Africans "cannot compete with Indians in business. Far from it. I don't think we'll ever pitch up to their understanding. Where merchants work it out for us its alright." The Chairman of the Durban Combined Advisory Boards, himself a trader, thought that Africans would make good businessmen if given the same opportunities as members of other races, though he did not want Indians as neighbors, "because they are too business-minded. But I don't hate them, I fear their competition."

In the situation of protected African trade within the locations of Durban, Indian-African rivalry is not too acute. Some traders express the same stereotype of Indians as applied to Jews in conditions of anti-semitism, and complain of Indian exploitation of African traders and customers. Others appreciate the interest of Indian wholesalers in African trade, and their assistance by way of credit, advice, and the delivery of small quantities which will not overcrowd the limited storage facilities. Or they recognize the service rendered by Indian retailers to African customers. The situation is different in the context of open competition, and it was in this context that Indian-African trade rivalry in Cato Manor found expression in extreme racialism. The circumstances were specially conducive to racial conflict.

Slum conditions themselves may be expected to stimulate violent reaction. In Cato Manor, before the policy of shack demolition became effective, Africans could escape from the tight control of urban African administration, even under the routine of daily police raids. Into the shacks flowed the many people who could not get proper accommodation in the locations, or who preferred the freedom of Cato Manor to supervised living in a location. And above all, for Africans not legally entitled to be in the area, Cato Manor offered a refuge, albeit hazardous since at any moment they might be caught in a police net and deported to their tribal areas, and since registering for employment would expose them to an automatic check on their right to be in the urban area.

Independent occupations provided a temporary solution, such as the illicit brewing of liquor by women, or other forms of illegal trade. There was in consequence much desperation among the residents of Cato Manor, and a general disorganization aggravated by shack demolitions, police raids, and the illicit liquor trade—circumstances conducive to the periodic outbreaks of violence.

African pressure for trading rights had been building up in Durban prior to the 1949 riots. In 1948, the Bantu Administration Department reported that sites were at a premium and that many were waiting to undertake the risks of private enterprise. As the demand for trading rights grew and was blocked by municipal control and Indian competition, there developed a force ready to erupt wherever the barriers showed signs of weakening. The riots effected a breach as the result of the destruction of Indian shops and the temporary disruption of African-Indian trade. Through this breach, illegal African traders emerged in the African areas of Durban, and more particularly in Cato Manor, where houses and stores had been burned, Indian men killed, and women violated. Before the riots, there were 22 licensed Indian traders and 11 licensed African traders in Cato Manor. In August of the following year, the number had increased to 26 licensed Indian traders, 18 licensed African traders, and 38 unlicensed African traders. Three years later (June 1953), the illegal African traders in the Cato Manor area numbered 105, almost exclusively dealers in foodstuffs, with about 10 of the shops having tinkers and hairdressers attached.

The causes of the 1949 riots are not clear, nor, for a variety of reasons, does the *Report of the Commission of Enquiry into Riots in Durban*[3] offer much enlightenment. In particular, it is difficult to say whether rivalry for trade and bus transport undertakings was a factor in the riots. Certainly, the African community was quick to exploit the consequences of the riots and the disruption of Indian trade. On February 19, 1949, shortly after the riots, a mass meeting of Africans in Durban resolved to support an Indian boycott movement, and instructed the African National Congress and the Durban Locations Advisory Boards inter alia to:

> impress on the Indians that African development is such that African economic progress can no longer be delayed or obstructed; ensure that whenever the African expresses willingness to take over the services at present in Indian hands in predominantly African areas, the Indian should give proof of his goodwill by disposing of these to the African at a reasonable price and that the African be given every facility to trade and to run buses to and from African areas; ensure that where Indian buses run or

3. Government of South Africa, U.G. 36/1949.

shops are established, and where these do not come under African management, African drivers and conductors and salesmen be employed [minutes of a meeting of the Combined Location Advisory Boards, March 8, 1949].

The attitude is that of the arrogant conqueror. The long-established rights of Indian traders and bus owners are disregarded. Indians must transfer their businesses as evidence of goodwill. There is no suggestion of reciprocity, except perhaps the suggestion that Africans will not riot again if Indians divest themselves of their assets.

The illegal traders presented their activities as guided by altruism, the desire to assist their people (memorandum to the Chief Native Commissioner, Durban, dated January 8, 1954), and maintained that both representatives of the Government and of the Corporation had encouraged them to trade. Whatever the situation in regard to encouragement, there can be no doubt that the Government and the Corporation condoned the illegal trading. Thus after a further outbreak of violence in September 1953, the Minister of Bantu Affairs expressed the following opinion:

> Evidently as far as possible, the root of the evil should be tackled rather than the consequences. In this connection the Indian share in trade and transport is first on the list. Going without saying is to give all new opportunities decidedly to Natives. Hereby those who are now trading illegally should not be victimised excepting those who are otherwise criminal. It seems that they are more technical offenders as they have not been able to obtain licenses or premises sooner. Two birds are killed with one stone if they can now become legal traders and bus owners. Otherwise with other Native traders they remain aggrieved element. It is best to lead existing trading in legal ways [contained in a letter from the Secretary for Native Affairs to the Chief Native Commissioner, December 11, 1953, and quoted in a memorandum by a departmental official dated January 11, 1955].*

As to the Bantu Administration Department of the Durban Corporation, it was opposed to illegal trading, but had modified its attitude in relation to Cato Manor because illegal trading had been virtually condoned for a considerable period after the riots and had become too entrenched for removal by a stroke of the pen, and because whatever action was taken at Cato Manor should be with a due regard to a judicious application of diplomacy, strategy, fairness, and firmness (memorandum of April 30, 1953).

It was difficult for the Corporation to follow a consistent policy, since

---

* Source could not be rechecked.

it was subjected to many cross pressures. It did not wish to condone illegal trading. On the other hand, African-Indian relations at Cato Manor were explosive: the Government sympathized with African aspirations in the area; Africans felt encouraged to pursue an aggressive policy; and sections of White public opinion in Durban favored the Africans in Cato Manor, no doubt assisted in this direction by anti-Indian sentiment. When twenty-three illegal African traders were fined and the Magistrate commented on the insufficiency of licenses, the *Natal Mercury* carried a leader (on May 19, 1953) that the Mayor was shocked by the prosecutions, since it was temporarily agreed that they be soft-pedaled, and the Mayor himself directed that means should be found immediately to provide Africans with lawful trading opportunities in Cato Manor. In July 1954, when some forty cases of illegal trading at Cato Manor were taken before the Magistrate, and the first accused, though found guilty, was cautioned and discharged, the prosecutor withdrew the balance of the charges as a protest against inadequate sentences.

The Corporation tried to regulate the situation by building shops for Africans and expropriating Indian shops in the Emergency Camp Area of Cato Manor. As legal trade developed, illegal traders were prosecuted; sometimes the shack premises used for trade were demolished. Illegal trade proved resistant, however, and in January 1957 there were still 120 illegal traders in Cato Manor, according to a census taken by the Cato Manor Welfare and Development Board. Parallel with the building of shops for Africans, the Corporation expropriated Indian traders in the Emergency Camp Area and allocated their shops to Africans—apart from some premises reserved for a post office, clinic, and child welfare and departmental offices. By January 1958, most of the Indian shops had been taken over.

The effect of these policies was to establish African traders in Cato Manor. The fostering of African enterprise in transport proved more difficult, notwithstanding support from the Corporation and the Bantu Affairs Commissioner, and notwithstanding African self-help through a boycott and the stoning of Indian buses. A number of African bus ventures burgeoned briefly and collapsed, or were liquidated, or disposed of their interests. In 1961, no Africans ran bus services inside Durban itself, though some provided services between Inanda and Durban, and between Umbumbulu and Durban.

African pressure for trading rights in Cato Manor was exerted by illegal traders, organized as buying clubs, presumably in an attempt to give legal cover to their activities. These organizations expressed and exploited African antagonism toward Indians; they exploited the Government's declared policy of encouraging Africans to monopolize trade in their own areas, and the anti-Indian sentiments of Whites; and they by-passed the Corporation in direct approaches to the Government on lines of appeal which they had reason to believe would be well received.

The Zondizitha (Hate The Enemies) Buying Club, with an original membership of about twelve to fourteen, which had increased to twenty-five in October 1952, appealed to the Mayor of Durban for relief. Their case was that they had set up small stores after the riots; that the Minister of Native Affairs had visited the area and permitted Africans to carry on trade; and that the City Council had refused to relax the health regulations, but had promised that Indian shops in Cato Manor would be given to Africans to conduct their business. This was not done, and now they were being prosecuted by the health authorities and for trading without a permit with heavy fines, thus increasing poverty and depriving Africans of legitimate livelihoods.

Previously they had sent applications for general dealers' licenses. Their agent had pleaded for the relaxation of health regulations, drawing a parallel with European trading in the early days of the century: "it was known to everyone that that time was not ripe for them to have business premises which were of concrete and burnt bricks." * Later, the same agent had written to the Manager of the City's Bantu Administration Department in accents of abject humility:

> Let us say that when you have a cow wishing to milk it and it runs away from you but at that time it changes its mind and comes to you I believe that you shall never neglect it because no matter where the beast may go it remains and vest in your powers; this being what applies to these Native Traders for they are yours and they shall always remain under you.*

In December 1954, Zondizitha was laying its grievances before the Governor-General.

More prominent than Zondizitha was the Zulu Hlanganani Association, which commemorates the 1949 riots in an annual celebration. A leading member of the African National Congress, who was associated professionally with Hlanganani, attended a celebration in 1951. He commented that there was nothing really anti-Indian about it: they celebrated on the grounds that they had focused the attention of the Government and of the Africans, with the result that there were now more traders. He did not think this anti-Indianism was something to worry about. It is difficult to agree with the informant. In August 1955, representatives of the Association presented the following petition to a central government official:

* Source could not be rechecked.

We the undersigned members of the Zulu Hlanganani Association of Cato Manor, here declare duly appointed representatives. It is the wish of the above Association to have the following matters cleared up. Consequently we appeal to the leader of the Bantu National Congress Mr. P. Makhene whose ideas are parallel with those of our Association and duly register ourselves with Bantu National Congress. The above area to our knowledge is proclaimed Bantu Area. The trading facilities and the everything are inherritage of the Bantu people. To our surprise trading facilities are in the hands of the Indians at this opportune time.

The above Association has fought tooth and nail to have these errors rectified with the officials of the Municipality of Durban. The responsible officials have since 1949 promised to rectify these mistakes but all in vain. It shall be remembered that in January, 14th, 1949, the riots took place between Bantu and the Indians in the said area. On the 18th January, 1949, the Municipal Officials pleaded for help from those that are prepared to help the Bantu residents of the mentioned area. Shortly after that a Commission was formed . . . to investigate the causes of the riots.

On the 5th December, 1950, another meeting was held in the Municipal Administrative Office . . . Mayor ——— declared that all trading facilities would be given to Bantu. From the genesis of the abovementioned area we have had promises which have never been fulfilled.

The Zulu Hlanganani Association has given several personal interviews and individual applications to the officials responsible for the area but all in vain. Trading rights are still in the hands of the Indians. We, therefore, present these grievances to you, Sir, so that they can be immediately rectified. It is not our wish to see another bloody war in this said Area but unless things can come our way within the short space of time it is possible that our respect and endurance shall no more prevail.*

The link with the Bantu National Congress is significant. This was an abortive political movement, mainly of African herbalists, which sought to win Government recognition by outright support of the policy of apartheid and a virulent anti-Indian campaign. The threat in the final paragraph is no trifle against the background of the 1949 riots and of the subsequent disorders in September 1953.

To phrase the matter conservatively, the rise of African traders in Cato Manor coincided with anti-Indian campaigns. In April 1953, a departmental official reports strong anti-Indian feeling as a result of Indian competition, prosecutions of Africans, and an Indian bus monop-

* Source could not be rechecked.

oly. In August 1953, there is a departmental report on complaints by
certain Cato Manor residents. Its findings are that there is little commerce between Indian men and African women, that it is rare to find
an African-Indian offspring, and that there was not a single complaint
of seduction. Nor was there any evidence of reckless driving and short
changing on Indian buses, but buses were unfairly distributed between
Indian and African owners in the Cato Manor area, about sixty-five
Indian buses to nine African. The report suggests that the trouble is
being engineered by illegal shopkeepers, illegal roadside vendors, African
shack landlords, unsuccessful applicants for transport certificates, and
persons illegally in the area. On September 20, 1953, there was a flare-up
against Indians in Cato Manor. According to a report in the *Natal
Mercury* (September 21, 1953), the riots started when an African attempted to board an Indian bus in Cato Manor, fell under the rear
wheels, and was killed. Thirteen or fourteen Indian stores and two
private Indian homes were set on fire, and one Indian bus was reduced
to ashes.

In March 1954, four members of the Cato Manor Welfare and Development Board handed in a petition from the residents of the Two
Stick and Langwane areas, complaining that an Indian had a shop, for
which a license had not yet been granted, yet he appeared to trade behind
closed doors. African women were admitted, the doors closed, there was
fear of indecent acts, and the situation might cause trouble at any
moment. Racialism always seems to resort to the play on sexual jealousies.

It was a dangerous weapon the Government unleashed in offering
new opportunities for African trade at the expense of vested Indian
trading rights. The two groups were set against each other in a situation
which invited Africans to take extreme racialist action. In this way,
no doubt, "two birds are killed with one stone." The implications
strike much deeper. The appeal of apartheid for the African trader
rests on racialism—a monopoly for one's own racial group and the
exclusion of other racial groups. It may be expected to predispose African
traders to the acceptance of a political philosophy, transcending Afrikaner dispensations, in which the power of the State vests in the African
majority and is exercised in its exclusive interests.

PART IV

The Organizational Milieu

CHAPTER 20

Voluntary Associations

WHITE CONTROL provides the basic structure of urban African life in South Africa. In large measure, the urban order is imposed on Africans. They are obliged to accept, or react against, or modify patterns set by an outside group. Their initiative and spontaneity are limited, and the range and form of their voluntary associations are controlled or profoundly influenced by Whites. The influence may be by way of the direct establishment or promotion of an African association, as in the case of the Location Advisory Boards and the Durban and District African Football Association, which will be discussed in the following chapters. Or the influence may be expressed indirectly by African imitation, as where African churches break away from a parent White mission church but adhere to the same beliefs, rituals, and communal forms. Or, paradoxically, there may be an indirect determination of spontaneous forms of African associational life. Thus I take the many mutual aid societies among Africans to be a consequence, certainly in part, of White urban and industrial dispensations and of inadequate provision for basic needs in a context of social change. In other words, there is a spontaneous movement of associational activities into the less structured areas of urban life.

The African residential pattern is set by Whites, with careful regulation of location, type of home, and form of tenure. Control is channeled through the Superintendents, and provision is even made for residents' associations in the form of Advisory Boards. The housing situation is only partly structured since accommodation did not keep pace with urban African migration, and the large illegal shanty towns temporarily bridged the gap. One important local movement in Johannesburg was based on an organization of shanty townsmen in search of homes, but the circumstances do not favor stable organization. In Cato Manor, for example, shanty dwellers initially lived mainly on land owned by Indian landlords, and their relationships, being based on individual contracts with different landlords, did not encourage joint action in residents' associations. Also many were uneducated, illegally in the towns, traditionally oriented. The population was shifting and unstable. Illegal brewers competed with each other, and there was a continuous invasion of the area by unattached African men and by the police, both in search of liquor, while shack demolitions and removals heightened the insecurity. From time to time, residents at Cato Manor have banded together in protection of their interests, but many of these associations probably owed their origin to the political organizations, in contrast to the spontaneous mass demonstrations, and were quite ephemeral.

African employment is rigorously controlled through the official procedures of influx permits, labor bureaus, and registration of service contracts, thus excluding the possibility of voluntary employment agencies. Even under the less rigid system of the past, Africans could hardly be effective in securing employment for their fellows, since they were not employers of labor and had low prestige with other groups: assistance hardly extended beyond that of kinsmen finding domestic employment for each other. In trade, opportunity is controlled by the authorities, thus encouraging dependent relations with Location Superintendents and Supervisors, rather than the independent organization of the traders themselves. It was in the unstructured situation of illegal trade and the disruption of Indian trade by the riots in Cato Manor that spontaneous trading associations developed in Durban. Two successful associations of illicit liquor dealers in Johannesburg also arose in a similar way, in the interstices, as it were, of ordered society. Partly as a result of the initiative and example of Whites, partly under pressure of disabilities specific to the African trader, and in some cases with the hope of promoting "Buy African" movements, African Chambers of Commerce are being established in a number of cities: there were also earlier instances of minor trading associations. At a conference attended by delegates representing more than 4,000 African traders, an African National Chamber of Commerce has now been formed (*The Star*, Overseas Edition, May 2, 1964).

African schools are the creation of the White man, and contained within his institutions. The training of African teachers, the objectives of African education, and the curricula and organization of the schools are determined by Whites. Even the participation of parents in School Committees and School Boards is regulated by statute. However there have been separate African teachers' associations for many years, the Natal African Teachers' Union, which had been founded in 1918, and the Cape African Teachers' Association in 1921. The segregated teachers' associations reflect the segregated nature of mission education, but not its denominational barriers, which the associations largely transcend.

Whites control the professions of law and medicine, and professional associations are thus provided for lawyers and doctors, including the small number of Africans. A spontaneous organization of non-European medical interns arose in the special circumstances of a movement against discriminatory salaries in King Edward VIII Hospital. At present, as a result both of pressure from the Government for comprehensive apartheid in the professional associations and of growing national sentiment among Africans, it seems likely that Africans will themselves establish a separate professional association. Nursing associations are governed by statute, and, again, it was a special circumstance, the imposition of apartheid in the nursing profession, which provoked the organization of an independent nonracial nursing association.

In religious organization, the basic structure was laid down by the mission churches. The ancestral cult, in which the services were performed by the head of the lineage in the ancestral home, provides no basis for religious organization in South African towns, nor was there an indigenous priesthood which could become an organizing group. The age structure in the towns, heavily weighted with younger men, would tend to exclude the heads of lineages. Nevertheless the traditional diffusion of religious responsibility at the level of the kin group may have been a factor in the proliferation of the small groups of Zionists to be seen in the streets of the cities. The churches and their subsidiary organizations provide an important area of association for urban Africans, promoting contact among strangers, and transcending tribal and class differences, though these may emerge in separate ceremonies and churches for different linguistic groups, or in a measure of separation between the educated and the uneducated in the subsidiary activities of the church. Women are the main worshippers, apparently experiencing great emotional fulfillment and a sense of significance in the release from traditional subordination. Women's associations flourish: the women often wear special costumes, and organize as a locality group providing sociability, mutual aid, and spiritual succor in times of need, a community of the elect.

It is probably in the field of religion that there has been the greatest development of African associational life, much of it outside the mission churches. This has been partly in reaction against White domination, the "Ethiopian" movement modeling itself on the dogma and ritual of a parent mission church, but asserting African independence.[1] The Ethiopian churches tend to reproduce themselves by fission as a result of rivalry for leadership, the desire for self-expression, disputes over property, and no doubt purely theological differences. They are

1. Monica Wilson suggests that splits occur where there is no strong sense of the Church as a Church, a corporate body distinct from a number of individual Christians meeting together (*The Coherence of Groups*, Durban, Institute for Social Research, University of Natal, 1962, p. 9).

essentially a product of the mission churches. In the case of the Zionist movement, Sundkler[2] comments that the initial force behind it was the Christian Catholic Apostolic Church in Zion, which was founded in North America in 1896. The influence of the mission churches in the Zionist and Bantu Messianic movements is, however, less direct and less pervasive: there is also a strong traditional influence, beliefs and rituals effecting a syncretism of Christianity and traditional worship.

Whatever the role of the missions, much of the impulse toward independent churches derives from the social situation of Africans. Sundkler links "the dramatic, hectic formation of Separatist Churches with an apocalyptic programme" to the quest for living space, for some security in terms of ownership of a piece of land, which became "the one burning question" after the promulgation of the Native Land Act of 1913. He sees the explosive development of the African independent churches as a consequence of what Africans came to regard as one of the great crises of this century. Of ritual, he comments that the Zionists and sections of the Ethiopians somehow stem from American Protestant churches, professing a sturdy individualism and democratic ideals.

> But let these democratic groups operate in a Bantu context in Natal and Zululand, and the result is paradoxical. Throw out the bishops in the name of democracy, and next day your cook or garage attendant will turn up as an Archbishop in mitre and vestments. Wrench the gilded crozier or pastoral staff out of the hand of your bishop, and next day you will find every member of the Zionist congregation with a staff and cross—not of gold this time, but of the wood of a special tree, the thorny *sondeza*.

And he shows the reaction to Whites in dogmas establishing an independent sacred genealogy for the Bantu churches, mystical and biblical credentials not derived from the Whites, and in the role of the Bantu prophet, the Bantu Messiah who stands at the Gate.[3]

In the field of formal recreation, Africans are largely dependent on Whites. Employers of African workers organize recreation by way of tribal dance or Western sport. Where such major facilities as sports grounds are required, Africans are almost inevitably dependent on the White authorities. Welfare services too are White. They were established by Whites and extended to Africans, discharging some of the functions performed by kinsmen in traditional society. Even though the scale of assistance may be low, the costs exceed the resources of most Africans. Where organizations provide interracial contact, the

2. Sundkler, *Bantu Prophets,* p. 48.

3. B. G. M. Sundkler, *The Concept of Christianity in the African Independent Churches* (Durban, Institute for Social Research, University of Natal, 1958).

initiative is almost invariably taken by the more privileged non-African groups. Presumably it is inevitable under conditions of racial inequality that initiative and leadership in interracial association should follow the hierarchical structure, more particularly where Africans command less organizational skill, though G. E. J. Brausch[4] mentions that members of the African intellectual elite in the Congo, encouraged by progressive Whites, had conceived the idea of interracial associations to foster fraternization.

It is almost only in the field of politics, not regarded as a role for Africans, that they have been free to create their own organizations and to develop their own ideologies. And even here, the influence of non-Africans has been profound. It is not surprising then, in the light of their general separation from the means of organization, that Africans hold back from movements initiated by the members of other racial groups.

Many of the associations fostered by Whites tend to be paternalist. The more spontaneous and independent urban African associations have arisen in response to needs which the official dispensations did not satisfy, or in reaction to crises, or, as discussed above, by way of rejection of White control.

In cases where few material facilities are required, and at the level of small groups, there are no real obstacles to the exuberant growth of African associations. Monica Wilson and Philip Mayer have described for Cape Town and East London the "home-boy cliques." In Cape Town, the home-boys are those who come from one district, village, or section of a village, and their cliques change in composition though continuing over time. "The district registration number for motor vehicles—C.F.D. or C.D.X. and so on, remains emblazoned over the door, the sign that here live the men from Alice or Middledrift, or wherever it may be." [5]

The prolific mutual aid societies, such as the "stockfairs," are of the same independent small-group type. Indeed, in Cape Town, the home-boy groups operate as friendly societies. The stockfairs generally consist of a few members, organized as a group with a chairman and secretary. They are often limited in membership either to men or to women. Each member in turn receives a small cash contribution from fellow members, thus helping to satisfy capital needs, which cannot

4. "The Problem of Elites in the Belgian Congo," *International Social Science Bulletin,* 8 (1956), p. 457.

5. Monica Wilson, *The Coherence of Groups,* p. 4. See also for Cape Town, Monica Wilson and Archie Mafeje, *Langa,* chap. 3, and for East London the full analysis of *amakhaya,* "home-people," in Mayer's *Townsmen or Tribesmen* (Cape Town, Oxford University Press, 1961), especially chaps. 5–7.

be met from the subsistence wages prevailing in the towns. The forms of the stockfair seem almost infinitely varied. Organization may be quite elaborate, based, for example, on a federation of small units, and assistance may be given by way of patronage of a drinking or supper party or in goods rather than cash. Stockfairs tend to combine sociability with mutual aid.

Some of the Zionist churches have a large membership, but most consist of small bands of devout believers. They are perhaps not unlike the diviner with his group of consultants in traditional society. In Durban, the pattern seems to be that of a man as leader, while the devotees are mostly women. Services are often held on an open piece of ground, within which the worshippers group in a narrow circle of hallowed land. The contraction of the circle, the intimacy of contact between devotees, and the trancelike inward quality of the group are suggestive of a close-knit community finding within itself a deep security in an alien world.

Small entertainment groups, in choirs or jazz bands or with penny whistles, express a native interest in music and sociability, encouraged to some extent by the hope of breaking through into the entertainment world. Whites respond warmly to African entertainers, and help to promote them.

Tribal associations in the towns may be promoted by the ruling houses of the traditional societies, and a leading personality—a prince or a relative of the chief—acts as the dominant figure linking the two societies. A common tribal identity may provide the basis for gangs, or for traditional dance teams in the towns. In Durban, the City Corporation has for a long time maintained diplomatic relations with the Zulu Royal House, and a representative of the Royal House functions within the administration. There appear to be no tribal associations whatever. This is unexpected, since there are small tribal groups, some far from home, in an overwhelmingly Zulu population (117,601 persons, over 86 per cent of the African population in 1951).[6] The Sothos celebrate a national day in dance and speech—Moshoeshoe's Day—and Sinyamo, an entertainment festival. The Nyassas will often delay a funeral to a Saturday in order that tribesmen may attend, but there is no formal organization. Monica Wilson[7] reports almost the identical situation for Cape Town.

Many of the small associations are a response to situations of crises, as, for example, women banding together in protest against the demolition of their shacks, or illegal traders exploiting riot and disruption. Some of the large independent associations, particularly the political,

6. Kuper, Watts, and Davies, *Durban: A Study in Racial Ecology,* p. 87.
7. *The Coherence of Groups,* p. 11.

owe their origins to threatening situations—some crisis has provided the stimulus and the occasion for their establishment. The Federation of Bantu Churches in South Africa may serve as a contemporary example of the crisis reaction and the binding force of threatened interests, though there would seem to be little prospect of an enduring association.

The independent African churches are dependent on the Government for recognition, and the consequent privileges of marriage officers, railway concessions, and sites for churches and schools. There is always this anomaly in African life in South Africa that all independence is spurious. In 1959, there were about 2,250 African churches without Government recognition, and 81 recognized churches (*Bantu Education Journal*, December 1959, p. 557: no doubt, some of the nonrecognized churches had ceased to exist). Both African and White churchmen are troubled by this fragmentation of African religious life, and doubtful of the Christian content in the teachings of some of the sects. The Interdenominational African Ministers' Federation, for example, expressed its objections to "the multiplicity of churches dotted all over the townships. This recurring decimal for self aggrandisement sometimes does more harm than good to the religious life of the people" (*baNtu*, April 1961, p. 174). African politicians have shown interest in the political potentialities of a united church. Thus Sundkler reports that a project for bringing together the separatist churches in a United National Church of Africa was taken over by the African National Congress, and an appeal issued under its aegis on December 16, 1931, suggesting this day as the annual day of the church.[8] The political interests are clear, December 16 being a national heroes' day for the Afrikaners on which they celebrate their victory over the Zulu people, consequent upon a covenant with their God. Conversely, some White politicians express anxiety over the potentialities for Black nationalism in the separatist movement. In any event, quite apart from political and religious considerations, the sheer numbers of these churches would have raised serious administrative problems and made difficult the allocation of sites in the urban locations. And in 1959, as a result of a Government circular, the nonrecognized churches were threatened with denial of sites for their congregations in the townships, and in some cases with expropriation of churches and parsonages. This threat has not yet been lifted.

Insecurity thus provides a basis, if not for the unification of the separatist churches, at any rate for a loose federation. But even this loose federation is likely to be unstable, because of the great diversity, and the exalted and sanctified position, of many of the religious leaders.

8. Sundkler, *Bantu Prophets*, pp. 50–51.

At the annual general conference of the Federation in May 1960, about 280 delegates attended (160 men and 120 women), representing some 200 sects. According to a tally made by an observer, there were among the men 51 bishops (26 of them on the committee), 39 prophets, and 58 ministers (the rest being laymen); and among the women, 10 bishops and 9 pastors. Educational levels varied, though generally they appeared not to be high: when the President spoke in English he needed two interpreters to convey his message.[9] How is such diversity and such sanctity of priest and prophet and divine revelation to be united in a single fold? Unification in groups of a few churches seems more feasible; for example the Ethiopian Catholic Church in Zion, threatened by the inability to secure recognition, merging with the recognized New-Church Mission in South Africa (*Ilanga Lase Natal*, April 15, 1961).

African political organizations derive to a large extent from situations of crises and from the denial of an effective political role for Africans. At the level of White initiative, only the Communist Party, founded in 1921, offered scope for Africans, until the establishment of the Liberal Party and the Progressive Party in the last decade. The Unity Movement, which has strong Colored leadership and is based primarily on the concept of non-European unity and a strategy of non-cooperation, did not come into existence until the Second World War. By this time Africans had already pioneered political associations: indeed, there were some small African political associations prior to Union. The African National Congress was founded in 1912 as a movement for democratic rights, and as a reaction to the denial of these rights in the constitution of the Union of South Africa. Similarly, the All-African Convention was established in response to a crisis, the contraction of African political rights under the Representation of Natives Bill, and the inadequacy of the allocation of land under the Native Land and Trust Bill. And, finally, the Pan-Africanist Congress, which arose in 1958 by fission within the African National Congress, expresses nationalist sentiments always present in the Congress movement as well as desperation over increasing racial subordination and the seeming failure of African political strategy.

A trade union role for Africans was never fully institutionalized, and the definition of "employee" under the Industrial Conciliation Act of 1924, as extended in 1937, effectively excluded the vast majority of African workers from participation in registered trade unions or in collective bargaining within the statutory machinery. Prior to this, in 1918–19, Africans had themselves pioneered the Industrial and Commercial Workers' Union. This was the first trade union for Africans

9. I am indebted to H. S. H. Ramaila for his analysis of this conference.

(including also some Colored members). It rapidly assumed the character of a political mass party of national emancipation, and as rapidly declined after a meteoric rise in the 1920s. The Communist Party actively promoted the organization of African workers in industry, and African trade union activity reached its peak in 1945. Inevitably it takes on an explicitly political character, since Africans are a proletariat in the classic Marxist sense and constitutional forms of economic and political redress are lacking. The Native Labour (Settlement of Disputes) Act of 1953 provides machinery for the emasculation of the economic and political potency of African trade unionism, while the founding of the South African Congress of Trade Unions (on a non-racial basis), and its affiliation with the Congress Alliance of political movements, is a frank avowal of the political role of the workers.

For the purposes of this study, with its interest in the race relations and political choices of the bourgeoisie, African voluntary associations may be distinguished first of all in terms of the degree of dependence on Whites. This may be conceived as a continuum, ranging from other-directed to self-directed associations, or from paternalist to independent. Second, the composition of the associations has relevance for race relations, whether membership is interracial or racially exclusive (or an ingenious combination of the two), affording or withholding opportunity for contact and community of interest. And, finally, associations may be classified on the basis of their goals in relation to the status quo: they may be conservative of White interests, or designed to secure change in favor of Africans, or neutral but with implications for social change.

The associations officially structured for Africans are paternalist, racially exclusive—under White control—and conservative with respect to social change, or if they involve social change then it is in a direction determined by Whites. The goals are externally defined in terms of official policies. This has a number of consequences. The associations tend to be rigid. In situations of protest or challenge, they are maintained by repression and change of personnel. The responsibility accorded Africans is limited, and deliberations may be unrealistic, since the major decisions are taken outside the association by White executives. Contact between White and African is on a basis of inequality, thus reinforcing the system of racial stratification. The leaders may appear to be representative, even elected, but by and large leadership is determined or controlled officially. Acceptance by African leaders of positions in the associations involves the acceptance of subordinate status, and a loss of initiative as a result of the commitment to externally defined goals. An aspect of the personality of the leader is as it were detached, and utilized under the direction of others. The leader may be alienated from himself in the same way as the worker from his labor. This is perhaps an element in the oscillation sometimes observed between servility and belligerency.

The intercalary position of the leader may have the same consequences. The leader is suspended between two worlds, that of his own people and that of the Whites. He has a responsibility toward, and no doubt an identification with, Africans, but he can do very little to help them. As tensions rise under acute racial conflict, his position becomes increasingly ambiguous, since he is rewarded by White patronage, and may be an instrument for executing the hated policies. In consequence, he is threatened with rejection by his own people. He is therefore obliged to manipulate two different systems.

He must maintain his affiliation to the Whites and abide by the rules of the game (or give up his position), and at the same time, he must ensure his acceptance within the African community. This ambivalence can be partly resolved by playing along with Whites in all essential respects necessary for continued membership, and yet displaying hostility toward them within carefully defined limits inside the association, but with less restraint outside. Here again is a source of oscillation between the servile and the belligerent states. Where opinion in the African community is divided, as in the case of school committees and school boards, the leader can identify with a section of his people, and face opposition with the greater security of some mass support. In Chapter 21, a case study is presented of a paternalist, officially structured, White-controlled, African association, the Combined Location Advisory Boards in Durban.

Tense issues of race relations arise also in the paternalist interracial associations, and in some situations the tensions are not very different from those in the paternalist racially exclusive organizations. Actually the term "interracial" is not precise, since membership may be open to all racial groups but segregated in the most varied and ingenious forms suggested by the sensibilities of racialism. The range is from the minor relevance of racial identity as in the interracial clubs (now closed by the Government) to its use as an organizing principle in, for example, the Methodist and Anglican churches of South Africa. In these associations, the key positions are generally held by Whites. Token positions of high prestige but little executive substance may be accorded Africans or they may be appointed vice-chairmen or vice-secretaries. Africans are now beginning to attain positions of high power, but for the most part, this is a recent development. Insofar as the associations are interested in securing change favorable to Africans, the approach tends to be gradualist, reformist, and benevolent.

Where the association exists for the sake of the interracial contact, Africans may in fact achieve positions well beyond their merits. An

African may be elected primarily because he is an African, and voluntarily offers himself, or has been persuaded to offer himself, for election. There is an element of patronage on the part of the Whites, and of clientage on the part of Africans, for whom the irksome restraints of urban African life may be somewhat eased by the friendly interest of Whites. The appeal of these race relations associations is essentially to educated Africans, who have mastered the techniques of White society. It is now more difficult to attract them. The paternalist interracial associations correspond somewhat to the trustee–ward concept of race relations, and both the paternalism and White initiative increasingly repel educated Africans. Under pressure, these associations may move away from paternalism toward equality, though shedding some of their conservative White members in the process.

There are few egalitarian interracial associations and they are still exploring equality of participation and nonracialism. The threat of racialism is always inherent in these associations, as groups both inside and outside the association exploit the racial differences between the members. The general rule of White or other non-African initiative in interracial association seems to apply, and this adds fuel for racial incitement.

The independent, racially exclusive African associations often include only a small number of members—essentially primary groups, and in some situations, almost a substitute for the kin group. Their leaders are often uneducated. Many of the small associations reflect the economic and social insecurity of the members, and they may be of short duration, having no investments or long term commitments to give them stability. In terms of goals and functions, they are largely adjustive.

The large-scale independent African associations are mainly religious, sporting, or political. In practice, their functions overlap. Because of the policies of apartheid, the lines between religion and politics and between sport and politics are not easily drawn. These associations generally emphasize their independence, and suspicions of interference are readily aroused. The leaders are educated men, though with exceptions, more particularly it would seem in some of the Zionist churches. Leadership tends to be oligarchical, with the same set of leaders perpetuating themselves, a process assisted by the gulf between the educated leaders, with organizational skills and a command of English, and the great mass of uneducated followers. The oligarchical tendencies are most strongly present in organizations which confer prestige or other rewards on their leaders, or which hold property rights, or in which the personality of the leader symbolizes the unity of the organization. Where leadership offers little prestige or other reward, and indeed vulnerability, as in the association of African teachers in Durban, there may be a

high turnover. There is a personality cult of leaders, rather than a
broad concern with ideologies, which may, however, be a preoccupation of the leaders themselves. Leadership style seems to be influenced
by chieftainship, both leaders and followers borrowing from the traditional pattern. The more highly educated intellectuals may be in the
wings, staging the performance and organizing the activities. Sometimes
they form an opposition.

The associations vary in their relationship to the status quo. So far as
explicit goals are concerned, it is rare for Africans to associate in support of apartheid, and the associations of this type seem quite insignificant. The main political organizations, the African National Congress
and the Pan-Africanist Congress, have as their aim the radical transformation of South African society. It would be superficial, however,
to emphasize only the explicit goals. An association may have political
significance though its activities and objectives are nonpolitical. Thus
some of the independent African churches may be indirectly accommo-
dative to apartheid or adjustive to racial domination in consequence
of a preoccupation with other worldly values, or conversely they may
challenge the structure of domination by their spiritual inflation of
the Black man. Moreover, under the conditions of contemporary South
African society, there are strong pressures on the nonpolitical or politically neutral independent African associations to become politically
involved. The reason for this is the pervasive dominance of the racial
principle under apartheid. The racial status of a man is his political
status. And since the associations have an exclusive African membership, and are thus protected from internal cross pressures by other
racial groups, the racial-political influences act with a certain purity
and elemental force. The racial conflict is so raw, and the political
thrust so powerful, that a purely African association can hardly avoid
political involvement.

The potential for political involvement, and the manner in which
circumstances may impel toward a subsidiary political role, can be illustrated in the case of the Interdenominational African Ministers' Federation. In 1952, during the Passive Resistance Campaign, the Federation
announced that it was not against the campaign, but that as an organization it did not wish to become involved in the resistance activities.
In May 1953, in a call for an African National Day of Prayer, the
Federation openly identified with African political aspirations, and appealed for "an African united front against all evils—persecution, oppression and all kinds of discrimination because of colour; these are
evils in the sight of God." [10] In May 1959, at the thirteenth annual
conference held at Sharpeville, the Presidential address placed the South

10. Leo Kuper, *Passive Resistance in South Africa* (New Haven, Yale University Press, 1957),
pp. 147–48.

African situation in the context of the continent-wide African revolution, and emphasized the need for a United Church (but not exclusively African) in the evangelization of Africa. A delegate declared that "we of the Church must now prepare to take over the leadership of the people. The African National Congress has been rendered all but impotent, not only by Government action, but by its own internal strife. It is up to us now to give a lead in the national struggle." And the conference itself denounced Government policy and decided to interview the Prime Minister for a review of the constitutional setup, with a view to having the segregationist South Africa Act scrapped (*Drum*, July 1959, pp. 27–29). Secret state police were present at the conference.

The racially exclusive organizations naturally offer a base for exclusive national movements, but this development is by no means inevitable, even in a situation of acute racial conflict. A purely racial association may work for nonracial integration. Thus the Durban and District African Football Association, which will be discussed in Chapter 22, gave its support to integration in football, and the racially exclusive African National Congress professed its goal to be a nonracial democracy. Perhaps the same argument might be advanced in regard to racial organizations as in regard to oligarchic associations. Just as the diversity and rivalry of oligarchically organized bodies may perhaps contribute to democracy in the wider society, so under certain conditions a racial organization of associations may perhaps contribute to nonracialism in the wider society. However, it seems more likely that a racial organization of voluntary associations will be linked with racially exclusive sentiments; and that African leaders will deliberately create a whole series of parallel African associations so as to promote the spirit of exclusive African nationalism. Indeed this process has already begun, though it is still rationalized by African leaders on the basis that the interests of Africans are different from those of other races, and hence require separate organization.

In the chapters that follow, I discuss in some detail three independent racially exclusive associations, and one statutory association for Africans under White control. They were chosen from the range of associations studied on the basis that they offer different opportunities for leadership and styles of leadership, that they vary in their relation to the status quo, and that they structure the alternatives of action and guide choice in different ways. The Combined Location Advisory Boards in Durban, discussed in Chapter 21, is a paternalist association within the framework of White domination, and compatible with apartheid, though it seems that the Advisory Boards will soon be replaced by urban councils linked with the tribal rural authorities. The Durban and District African Football Association (Chapter 22), for many years one of the major independent African associations in South Africa, has fostered a traditional type of leadership and oligarchical control. Though neutral with respect to social change, its policies and activities have relevance for the racial integration of sport and political relevance for race relations. The political associations, the African National Congress and the Pan-Africanist Congress (Chapter 23), are specially relevant to this study, since they directly confront the issues of racialism and nonracialism, and of violence and nonviolence, and propagate among Africans their choice between these alternatives of ideology and action.

CHAPTER 21

Advisory Boards: A Case Study in Paternalism

THE *Sunday Times* of February 7, 1960, carried the following report:

> A meeting of Durban's ultra-conservative Combined Native Advisory Boards ended in an uproar on Thursday after the chairman of the City Council's Bantu Administration Committee, Mr. A. S. Robinson, M.P.C., had referred to the board's Native chairman as "boy."
>
> The Native chairman is 67-year-old Mr. A. W. G. Champion, one of the country's best-known non-White leaders and a man whose opinions have been sought by prominent members of Sabra.
>
> Members of the Combined Advisory Boards are incensed over what they call an insult to Mr. Champion.
>
> They told me today that they regard this as confirmation of their opinion that Mr. Robinson is unsympathetic toward Natives and "a most unsuitable person to be chairman of the Bantu Administration Committee."
>
> Mr. Robinson, who was accompanied by a handful of European officials, took the chair at Thursday's meeting.
>
> When the meeting opened Mr. Champion proposed that the recent Cato Manor disturbances be discussed.
>
> Mr. Robinson refused to accept this motion and said, "Champion, my boy, sit down."
>
> Mr. Champion sat down.
>
> Another Native Board member then asked on a point of order whether Mr. Robinson should have referred to Mr. Champion as a boy.
>
> Mr. Robinson, who is several years younger than Mr. Champion, said: "It is in order—he is a boy."
>
> Grey-haired, dignified Mr. Champion then asked: "Mr. Chairman, are you sure you called me a boy deliberately? Were you not joking?"
>
> Mr. Robinson: "No, I was not joking."

There was an uproar and Mr. Champion moved the adjournment of the meeting. This was solidly supported by the Native members, and Mr. Robinson then strode from the room, followed by other Europeans.

The minutes of the Combined Native Advisory Boards indicate that the "my boy" incident was preceded by some friction between the Chairman and Mr. Champion. The Chairman was opposed to a discussion of the Cato Manor disturbance and expressed the view that it was a matter which solely concerned the South African police. Mr. Champion deprecated the Chairman's views and pointed out that the position was serious, as nine policemen had died. The Chairman submitted that the police had in fact been murdered. (According to one account, the Chairman said, "They were murdered, my boy," and not "Champion, my boy, sit down.") Mr. Nkwanyana felt that the Chairman's remarks were not in good taste. He deprecated the fact that the Chairman had also seen fit when replying to Mr. Champion to refer to him as "Champion, my boy" and inquired whether in fact Mr. Champion was the Chairman's "boy." (There may have been an innuendo here, since many Africans claim that Mr. Champion works closely with the Corporation.) The meeting adjourned at 8.22 P.M. after a session of only 22 minutes.

At the next monthly meeting of the Advisory Boards, the African members remained seated when the White Chairman, followed by other White officials, entered the committee room, and took his place at the head of the horseshoe (*Sunday Times,* March 6, 1960). Their normal practice is to stand. The Chairman greeted the members, but received no reply. When the minutes of the last meeting were presented for confirmation, Mr. Nkwanyana objected on the ground that the Chairman's reference to Mr. Champion as "boy" had not been recorded, nor Mr. Champion's question whether the remark was made in a serious strain. Mr. Mbhele moved confirmation of the minutes at the request of the Chairman, on the grounds that verbatim records were never made. The minutes were confirmed as presented. Then Mr. S. K. Ngobese, an elected representative of the S. J. Smith Location for male Africans, a university undergraduate, formerly self-employed as a general agent and later working in the office of an African attorney, proposed the following resolution:

> That whereas in a caucus meeting presided by Mr. Champion, its Chairman, it has been agreed that in the light of the fact that despite attempts by Mr. Champion urging the Chairman to withdraw his remarks against him viz: calling him a "boy," he failed or refused to withdraw and in further view of the facts that members of the Boards had invariably complained about his attitude and

hostility against African people and also that during the Boards' visit for inspection at Kwa Mashu he showed a spirit of unco-operativeness, therefore, these Boards find it necessary to ask the Chairman to resign forthwith. [There was a complaint by Advisory Board members that the Chairman sat in his car during the tour of inspection, instead of conducting it.]

This was seconded by Mr. S. N. Mbhele, formerly a school principal and Sunday School organizer and then a trader in the S. J. Smith Location, which he represented as an Advisory Board member nominated by the City Council. According to one report (*Sunday Times*, March 6, 1960), the White Chairman, accompanied by the White officials, "strode angrily from the room"; according to another report (*Natal Mercury*, March 7, 1960), he "stalked out of the meeting." The meeting ended, in any event, abruptly at 8.11 P.M.

Mr. Champion commented: "We are treated like small boys in a classroom. I would rather the Government abolished the Advisory Board system in Durban than continue to serve under Councillor Robinson." Mr. Mbhele, African Vice-Chairman under Mr. Champion, expressed the conflict of duties he experienced: "As a Council nominee I am in a difficult position. I seconded the resolution because I thought it was in the best interests of the African people."

The White Chairman felt that the press criticism reflected unfairly on him as "a man who has fought for the rights of the underdog for years" (*Natal Mercury*, March 7, 1960). The Mayor supported him, commenting that the affair "appears to be a misunderstanding among African members of the board. To say that Mr. Robinson is unsympathetic to African aspirations is ludicrous, particularly when viewed against his background of loyal and worthwhile service in the cause of the needs of Africans for so many years" (*Natal Mercury*, March 8, 1960). Some Councillors apparently did not share the Mayor's view. A *Sunday Times* reporter wrote: "Councillors told me this week that there was a growing uneasiness about Mr. Robinson's attitudes to non-Whites. Several said they were embarrassed at his references at committee meetings to Natives and Indians as 'kaffirs' and 'coolies.' They said this seemed to indicate a lack of sympathy on his part" (March 6, 1960). The Bantu Administration Committee, however, which is the all-White parent body to the Advisory Boards, passed a unanimous vote recording its utmost confidence in Councillor Robinson as Chairman of the Boards.

At the next meeting of the Advisory Boards, the Mayor delivered a written speech designed to restore harmony. First, he valued the Advisory Boards: they seemed to be the only bridge between us "where we can learn your views on our many problems and difficulties and your

views as to the best ways of making progress against them." And
second:

> I want to tell you—for I think you might not know this—
> that the words "my boy" are commonly used in this way by
> English-speaking people. They are used *between equals* and convey
> *feelings of friendliness*. They do not denote a feeling of superiority
> or condescension, or anything of that sort. They are not regarded
> as offensive, but rather the opposite. It is common for me to say
> to your Chairman, for instance, "Robbie, my boy, I disagree with
> you," or something like that; and he knows that all I am doing
> is to show that I feel friendly towards him, and accept him as my
> equal in the conversation.
>
> I am quite sure that the Chairman used these words in that
> way (in fact, he has said so to me); that he did not mean to give
> offence in any way; and that no offence should have been taken
> at what he said.

The underlining of *between equals* and *feelings of friendliness* are in the
minutes, and indicate that the Mayor attached great importance to
these phrases, apparently his trump card. Members of the Boards were
unimpressed. The Mayor, Mr. Champion complained, had prejudiced
the position by releasing a press statement in support of the Chairman.
The "my boy" incident had merely been the spark which had kindled
the flame of feeling the Boards had nursed for some time against their
Chairman. "For years Councillor Robinson had treated Board members
in a derogatory fashion as 'his boys.' He should now accept the views
of the Boards in this regard and resign. There was no contact between
the Boards and the City Council as Councillor Robinson was Chairman
of both the Board and the Bantu Administration Committee and the
Boards' views were never represented to the City Council as they
should be."

The Mayor played his trump card again, explaining that, on occasion,
he addressed both Councillor Robinson and Councillor Shearer (the
Chairman of the Council's General Purposes Committee, who had accompanied him) as "my boy"—just showing friendliness and accepting
them as equals in conversation. The incident, he said, was a small one
compared to the larger issues confronting the Board, and he asked them
to hear Councillor Robinson. This provoked the reply from Mr. Champion that the issue was not a small one in the eyes of Board members,
"and he appealed to the Mayor not to treat members as young boys."

A member of the Board pointed out that Councillor Robinson had
had two months in which to give an explanation of his conduct in this
matter, but instead he had brought a "Saracen," the Mayor, to the
meeting. (Reference was to the patrolling of African areas by armored

cars, a show of force which was becoming the most convincing argument in the administration of Bantu affairs.) Another member drew attention to the fact that as a result of the recent incident, Board members were now subject to insults by fellow Africans.

Councillor Shearer then intervened, basing his appeal apparently on concepts of what was cricket and what was not cricket. As Chairman of the General Purposes Committee, he must hear the Boards' reaction to Councillor Robinson's statement of his case. If the members would not let him hear Councillor Robinson's side, then he would have to support the decision of the Bantu Administration Committee (i.e. a vote of utmost confidence). Advisory Board members still remained adamant, and the Mayor was left with no alternative but to declare that he would report to the Council their refusal to accept Councillor Robinson as Chairman and to hear his point of view. "The Mayor felt that the Boards had not debated this matter in a democratic way" (a strange comment from the Mayor of a City Council with wide executive powers to Africans representing the voteless masses of their people in a purely advisory capacity). The Bantu Administration Committee was therefore obliged to reconsider its attitude, and a special meeting was held on April 1, 1960.

While this dispute was going on, there had been a series of disturbances throughout the country, including Durban. Many non-White political leaders were arrested, police and armored cars patrolled the streets, and a general state of emergency was declared. Under these conditions of a critical deterioration in the relations between Whites and Africans, the Bantu Administration Committee sought a more radical solution in proposals for the reconstitution of the Advisory Boards. European chairmanship would be withdrawn both from the combined and the local Advisory Boards, which would therefore meet under their own elected African chairmen, and the African chairman and vice-chairman of the Combined Advisory Boards would be admitted to meetings of the Bantu Administration Committee, but only when Advisory Board minutes were discussed.

Here then was a sharp conflict between the African members of the Advisory Board and the White authorities. The immediate precipitating event was the use of "my boy" in reference to the African Chairman, and the failure of the White Chairman to withdraw the phrase. From the point of view of the White persons involved, the incident was apparently of little significance. For the African members it was so deeply wounding that they appeared ready to risk the displeasure of the White authorities and to forfeit their positions as Advisory Board members, Chairmen of standing committees, and so on, for which they had worked, and which many of them cherished. This sharp conflict of values can only be understood in the context of the role of the Advisory

Boards, and the changing situation of its African members in the wider society.

The Advisory Boards are one of the many African statutory bodies which include School Boards, School Committees, Native Labour Committees, and Bantu Authorities. They all share in common the subordination of Africans to a general policy over which they have no control, and to administrative and executive domination exercised by members of a different racial group.

From the point of view of the White authorities, participation in the statutory bodies implies acceptance by the African members of a racially subordinate role and a restricted field of action. Discussion of broader issues transcending the prescribed limitations constitutes political action, which is heavily taboo for Africans generally, and under strong repressive sanctions. For Africans, participation does not necessarily imply subordination. Positions on the statutory bodies could be used as bases for undermining the structure of domination. They provide opportunities for organizing the people, and there are small advantages to be gained in the improvement of living conditions. The main lines of policy cannot be changed directly, but pressure can be exerted in this direction by skillful organization and sabotage.

In the early 1950s, when the Government created a variety of new statutory bodies, African political circles hotly debated the possibility of playing roles in the statutory bodies, not as docile subordinates at the lowest levels of the White bureaucracy, but as fighting advance guards of the non-White liberation movement. Two opposing views crystallized, one that all available means should be used, both protest and compromise, the other, that there must be no cooperation in the instruments of oppression, that such mechanisms as the statutory bodies must be boycotted, since they are designed for the domestication (enslavement) of the African people.

The policy of a boycott was not feasible at the time, because of a lack of unanimity among the African leaders, the temptation of rewards, and the existence of politically sterilized categories of Africans, such as civil servants and traders in municipal institutions, whose livelihood might be jeopardized by a refusal to serve on the statutory bodies. An African school inspector, for example, is not in a position to decline an appointment as a lecturer in one of the tribal university colleges, even if he feels poorly qualified for the post, entirely opposed to the policy of separate tribal universities, and sensitive to the stigma of serving in an institution rejected by many of his people.

The result is that these statutory bodies function, and the positions are filled by Africans. At best, their participation is tolerated by the militant movements. The African National Congress allows its members freedom of choice, and active members of Congress are to be found on the statutory bodies. At worst, the African members are despised as "stooges," "sell-outs," betrayers of their people. The "sell-out" definition of the situation, in the past a somewhat exclusive vituperative epithet, under the copyright of the Unity Movement, is now widely diffused and dominant, symbolizing the growing distrust and antagonism between the racial groups.

The history of the Advisory Boards spans the period from African acceptance of the techniques of compromise—cooperation in subordinate positions under White patronage, humble deputations, petitions, prayers, pleading for concessions—to the present militant challenge of White rule. It spans a period when African leaders were willing to serve on statutory bodies to the period when most of them would feel hopelessly compromised by such service. The change can be traced in the evolution of the political outlook of Chief Albert Luthuli, who preferred to be deposed from his position as elected chief rather than to renounce his role as Natal President of the African National Congress in the campaign for the defiance of unjust laws.

> Previous to being a Chief I was a school teacher for about seventeen years. In these past thirty years or so I have striven with tremendous zeal and patience to work for the progress and welfare of my people and for their harmonious relations with other sections of our multi-racial society in the Union of South Africa. In this effort I always pursued what liberal minded people rightly regarded as the path of moderation. Over this great length of time I have, year after year, gladly spent hours of my time with such organisations as the Church and its various agencies such as the Christian Council of South Africa, the Joint Council of Europeans and Africans and the now defunct Native Representative Council.
>
> In so far as gaining citizenship rights and opportunities for the unfettered development of the African people, who will deny that thirty years of my life have been spent knocking in vain, patiently, moderately, and modestly at a closed and barred door?
>
> What have been the fruits of my many years of moderation? Has there been any reciprocal tolerance or moderation from the Government, be it Nationalist or United Party? No! On the contrary, the past thirty years have seen the greatest number of Laws restricting our rights and progress until today we have reached a stage where we have almost no rights at all: no adequate land for our occupation, our only asset, cattle, dwindling, no security of homes, no decent and remunerative employment, more restrictions to freedom of movement through passes, curfew regulations, influx control measures; in short we have witnessed in these years an in-

tensification of our subjection to ensure and protect white supremacy.

It is with this background and with a full sense of responsibility that, under the auspices of the African National Congress [Natal], I have joined my people in the new spirit that moves them today, the spirit that revolts openly and boldly against injustices and expresses itself in a determined and non-violent manner. . . .

It is inevitable that in working for Freedom some individuals and some families must take the lead and suffer: the Road to Freedom Is Via the CROSS. [Statement issued by the African National Congress and the Natal Indian Congress, November 1952.]

Legislative provision was made for the establishment of Advisory Boards under the Natives (Urban Areas) Act No. 21 of 1923. Section 21 of the Natives (Urban Areas) Consolidation Act No. 25 of 1945, as amended, governed the position for the country as a whole. The rapid and haphazard urbanization of Africans, and the indifference of many local authorities, had resulted in poor conditions of living, and the Act was designed to ensure more adequate accommodation for Africans in segregated areas as well as control over their movement into the towns. The Advisory Boards were to be the mechanism for consultation between the local authorities and the urban African residents on matters affecting their welfare.

Their duties are to consider and report on regulations proposed by the local authority, on estimates for revenue and expenditure of the Native Revenue account, and on matters referred to them by the local authority or the Minister of Native (Bantu, African) Affairs. The Boards may also initiate reports on any matters affecting the interests of Africans in the urban area, and recommend regulations. The City Council is under an obligation to consider the report of the Advisory Boards on proposed regulations, and to transmit the report to the Minister. The Board also has certain rights of consultation in respect of beer brewing.

The Durban City Council established a "Goodwill" Advisory Board in 1930, but did not comply with the provisions of the Urban Areas Act until 1937. Seven Advisory Boards were finally established, three for the family locations of Lamont, Chesterville, and Baumannville, four for the male barracks of S. J. Smith, Dalton Road, Somsteu Road, and Jacobs. (The Advisory Boards for Baumannville and Somsteu Road locations have now been discontinued because of the removal of their populations from the central areas. In the shack sections of Cato Manor there is an Emergency Camp Welfare and Development Board, which functions separately and in the manner of an Advisory Board, and the new satellite townships of Kwa Mashu and Umlazi have a form of residents' representation, but not yet Advisory Boards.) Each of the Boards has three elected members (with the exception of Lamont Location, which has four) and two nominated members. They meet separately once a month with their Location Superintendent, jointly but severally as the Combined Advisory Boards, and in a number of Board subcommittees (General, Welfare, Employment and Registration, Location Affairs, and Trading).

The procedure at the meeting of the Combined Boards is for the African members to assemble an hour in advance under their own Chairman. This represents the caucus. Then the European Chairman enters, accompanied by the Director of Bantu Administration, his personal assistant, the Deputy Director, the Assistant Director, and the Committee Clerk. At present there is a standing invitation to representatives of the Chambers of Commerce and Industries, who also attend. City Councillors sometimes attend the meetings. The African members stand until the Chairman takes his seat at the head of the horseshoe, surrounded by the White officers. The horseshoe, chairs, and committee room are of good solid construction, symbolizing the substance and dignity of the city of Durban. And the meeting itself is conducted through highly formalized, twentieth-century, business executive committee procedures, in strong contrast to the free and full oratory of traditional African debate. There is insistence on correct procedure, and some of the African members become preoccupied with the formal techniques of correct debate rather than the substance: denied substantive power, they become absorbed in its symbols and trappings. When the meeting adjourns for tea, the White men retire to an adjoining parlor, while the Africans are served tea in the committee room.

The Advisory Board must "act entirely in an advisory capacity." The Board may pass outright resolutions in regard to such matters as confirmation of minutes, quorum, and deliberations of its subcommittees— that is to say, its own internal organization. For the rest, the form of resolution is "Resolved to Recommend." The body to whom the Advisory Board recommends is not the City Council, but one of its Committees, the Bantu Administration Committee, which consists of five White city councillors and the Mayor ex officio, assisted by White officials: the Director of Bantu Administration may be present in an advisory capacity. African Advisory Board members have no direct link with the parent committee. They are dependent on the interest and sympathy of the White Chairman of the Combined Advisory Boards, who is also Chairman of the Bantu Administration Committee, and of the Director of Bantu Administration. The Bantu Administration Committee may see to it that the proposals reach the City Council, or it may "cut, cut, cut. . . . When a man just notes things and no results come, we feel we are treated like school children." The White Committee is the gatekeeper, closing out the physical presence of the subordinate

African, ensuring that executive decisions affecting his welfare should be taken for or against him, but never with him—"many European officials, including magistrates, to save their face, will never consider any proposition we may make, in our presence"—and acting either as a channel for, or a buffer against, the transmission of his wishes to the arbiter of his destinies. Only a limited protection is accorded the Advisory Boards by the provision that their reports on certain issues should be transmitted to the Minister.

The Director of Bantu Administration, like the Chairman, can act as a bridge between the Advisory Boards and the City Council, through its Bantu Administration Committee, or he can act as a moat. In the bureaucracy, he is regarded as the technical expert on the administration of Natives. This introduces the first ambiguity in the position of the Director. Technical standards of competence can be specified for the City Engineer, or the City Architect. No standards of competence are available for testing the efficiency of a person whose task is the administration of human beings in the basic aspects of their lives, in fields of action where individuals normally exercise a measure of free choice. No standards of competence exist for the position of arbiter of the fate of other men in the routine of living, and in its elaboration.

Nevertheless, the Director of Bantu Administration plays the role of expert on Black humanity. As such, he draws the technical plans for the implementation of policy. In the same way as other experts, he must secure the acceptance of his plans by the authorities. This is often a serious problem in the work of local authorities, since the technical expert is likely to be confronted by a panel of changing councillors relatively ignorant in the field of his own specialization. He may solve the problem by gaining respect for his expert knowledge as a kind of sacred mystery, or he may take part in the power politics of the local authority, winning over influential members. In either event, his planning may be frustrated by the impassioned rejection of the voters, acting through the City Councillors. For the bureaucratic expert, the people for whom he plans are a nuisance. They have views of their own, interests of their own, and the power to express them effectively.

The Director of Bantu Administration, like other bureaucratic experts employed by local authorities, is confronted with two sources of frustration, the local authority whom he serves and the people for whom he plans. In other respects, his situation is different, since the Africans he administers have no vote and therefore cannot effectively exert pressure through the City Councillors. The latter are responsible not to Africans, but to the electorate, that is to say the White voters. They would naturally be concerned to avoid the unpopularity of rising municipal rates and hence to finance expenditure on Africans solely from the revenue which can be derived from them. Since Africans are the poorest section of the population and their needs have been neglected for many years—an inevitable consequence of the lack of franchise—the Native Revenue Account is always inadequate even for the provision of minimum standards. City Councillors will support the Director in maintaining administration at the traditional low level of concern for African Welfare, or in introducing minor improvements. If he wishes to raise standards appreciably, he must rely on the sympathy and conscience of the City Councillors, a sympathy and conscience which lack the ballot box to activate them, though the role of ballot box is sometimes taken by such exasperated pressure groups as the Chambers of Commerce and Industries, or the violent despair of the African populace. It required a major riot in June 1959 to focus attention on the impoverishment of the African population.

The Director's powers are restricted in another direction. The executive members of the Bantu Administration Department—the Director, the Deputy Director, and the Assistant Director—are the employees of the Council and at the same time the licensed officials of the Minister of Bantu Affairs, who protects them against removal from their position or reduction in their emoluments. The Director thus risks the withdrawal of his license, and hence the loss of his post, if he fails to implement Government policy. The City Council's parsimony and indifference and the Government's repression and domination converge in his position, and it is natural therefore that in times of crisis he should be the personal target of resentment. It is useless for him to protest that he does not determine policy, that he is sympathetic to the aspirations and grievances of the African people. Indeed it becomes difficult for him to identify with the Africans he administers, and hence to respond sympathetically to their grievances, since his position is dependent on his being responsive to the political pressures from Government and City Council, and the policy he carries out is based on the subordination of Africans. His situation is as ambivalent as that of an African chief, and he is liable to become estranged from African points of view, as the following incident shows. In 1958, during the national election campaign, the African National Congress proposed a "stay-at-home" demonstration, as the only way in which a voteless people could make its voice heard. At the meeting of the Combined Advisory Boards in April 1958, the Director lectured the members on the irreparable harm of such a policy. The threat of a strike had been linked to the election. Natives, he said, had no right to vote, and therefore should not take sides in the election issue. Implicit in his homily is the paternalism of the White man, who knows what is best for the Black man: it should be a matter of indifference which group of White fathers administers him and under what policies.

Africans, almost up to the time of writing, did not represent a political force to which the Director need respond. Nevertheless, they could be troublesome, and interfere with the carrying out of his duties, as measured by the demands of the Government and the local authority, and by criteria of efficient administration. The Combined Advisory Boards might delay implementation of plans by being obstructive in committee, or challenging decisions in court. The residents themselves are readily raised to a pitch of protest, noncooperation, and violence because of their routine sufferings. Hence the Director may be exposed to the temptation of eliminating the "agitators" and of surrounding himself in the Advisory Boards with docile types, "good boys" who will help him to execute his plans. The extensive powers of the Director facilitate victimization of the outspoken critic.

The Superintendents of locations are the replicas of the Director at the local location level. They can use their extensive powers to establish themselves as minor despots, and they are even more exposed to the temptation to eliminate flaws in the machine. They are in direct contact with the people they administer, and "intransigeant" elements emerge as known persons. There is also a greater likelihood of incongruities in status, hence feelings of animosity, as between a highly educated African and a relatively uneducated Superintendent, for example. Until recently, when a minimum of matriculation or equivalent was introduced, there were no standards of qualification for Superintendents. Unlike the Director, they may be men of limited education, men who might find difficulty in achieving recognition in their own White society. As administrators of the subordinate Africans, their prestige in the company of Whites is probably diminished by a sort of contagion. The Director also administers Africans, but his status has been progressively raised over the years, and his contacts are mainly with the higher echelons of White officialdom. The Superintendents, on the other hand, are in close contact with the African people, and the taint to prestige probably arises from this intimacy, as it might for workers in an abattoir. This impedes the recruitment of top administrators, thus accentuating the status incongruity. It is natural that in these circumstances Superintendents may feel the temptation to exercise their powers fully, and find themselves in conflict particularly with well-educated Africans, from whose ranks the more articulate critics will be drawn.

These then are the circles of power within which the Advisory Boards operate. The elected members in particular are faced with a basic dilemma: they are accountable to the people they represent, and yet they can do very little to remedy their urgent grievances. Power rests in other representatives, accountable to other groups, and the role of the Advisory Board members is often that of pleading. They can do nothing at all about the major Government policies which bear so heavily on their people, such as influx and efflux control and the payment of economic rentals; these policies are sacrosanct. On other issues, improvements can be won but often at the expense of long, drawn-out struggle. Many items recur over months or even years, such as accommodation for visiting wives at the men's locations, the provision of bus shelters, and of inner doors in the houses. Sometimes apparently reasonable proposals on matters of detail are not accepted—proposals that transport to attend meetings should be made available for members whom the City Council had moved from their previous location homes to Kwa Mashu, that a new location should be named after two African leaders, that the Native Administration Department should be renamed the African Administration Department. The withholding of transport, the naming of the location after a leading White sugar farmer, the reaction that change in the name of the Department was not considered desirable[1]—all these decisions emphasize, by the very pettiness of the issues, the hollow role of the Advisory Boards. Some redress is possible by direct appeal to the Minister or his representatives, but this has not materially affected the administration of the Advisory Boards by the Durban Corporation.

The procedure is that the Director reports to the Bantu Administration Committee on the minutes of the Advisory Boards, dealing with them item by item. He is the executive official, shaping the decisions of the Bantu Administration Committee. In fact it is clear that he does not regard himself as in any way the servant of the Advisory Boards, but its master, sometimes sympathetic, as in his recommendation that the allowances of members be increased, sometimes peremptory, as in his rejection of complaints against his department.

There is a close working relationship between the Director and the Committee. Reading the minutes gives an impression of a group of insiders working harmoniously together. The prevailing comments are that the recommendation of the Advisory Boards be referred to the Director for investigation and report; that the report of the Director be referred to the Advisory Boards for information; that the request be not acceded to; that the request be referred to the Director for attention. Much of the work of the Advisory Boards seems to be resolved in this internal,

1. The Native Administration Committee was prepared to accept renaming as the African Affairs Committee. The issue was complicated by the fact that such names as Kaffir Beer and Native Advisory Boards appeared in statutes, and to change them would have required statutory amendments. The Department and the Committee are now named the Bantu Administration Department and the Bantu Administration Committee. The Committee itself generally used the term "Native" in reference to the people it administered. The word "African" occasionally slips in, and the Committee was probably moving toward use of the word Bantu, since this is favored by the Government. Habituation to the term "Native" dies slowly. The difference between these terms is that Native implies something in the nature of the flora and fauna of the area, and inferiority and subordination; Bantu is the same inferiority dressed up in comic opera, in "coon carnival" clothes, a museum exhibit of folklorism; while African implies recognition of the movement toward equal rights. In the case of transport to the Advisory Board meetings, the attitude of the Corporation was that it could not collect members from all over town, but only from the institutions they represented, wherever they might in fact be living.

introspective, circular way, though some recommendations are accepted and implemented. There is a striking contrast between the deliberations of the Advisory Board and those of the Bantu Administration Committee. The former suggest a talking shop; the latter, even though the Committee's plenary powers are very limited, lead to action. It is in the Committee that policies are shaped and direction given to new projects. The Advisory Board members are virtually advisers to the Director, or a sounding board by which he assesses the needs and disaffections of the people he administers. When faced with criticism by the Boards, the Committee often closes like a charmed circle.

The impotence of the Boards, the interminable delays in the handling of their recommendations, the minor victories in a setting of major defeats, are an inevitable source of frustration for the location residents and of mounting resentment against the members as agents of the Corporation, as "stooges" and "sell-outs." This was expressed dramatically in the burning down of Mr. Champion's shop during one of the Cato Manor riots. The more general manifestation is of apathy in the locations toward the Advisory Board elections, with the possible exception of Lamont Location: and even in Lamontville, there was a substantial boycott of the 1962 elections (*New Age*, October 18, 1962).

Here in Lamontville, a two-party system and the exploitation of antagonism between the educated and the uneducated lent some vitality to the Advisory Board elections. Rightly or wrongly, the Sikhumba ("Hide") Party was regarded as the party of the educated, the opposition as the party of the illiterate. Certainly the leaders of the Hide Party were more highly educated. In 1959, their candidates, described in their campaign leaflets as:

A. R. Ntuli	T. E. Mapumulo	Solomon Ngobese	C. Mtyali
(My Blue Brook)	(Eugene)	(Solly)	(Skali Uyashishiliza)
			(Sliding Drinking Mug)

were educated men of middle-class occupations. Actually the supporters of both parties are drawn from the educated and uneducated, even though, according to a Sikhumba supporter, his party was "supported more by enlightened and educated people." There was nothing in the policies of the Hide Party which would stamp it as the party of the educated. The 1959 election manifesto of "the hide that beats tanners" referred to very general matters—the position and salvation of buyers at Nylon, economic rentals, and things that militate against harmony and the welfare of the people. Probing failed to reveal policy differences between the parties, and the basis of division seemed to be that of rivalry between leaders, though Hide Party supporters claimed to have a democratic representative leadership and organization in contrast to the governing party, which they regarded as providing a traditional type of leadership, imposed from above.

The division between educated and uneducated was exploited at election time. The leader of the Sikhumba Party complained that his opponents used the propaganda theme among the illiterates that these educated people would deceive them. "In other words, they are saying that the people must not vote for us because we are educated." There was the feeling at one time among members of the Sikhumba Party that the Superintendent, being a man of modest education, favored the party of the illiterates, and used his powers and the services of the indunas employed in his office to advance their interests.

It was only at Lamont Location that the party system was highly developed. There are embryonic suggestions of party organization in other locations, where candidates may work together as a team without forming a party. The effects of the two-party system seem to be disruptive. The scope of the Advisory Boards is so limited that there cannot be any real policy differences. Divisions inevitably follow personalities of the leaders, creating animosity and the possibility of playing off the different sections against each other, when the situation is such that little can be achieved, save by a common front.

In all the circumstances, it is surprising that candidates should be found for the elections. The desire to serve their people, which some members offer as an explanation, is certainly a factor. The Advisory Boards also provide scope for leadership in a world where Africans have few opportunities to lead. There is the excitement of elections, interest in the procedures of civic government, and the opportunity to lift the veil, as it were, from the sacred mystery of remote control, and to speak directly to the White man in command. There is the challenge of a seat around the horseshoe. The average White voter looks with a measure of condescension upon his elected City Councillors and the paid officials and civic ceremonial. For the African to confront, around the horseshoe, the wielders of despotic powers, and to stand candidly for his point of view, is a test of manly courage. And then there are the personal rewards. The remuneration of £3.3.0 per month, later raised to £4.10, can be important in the budget of an African family. For some, membership in the Advisory Boards has been a steppingstone to a highly prized trading site, and the contact with officials may be a source of influence and other personal advantages.

A more general explanation of the participation of Africans is that the Advisory Boards correspond to the interests of sections of the bourgeoisie. This is shown by the social background of the members and by the issues they raise in committee. They are almost all Christians, from established denominations. They are predominantly white-collar workers, small traders and professionals, and they tend to have more than average education. There is a minority of manual workers and of poorly educated members, with perhaps some cleavage between them and the educated. The latter tend to be highly conscious of their education, and to feel that it equips them to present to the White authorities the views of their people. Uneducated Africans often distrust the educated, who can speak a type of English they cannot understand, and who are often used by White officialdom in the apparatus of the State. There may be substance to the observation by an educated member that uneducated members never follow properly the proceedings of the combined Advisory Boards which are conducted in English: though an interpreter is present, he is rarely used. There may be substance also to the complaint that "these uneducated members are always very afraid of the White man," and that "when the elections are on, these [uneducated] board members would make fiery speeches, but when they come before the authorities they would be tame and quiet."

Inevitably the Advisory Board members express the general interests of the urban location residents among whom they live and to whom they are accountable. They are equally subject to the policies which grieve the population, even though their higher economic position may enable them to mitigate some of the consequences. Regularly recurrent grievances are the policy of influx control, the imposition of economic rentals, police raids, the arbitrary powers exercised by the authorities, and indignities suffered by Africans. The following resolutions, by way of illustration, express something of the disorder and anguish of urban African life. In August 1949, the Advisory Boards objected to a proposed increase in rents at Chesterville Location, and the African Chairman commented that since the police could raid at any time, location homes were not really private homes, but the property of the City Council, which should bear the losses; it was not the desire of the Native people that they should be placed in locations. In August 1958, the Boards objected to the proposed housing policy at a new location.

> In view of the fact that families of unmarried couples, unmarried mothers, widows, female divorcees and single females with dependents will not be allocated accommodation at Kwa Mashu township in view of the present policy of the department to accommodate married families only thereat, and as the classes of families referred to constitute the majority of the total number of families in Durban, the Boards wish to record their inability to support such a policy. Furthermore, the Boards wish to express the view that if the success of the scheme is to be measured by the amount of human misery and breaking up of families it will cause as against the benefits of the handful of families, it will fail in its object, namely,

the improvement of living conditions of families of Durban workers, regardless of sex and marital status of such workers.

The charge often leveled at members that they do not take up the
grievances of the people is without foundation. Nevertheless there is
considerable preoccupation with the interests of the bourgeois class from
which the members are largely recruited. They crusade strongly for increased trading facilities; they raise the issue of freehold tenure of land;
they seek to expand the opportunities for more responsible and remunerative employment in the Bantu Administration Department, and
they express the view that Africans should gradually replace White
officials in conformity with the declared policy of the Government, as
the high salaries paid to White officials constitute a large drain on
revenues. In private discussions, the monopoly of senior posts by White
officials is deeply resented, partly on the grounds that the administration
of Africans should be reserved for Africans, and partly because of the
incongruity in the qualifications and power of highly educated Africans
subject to control by poorly educated Location Superintendents.

> Then comes Mr. ————. He was also cross-examined in court, . . .
> he revealed that he had gone no further than standard 6. . . . His
> views are typically those of a White South African, viz., that an
> educated African is useless and no more than a trouble monger
> among his people. . . . In the final analysis of things, the object in
> view of the members of the Advisory Board has always been to
> point out the aforesaid discrepancies, viz., to put the African in
> his proper place and let him replace all Europeans who after all
> have no education in most cases. The authorities have always given
> that approach a deaf ear, dubbing each member who brought those
> grievances as an agitator and even go to the extent of working
> behind the scenes for the elimination of that person.

> The Superintendents are against any progressive thing. The Native
> Administration Department gets a retired policeman who can speak
> Fanakalo, but a policeman has seen only the worst side of Africans.
> These men are worse educated, and worse off economically than
> many of the men they rule. They perform the functions of an
> illiterate chief in the reserves, but get paid much more. [Quotations
> are from interviews with board members.]

And, finally, the members show an awareness of class structure. In
May 1956, the Boards recommended that the main beer hall in town be
divided into two partitions so as to accommodate (1) civilized class and
womenfolk and (2) the public in general; that clean tables, plastic jars,
and civilized caterers be provided for civilized class and womenfolk, and

that a general review be made of the present vessels used by beer drinkers. In September 1958, they asked that certain classes of Africans be
permitted to buy European liquor. In March 1959, they commented on
the unsuitability of dormitory accommodation for Africans such as
lawyers, doctors, teachers, social workers, and other educated Africans
and requested provision of single rooms for this class of persons. And in
May 1959, they took up the difficulties of civil servants (teachers, policemen, and clerks) transferred to Durban, who thereby lose the right of
accommodation for their families in the areas they leave, without acquiring it in Durban for a period of two years.

Service on the Advisory Boards is, however, deeply frustrating, because of the disproportionate effort expended for small gains. Only five
of the thirty-five members interviewed on the working of the Boards
over a long period of time expressed approval. Another eight members
gave a qualified approval, which may be summed up in the phrase used
by one of them—that the Boards were "never altogether futile." The
remainder attacked different aspects, and indeed the system itself, though
sometimes acknowledging minor achievements.

Some officials were described as favoring particular candidates and interfering in the elections. According to an informant, the Superintendent of one of the locations told a meeting of residents that they should
not vote for a particular candidate: the candidate "then got the biggest
majority ever" (indicating that disapproval of an African by the authorities is an honorable citation in the eyes of his people). At a subsequent
election the same candidate was said to have been excluded from the
nomination list on a variety of changing grounds (that he had not paid
his rent, when in fact he held the receipt; that he had no right to be
living in the location, an invalid basis for exclusion; and finally, as a last
resort, that he was an "undesirable native"). Whatever the merits of the
case, residents responded with so effective a boycott that only sixteen
residents in a population of over 4,000 cast their votes.

Interference in the elections is one aspect of the more general charge
that some officials use their extensive powers to surround themselves with
"good boys," with advisory eunuchs, intimidating those who speak up
for their people. The case of the candidate mentioned in the last paragraph was cited. According to his own version, he was arrested on a
charge of being illegally in Durban and thrown into the cells, without
an opportunity to consult his attorneys. Released on bail, he returned to
the location and was immediately arrested for being in possession of
dangerous weapons. He was released when he gave his explanation. Then
followed a criminal charge for failure to comply with a notice to vacate
the hostel. Again, he was acquitted. Later, the same charge was laid
against him, and, after conviction in the court of first instance, he was
acquitted on appeal. Meanwhile, in July 1959, during the disturbances

at Cato Manor, the Bantu Administration Committee included his name in a list of Africans to be deported from the city under arbitrary powers which exclude the rule of law and the right to contest the decision, but he was saved by the City Council's refusal, on a narrow majority, to exercise these powers.

He finally failed in the Appellate Division on the charge of being illegally in the city and was given an extended period within which to register, the Court expressing the opinion that "as he has resided in Durban for some time, and is a member of a location advisory board, it may well be that he will be granted permission to remain if he applies for it." He applied unsuccessfully for permission, and there was a further appeal pending from a conviction in the Magistrate's Court of being illegally in a municipal hostel. Shortly after, during the general disturbances in Durban, he was charged with incitement. Released on bail, he was imprisoned under the emergency regulations, and this was by no means the end of his tribulations. He was later charged and fined for incitement.

The issue raised in this discussion is not that of determining whether some of the officials of the local authority victimize and intimidate their outspoken critics. This is a matter better left to a judicial commission. Irrespective of its validity, however, the belief in victimization is a significant element for the understanding of the Advisory Boards. This theme recurs in the interviews.

> Anybody who has a lot to say within the Combined Advisory Boards is regarded as an enemy of the City Council and consequently an undesirable Native who should be deported out of the urban area to the place of his domicile. There is a glowing example of this—a gentleman by the name of ——— [the case referred to above] has earned himself a lot of enmity with the City Council of Durban, by reason of submitting a lot of grievances each time the Advisory Board meets. This gentleman was in fact one amongst the crowd that was recommended for deportation from the urban area of Durban. . . . Actually, 39 people had been recommended for deportation. It is common cause that most of those who had been recommended were people whose views were outspoken about the bad conditions under which the African lives here in Durban. . . . The underlying motive of those in authority is none other than to get rid of him because he had a lot to say within the Advisory Board context. The history of this gentleman indicates that he is one of the true sons of Africa. He is most law abiding and has never been charged with any of the serious offences committed by rogues in the urban areas, but he must leave the area of Durban, and he must leave behind him people who are a menace

to both Blacks and Whites. Those who had been recommended for deportation with Mr. ——— comprise decent Africans who are not rogues at all, but whose only default is that of pleading for the underdog.

Other informants express the same feeling, that you incur enmity if you voice criticism.

In relation to the municipality, if you point out facts as they stand you are an agitator. The municipality wants groups who are on the moderate side and on the municipal side.

If the municipality finds that you are liked by the people and wield some influence, they tend to hate you. . . . People who don't talk and who don't criticize the bad conditions under which the people live in these locations are considered good, and they are said to represent the true interests of the Africans. If you talk a lot then you earn yourself the name of a Communist. If the people who are elected to the Advisory Board were not afraid to talk they could achieve something.

Some informants believe that the Corporation uses the grant of a trading site as a means of taming outspoken critics, and its refusal as punishment, or that effective elected leaders are sterilized by conversion into Corporation nominees. The latter course would certainly diminish their influence, since there is a measure of antagonism between the elected and the nominated, both groups tending to feel that the nominees are the agents of the Corporation rather than the representatives of location residents.

There seems to be some justification to the complaint that the Corporation tends to reject criticism, and to regard grievances as the trouble making of agitators. The explanation is not to be found merely in remote control, and the soft illusion of efficient committee procedures. It lies rather in the nature of arbitrary rule, since criticism reflects on the qualities of the rulers and undermines the legitimacy of their rule, which rests not on representation, but on claims to greater wisdom and civilization. An extreme illustration of the resistance to criticism is provided by the handling of a resolution of the Advisory Boards in March 1959, asking for a commission of inquiry into factors giving rise to grievances of Africans against the Department of Bantu Administration. The Director commented on this resolution in his report to the Bantu Administration Committee, and the Committee's resolution followed the Director's recommendation. It was resolved

that the Native Advisory Boards be advised that this Committee is unable to accede to the Boards' request for the appointment of a Commission of Enquiry to investigate factors giving rise to grievances of Africans against the Department of Bantu Administration, in view of the fact that this Committee is not aware of any "seething discontent" amongst Africans in Durban, but is aware of agitation caused by disgruntled individuals most of whom are illegally in the urban area [April 15, 1959].

Not three months later (June 18, 1959), the residents of Cato Manor were expressing their resentment against the Corporation by burning down the symbols of Corporation rule—its administrative offices in Cato Manor and other Corporation buildings. The life of the Director himself was threatened, and it was dangerous for him to meet the women of Cato Manor, save with massive police protection. There was picketing of beer halls and a series of disturbances throughout Durban. Even the police did not want to be associated too closely with the Corporation for fear of the contagion of its unpopularity.

> The Deputy Commissioner of Police intimated that it was his intention to reduce the scale of his liquor raids to sporadic raids only. He gave two reasons—first that such raids were too great a strain on his force, and second, that his force was becoming identified with the City Council and was losing prestige and popularity with the Native population on account of these raids [minutes of the Bantu Administration Committee, July 24, 1959].

And a year after the Committee's resolution, Durban was like an armed camp, and the African areas like occupied enemy territory.

More fundamental than complaints against the administration of the system are attacks on the system itself, on the constitutional powers of the Advisory Boards—"guns without bullets," as one member described them. Informants say they are purely advisory without executive powers; in fact, they do not fulfill their advisory functions, since their advice is ignored. Advisory Board members are used by the authorities as "rubber stamps." Normally the people who advise you know more than you do, but here it is the reverse. The Boards do nothing whatever to cater to the interests of the African people, but are there merely to justify the White man's contention that South Africa is a democracy. The position of the Advisory Boards is an impossible one. Members are told about laws after they have been passed; some of the laws are bad, and the Boards must try to make them workable. Yet at the same time they are responsible to the people they represent, they must bring forward their grievances, which are then dismissed as unfounded, or answered with promises. Informants complain that they can do nothing about the laws or the grievances arising from the laws, and, in consequence, that their mandate from the voters cannot be fulfilled: they are obliged to face the anger of the masses.

Indeed, some of the critics go further and regard the Advisory Boards not merely as futile but as positively damaging to African interests. "It is one of those useless institutions which only serve to create unnecessary divisions amongst African people. It also serves to mislead them and divert their attentions from the real problems facing the African people." The authorities are charged by some with using the Advisory Boards as a means for implementing policy.

> It was made to enable the Corporation to know how we feel about certain things, so that the authorities could frame their policy accordingly.

> I regard the Advisory Board as nothing but the helping hand of the Europeans in everything they want to do to us.

> It is a way for the Europeans to sound feelings and see how to get their way with no intention of remedying grievances.

> The Advisory Board is intended to serve the interests of the White man and not the African. You are always expected to show due respect to your Superintendent. We were merely intended to advise the authorities and never to suggest or alter what they thought was right.

They feel the role of the Advisory Board members to be that of dummy, stooge, or sell-out, and this point of view is held much more widely outside the Advisory Boards than inside them.

This then is the background for the incident in which the African Chairman of the boards was addressed as "my boy" by the White Chairman. The latter almost certainly intended no insult. When he was asked whether it was in order for him to refer to Mr. Champion as a boy, he said it was in order—"he is a boy," presumably carrying on the pleasantry and not aware of the reactions of those present. Yet when Mr. Champion gave him the opportunity to say he was joking, he declared that he was not joking. (There are, as a matter of fact, different versions of what actually transpired.)

Mr. Champion, it seems, might have brushed the whole matter aside as a joke, and this is of some interest. He was a leader of considerable stature and, under other conditions and in other countries, could have hoped to attain a position beyond the reach of the White Chairman. He could hardly fail to be conscious of this, and the present incident was not the only one in which Mr. Champion had been involved with the Chairman of the Boards. Joking is one of the ways by which the discomfort arising from incongruity in status may be bridged, releasing tensions. By some oddity, the joke often goes near the bone, probing precisely the painful wound—nevertheless, it appears acceptable.

The initial insistence of the White chairman that he was serious in his use of the phrase was possibly due to a failure in judgment. His persistence is more difficult to explain. It would have been simple enough for him to say that he intended nothing derogatory, and that he withdrew the words. Yet quite a far-reaching reconstruction of the Advisory Boards was proposed as a solution to the impasse. This reconstruction might have been proposed in any event. The amendment of the regulations was under consideration. A number of complaints against the system had been taken into account, in the suggestions, for example, of a longer tenure of office and the abolition of nominees. But it would seem from the occasion which provoked the proposed reconstruction that it was a face-saving device. Could it be that the pattern of domination might be disrupted if a White man apologized to a Black man, particularly when the request for an apology was initiated by the Black man?

The anger of the Advisory Board members can be understood in the context of their position. The balanced point of view on the value of the Boards is that they do achieve something for Africans in a rather circumscribed field of local welfare. Members of the Boards have themselves pointed to many achievements—the right to examine estimates of Council expenditure before they are passed, some expansion of trading facilities, bus shelters after many years, and so on. Yet the majority of the members interviewed were preoccupied with the debit items. The slow pace of minor welfare reforms in a context of humiliating frustration is overtaken by the increasing sufferings of the African people and is obliterated from their perspective.

The members too feel somewhat guilty about their role. They know that they are regarded as stooges by many Africans, and some do indeed feel their role to be that of the sell-out. The charge is in fact not true. Certainly, some of the members play the role of Corporation agents. Yet the Boards as a whole have taken up the major grievances of their people—poverty and influx control. In September 1956, the Government refused to allow Native Revenue Account to be used for traveling expenses to the national annual congress of Advisory Boards. They had become too political, in the Government's view, having taken up such political matters as education policy.

In the context of the despotic powers available against Africans, and their feeling that these powers are abused to silence criticism, many of the members have shown considerable courage. But the role is an ambiguous one. It requires cooperation with the Bantu Administration Department, and the policies applied by the Department weigh heavily on the Board members and their fellow men. There is pressure to conform. And as Africans increasingly regard the Government and the Department as enemies, it becomes dangerous to be associated with official policies.

Driven by their own people and by their own desire for recognition, at a time when African states around them are achieving independence, the word "boy" becomes a symbol of an intolerable subordination both inside and outside the Advisory Boards. As a leading member explained:

> I am the last man to take offense. I am not easily provoked, but in that case I felt we were belittled and humiliated. I felt it was not Mr. Champion alone who had been humiliated. There was a great deal of heat produced and at last Mr. Champion stood up. He was not the man who had asked the Chairman to withdraw the word "boy." Everybody had been enraged. I also felt injected. Mr. Champion stood up and said: "Mr. Chairman, in calling me a boy you are passing a joke or what?" The Chairman said, "No, I mean it. If I say you are a boy I mean it. We are used to that, we say that between ourselves." "But you see, Mr. Chairman, we don't like that you have aired." He said he was not apologetic.
>
> The resolution was prepared by the caucus before the meeting commenced. We agreed that if he does not apologize we should resolve to adjourn the meeting. It was suggested that if the resolution was proposed a strong man should support it and that is how it came about that I supported the resolution. Everybody was looking at this stooge to see if he would support the motion. I stood up to second the motion. When the press people phoned me, I told them I did support the motion, even though I was feeling sorry. If I were to agree that our Chairman be called a "boy," my people would stone me to death.

The deadlock was finally resolved at the end of 1960, some nine months after the initial incident. Changes in the membership of the Board, following the elections, and a diplomatic statement by the White Chairman helped to effect a reconciliation. It would seem that in a situation of growing antagonism between White and Black, both sides felt the need for some means, however inadequate, of resolving conflict.

CHAPTER 22

Politics of Football: The Durban and District African Football Association[1]

FOOTBALL AND POLITICS are major interests of Africans in Durban. Football is the more efficiently organized and disposes of greater resources, since African sportsmen have a freedom of association which is denied African politicians. The game has a relatively long history in Natal. It was already being played in some of the mission stations before the end of the nineteenth century; and in 1916 it had advanced to the stage of a formally constituted association of clubs in Durban and its districts, under the name of the Durban and District Native Football Association (changed in 1932 to the Durban and District African Football Association). The Association took the initiative in promoting first the Natal, and later the South African, African Football Associations. It encouraged tennis and boxing, as well as cricket, which is, however, not yet fully established. By the 1950s the Association was strong enough to organize a match in Rhodesia at a cost of over £1,000, and to enter into an agreement for the purchase of more than 50 acres of land in Inanda, near Durban, at a price of some £7,800. For a period, the Association employed the services of a White professional coach. The number of affiliated clubs stood at 256 in 1959: membership was over 5,000 and the annual gate takings, according to one estimate, about £12,000 per year.

All this represents a specifically African achievement. White paternalism was not a feature of the Association. The reason is partly that the American Board missionaries, who promoted African football in the coastal areas of Natal, encouraged African initiative. Though the first President, from 1916 to 1923, D. Evans, was a White man, employed by the Durban Corporation, he appears to have identified with Africans: he coached players, acted as referee, and sometimes played on the Association's teams. An illuminated address, presented to him on his retirement as President, described him as a "European President

---

1. I am greatly indebted to Bernard Magubane for his analysis of football in "Sport and Politics in an Urban African Community."

who had the interest of the Native at heart," and he remained an Elder of the Association and Honorary Life President.

The role of White persons became an issue in connection with Mr. Evans' presidency. This was during the negotiations for the founding of the Natal African Football Association. The Pietermaritzburg group refused to enter the provincial organization while Durban had a White President, and Durban was not prepared to discuss the matter because of loyalty to a President who had served so well. The Natal Association was therefore established in 1920 without the affiliation of Pietermaritzburg. The later resignation of the White President was linked with this issue: he explained in an interview that he did not wish to stand in the way of the development of African football, and he felt that the Durban Association was well on its feet. Apart from this early period, the Association has been under direct African control, and its members highly prize their independence. They cannot be fully independent, since they must rely on the Durban Corporation for facilities until such time as the Association can establish its own playing fields at Inanda.

Though the Association is specifically African, there are no constitutional barriers to the admission of members of other races. Relations with interested White sportsmen are cordial. But the Association is sensitive to any suggestion of White patronage. And it is vigilant in maintaining and asserting its independence, and highly suspicious of the Durban Corporation, which has the means to interfere with the autonomy of the Association through its control of playing fields. Relations have been guarded since the earliest days. The Association would clear land and prepare grounds, only to be moved out again into the bush. A White official of the Native Recruiting Corporation, donating a trophy to the Association, commented that the Native footballers had been booted out by the Durban Corporation from one football ground to another, from Western Vlei to Lords Grounds, and from there to the Eastern Vlei, and that each time this happened, Europeans or Indians followed to occupy the grounds. In 1931, the Association initially rejected affiliation with the Bantu Recreational Grounds Association, formed by the Corporation to coordinate sporting activities and to regulate the allocation of facilities. It now serves guardedly on this body. An issue between the Association and the Corporation was the desire of the latter for a larger share of gate monies as a contribution to help defray costs of maintenance.

Something of the quality of relations between the Association and Durban's Bantu Administration Department is conveyed by an incident which occurred in 1956 when the Department asked that its representatives be coopted to the Association's committee. The Association replied that it did not understand on which committee the officials were to be represented, and that its constitution made no provision for coopted members. Then followed discussions in which

> the president had pointed out that the N.A.D. were introducing politics into football and had pointed out that the Africans were sceptical about the motives of the N.A.D. in seeking representation, and that hitherto no interest had been taken by the corporation until just lately, when the Association was well on its feet [report in the minutes of the Association, August 9, 1956].

The Welfare Officer of the Corporation, according to the report, then asked for consultation on controversial matters, to which the President replied that the N.A.D. wanted to employ a paid sports organizer, who would make a living on what Africans had achieved unassisted by the White man, save the Honorable Councillor, Mr. D. Evans. Thereupon the Welfare Officer raised the question of Mr. X, a White sports official employed by his Department, and the President answered that the Association resented the attitude of Mr. X toward Africans at the sports grounds "when he seemed to boss everybody."

The influence of Whites, though rejected at the level of control, is of course most marked in the game itself and to a lesser extent in the style of administration. The rules, as applied by the Association, are those governing international soccer. At the time of the adoption of the constitution, the White President explained that "from the very word go we followed European rules and the Africans did not introduce anything. We took all the English rules and introduced them into our constitution as they were." Administration, by contrast, though Western, incorporates traditional elements in such a way as to give the Association its own special character. Traditional patterns, for example, are reflected in the position of the Elders, that is to say, the founding fathers of clubs who act as advisers or to effect reconciliation in disputes, sometimes adjusting social relationships in much the same way as might a traditional court. At times, too, the role of President seems to have taken an imprint of chieftainship. Western elements are expressed in the apparatus of committee procedures, in impressions of parliamentary debate, and in the judicial process. There is mention in the records of the "bench," the "house," and the "cabinet"—the latter referring to the President, Vice-President, Secretary, and Treasurer. Select committees are appointed with power to constitute themselves as commissions of inquiry. Complaints are often handled in the manner of a magistrate's court, as shown in the following report of the Misconduct Committee:

> By order of and as had been duly appointed by the Monthly Committee meeting, sitting on the 7th May, 1931, the above com-

mittee, consisting of Messrs. A. R. Ntuli, A. B. Ngcobo, I. Lutshozi, H. S. Goba, and J. S. Malinga, sat on Wednesday 13th May, 1931; and Mr. A. B. Ngcobo was mutually appointed to act as Chairman for the meeting, and the meeting was declared opened at 6:50 P.M. instead of 6 P.M. owing to the preparation for the Rand tour in which the Secretary was engaged.

The following accused answered to their names being called as present in compliance with the summonses that had been issued for their attention of this meeting: Messrs. Springboks F. C., Makanya of the Swallows F.C., The Vultures F.C., and the Klip River County F.C.

The Springboks F.C. were charged with having contravened Rule 12 under Constitution and Rules of the Association, by having failed to fulfill an engagement against the Wanderers F.C., on the 4th April, 1931, this being an authorised competition match under the jurisdiction of the Association, reported their inability to attend personally owing to work; and no pleadings were filed on their behalf. On investigation further, it was ascertained that they had not scratched in terms of Rule 6 under Cup Competition Rules, but had written a letter to the Association Secretary reporting that they shall not have been able to play their match of the 4th April, as their men will be working in the morning, this being not a recognised public holiday.

Judgement: Seeing that the Springboks F.C., had not scratched in terms of Rule 6 under Cup Competition Rules, they were held to have unconstitutionally failed to fulfill an engagement and were declared to have forfeited the points, which were awarded to their opponents, the Wanderers F.C.

The officials were dedicated to the Association. In the early days, meetings sometimes lasted all night. Attendance at executive meetings was enforced, and failure in some duty without a satisfactory explanation might be punished by fine or suspension from office. Defalcations of funds, not uncommon, were sometimes reported to the police, or settled within the Association out of consideration for the defaulter and to avoid unfavorable publicity. Mishandling of funds is probably not more common in African associations than in those of other groups, though Africans seem to regard the administration of funds as synonymous with their maladministration, and freely voice their suspicions.

At meetings, the committee procedures often take on an independent life, and the work of the Association is enmeshed in the most complex and obdurate debate. In April 1932, three pages of the minutes were devoted to an argument as to whether the meeting might proceed constitutionally without the minutes of the previous meeting having been read. "Mr. Kuluse, for Mountain Blues, commented on the intentions and interpretations of the word *shall*, contending that, it impressed on order Imperative, and without any alternative on the contrary." One member suspected that the Chairman had deliberately rearranged the agenda. "The Chairman, in clearing the suspicion thus aroused" and having been "favourably grunted on by the meeting generally," gave his reasons. In June 1933, there is the following minute:

> Mr. Sitebe speaking in the Imperative mood remarked that minutes were incorrect but couldn't advance reasons and solution of rectifying them, he was ordered out of order by the Chair but he persisted on repeating himself on his Theatrical dodgings. . . . The Chair applied the Subjunctive mood that, if you Sitebe have ready made Explosives which are inverterating your Cause, you better say so, and I warn you that you are labouring under extreme misapprehensions.

With the passage of time, the minutes become businesslike, but there is still much sterile debate. This arises in part from the desire to display procedural virtuosity and from a lack of familiarity with the rules. But the emphasis on ritual also shows the importance attached to the organizational mysteries of the White man. Magubane describes the obsession with constitutional procedures as an overconformity, enabling Africans who are barred from assimilation to identify mentally with the practices and outlook of the dominant White group; and he refers to some of the judicial procedures as vicarious participation in the European social structure. From another point of view, it seems as if the symbols of power represented by the committee procedures of the White man become a substitute for the exercise of power, and that political energy, denied other expression, is projected into the Football Association. Certainly, there is much rivalry for position.

Leadership in the Association and the affiliated clubs is highly prized, and for important matches sport administrators often lead their teams onto the field in proud parade. Rivalry for leadership at the club level is ultimately resolved by fission. The tendency is of course more marked in the leading clubs, where the prestige of the club and its larger membership provide both greater incentive and greater opportunity for rivalry: thus Magubane reports that fifteen clubs had split off from the Wanderers Football Club and that the process was still continuing. The trainer of the Bush Bucks, a leading team, explained the reasons for the split in his own club.

> There were now many stresses and strains in our club. After our defeat by the Wanderers, I was accused of having sold them our

lucky charm, and besides it was alleged that I had embezzled the funds of the club. After a drawn battle for my suspension from the club, I was finally dismissed. It was then that I formed my own young club called the Black Spades. From those internal stresses and strains, the Bush Bucks never fully recovered, and last year they suffered a major split, when about half the members broke away to form a club they called Carlton Bucks. I had built up the Bush Bucks to a wonderful team, and had created among the players a wonderful discipline, and I felt myself very important, and in the Bush Buck Club I was a demigod, and envy and jealousy began to grow amongst the officials, and with encouragement from the President of the D.D.A.F.A., I was ousted from the Bush Bucks.

Monica Wilson[2] reports a somewhat similar process of fission in Cape Town. She writes:

> Father Botto's evidence suggests that as soon as a rugby club has enough members to field two teams it is in danger: the average size of a rugby club in Langa is only 36 members. Soccer clubs are rather larger, possibly because soccer does not carry as high a social status, and the competition for leadership is less. There are 35 African rugby and soccer clubs in Cape Town and the size is considerably smaller than in corresponding white clubs.

In Durban, where soccer (football) carries high prestige and rugby is hardly played, an upper limit is placed on fission at club level by the rule that only constituted clubs of not less than 20 members (16 of whom must be playing members) are eligible for affiliation to the Football Association.

At the level of the Association, the structure provides a ready basis for fission. The situation is analogous to that of the segmentation of a lineage, a group of clubs offering the same opportunity for breaking away as a group of kinsmen. Probably the main factor restraining the tendency to fission was one external to the Association, namely that the Durban Corporation, on whom the Association depended for the use of playing fields, recognized only one body in each field of sport. Within the Association, there are other factors promoting cohesion. The members have an interest in the Association itself as providing the necessary organization for interclub competition. They find scope for leadership in consequence of a multiplication of offices within the Association. They take pride in its achievements and in the demonstration

---

2. *The Coherence of Groups,* pp. 9–10. Pauw regards the tendency to fission in associational life as reflecting a transitional stage between leadership based on ascriptive status and leadership based on mutual consent (*The Second Generation,* pp. 175–76).

that Africans can successfully manage their own affairs. And they feel, or formerly did feel, a need to maintain a solid front against the Corporation. Dissension among leaders and charges of maladministration are seen as threatening the autonomy of the Association, since they might provide a pretext for interference in its domestic affairs. Magubane[3] suggests that many members "believe that it is better, so to say, if the finances of the Association are 'eaten' by an African, than by a White man. Thus they condone flagrant irregularities. The officials often play on this sentiment. Those who voice criticism of the ruling clique are immediately branded as 'selling' the Association to the White man."

These restrained tendencies to fission are combined with marked oligarchical tendencies. Since 1923, there have been only six African Presidents. A relatively small circle of educated men share between them most of the positions on the executive and its subcommittees, and act also as representatives of the Association in the provincial and national organizations. During the period 1924–60, half the members of the various committees had served for more than ten years. Loss of office was apparently a severe blow to pride. Thus in 1932, there was a move for changes in the executive. A. J. Luthuli, then Vice-President, was elected President, "Telephone" Ngcobo, the former President, was elected Treasurer, and A. R. Ntuli, Vice-Secretary. Luthuli declined office; because of his duties as a teacher, Secretary of the Natal Native Football Association, and Secretary and Treasurer of the South African African Football Association, he felt his hands were full. Ntuli declined; "Seeing that I have been elected Vice-Secretary, I feel the meeting has indirectly trespassed on my name, hence I feel compelled to decline the office." Ngcobo said, "In the same way of the inferiority of the office of Treasurer compared with the office he holds with the N.N.F.A. and S.A.A.F.A. he decided to decline the acceptance."

Many circumstances promote the oligarchical tendencies. English is the language of debate, because "if Zulu were to be used other nationalities would suffer." The constitution specifically provides that the official language at meetings shall be English, save with permission of the Chairman. The use of English and the need to master the complex procedures of debate and administration virtually exclude the uneducated or inexperienced. The mass of members, though loyal to the Association and ready to submit to its rules and discipline, are apathetic at meetings. They are interested in the sport and not in the organizational work, which they find difficult to follow. Their apathetic reaction to a role in the government of the Association encourages rule by the few, and the struggle for power takes place within a narrow range of members. The situation is analogous to that of a one-party govern-

3. "Sport and Politics," p. 39.

ment with conflict of interests expressed in factions. Rival leaders represent affiliated clubs. This is the basis of their power, which they may seek to augment by promises of preferential treatment for influential clubs. It is also a source of conflict because the leader's involvement in the affairs of his club may obscure his recognition of the broader interests of the Association.

The first split in the Association in 1932 or 1933 followed the abortive attempt to elect Chief Luthuli as President. Some clubs broke away to form the Durban and District Bantu Football League, but they could not survive because of lack of facilities. In 1941, there was an attempted rebellion in an atmosphere of intrigue. Nine clubs petitioned a meeting to censure the officials of the Association for "incompetency, dishonesty, subjugation, and disobedience." The executive anticipated the meeting and appointed a commission of inquiry, which found that neither the secretaries of the clubs nor the man who asked them to sign the petition knew its contents. Mr. X., who was actually responsible for the petition, was suspended by the executive for five years on the grounds of contrivance, but this suspension was set aside by delegates of the Association, who asked that Mr. X. be reinstated by the executive. The commission of inquiry appointed in 1942 recommended that the constitution be revised and that the executive be not allowed to dictate.

During the last decade, oligarchical tendencies have become more pronounced. This seems to be a consequence of growth in membership and resources and of the policy of paying allowances to members for work on behalf of the Association. The present schism, the most serious in the history of the Association, has its roots in dissatisfaction with the President and the seeming impossibility of unseating him. Opponents of the regime felt that they were being arbitrarily suspended from the Association. Suspension is presumably the sporting equivalent of political banning or the religious heresy trial. The rebellious groups met in secret, at night, and in the most obscure places. This became known, and at the annual general meeting in 1958, delegates resolved to charge, before the Misconduct and Protests Committee, those who had attended the meetings with suspended members.

In February 1959, at a meeting of the Association, three members of the executive made a series of complaints against the President. The President replied for three hours, and after some angry exchanges the delegates decided to appoint a commission of inquiry. The report of the commission, carefully presented and documented, was highly critical of the administration. The Association rejected the report on such grounds, among others, as that the chairman of the commission, when he was President, had left only one shilling and sixpence on expiration of his term of office. Powers of suspension were exercised against the members of the commission for the alleged failure to return certain vouchers. By February 1960, tension between the "Russians" (the Government) and the "Japanese," or "Tokyo" group (the dissident elements), was acute. There were further suspensions, some delegates only learning of their suspension when they presented themselves at the February annual general meeting. Nevertheless, the Japanese were there in strength. When a crowd burst into the hall, the South African police were summoned, and they came immediately armed with Sten guns and revolvers. The meeting ended in an uproar, and the President, on the advice of the police, declared the meeting closed. The police escorted him from the hall, accompanied by shouts of "We don't want you" and "You must resign."

The Japanese thereupon secured an interim interdict from the Court, restraining the use of the assets, and calling on the Association to show cause, inter alia, why the annual general meeting should not be reconvened and elections held. The Association then called a general meeting in May 1960, to comply with the terms of the interdict. As a result of the Japanese decision to boycott this meeting, the President was in full control. He allowed the use of the vernacular, as he had done at the February meeting. "Your constitution binds you to speak in English but I will give a special dispensation for the use of the vernacular. For people who are trying to build up a nation, I find it a shame that you despise your language and speak in a foreign language, English." This was obviously an appeal to sentiment, more particularly of the less educated. The leaders of the rebel Japanese group represented a better educated stratum, and the play on the suspicions of the less educated emerged again as an element in the struggle for power.

The President declared both his dispensability and his indispensability:

> I don't want a single one of you to regard me as a king. If you remove me from office well and good. There are people who go about saying that I am refusing to be removed from office. You did not elect me because I had better brains than you have and my presence here is not because I am better. You chose me like an old man would do when he chooses his herdboy. He will choose him not because the boy will be better than others but because he likes the way he looks after the sheep. You are still the final arbiters and what you say holds true.

But at the same time, he had made a valuable contribution.

> This Association has built up your spirit of nationhood and during the last eight years you have grown up to be one of the biggest associations. At one time you used to be beaten by the Indian football teams and by the Transvaal teams. To improve the stand-

ard of soccer among the boys I went to invite Topper Brown to
train you and the result was that you beat the Indians and the
Transvaal. After all these good things you have decided to break
and form a splinter association. . . . I ask you do not destroy
your Association, but remove [the President] if he is a stumbling
block. You know that you have enhanced your status even in the
eyes of the European Association, which invites you time and
again to go and play at Kingsmead, and I as your President, I am
invited to Kingsmead whenever there is a big match. Have you
had another President who has enjoyed the confidence of the White
sporting body? You must be proud and do not destroy your Association. I am asking you like a father would do when he asks his
son to behave well. . . . You have all the powers in your hands
and you can still build up this Association. I don't think that
those who have broken away have better brains than you have.

Before the elections, the Vice-President emphasized that in electing
office bearers, delegates should use their good judgment: they must
know that football is one sphere where African people can and must
prove to the world and the Europeans in South Africa their ability
to manage their own affairs. The President and Vice-President were
then re-elected unanimously. The officials themselves led the vote for
men they wanted by standing up and indicating with their hands that
the delegates should stand up, until the Vice-President remarked on
the unfairness of the procedure.

The results of the election appear not to have been unanticipated.
The same President is in power and the rebel Japanese group is now
established as an independent association, the Durban and County
African Football Association, with a substantial club membership. There
have been two further fissions on a territorial basis, in response apparently to local availability of grounds and problems of distance—the
Durban North African Football Association and the Western Areas
African Football Association. The parent Association has now greatly
declined in power.

Notwithstanding these internal conflicts, the basic role of the Association, and of the seceding associations, is integrative. The competing
units are the clubs, and their competition is regulated by the rules of
their Association and the rules of the game. Sometimes, more particularly in the case of the leading clubs and their supporters, competition
bursts across the legitimate bounds into open conflict. There are assaults
on referees, players, and officials of the Association, and faction fights
between the supporters. These conflicts tend to assume a tribal character, where the clubs are linked with particular areas and groups: for

example, the Bush Bucks are often nicknamed the Pondos; the Zulu Royals have the Paramount Chief of the Zulu nation as chief patron, and are linked with Zululand, and the Wanderers with the Abaqulusi around the Newcastle-Nqutu-Dundee area. Disciplinary action is immediately taken by the Association against the offending clubs and a sporting relationship re-established among them, in serious cases after a period of suspension. Conflict is contained, and a measure of integration achieved at the local level. This process is repeated throughout South Africa, the competition between cities giving vitality to the provincial associations, and the provincial associations sustaining the national body. Thus the South African African Football Association brings together Africans from different regions and of different background, providing a basis for a common sentiment transcending tribalism and Bantu Authorities.

In race relations, the Association formed part of a movement for racial integration in sport. Generally in sport, a strong, though not absolute color bar is raised between White and non-White. White sports administrators tend to regard this as nonpolitical, simply one of the customs of the country, and they often characterize attempts to remove the color bar as the intrusion of politics into sport. The more militant non-White sportsmen see apartheid in sport, and the monopoly of national colors by Whites, as obviously political, and part of systematic political discrimination. Though the movement for the deliberate racial integration of sport is recent, interracial football has a relatively long history among non-Whites. There were already interracial matches in the 1930s, and these led in 1946 to the founding of an Inter-racial Soccer Board in Natal, consisting of Africans, Coloreds, and Indians. Similar boards were in existence in the Cape and the Transvaal. In contrast to the matches between the main African clubs, the interracial matches in Durban only once erupted into race violence between Africans and Indians. This was in July 1960, and immediately led to a reaction against racial match competitions. The greater peacefulness of the interracial matches is difficult to interpret. African and Indian crowds identify with the teams of their own race, and there appears to be a deep emotional involvement. Whether this is as intense as the involvement of Africans in the fortunes of the clubs they support, it is impossible to say. There is much latent hostility between Africans and Indians, and competition in a game taken as seriously as football would seem to invite race riots. Perhaps it is the greater danger of a conflict between two large racial groups which more effectively restrains violence. Or perhaps the competition between African clubs is a substitute for intertribal clashes. African clubs are of course not unique in their occasional outbursts of violence on the playing fields.

The organization of interracial sport was on racial lines, the teams of Africans or Indians or Coloreds being managed by their own racial associations. In this respect, the organization of sport followed the same pattern as the political organization of the Congresses. And this basic racial pattern persisted when the South African Soccer Federation was founded on September 30, 1951, to coordinate interracial football and to seek international recognition. The federated foundation units were the racial associations of Africans, Coloreds, and Indians. The Federation promoted interracial football, arranging matches for the Kajee Trophy, and negotiated with the Football Association of Southern Africa (F.A.S.A.), a White association enjoying international recognition, for the merging of the two bodies into one national unit. When these negotiations failed, the Federation sought the disaffiliation of F.A.S.A., and its own recognition by the Federation of International Football Associations (F.I.F.A.). Its argument was simple and cogent —that F.A.S.A. was not a national association since it represented only 18 per cent of the population, and practiced racial discrimination, contrary to the statutes of F.I.F.A. After protracted negotiations, F.A.S.A.'s membership was suspended, on pain of total exclusion if it did not remove racial discrimination within a period of twelve months.

Meanwhile the South African Soccer Federation was under some compulsion to reorganize football on a nonracial basis, since a federation of racially constituted bodies is hardly an ideal basis for the rejection of White racialism in sport. The appeal to the higher international tribunal calls for some inner purification. And in July 1961, a conference of the Federation took a resolution for the abandonment of racial designations and for full integration between African, Colored, and Indian players from the club level to national associations. Existing national associations were asked to dissolve not later than May 1962, so that the Federation might be reconstituted on a nonracial basis. Thus it is that the higher international tribunal, with effective sanctions in the form of recognition and its attendant privileges, strengthens the forces of nonracialism among non-Whites. The Federation is now pursuing a policy of deracialization, that is to say, the organization of football on a territorial basis, with membership of the territorial associations and of teams on an interracial or nonracial basis.

This process extends beyond football to sport in general. The South African Sports Association, which held its inaugural conference in January 1959, seeks to eliminate racialism in South African sport. In its representations to the Olympic Council in 1959, the Association contended that all sportsmen had the right to be considered on merit, and that the exclusion of non-Whites by the South African national bodies flouted the canons of sportsmanship. Non-Whites, the memorandum stated, had no desire to see their White compatriots excluded, but they insisted that merit should be the criterion, without consideration of such extraneous issues as color, race, or creed. To establish that their exclusion from nationally representative teams was not simply a matter of the greater athletic prowess of Whites, they cited a case of non-White sportsmen who had passed as Whites and traveled with the South African team of boxers and weightlifters to the 1956 Olympic Games, but were later asked to retire (memorandum of the South African Sports Association to the World Olympic Council, presented in May 1959). In October 1962, the South African Non-Racial Olympic Committee was established, and the conflict—in foreign affairs for international recognition and domestically for desegregation and nondiscrimination—is now extended to the whole range of sport.

The ensuing struggle reproduces almost all the forms of the political conflict. In the international forums of sport, as in the international forum of the United Nations, the issue is whether effective sanctions will be applied against South Africa. Non-Whites were encouraged by the early international recognition of the nonracial South African Table Tennis Board of Control and the disaffiliation of the parallel White association. This gave impetus to the whole movement for international recognition. White sports administrators are now on the defensive. They have a difficult case to argue before international multiracial tribunals. The suspension of the football association brought home the power of international sanctions more effectively than disaffiliation in the minor and somewhat genteel sport of table tennis. And the loss of Commonwealth recognition, as a result of South Africa's political withdrawal from the Commonwealth, increases the threat of isolation in sport. However South African White sportsmen are not defenceless, and the lifting of the suspension of the football association in January 1963 is a reminder that South African Whites have powerful friends in international sport, as in international politics, industry, and commerce. The comment that the lifting of the ban was a "defeat for communism" (quoted in *South African Digest*, January 31, 1963), suggests that also in sport South Africa may begin to project a propaganda image of herself as the bastion against communism.

Within South Africa and among non-Whites, the issues are complicated by internal divisions. In much the same way that certain chiefs support the Government's policy, so too there are non-Whites willing to serve in paternalist associations, directly or by affiliation under White control. There is some possibility that the Durban and District African Football Association, consequent on its decline in strength, may move into the circles of White patronage. Whites can offer attractive incentives to non-White affiliates and conversely they can exert pressure against nonaffiliated associations, as indeed they have done in some cities, through municipal control over sports facilities. Many White sportsmen are sincerely interested in promoting non-White sport, but at the same time they subordinate and segregate non-Whites. The relationship of the affiliate is within the framework of White domination. The result is antagonism by the more militant non-White sportsmen toward those of their fellows they regard as "selling out" to Whites, an antagonism analogous to that between the militants and the collaborators in the political field, though less intense.

The issue for White sportsmen is not so much internal dissension as the dilemma of satisfying the absolutely opposed requirements of the South African Government and of the international sports tribunals. Traditionally White sportsmen followed a policy with reference to non-White sport which might be described as the equivalent of the political philosophy of trusteeship. Though they had introduced Western sport among Africans, showing a varied interest or indifference in its promotion, for the most part they would not have conceived it as appropriate, save in a remote future, that White and non-White should belong to the same associations and play in the same teams or against each other, or that non-Whites should be considered eligible to represent South Africa or to direct national sport. Yet these are precisely the expectations of the international sports tribunals. And the White associations must now comply with these expectations and demonstrate that they are nationally representative and racially nondiscriminatory, that is to say, they must radically transform their traditional policies. But this they cannot easily accomplish, by reason both of the outlook of many of their members and the attitude of Government. Hence they are obliged to present the appearance, since they cannot present the reality of national representativeness and nondiscrimination; the issues become infinitely complex, and obscured by shrewd compromise and skillful advocacy.

The appearance of national representativeness, but within a context of White control, may be projected by various types of paternalist associations similar to the Advisory Boards and Advisory University Senates, or by means of affiliation with subordinate status. Thus the South African Bantu Amateur Athletic Association, a paternalist association, was affiliated on roughly the model of the African parliamentary representation introduced in 1936—that is to say, limited representation by Whites at general meetings of the governing White association: the conditions of affiliation also expressly stipulated acceptance of the recognized policy of trusteeship. Securing an appearance of nondiscrimination is somewhat more complex, with much polemic and political argument. The past exclusion of non-White athletes, for example, is justified on the ground that non-White standards were too low for national representation. This is the old rationalization for withholding the vote, that non-Whites are not yet civilized, and it submerges the accomplished non-White in an undifferentiated, stereotyped mass. Or again the charge is made that the movement for nonracialism in sport is politically inspired, that is to say the work of "agitators," and does not represent a legitimate grievance: or that it is dominated by Indians, thus invoking the traditional scapegoat, inciting antagonism, and again dismissing the movement as not grounded in legitimate complaint. Above all, the White associations seek absolution on grounds of necessity, that they are complying with the laws of the land—a contention refuted by their opponents—and they rely on the Government to shield them from responsibility.

These arguments and arrangements would prevail inside South Africa and before White umpires, but they are not likely to be too persuasive in international forums and under vigorous criticism by South African non-White representatives. Also they offend the sentiments of liberalism and integrity of those White sportsmen who genuinely reject racialism in sport. And they conflict with the ethos of sportsmanship which encourages ideas of fair play, equal opportunity, and open competition. Consequently, under international pressure, White sportsmen incline, though in complex and obscure ways, toward less racialism in sport. At the level of organization, there is now direct representation by non-White affiliates in F.A.S.A. In May 1962, the President of the South African Bantu Football Association accompanied White officials of F.A.S.A. to a meeting of the international football federation.[4] In October 1963, an African sports official was South Africa's second delegate at the International Olympic Congress. There have been demonstrations of a willingness to engage in interracial sport by the staging of events outside the borders of South Africa, and by such actions as the admission of an Indian golfer to national and provincial open golf championships. Non-Whites are assured that selection for international athletic competitions will be on the basis of merit. In the case of football, there is to be alternate selection of White and non-White teams for World Cup competitions, and a decision was taken that South Africa would "be represented at the next World Soccer Games in 1964 by an entirely non-White side" (*The Star*, overseas edition, March 2, 1963). An impulse has been given to nonracialism in sport, and students of the English-speaking universities have already formed a nonracial National Student Sports Association.

The trend away from racialism in sport creates a dilemma for the Government. It dare not allow apartheid to be undermined by nonracialism in sport, and yet it cannot act, by legislation or repression, in so forthright a manner as to provoke the exclusion of White sportsmen from the international arenas, particularly since sport is a major value in South African life. Hence the Government is obliged to counter

---

4. See the full discussion by Mary Draper of *Sport and Race in South Africa,* South African Institute of Race Relations, 1963.

integrating tendencies, while supporting the international aspirations of White sportsmen. The resultant restraints and compromises appear in the policy of the Minister of the Interior, whose portfolio includes the regulation of racial contact. The acceptable organizational pattern is one of White paternalism domestically and of White representation in foreign affairs.

> For the purposes of administration and control, it would be in accordance with Government policy for non-White associations to exist and develop alongside the corresponding White associations.
>
> In considering matters affecting non-White associations, one or two members of the White executive committee of the chief organisation could attend meetings of the non-White organisation's executive committee when requested to act as a link between the committees and to inform the White committee about the opinions of the non-White committee when matters of concern to the non-White committee were being dealt with.
>
> If this method should appear impracticable for some or other reason in a particular instance, one or more members of the non-White body could be co-opted or elected to serve on the White executive committee in an advisory capacity when matters affecting the non-White organisation were discussed to represent the interest of the non-Whites.
>
> The White executive committees could serve on a high level as co-ordinating bodies between the associations and as representatives in the corresponding world organisations.

Sport within South Africa must not involve contact between Whites and non-Whites.

> South African practice is that within the country's borders, Whites and non-Whites practise their sport separately and this practice must be upheld.
>
> This means that within the country's borders Whites and non-Whites must not compete with one another, whether in individual items or as teams or part of teams.
>
> South African sportsmen can compete beyond the country's borders with sportsmen of different races who are not South Africans where this is the custom in those other countries.
>
> Where sport beyond the country's borders is concerned, the Government will observe the customs of other countries.
>
> But it desires that others, when visiting South Africa, should observe South Africa's customs. In other words, within South Africa's borders Whites should compete with Whites and non-Whites with non-Whites.

South Africa is not a nation—this is, of course, implied, not explicit—and there cannot be national representation overseas but only racial representation.

> Participation in international sports tournaments or competitions of mixed teams as representatives of South Africa as a whole cannot be approved.
>
> Where, for example, Whites participate individually in such tournaments, they must do so as representatives of the Whites of this country and, similarly, the non-Whites must take part as representatives of non-White South Africans. [Quotations are from the summing up of policy by the Minister of the Interior as reported in *Natal Daily News*, February 4, 1963.]

In effect, under this compromise solution, non-Whites would represent South Africa in international competitions, though as members of a contingent, not a team, or as representatives of their own races and not of South Africa. Indeed this did occur, when a contingent of White and non-White boxers fought in the United States of America and Lukas Matseke won the amateur flyweight championship for 1963. And it is inevitable that White South Africans should take pride in the athletic prowess of their non-White countrymen, thus forging another link with non-racialism—that is assuming the process is not overtaken by civil war. A proposed athletic tour of Europe by nine White and two non-White athletes was however canceled, apparently by way of reprisal against the International Olympic Committee, which had required a declaration renouncing racial discrimination in sport from its South African affiliate (*The Star*, Overseas Edition, June 27, 1964).

Though the Government shows relative restraint in the handling of sport, this does not exclude the conventional political reprisals. The secretary of the non-White Soccer Federation was detained during the emergency in 1960: since no charge was preferred, it is not possible to say definitely that this was a reprisal for his stand against racialism in sport. The militant secretary of the Sports Association has been banned for a period of five years (and arrested). Passports were withheld from the non-White table tennis team which was to compete in international championships. Militant non-White sportsmen seem to be exposed to the same dangers as militant non-White politicians. And the possibility of explicit legislation cannot be excluded. But the Government has exercised more than customary restraint, because it is acting under the close scrutiny of international tribunals which have demonstrated their preparedness to withhold valued recognition as a sanction against racialism.

It is not surprising that similar processes should be observed in sport and politics, and indeed in religion, since they are all related within the structure of South African society, and influenced by the systematic and overriding emphasis on racial separation. And for the same reason, it is not surprising that sport, religion, and politics in South Africa should all be matters of international concern.

In sport, and in religion within the English-speaking churches, the ethic now encourages deracialization. This process is particularly favored in sport by the role of the international tribunals. In religion, the discrimination is mainly within the Protestant churches, and World Councils of Churches can hardly be so effective in sanctioning the behavior of Protestants who relate themselves directly to the divine. The international religious organizations can only withhold their approval: they control no values comparable to the control of international competitions. And in any event they would be more inclined to pray for a change of heart in their White brethren than to exert pressure. If a South African church becomes disturbed by resolutions of a World Council of Churches, it can resign, as did two sections of the Dutch Reformed Churches, apparently without too great sacrifice.

The role of international sanctions is obviously crucial in the case of sport, as analyzed in this chapter. The important difference between the world organizations in sport and religion is that the former can exercise effective sanctions. Clearly in political life the United Nations is also in a position to apply strong sanctions by the withholding of major values, particularly in trade. I am not suggesting that politics is to be equated with sport and religion. Many Whites would be more ready to make concessions in sport and religion: they would feel that games and spiritual concerns have minor relevance compared with the realities of power, property, and prestige, or as they would phrase it, the realities of survival. But I am suggesting that the same processes operate. And I would regard it as certain that, as in sport, the withholding of highly prized values by the United Nations would stimulate processes of compromise and adjustment in the direction of racial cooperation, and thus counter the present trends toward racialism and civil war.

CHAPTER 23

Political Choice—Racialism or Nonracialism, Violence or Nonviolence

IN THEORY, the political choices of African leaders are almost unlimited. The older leaders have experienced many political systems, not only intellectually and in the abstract but quite concretely and in the routine of living. Inevitably, they have an expert knowledge of types of domination, whether linked with the concept of trusteeship and ultimate emancipation, or with Afrikaner nationalism and the policy of tribal self-development, or "Balkanization," as they sometimes describe it. They have seen at work a Western type of democracy, based on elections and parliamentary representation for a small sector of the population: and indeed, they have participated in this system in a limited and a nondemocractic way. At the same time, their own lives are subjected to totalitarian control, under a highly organized exclusive nationalist movement. Many have views as to the effects of liberal policies on African progress: and they could hardly fail to be aware of the policies and techniques of the Communist Party, and of the workings of capitalist society.

At the level of techniques of political action, there is the same diversity. A wide range of violent and nonviolent means has been used in the struggle between the races. In his comments on the Sabotage Bill and the greater responsibility of Whites for all the evil that was being done, Chief Luthuli expressed this diversity of political action as follows:—

> This does not mean that the Non-White peoples must now hope for their salvation through the ballot box. Theirs is the role of continuing the struggle which began with our forefathers. They must draw inspiration from the great battles and the sacrifices of Tshaka and Moshesh, of Gandhi and Hintsa. They must also draw inspiration from our more recent martyrs who fell at Sharpeville and Langa, at Pondoland and Cato Manor, at Zeerust and Sekhukhuneland.

They must draw inspiration from the hundreds who rot in exile in the far corners of our beloved country and those who languish in prison because of their love for freedom. They must draw inspiration from their many gallant leaders who have been gagged and restricted because of their role in the struggle for freedom for all in South Africa.

In the dark and difficult days that lie ahead of us, we must not only draw inspiration from our martyrs for freedom—past and present—we must also re-dedicate ourselves for the bitter fight ahead. We cannot and must not allow fascism to take root in our beloved country. We must not allow the despotism and degradation that befell the peoples of Nazi Germany, Fascist Spain, and Portugal [*New Age,* June 21, 1962].

In recent years, African leaders have experimented with many non-violent techniques, ranging from such forms of submission as deputations, petitions, and humble prayers to militant action by way of boycotts, strikes, demonstrations, civil disobedience, and days of mourning and of dedication to the heroes and martyrs of the liberation struggle. Interwoven with these campaigns was the spontaneous violence of intermittent mass movements. And today, the group known as Umkonto we Sizwe (Spear of the Nation) is specifically organized for sabotage and has launched its first ventures into scientific violence.

Quite apart from the diverse forms of direct political action in which Africans have taken part, their varied experiences of life might be expected to shape very different political perspectives. Different occupations offer different rewards and frustrations. Sects and separatist churches and mission churches have their distinctive social contexts and world views. The segregated universities provide a narrower basis for social and intellectual perspectives than the racially open universities. Age profoundly affects the quality of life experience. Some of the younger men have virtually spent their lives under apartheid. As they came to intellectual awareness they found themselves in a world governed by the domination of the racial concept, and regulated by force and violence. In interviews and discussions with these younger men, it sometimes seemed that only a narrow segment of life was represented, one hedged in by the racial group, turned inward and devoid of satisfying contacts with the outside world. Their experience, in contrast to that of many older men, is of a society systematically organized by the principle of racial cleavage.

Now this diversity of experience and knowledge of political forms and techniques, and of social milieus, is not expressed in the range of choices offered Africans by their political organizations. The situation is so raw and compelling, and so governed by racial ideology and domination, that it is the perception of race relations which becomes the overriding factor and shapes the political ideologies, both of the parliamentary parties and of the non-White extraparliamentary movements. For many Africans, the varied possibilities of political and economic organization—Western democracy, totalitarianism, capitalism, communal ownership of the means of production—seem of minor or less immediate significance. The theoretically wide range of political choice was in practice limited by the main African political organizations first to liberation from White domination and then to the choice between violence and nonviolence, and between an exclusive African nationalism and an inclusive South African nationalism—alternatives which I equate, in the context of a multiracial society, with racialism or nonracialism. In 1960, the alternatives of racially exclusive or inclusive nationalism and of violence or nonviolence were represented by the African National Congress pledged to racial cooperation and nonviolence, and the Pan-Africanist Congress, racially exclusive and without commitment to nonviolence. Yet this distinction is only accurate at the level of the proclaimed ideology. There were currents of racialism in the African National Congress and of nonracialism in the Pan-Africanist Congress.

The ambivalence within the African National Congress has deep historical roots. The dominant trend of nonracialism rested on the needs of the African people as perceived by their leaders, the role of intellectuals in the movement, and their commitment to ideals of human equality and of the human personality. The appeal of racialism derived from the situation of conquest and domination by a foreign power, the suffering and humiliation of racial discrimination, and their heightening under apartheid.

Founded in 1912, the African National Congress was a reaction against the exclusion of Africans from democratic participation in the newly constituted Union of South Africa. In conception, it was a "Union of Black South Africa." Organization and procedures were modeled on the parliament for Whites. The Chairman of the Select Committee which framed the original constitution acknowledged his debt of gratitude for the loan of Palgrave's Book on Parliamentary Practice, this having provided the basis of the Standing Orders in the constitution. Officers at national conventions included a Speaker, Clerk of the Convention, Senior and Junior Chaplains, and Sergeants at Arms, and there was also an Upper House or House of Chiefs, analogous perhaps to a House of Lords, with positions held for life. The constitution however declared the Congress to be "without legislative pretensions." Elements of the parliamentary play persisted throughout the years, even though the role of Congress was extraparliamentary—

indeed perhaps precisely because it was denied effective parliamentary functions. The Upper House of Chiefs no longer exists, and there is now a basic conflict of interests between tribal chiefs and national political leaders.

Lionel Forman[1] comments that Congress could not have come into being at that time without the support of the chiefs, since tribal traditions were still strong and national and political consciousness weak. The special position accorded the chiefs in the constitution was an acknowledgment of their power: they were allowed the distinction of Honorary Vice Presidents, assigned a separate place of honour and respect at meetings, and vested with rights of veto (Clause 31). Congress was an alliance between a small professional elite and the traditional elite of tribal society. As industrialization undermined the traditional societies and created a more politically conscious urban population, and as the chiefs were transformed into minor civil servants and later into the agents of retribalization under apartheid policy, the chiefs and political leaders came increasingly to represent diametrically opposed ideologies and class interests. This cleavage is a major weakness in the African national movement. It is exploited by Government officials, and threatens African solidarity with a resurgence of tribal sentiments.

One of the major goals of the Congress was the forging of the tribes into a single political unity. The initial objectives in the constitution included the following:

> To encourage mutual understanding and to bring together into common action as one political people all tribes and clans of various tribes or races and by means of combined effort and united political organisation to defend their freedom, rights and privileges;
> To discourage and contend against racialism and tribal feuds or to secure the elimination of racialism and tribal feuds, jealousy and petty quarrels by economic combination, education, goodwill and by other means.

This still remains a primary objective. In the revised constitution dated January 1958, the first stated aim is: "To unite the African people in a powerful and effective instrument to secure their own complete liberation from all forms of discrimination and national oppression."

The rejection of racialism, as distinct from tribalism, was clear from the third aim of the revised constitution, namely to strive for the attainment of universal adult suffrage and the creation of a united democratic South Africa on the principles of the Freedom Charter. The latter document declared that South Africa belongs to all who live in it,

1. *Chapters in the History of the March to Freedom* (Cape Town, New Age Publication, 1959), pp. 19–20.

Black and White, and that only a democratic state can secure to all their birthright without distinction of color, race, sex, or belief. Congress leaders persistently attacked racialism, and the President-General, Chief Luthuli, used his prestige and power to promote racial cooperation. His presidential address to the 46th annual conference in 1958, explaining Congress policy, stressed multiracialism, and attacked the racialist sentiments crystallizing in the Africanist movement. He declared that Congress had no desire to dominate over other racial groups by virtue of the superior numbers of Africans, and that it stood for Free Democracy.

> It is as opposed to a racial majority masquerading as a democratic majority, as it is opposed to a minority of any kind, racial or otherwise, dominating over others because, for some reason, it seized the full control of the State. We say that in a truly multi-racial country democracy should, by the nature of things, be colour-blind. . . . [Even with African potential] to go it alone in the struggle for freedom, respect for other freedom lovers in other racial groups in our country would demand that we invite them to be our comrades-in-arms in the fight for freedom, if we are to cooperate with them as equals and with a deeper appreciation and trust of one another in the truly free democratic South Africa we are working for. Such a cooperation, born of comradeship in the struggle would be the surest guarantee against the arrogance, now and after victory, of would-be political exclusivists-dictators.

Yet African unity on the one hand, and a nonracial democracy on the other, do not lie easily together. It is sometimes argued that the sentiments supporting tribalism are of the same nature as the sentiments which support racialism, and that an African unity based on racial antagonism to other groups will be unstable, and fragment again into tribalism when liberation is achieved. This may be true. But the initial task of forging the tribes into an African unit, without the focus of a hated alien group, is most difficult, since the principle of unification is an abstract ideal, not a human passion.

The adherence to democratic principles may indeed have retarded the growth of the African National Congress. The movement was essentially nonrevolutionary. Its policy was to extend the area of freedom, to gain more rights for Africans within the existing system, and the strategy was constitutional, such as would be acceptable to leaders recruited from the professions and having some stake in the society. Probably Congress could follow no other course, given the tribally fragmented condition of African society, and the small numbers of educated men and of the urban proletariat. The more militant campaigns for full equality had to wait upon industrialization, the extension of education, the hopes raised by the Second World War, and their frustration under the regime of apartheid. But in the 1950s, the goal was still the sharing of power, not its transfer, and democratic ideals were widely proclaimed in Congress circles. This adherence to democratic values no doubt derived in part from the social situation of Africans: it certainly accorded with the class interests of the educated leaders. Salvation lay in the extension of the democratic principles which the White rulers professed, and used to regulate their own participation in government. But there would also have been an exposure in the mission schools to democratic ideals; and the conversion to Christianity, the movement from tribal village into mission station, and the entry into a community of believers, meant the renunciation of the ties of blood in favor of new and more universal principles of association. (See Jordan Ngubane's[2] reference to this point).

Nevertheless, there is also a long tradition of exclusive nationalism in the Congress movement. Ngubane discusses, in Part II of his book, the two moods of African nationalism. The Rev. John L. Dube, the first President of the African National Congress, thought explicitly in terms of restoring to the African what was his. He declared his policy in the phrase: *"lapho ake ema khona amanzi ayophinde eme futhi"*—"where there was once a pool, water will collect again." Power will return to Africans. From this point of view, what appear to be the negative methods of the early Congress leaders, based on the mistaken assumption that constitutional political action could be effective in a situation where the African lacked political power, might be interpreted as a policy of biding time in order to build up reserves of power.

From its inception, Congress included representatives of exclusive nationalism, that is to say Africanists, with two consequences in later years—the eruption from time to time of Africanist sentiments and movements; and the inhibition of Congress, and restraint upon it, for fear of antagonizing these Africanists.

In 1952, there was a secession in the form of the African National Congress (National-minded bloc), as a reaction inter alia against co-operation between the African and Indian Congresses in the planning of the Campaign for the Defiance of Unjust Laws. This by no means drew off the Africanists in the Congress ranks. They came increasingly into the open, protesting against the Freedom Charter and political alliance with other racial groups. And even with the final secession of Africanists in 1958 and the establishment of the Pan-Africanist Congress in 1959, there were still Africanists within the African National Congress. They criticized the secession, not on principle, but on grounds of expediency, claiming either that the Africanists should have worked for their point of view within Congress, or that the assistance of other races was still necessary in the struggle against apartheid. Indeed the matter was more complicated: Africanism had an emotional appeal for

2. *An African Explains Apartheid,* p. 92.

Africans, even where the intellectual commitment was to a nonracial democracy.

In consequence, the African National Congress showed an ambivalence, particularly marked at the level of organization. Technically, Congress was open to all persons over the age of eighteen who accepted its principles, policy, and program and agreed to abide by its constitution and rules: and apparently a few non-Africans were admitted as members of Congress. In practice, however, Congress remained a racially exclusive organization which stood for nonracial democracy and proclaimed racial cooperation, but denied these principles within its own organization. The arguments advanced by the Executive in its report to the 1959 conference, justifying racial exclusiveness, have a decidedly Africanist ring.

Congress was founded, so the argument runs, to unite and voice the views of Africans, and not for the primary purpose of building a "multiracial" or "non-racial" society.

> Let those who will, call this racialism. But most people who look at our achievements honestly and without malice will realise that the building of an all-Union organisation of Africans, built in the teeth of every obstacle that governments could muster against it, and the leading of that organisation to become a mighty power in the land is an achievement from which not only Africans but all democratic South Africans can draw pride and satisfaction.

This is a complex proposition. Probably within South Africa only the unity of Africans can provide the volume of power needed to displace Afrikaner domination. But there is no reason to believe that African unity as such would furnish a more effective guarantee for democratic rights than Afrikaner unity.

The argument continues that Congress has been far-sighted enough to join hands with other groups representing other oppressed peoples, but that this does not mean that Congress intends to abandon its functions as a national organization of Africans. Then follows a typically Africanist twist to Marxist theory. The thesis is that however other groups are oppressed,

> Africans are oppressed in a special way, by special laws which affect them in special ways. As a result the immediate grievances, aims, and outlook of Africans, their daily needs and aspirations are not identical with those of other racial groups in South Africa, however identical their long-term aim of liberation might be.

Hence, the conclusion is drawn that the special interests of Africans demand a purely African organization. The anomalous position arises that a nonracial democracy is to be established by an alliance of racially exclusive political movements, and that Congress is more radical in its demands than either the Liberal Party or the Progressive Party, but more conservative in its organization.

Added to this is a characteristic Africanist threat to the White group. The long-term interests of Whites working in the Congress movement and organized separately as the Congress of Democrats are described as identical with those of Africans, but not their immediate interests. They are "not an organisation of an oppressed community, but rather an organisation of non-conformists from the ranks of the oppressor caste." Their immediate interests are said to be, first, that of breaking through the iron-hard core of European color prejudice and racialism, and second, that of establishing "by their deeds the right and justification for White South Africans to become part of the native people of a free South Africa, and not like the British in India or the Dutch in Indonesia— an alien community for whom there is no place in the years after liberation."

The purpose of this discussion is to establish that there were strong Africanist sentiments within Congress, and a potential for racialism, and that these sentiments explain the continued racial exclusiveness of Congress in the last decade. No doubt, there were also other reasons for racial exclusiveness, such as fear that a more sophisticated leadership from non-African groups might dominate African political development and deflect it toward goals not in accord with African aspirations. But the effect, in any event, was to impose communalism on the extra-parliamentary political movements, since the refusal of the major organization to deracialize deprived the other organizations of valid reasons for interracial merger. There was thus a sharp contrast between the situation in the political field and the sporting world, where there is de-racialization and where the mark of a patriot and a democrat is the rejection of racialism in sport: and presumably one reason for this difference is that the international tribunals reward nonracialism and punish racialism in sport, but not in politics.

Congress handled the threat of racialism by its participation in the Congress Alliance. The members of the alliance were the South African Indian Congress, the small South African Coloured Peoples Organisation, the Congress of Democrats (communal organizations of Indians, Coloreds, and Whites), and the South African Congress of Trade Unions. All these subscribed to the Freedom Charter, which was the Magna Carta of the alliance. A Consultative Committee, based on equal representation and unanimity of decision, coordinated the activities of the organizations, thus providing a basis for racial cooperation. Sentiments supporting racial cooperation were heightened by interracial mass meetings and campaigns. In these activities, Congress leaders proclaimed their faith in interracial cooperation and promoted the ideals of nonracialism. The claim of Congress in 1959 that "the high-water mark of racial fraternity and cooperation in South Africa today is the Congress Alliance" was not extravagant. Yet the balance between racialism and nonracialism was an uneasy one. Joe Matthews, one of the Congress leaders now in exile, described the situation in an interview as follows:—

> The African National Congress will always have a potentially powerful nationalist feeling and Congress could switch at any time. It is an illusion to think that with the Africanists out, the bad nationalist sentiment is out. Many African nationalists would regard the Africanists as blunderers who have let the cat out of the bag too early whereas at this stage they would say we should work with other groups. The Africanists have not succeeded because there is nobody in the Africanist group of sufficient prestige to put it across. The extent of the nationalism can be seen from the fact that you cannot get support for the idea of one Congress, the leadership dare not do it. The forces at work in the society as a whole are constantly poisoning the atmosphere and creating nationalism. The only way you can keep it down is by having the people so busy fighting the [Afrikaner] nationalists. The group of antiracialists is very small and they are only followed because they have rendered services in the community. The people don't follow them because they believe in nonracialism themselves. When you put the case for nonracialism, you have to give them reasons, as for example that the outside world would not approve [of racialism]. It is difficult to put it on the basis that it is intrinsically the correct, the moral outlook.

The Pan-Africanist Congress, in contrast to the African National Congress, makes a virtue of racial exclusiveness both in organization and mode of struggle. It is difficult to describe precisely the Africanist ideology, since there was little time for crystallization in the period between secession in November 1958 and submergence underground as a result of proscription in April 1960. The emphasis is on racial struggle. In an article in the *Golden City Post*, December 7, 1958, Leballo and Ngendane, at that time Chairman and Secretary of the Africanist Movement (Transvaal), contend as Africanists, that:

> the wars our forefathers fought during the 18th and 19th centuries against the foreign invader, never came to an end. What happened was that new methods of struggle were involved. Thus the close of the 19th century saw, generally, an end to military struggle between Black and White in this country and the beginning of a new phase—the political.

This is a valid historical perspective, and one prominent in Afrikaner nationalist thought. Its effect, however, is to set aside as irrelevant the period of contact, and the many relationships and cross-cutting loyalties between persons of different races, and to emphasize the racial struggle.

The same writers reject class distinctions among Africans as non-existent, since "they are all non-citizens because they do not have the franchise." Similarly White persons, rich and poor, educated and illiterate, urban and rural, are not differentiated—they are all masters in South Africa. "On the material level, therefore, there is no basis for co-operation between Black and White." The structure of South African society is thus reduced to White masters and Black servants. There are in consequence no class divisions within African society which might impede unity and no class bases for cooperation across racial lines. This Leballo makes explicit when he writes that "we believe the African people are oppressed as a nation, not as a class, and must therefore struggle as a nation to overthrow white domination" (*Contact*, November 1, 1958, p. 10). So too, the President of the Pan-Africanist Congress, in an article outlining policy and goals "authoritatively and un-ambiguously" declares that "the Africans are the only people who, because of their material position, can be interested in the complete overhaul of the present structure of society." He writes that White persons cannot completely identify with that cause, because they benefit materially from the present situation; and they stultify and retard the movement of Africans, because they are consciously or unconsciously protecting their sectional interests (*Contact*, May 30, 1959, p. 9).

The functions of this ideology are to heighten the racial aspects of the conflict and to detach Africans from other racial groups in the political struggle. The basic assumptions as to the influence of material factors on political consciousness are essentially Marxist. But the conclusions are non-Marxist, that the conflict is a racial conflict, not a class conflict; and the Pan-Africanist Congress is anti-Communist. It would seem that the identification of class and race, or the submergence of class distinctions in racial distinctions is readily made in situations where, as Rupert Emerson[3] phrases it: "The relation of the non-White worker to the alien white boss parallels the relation of the non-white subject to the alien white ruler." In South Africa, the elimination of class distinctions on the ground that they are subsumed in the racial divisions, or the identification of class with race, is complicated for the Africanists by the presence of other non-White groups also subject to political and economic discrimination. Since Africans are not the only oppressed people in South Africa, it becomes difficult to rationalize African political exclusiveness on other than racial grounds.

The President of the Pan-Africanist Congress sought a solution for

3. *From Empire to Nation* (Cambridge, Harvard University Press, 1960), p. 183.

this problem in relation to Indians by distinguishing classes within the Indian minority, a merchant class tainted "with the virus of national arrogance and cultural supremacy," and the poor Indians of the sugar plantations, who, because of their material position, would be interested in the establishment of a "genuine Africanist democracy." But the poor Indians must first reject the opportunist leadership of the merchant class, produce their own leadership (*Contact*, May 30, 1959, p. 9), and in fact accept African leadership (*The Leader*, June 26, 1959). At a meeting of the Pan-Africanist Congress in Durban in June 1959, the President repeated the argument in relation to the class structure of Indians, and said that the poor Indians might remain because they did not have money to go anywhere; and as for the Coloreds, he accepted them as part of the indigenous people of Africa, with no other home. The important thing was origin: Europeans had a home of their origin just as the Indians had theirs. Here the extreme severity of racial exclusiveness is mitigated by the application of class distinctions to the Indian people, in such a way as to exempt the impoverished Indian from repatriation.

A more radical basis for excluding other non-Whites and for identifying Africans with the proletariat and non-Africans with the bourgeoisie, was provided by an African doctor in an interview. He explained that the concept of land rights as the basis for class stratification was important in his Marxist thinking.

> The difficulty is that the proletariat is composed of Black people and the bourgeoisie of Whites. One could not help being racialistic. There is a proletariat on the one hand and the bourgeoisie on the other, and dividing these is the color line and racial barrier. The Land Act of 1913 meant that no Native could own land, whereas Indians, Coloreds, and Europeans owned land and therefore fall out of the proletariat. So that whatever racialism I have now stems from my identification with Africans.

This is an ingenious argument, substituting the right to own the means of production as a criterion of class in place of the actual ownership of the means of production. In consequence such poor Indian laborers as street cleaners become members of the bourgeoisie.

Thus the rationalization of racial exclusiveness is based in the first place on arguments as to the unique situation, material and political, of Africans in South African society. A second basis is to be found in a cluster of factors somewhat connected with the concept of the "African Personality." The approach is that there can be no general cooperation with other racial groups until Africans have liberated themselves by their own efforts: nor can there be any firm commitment to ideologies, espoused by other groups, prior to emancipation. This rests again partly on Marxist premises, that the class interests of other racial groups con-

flict with those of Africans, and are likely to prevail in interracial cooperation because of the subordinate position of Africans. But there
seems also to be some idea of rebirth, of purification from the humiliations of domination. Africans are oppressed: first they must break their
chains and then they can decide on the future of the country or
negotiate with the White man. And they must do so by their own un-
aided efforts. Only in this way can they express the dignity of the
African Personality, and only when they have thus liberated themselves
can they cooperate with other groups. Against this background, it is
significant that the Africanists initially planned, as a first campaign, a
status boycott, designed to secure courteous treatment. As the President
explained:

> We are reminding our people that acceptance of any indignity, any
> insult, any humiliation, is acceptance of inferiority. They must first
> think of themselves as men and women before they can demand to
> be treated as such. The campaign will free the mind of the African
> —and once the mind is free, the body will soon be free [*Contact*,
> August 8, 1959, p. 2].

An advance commitment to foreign ideologies would detract from the
full expression of the free person. The Africanists, it is true, freely borrowed their concept of the African Personality and their policy of
positive neutrality from the North. They chose from current political
philosophies a planned economy, within the framework of political
democracy, and with the most equitable distribution of wealth. But in
thus selecting the best from East and West, "we nonetheless retain and
maintain our distinctive personality and refuse to be the satraps or
stooges of any other power" (from an address at the inaugural conference by R. M. Sobukwe, who was elected President—*Contact*, April 18,
1959, p. 8).

Leaving aside any rationalization of racial exclusiveness, the racial
hatreds and oppressions in the society are such as to make an Africanist
movement inevitable. And there are strong political pressures in the
same direction, since the emotional appeal of nationalism is likely to be
the most effective rallying point for a militant African unity. The
Africanists are explicit on this point.

> It is our contention that the vast illiterate, and semi-literate masses
> of the Africans are the corner stone: the key and very life of the
> struggle for democracy. From this we draw the logical conclusion
> that the rousing and consolidation of these masses is the primary
> task of liberation. This leads to the conclusion that African nation-
> alism is the liberatory outlook to achieve this gigantic and historic
> task, and that the philosophy of Africanism holds out the hope of

a genuine democracy beyond the stormy sea of struggle. [Authoritative statement by the President, *Contact*, May 30, 1959, p. 9.]

In his inaugural address, the President declared that the African people could be organized only under the banner of African Nationalism in an all-African organization where they would by themselves formulate policies and decide on methods of struggle without interference from either of the so-called left-wing or right-wing groups of the minorities which arrogantly appropriate to themselves the right to plan and to think for the Africans.

But in a multiracial society, an exclusive national movement based on racial membership must be racialist, whether the movement is one of Afrikaner nationalism or of African nationalism. And it is not difficult to demonstrate racial antagonism within the Africanist movement. Thus the President of the Pan-Africanist Congress appears to have assumed that the African masses would be motivated by hatred for Whites. According to a report in the *Golden City Post* (March 29, 1959), he had written, prior to the inaugural conference of the Pan-Africanist Congress, in a journal circulating among its members, that in every struggle, national or class, the masses do not hate an abstraction. They do not hate oppression or capitalism. They make these things concrete and hate the oppressor—in South Africa, the White man. But they hate these groups because they associate them with oppression. Remove the association and you remove the hatred. Once White domination has been overthrown, there will be no reason to hate the White man and he will not be hated even by the masses. This is a very different principle from that of Mahatma Gandhi—hate the sin, but not the sinner—and it seems to be based on the conception that racial hatred can be neatly controlled, once it has served its political purpose. Or by way of further example, at a public meeting in Durban on January 31, 1959, an Africanist leader of extreme views, who later withdrew his oath of allegiance to the President, expounded the doctrine of God's apartheid—the Father God had given us houses, given us the continents: Europe to the Europeans, Asia to the Browns, Africa to the Africans. And he explained that civilization started in Africa and then went on to the Whites. "The civilization of the West means greed, killing. You can go into any kraal and they will not call the police—they will give you what you want free —that's what *we* mean by civilization." At a later meeting in Durban in May 1959, one of the speakers described the human race as being divided into the Caucasoids, Mongoloids, and Negroids. "Africa belongs to the Negroids. They are the people who are me and you . . . the soul and flesh of the Negroids has been annihilated by the Mongoloids and Caucasoids. . . ." (*The Leader*, May 29, 1959). There are references in speeches to Indians and Whites as foreign minority groups. And a special antagonism is expressed toward Indians, the obvious immediate scape-goat for racialism.

Moreover, the democracy offered by the Africanists is conceived in racial terms. It carries the principle of universal adult suffrage to the conclusion of rule by the African majority. Politically Africanists stand "for government of the Africans, for the Africans, by the Africans." This is the principle Chief Luthuli described as "a racial majority masquerading as a democratic majority." Members of other racial groups are not excluded from the Africanist democracy. Everyone who owes his only loyalty to Africa, and accepts the democratic rule of an African majority, will be regarded as an African (according to the President's authoritative statement, *Contact,* May 30, 1959). The obligation of the non-African is to accept the primacy of African interests and to identify with Africans, to become in emotion and perception an African. This is a different concept of Africanization. It is not the change in the incumbency of civil service and other positions from European to African, as in the independent states of Africa. It is the psychological transformation of the non-African, the *evolué* policy of the French in reverse. Much as the passport to French citizenship was not the quality of the African but of the French culture within him, so too the passport to Africanist citizenship is not the personal quality of the non-African, but the generalized African within him. The Africanists will accept themselves.

The combination of nationalism and racialism is familiar to South Africans; they have spent much of their lives under it. The celebration of National Heroes' Day, the going down the corridor of time and renewing acquaintances with the heroes of Africa's past, the appeal to the spirits of Hintsa, Tshaka, Khama, Msilikazi, Sekhukhuni, and Moshoeshoe, possible experiments with traditional costume offer the occasion for building up the dignity of African history and personality. Paradoxically, the Government uses somewhat similar techniques to retribalize Africans. The emotional appeal of nationalism is a more effective technique for unification than the abstract principles of the African National Congress, and the infusion of racialism provides a hated out-group as a focus for crystallization of national sentiment. And yet there is strong ambivalence within the Pan-Africanist Congress.

Most political organizations use formulas indicative of high moral purpose: the appeal is rarely in terms only of naked self-interest. The exclusive nationalism of Afrikaners is linked with the idealization of the ethnic group and with the promise of self-development and, indeed, independence. A purely racialist ideology would no doubt seem repugnant to many Afrikaner leaders. The Africanists are less exclusive in some ways than the Afrikaner nationalists, since they declare that in the future democratic society they will be ready to accept the non-African who identifies with them. But racial distinctions are also crucial for the Africanists. At the same time, they feel ambivalent about racialism. Many of the leaders are intellectually uncomfortable with racialism, they have suffered all their lives under it, and they cannot idolize racial identity. The ambivalence is not to be resolved by so simple a formula as an ultimate willingness to accept identifying non-Africans as Africans. Hence the leaders are driven to seek more inclusive formulas, or to represent themselves and their movement as motivated by more universal moral principles.

It is against this background that the ideological conflict between the Africanists and the Congress leaders must be interpreted. In their debates, the Africanist leaders sought to project themselves as standing for true nonracial democracy in contrast to the undemocratic multiracialism of Congress. Their argument comprised the following ideas. There is only one race, the human race. The word race, as applied to man, has no plural form. To view South Africa as a multiracial society is to acknowledge the existence of races, and hence to be guilty of racialism. Even to admit the existence of other races is a sign of racialism. For the true democrat, that is to say the Africanist, racial differences do not exist. The African National Congress stands for multiracialism and is a member of a multiracial alliance. Multiracialism involves the perpetuation of racial differences, the protection of the rights of racial minorities. It is racialism multiplied. There will be no need for the safeguarding of minority rights under the democratic rule of the African majority, because Africanists think in terms of individuals, not of groups. And in phrases reminiscent of the Marxist concept of the prophetic role of the proletariat, whose emancipation would be the emancipation of mankind, the Africanist President declared in his inaugural address that the freedom of the African means the freedom of all in "South Africa, the European included, because only the African can guarantee the establishment of a genuine democracy, in which all men will be citizens of a common state and will live and be governed as individuals and not as distinctive sectional groups."

For the supporters of the African National Congress, the distinction between nonracialism and multiracialism was simply semantic hair splitting, and they accused the Africanists of racialism disguised as nonracialism. Each side charged the other with racialism, and proclaimed itself dedicated to the ideal of a society in which race would be irrelevant. There was thus an apparent convergence of viewpoints between these sharply opposed antagonists. The fact of the matter is that the two groups shade off into each other. They are driven by similar aspirations and they have a similar background of experience.

In the past, the political aspirations of educated Africans were directed toward the extension of democratic rights and the sharing of power, and the educated still emphasize universal criteria of evaluation, the acceptance of the individual on his merits, regardless of race. This political conditioning was common to many Africanist and Congress leaders: the equality of persons was idiomatic in political discourse. African domination by virtue of numbers, the democratic rule of the African majority, the transfer of power rather than the sharing of power, only became a realistic goal with the emergence of independent African states, and the extensive participation of Africans in the urban and industrial society of South Africa. The Africanists, apparently recruiting a younger leadership, responded more immediately to this goal. But Congress leaders are also absorbed in the struggle for the conquest of power. The leaders and members of both the African National Congress and the Pan-Africanist Congress have been exposed to the same discrimination and humiliation. They recognize that they have been indoctrinated with inferiority or that in other ways their people have accepted inferiority. The assertion of their dignity, the reinterpretation of South African history, the idealization of the African heroes they had been taught to reject, have an emotional appeal regardless of the parties to which they belong. They are emancipating themselves from reliance on the White man. This is expressed in extreme form in the Pan-Africanist Congress with what appears to be a compensatory racial pride, but there is also present in the African National Congress a distrust of White initiative, and, indeed, of initiative from other racial groups, and increasing racial self-assertion. Again, the two organizations have much in common.

Economic policy is not a matter of immediate contention between African politicians, and is not central to the political divisions among Africans. The Pan-Africanist Congress is anti-Communist, whereas Communists held many key positions in the Congress Alliance, and some of the younger Congress intellectuals have been recruited to Communism. The trade union branch of the alliance, the South African Congress of Trade Unions, is affiliated to the Communist-dominated World Federation of Trade Unions, and was a founding member of the All Africa Trade Union Federation, launched in Ghana; while the Africanists have their own trade union organization, the Federation of Free African Trade Unions of South Africa, affiliated to the International Confederation of Free Trade Unions.

All the circumstances would seem to favor the development of Communism—a country in rapid process of industrialization, large numbers of peasants seeking absorption in the industrial system, low and discriminatory wages, poverty and oppression, and theoreticians to crystallize Communist interpretations and solutions. Yet Communism appears to have made only a small impact on Congress members and on Africans generally. The differences between the two organizations on this issue may not be so fundamental. The Freedom Charter, adopted by the African National Congress and its allies, speaks of the national wealth of the country being restored to the people, the mineral wealth transferred to the ownership of the people as a whole, and the land redivided among those who work it. The President of the African National Congress declared himself personally in favor of a democratic social welfare state, and the President of the Pan-Africanist Congress avowed his preference for socialism and Western democracy. Both organizations have in common the sentiment that the wealth and land of South Africa have been unjustly appropriated by Whites; a redistribution of national resources must inevitably form part of the programs of African political parties in South Africa.

The leaders of the two organizations share the rejection of the Bantustan policies, the Balkanization or fragmentation of Africans. Similarly they experience the excitement of moving outward toward the world in contrast to the Whites, contracting into their laager. Developments in Africa heighten African feelings of deprivation within South Africa, and African hopes and aspirations for the future. It is the conflict between the present reality of discrimination and a future of national independence and international recognition which gives the struggle a great sense of urgency for both Africanists and Congress. The boast of a leading member of the African National Congress that "nowadays when Black Africa sneezes the whole world seems to be catching a cold" has its counterpart in the more sober statement of the President of the Congress: "Whether anyone likes it or not, the voice of Africa, claiming a place of honour for her children will be heard with growing insistency and force in the coming days" (presidential address, 1958), and of the Africanist President: "Afrikaner Nationalists need only look at their own history to know what force they are dealing with. But in this case it is not only a small, sub-continental force but a continental force. . . . And we Africans are not demanding it [self-determination] regionally but continentally" (*Sunday Times*, April 12, 1959). The major difference is that the Africanist world is primarily that of Africa, while the Congress world is more international. Both organizations are deeply identified with Africa and African liberation.

How then is the secession of the Africanists to be explained, since the two organizations have so much in common? Is it a struggle for leadership, as Congress claimed, a group of ambitious unrecognized men separating in umbrage? Many of the Africanist leaders are young untried men, in contrast to the seasoned leaders of the Congress. There are marked oligarchical tendencies in Congress: the role of leader in Congress is highly personalized, and Chief Luthuli has the status among his followers of a national hero, a paramount chief, a political martyr. Sometimes, at conferences in Natal, as I observed his followers bringing in

Chief Luthuli in a procession of song and rhythmic movement, I was reminded of the prophet and his disciples.

Certainly, the Africanist leaders were reacting against Congress leadership. They specifically chose, as their major campaign, the defiance of the pass laws, thus repeating the Congress defiance campaign of 1952. And they emphasized that in contrast to the Congress leaders, they would be the first to court imprisonment, as indeed they were. The result was that the main Africanist leaders were removed from active participation, and the general situation deteriorated, with the proclamation of a state of emergency. Precedents of violence and suspension of legal process tend rapidly to become routine in South Africa. The Africanist campaign thus duplicated the defiance campaign with somewhat similar results. Only the preoccupation with the leaders of the Congress could have so clouded the perception of the Africanists.

The issues, however, go much deeper. The Africanists reflect a new mood of nationalism, more aggressive, more exclusive, more racially antagonistic. They are the product of a deteriorating situation, of a different life experience from the older leaders. The repressions and humiliations and discriminations have nurtured a heightened awareness of race, a deeper resentment, and a more profound disillusionment. It is these sentiments which the Africanists direct toward racial hostility and revolutionary change. And the main difference between the ideologies of the two organizations, prior to their proscription, lay in the Africanists' refusal to be committed to nonviolence and their rejection of racial cooperation as a principle of struggle.

Today I would think that the differences between the followers of the Pan-Africanist Congress and those of the African National Congress have narrowed, and that the political choice for both groups has moved toward violence and racial exclusiveness. I can, however, only speculate on the position. The Congresses work underground and their members are subjected to the most intense repression. It becomes difficult to chart their activities beneath the floods of emotionally laden propaganda, or to disentangle directed political action from the undisciplined and haphazard activities of random gangs. The following comments are purely tentative.

Violence seems to propagate itself. I am not referring only to the violence of the State provoking counterviolence among its opponents. Violence may become so well established in a society that casual groups are encouraged to band together as saboteurs or terrorists by a process of private election, in much the same way that small sects proliferate under the influence of a separatist church movement. The readiness to commit violence becomes an accepted social mode of relationship. Privately incorporated groups arise outside of the political organizations, pursuing purely private nonpolitical ends, or harassing the enemy by arbitrary and unrelated acts of violence. The political organizations may seek to yoke these groups into political harness or they may themselves promote sabotage and terrorism: or some of their members may found groups for the practice of violence and then confront the organization with the problem of acknowledging paternity. The society begins to erupt with private and public vendettas, and with selective and haphazard violence.

This is the contemporary situation in South Africa. Violence is of course increasingly manifest in the State, under a masquerade of uniforms and legal process. It has also been manifest for many years in the urban locations and cities. And it has now become manifest in sporadic acts of murder and arson as an extraparliamentary opposition to the Government and its policies.

At the political level, violence is encouraged, among those who propose its use, by belief in its inevitability and its legitimacy. Colin Legum in his article "The Roots of Violence" (*The Observer*, May 5, 1963) comments on the fatalistic acceptance of the inevitability of violence on all sides in South Africa. He writes that Government spokesmen lead opinion in preparing the public for what lies ahead, and that violence has also become the language of the Africans—from Congress leaders to women domestic workers. Presumably belief in the inevitability of violence encourages the resort to violence.

The legitimacy of violence would hardly be an issue for the Government. Its political goals are blessed by its churches; and its holy mission, conceived as the preservation of a Christian and civilized way of life against the forces of barbarism and Communism, would clearly sanctify carnage. As for the African political organizations, I think I am right in saying that the legitimacy of violence was also never an issue for the Pan-Africanist Congress, and that the major change has been in some circles which followed the African National Congress and now increasingly legitimate violence on the grounds of intolerable oppression and the proven inefficacy of nonviolence.

The turning point appears to have been the demonstration in May 1961 against the establishment of the Republic. When the Government repressed this demonstration with massive force, the Congress leader and organizer of the protest, Nelson Mandela, declared that "the events of today close a chapter as far as our methods of political action are concerned" (*The World*, June 3, 1961). The "new methods" which were announced, however, basically noncooperation in the instruments of oppression, were the methods advocated by the Unity Movement consistently over a generation, although industrial action was also contemplated. These methods could hardly be satisfying to militant young men, spurred on by the humiliation of apartheid and by the increasingly realistic expectation of independence. Moreover the Government was continuing to mobilize violence and repression against all possibility of nonviolent action for social change. In fact, it was at this time that the decision was taken to form an organization for sabotage, Umkonto we Sizwe (Spear of the Nation).

A leader in exile of the African National Congress, Oliver Tambo, in a paper on "Passive Resistance in South Africa" given to a conference of the American Society of African Culture in April 1963, describes the Verwoerd Government as having abandoned the political fight and taken to arms at the time of the anti-Republic demonstrations. He writes that today the oppressors are arming feverishly. He comments on a peacetime "defence" budget of over sixty-four million pounds; the boast by the Minister of Defence that 250,000 White men and women could be put into action at any time; the rapid increase in the police and regular army; the establishment of arms munition factories in South Africa; the supplies by Britain and France of a substantial range of death-dealing war weapons and military aircraft; and the "Anti-Sabotage" Act of 1962, which keeps the executioner's axe poised within easy reach of the neck of everyone who engages in anti-apartheid activities. And he concludes that this leaves "our people with no alternative but to pursue the goal of freedom and independence by way of taking 'a tooth for a tooth' and meeting violence with violence." To this he adds, "it is hardly necessary to make the point that we should rather have avoided this course."

The relationship between the Communist Party and the African National Congress has been the subject of much Government propaganda. I would think that the Communist Party's influence on the African National Congress over the last decade has been in the direction of non-racialism and nonviolence. And it would seem that in respect of nonviolence, there has been a change in policy. To be more precise, recently the South African Communist Party issued a draft program of principles in which it declared that it carries on the traditions of the former Communist Party of South Africa. The people's leaders, it explained, had followed a policy of nonviolence, with the full support and approval of the Communists, because they wished to avoid the bitterness and bloodshed of civil war. The Nationalist Government had, however, invariably replied to nonviolence with violence. The masses would still prefer to achieve their liberation by nonviolent means, but, as every avenue of peaceful change was closed by the Government, as one act of oppression and repression was piled up on another, the people would have no alternative but to meet force with force.

> However the Communist Party does not believe that there is no longer any prospect of peaceful advance to the democratic revolution in our country. It will continue to work for and make use of every possibility for traditional forms of political struggle, non-

collaboration, strikes, boycotts and demonstrations. But at the same time, it calls upon the peoples of South Africa to prepare themselves for other methods in the face of the terrorist dictatorship of the Nationalist government.

The acceptance of and commitment to violence thus grows on all sides, Government and non-Government. Terrorist and sabotage groups confront the terrorism of the State. In "The Gathering Storm" (*The Observer*, May 12, 1963), Legum classifies as terrorist the "Hill Movement" in Pondoland (referred to as "mountain committees" in Chapter 3), a second group in part of Tembuland, and Poqo in the Transkei and Western Cape. He comments that the precise relationship between Poqo and the Pan-Africanist Congress is unknown. The Government, supported by the interim findings of a commission of inquiry into disturbances at Paarl, treats Poqo (meaning "exclusive" or "only"—i.e. exclusively African) as synonymous with the Pan-Africanist Congress, and characterizes it as a movement of the same type as Mau Mau. Some observers regard Poqo as a secession from the Pan-Africanist Congress of more extreme and less sophisticated elements in the Western Cape and the Transkei. In a Fabian Society tract, *The Coming Struggle for South Africa*, Sandor[4] suggests that Poqo terrorism is a product of the Government's intensified efforts to remove Africans from the Western Cape to the Transkei, and comments that "it is probably truer to suggest that the P.A.C. is trying to establish control over Poqo than that the P.A.C. leadership inspired and controls its activities."

Under the heading of sabotage groups, Legum[5] lists the National Liberation Committee (about which he writes that "its interracial membership was originally drawn from all parties, but later became confined largely to liberals, many of them whites, who are not members of the official Liberal Party. It is now relatively inactive."): a second group started by the Pan-Africanist Congress and concentrating on the training of saboteurs: and Umkonto we Sizwe (Spear of the Nation) which "declares itself to be in support of Chief Luthuli's African National Congress [A.N.C.] and accepts its leadership. In its most recent declaration, the Spear announced a policy of 'an eye for an eye, a tooth for a tooth and a life for a life until final victory is won.' " The Government equates Umkonto with the African National Congress. In June 1964, some of the leaders of Umkonto we Sizwe, including Nelson Mandela, were found guilty of organizing and committing extensive sabotage, and sentenced to life imprisonment.

The forces impelling African organizations toward violent methods of struggle, exclusive nationalism, and an African conquest of power

4. Fabian Tract 345, June 1963, p. 26.
5. "The Gathering Storm," *The Observer*, May 12, 1963.

are likely to be reinforced by African leaders on the continent. Within the context of South African society, five million non-Africans are a strong argument for accommodation. From a continent-wide perspective, or from the perspective of almost exclusively African territories, they do not disturb the image of Africa as a specifically African continent. The full realization of African independence in the free states of Africa is frustrated while Africans suffer racial subordination in South Africa. Hence African leaders will seek to influence the African political organizations in South Africa to project a purely African image and to engage in a militant African conquest of power.

It is the consummation of violence and racialism in the National Party Government, and the near consummation of these forces among many Africans; and it is the so-called granitelike commitment of the Government to apartheid and the African commitment to emancipation, which lead observers to view the South African situation in terms of an inevitable and irreconcilable conflict of exclusive nationalisms. This is no doubt the overwhelming fact, but it represents an oversimplification in at least two main respects.

The granitelike commitment to apartheid cannot be taken for granted. The mores of a dominant group may be highly responsive to changes in the distribution of power. In the decade and a half of National Party rule, the political formula for apartheid has undergone the most remarkable transformations—from White domination and racial separation to separate and autogenous development, and now to self-control and self-government.[6] These changes are a response to internal and external pressures. Self-government for the Transkei, however misleading the term may be, and the great haste in advertising this policy overseas, are signs of changing mores under fear of sanctions. The political formula of apartheid is in a continuous state of flux.

The assumption of an inevitable violent conflict between Afrikaner and African nationalism also overlooks another aspect of the situation, namely the many forces making for an accommodation between the races. These have built up over three centuries of contact, and extend far beyond purely economic interdependence. Innumerable social relationships link people of different race. The presence of a non-African population of five million, and the complex interweaving of the races in a wide range of activities, would seem to impose the necessity for interracial accommodation. The processes of deracialization, in, for example, non-European sport or the English churches, are by no means negligible. Members of the many minority groups—Indians, Coloreds, Jews, English—may have an interest in finding nonracial solutions. And

6. The Prime Minister, in his reply to the debate on the motion of "no confidence" in 1963, argued, on the contrary, that apartheid policy had maintained a consistent course. I see no reason to amend what I have written.

the values of the outside world, expressed in the world organizations, act within South African society to reinforce nonracialism. Racial civil war may in fact devour South Africa, but I question its inevitability.

Life Chances of the Bourgeoisie

CHAPTER 24

Life Chances of the Bourgeoisie

SOUTH AFRICAN SOCIETY is now so saturated with racialism that there are few situations in which race is not relevant. Immediate perception is in terms of race, at any rate as socially defined. Where the obvious cue of physical appearance is not adequate, as, for example, to distinguish between the Afrikaans and English White "races," then indications in dress, physique, accent, or name are assessed. Individuals are located racially with great speed, and, their racial identity established, the appropriate patterns of behavior are defined. Race is not the only definition of social situations, but it is certainly a dominant definition, and so pervasive that the same strands run through the different institutions, and the same rationalizations ramify. Racial aspects of the political struggle are reproduced in sport, education, and religion, and institutional interests coincide with racial membership to effect division by race.

Racialism is expressed in institutional and social cleavages, and is heightened by them. But the cleavages are not complete, save in apartheid design and legislation, and even then with substantial reservations in the economic system, and subject to an over-all regulation. White and Black are not solidly arrayed against each other in irreconcilable conflict. Numerous structures draw together people of different race. Some of these structures are themselves a reaction against the increasing institutionalization of cleavage. Racial solidarity is fragmented in the most complex and varied ways. Anti-Government sabotage, for example, is not exclusively African, and racially integrative mechanisms are built by the Government itself to bring about the cleavages under apartheid. Nevertheless, many integrative structures, at any rate between White and non-White, may prove unstable as conflict heightens, and become submerged or latent, being renewed under more favorable conditions in much the same way that the more moderate may take over after the first phases of revolutionary violence.

It is difficult to assess the strength of the interracial structures and trends, and it may be optimistic to attach great significance to them. Certainly the overwhelming reality is that of racial cleavage and con-

flict. The most irrelevant situations provoke the crystallization of racialism. Cooperation becomes difficult. Even where there is racial good will,
sympathy and understanding are precarious. There are conflicts in basic
values. Opposite reactions to the same events make this manifest, as, for
example, the suspension of the Football Association of South Africa,
encouraging to many non-Whites, and threatening to Whites; or the
White man's image of the Congo, at the time of its independence, as a
country in chaos with unspeakable racial atrocity perpetrated by barbarous Black hordes and proof of African political incapacity and need
for White rule, as contrasted with a frequent rejection by educated
Africans of the press accounts as propaganda, and a tendency to hold
Belgian oppression responsible for African violence. As one African informant commented:—"The evils that they teach us, we will execute."

The heightening of racial conflict and the failure in consensus are
shown further by the increasingly repressive laws affecting race relations,
the mounting political persecutions, the improved lethal capacity of
police and military, the rising appropriations for defence, the growth of
sabotage and terrorism, and the many violent encounters. In the process,
race relations become more deeply charged with enmity. It is as if the
events accumulate, each adding an intensity to an endless history of
racial conflict. The spirit of violence spreads. The most trifling incident
may spark off a racial conflagration. Whether or not apartheid has raised
the very dangers it was designed to avert, lives, property, and privilege
are now threatened. A numerous and well-armed ruling class, partly
fortified by the religious sanctification of apartheid, may be expected to
fight for survival with great determination and ruthlessness. As for the
non-Whites, the systematic oppression creates a situation in which
they begin to feel that only the most radical measures will effect change.
And so the conflict moves continuously to greater extremes.

In these circumstances, detachment and neutrality are inconceivable.
All groups and all strata are drawn into the racial conflict. Members of
the African bourgeoisie cannot escape involvement, and indeed it is
under bourgeois leadership that the main African political organizations
move toward racial exclusiveness and violence.

The political formulas of the African organizations are, however,
ambivalent. There is for example the curious alchemy of achieving nonracialism through racial exclusiveness, or the sophistry of equating
nonracialism with rule by the African majority. Because of the pervasiveness of racial criteria in South African society, the political
formulas in fact express race attitudes, and the ambivalence in race
attitudes is thus projected into political ideology. The impression is often
of strong emotions of racial hatred struggling with a reasoned rejection
of racialism, though racialism begins to prevail.

Ambivalence in racial and political attitudes was characteristic of many of the intellectuals in this study. Thus medical students hoped for a racially integrated society, which they phrased as a society in which race has no place; in which intermarriage has no meaning, one human being marries another human being; in which everyone is regarded as a human being (with the obvious implication that non-Whites are treated under present conditions as nonhuman); a society based on individual merit, multiracial in everything, integrated in all spheres. Only two students, of thirty-one, deviated from this pattern. Yet the same students freely stereotyped other racial groups with much antagonistic comment. Half the students perceived the English-speaking White man as cunning, hypocritical: "he is too cunning, like a rat he bites and soothes at the same time"; and "they give you a bitter sugar coated pill; you are not aware of the thing that hurts you when he does it." Some students contrasted the hypocrisy of the English with the openness of the Afrikaner,[1] open, that is to say, in the sense of frank domination. The main stereotype of the Afrikaners was in terms of racial arrogance, oppression, and brutality: "they regard themselves as the chosen friends of God"; "the Afrikaner tells you you are a Kaffir and you have to keep saying 'Baas' to get anything out of him"; "in their eyes the African is just a dog and not a human being at all"; and "the Afrikaners seem to have savage cruelty." In general, students reacted more favorably to the English, reflecting the fact that apartheid is a product of Afrikaner society and that students have a different experience of contact with English and Afrikaner. Many of the students educated at mission schools had become acquainted with English-speaking Whites as school teachers or ministers, while their contacts with Afrikaners would have been largely with the lower strata of the bureaucracy and police force. The stereotypes are related in part to the contrast between middle-class Englishmen as teachers and ministers of religion, and lower-class Afrikaners carrying out the rituals of domination. And the charge of hypocrisy is made precisely because of the greater identification with, and respect for, the English.

There was more reluctance to stereotype Indian fellow students or Indians in general, and a greater readiness to interpret behavior sympa-

1. This seems strange, since there is a wide gap between the practice and the promise of apartheid, and I attempt an analysis of the apparent anomaly in Appendix C. Much the same distinction of frankness and hypocrisy was made by African university students in the humanities section, between the National Party and the United Party opposition—this may be a further source of the ethnic stereotype. P. L. van den Berghe reports a tendency for non-European students to dichotomize between the imputed blunt oppressiveness of the Afrikaner and the subtle and hypocritical snobbishness of the English in "Race Attitudes in Durban, South Africa," *Journal of Social Psychology*, 57 (1962), 61, and E. A. Brett, in *African Attitudes*, (South African Institute of Race Relations, No. 14, 1963), p. 59, reports the frequent rejection of the United Party as little better than the National Party.

thetically. Some students commented on cultural differences—a tendency, as they perceived it, for Indian students to ingratiate themselves with those in authority and for African students to suspect anyone close to authority; a quiet Hindu reserve as contrasted with a boisterous African sociability; and an exclusiveness and submissiveness trained in the Indian home. Or they saw an ambiguity in the position of Indians as a minority, under pressure to play both sides, the controlling Whites and the African majority (responsive, that is to say, both to the present and future sources of power). But even with this more complex and sympathetic reaction, the conventional Shylock stereotype of the foreign petty trader emerged, and an image of Indians as opportunist and insincere. Moreover, in times of stress, tension may be directed against Indians, as during the graduation boycott, or under competition in examinations, when a charge of racial favoritism may compensate for feelings of inadequacy. Thus sentiments of racialism are interwoven with ideals of nonracialism, and medical students who express acceptance or indeed approval of interracial marriage may nevertheless resent friendships between Indian men and African women.

In the humanities section, students showed the ambivalence between racialism and nonracialism in their political affiliations. At the time of our interviews, there was much ferment over the issues of racial cooperation and nonviolence, and some movement toward the newly formed Pan-Africanist Congress. Supporters of the African National Congress were the most firmly committed to nonracialism. The Sons of Young Africa (a division of the Unity Movement) repudiated racialism, but nevertheless unleashed racial antagonism by means of a political formula which equated Whites with the oppressors and non-Whites with the oppressed. Nonracialism was in effect, though not in theory, identified with non-White unity. By contrast, the Pan-Africanist Congress equated nonracialism with Africanism, that is to say an exclusively African struggle for liberation and the primacy of African interests. In practice, commitment to the nonracialism of the Pan-Africanist Congress and of the Sons of Young Africa encouraged the expression of racial antagonisms, while commitment to the nonracialism of the African National Congress imposed restraint.

The following extracts from interviews illustrate some of the ambivalences in the different political ideologies.

African National Congress

It [the A.N.C.] believes that everybody belongs and must live in this country. . . . The Whites are here to stay and we must never run away from that fact. We must love those neighbors whom God has given to us and not love those whom we want. It was God's plan that they be our neighbors and that is the policy of the A.N.C. As things are at the moment, and when we are faced with an unreason from above, that is from a Government which has been indoctrinated with the policy of separation, you cannot reason, and even if you tried, it would be a waste of time. The only way to reason with them is by adopting a new policy altogether. A political body like the P.A.C., which advocates a policy of Africa for the Africans, I think of violence as the means to achieve this, are the people who can give us something to work upon. If we can or were to attack the Whites, we can put them in a state of awareness, that we want something, and that we mean business. The policy of violence can't work forever, and if it does work, it will lead to a dictatorship. I think when this policy has put sense into the Whites, then moderates can come to the scene. The Whites are using force against us and we must also use force. We can't settle anything peacefully. Violence must be met with violence. No country has and will attain its freedom without having shed blood.

Sons of Young Africa

In any case what I discovered was what I had already known, that all Whites are for the oppression of the non-Whites and this segregation is a symbol of it. About the future I feel that it is not long before there is a revolution in South Africa. I feel ultimately everybody shall achieve something from it, e.g. equality. Political guidance is needed for the non-Whites when this revolution comes about. As it is now—if the Africans were to continue struggling the way they do without Indians and Coloreds—it will mean a great loss of human life and that won't achieve much, without the members of other racial groups not participating and assisting. Let us assume also that the Africans got their independence on their own without the help from other racial groups, then you cannot expect democracy in the true sense of the word under these circumstances, because no African would allow the Indians and Coloreds to enjoy the freedom for which he has suffered and the result would be endless feuds and warfare. The split in the United Party [i.e. by the formation of the Progressive Party] is insignificant as though it did not exist in the sense that it reminds me of the people in the Bible, who tried to share Jesus' garment. They are not quarreling on whether they should oppress us or not, but on what amount of assistance should be given to the Nationalist Party of this oppression. They know they are oppressing us, but what they are not sure of is whether by oppressing they are more kind to the non-Whites or to the Whites, but only if they can or cannot get the next election. The question of others being called Progressives is nonsense. They are all moving backward.

Pan-Africanist Congress

This extract is from an interview with a student who at the time was a supporter of the African National Congress. When interviewed in the following year, he had moved over to the Pan-Africanist Congress.

I like what the A.N.C. is doing. . . . One thing which Congress does and with which I don't agree is that it is disowning the African of his heritage, which is the ownership of the country as such. They say this is an interracial country where everybody shall have equal rights. I am not in favor of oppressing anybody and I think they should be telling the African what his rights are. There are Africans in England and America, who have been granted full citizenship rights there, but I don't think those Africans can now claim England as their country. They will still remain Africans. They can enjoy the rights and privileges given them, but they can't claim England as their country. That is what I disagree with in the policy of the Congress. I am not a member of Congress.

And from another student, sympathetic to the Pan-Africanist Congress:

I don't like the idea of including members of the other racial groups in our struggle. They do not only retard the course of our progress, but they destroy it. They are going to use the A.N.C. to achieve their own ends. If by multiracialism they mean nonracialism, I have nothing to oppose in that. By nonracialism I mean that, because the Africans are the predominant race numerically they should also predominate in the agents of government. Multiracialism, if it will safeguard the rights of minority groups as groups and not as individuals, then I am opposed to it.

The teachers expressed grim forebodings of racial civil war. Some saw violence arising from the rigidity of White policies, so that Africans would be forced to destroy White supremacy by violent means: others saw South Africa heading for another Congo, and Africans driving Europeans from South Africa:

"there will be peace and quiet and things shall be as they are in the Belgian Congo." There was the expectation of a period of chaos, bloodshed, and revolutionary change; "a civil war—those for universal happiness against those for sectional happiness"; "civil war-Afrikaners versus Africans and European sympathizers"; "to survive—one group is bound to kill the other—the Whites may kill all the Blacks or vice versa"; "Africa will be controlled by the Africans, if not by persuasion, by force"; "Europeans will be forced to quit the country because we shall have gained freedom or they will be suffering under us."

Most teachers (86%) felt there was a deterioration in race relations, with growing race hatred, separation, and discrimination. Many perceived the older school children as affected by extremism, racialism, and anti-White sentiment, or as politically conscious, or as emancipated from the fear of, or inferiority to, the White man, so characteristic of their own generation.

The expectation of racial violence is consistent with Pan-Africanist sympathies, since racial antagonisms seek an outlet in violence, which is also the means of social change. But it must be a source of ambivalence for the majority of the teachers, who hoped for a nonracialist democratic society as a solution to the South African race problem. And so, too, hostile stereotypes of other racial groups must be a source of ambivalence, and teachers showed the familiar readiness for racial stereotyping. This was particularly marked in relation to Indians, with a volume of response, much of it adverse, and with play on the Shylock image. About half the sample offered characterizations of Whites, mostly as having a superiority complex or as being racist or oppressive, and of the English-speaking as gentle, courteous, refined, and kind, but also sly and cunning. Characterizations of the Afrikaner were more voluminous, couched in much the same terms as those given by the university students; and again the frankness of the Afrikaner (in his racial attitudes) was contrasted with the hypocrisy of the English.[2]

Most teachers accepted the invitation to rate Afrikaner, English, Indian, Sotho, Xhosa, and Zulu in terms of intelligence, honesty, human kindness, and respect for authority, thus presumably again demonstrating the tendency to stereotype. But the ratings do not show crystallized racial antagonisms: they are not anti-White. The Afrikaners are rated lowest in all save honesty, where there is the ambivalence of honest in oppression, while the English are accorded a very high rating.[3] Nor is there marked Africanism: the Xhosa, for example, are given a lower valuation than the English and Indians. And even ethnocentrism is restrained: though informants are mainly Zulu, they do not consistently rate the Zulu highest in all qualities, but accord a low rating in intelligence, apparently equating intelligence with education. (See Appendix D, Table 10).

Group prejudices are apparent in the ratings but not in consistent crystallized patterns. Throughout there is ambivalence and ambiguity. It is against this background that the political debate between Congress and the Africanists gains significance. Most teachers were keenly aware of the issues, which they phrased mainly in terms of multiracialism or Africanism, and moderate or resolute (precipitate) action, sympathy

---

2. For example:

The Afrikaner is crude in speech and appearance. The English is refined and a real gentleman. The Boer is very open. He does not hide that he doesn't want you. An Englishman covers up his hate. I prefer a Boer because he is our open enemy.

The Afrikaner tells you point blank if he does not want you, but with an Englishman he pets you and never shows and tells you the truth. A European will always be a European.

The Afrikaner people are a people who have hatred against us—such hatred that they fail to conceal it.

The Afrikaner is very open: he hates everybody but himself, especially the Black man.

He [the Afrikaner] hasn't the true love of another race even though he may be a missionary.

The question to teachers was confusing: "What are the characteristics of the White man? Do you draw a distinction between English-speaking and Afrikaans-speaking? If so, what?" and elicited one unexpected distinction: "I don't draw any distinction. A White man is polite —the Afrikaner in most cases is crude," and: "The Afrikaner speaks forcefully and the European has a milder tone." On inquiry there appeared to be a traditional distinction among Zulu people between *abelungu* (Whites) and *amabunu* (Boers, Afrikaners).

3. Brett in *African Attitudes* and van den Berghe in "Race Attitudes in Durban, South Africa" also report a relatively high rating of English-speaking Whites.

governing the precise phrasing. These political debates are of great significance, because it is through them that strong influences are exerted on African race attitudes.

While there is a universal involvement in the racial struggle, the nature of this involvement for particular groups is likely to vary with differences in their social situation. Members of the African bourgeoisie in particular are affected by two distinctive characteristics:—first, by a basic incongruity in status,[4] especially of the professionals and the educated, and second, by the specific nature of their professional and trading occupational milieus.

Incongruity is inherent in the position of an African professional. The successful African doctor, for example, can differentiate himself from other members of his group by a higher standard of living and material possessions. But he cannot own a home in the "White" town in which he practices, nor easily find an exclusive area of living, away from the common man, as does the White doctor with whom he trained at the University. He has acquired the culture of the White man, but is largely excluded from association with him. And in respect of civic rights, or personal liberty, and in respect of the obligation always to carry papers, which can be demanded at any time and in any place by any policeman, he is in a similar position to the impoverished and illiterate African laborer. This is the inherent incongruity in his position. After many years of education in which his achievement is marked by a ceremonial ego-enhancing graduation, and having dedicated himself by the Hippocratic oath to the self-sacrificing ideas of a noble profession, which at the same time offers high economic rewards and bourgeois fulfillment, he is relegated with his fellow Africans, in an undifferentiated way, to the status virtually of a minor and of a potential criminal.

This inherent incongruity is heightened by two further factors. Since relatively few Africans have achieved high occupational and educational status, they enjoy an exaggerated prestige in the African community, thus emphasizing and indeed widening the gap between occupational and civic status. And second, the meanest White man in terms of education, moral standards, occupation, personality, or basic courtesy, enjoys precisely those fundamental human rights denied the African professional, thus sharpening the sense of deprivation. It is as if two perspectives converge in the position of the professional—an exaggerated adulation of his achieved status by his own people, and a contemptuous denigration of his ascribed racial status by the Whites.

Race domination gives rise to an incongruity of status not only within

4. See R. J. Pelligrin and F. L. Bates, "Congruity and Incongruity of Status Attributes," *Social Forces, 38* (1959), 23–28.

the ranks of the African bourgeoisie but also among the White members of the large bureaucracy which rules over all aspects of African life. It seems that many members of this bureaucracy are recruited from the less qualified and able sections of the White population. Africans are held in low esteem, and the stigma attaching to Africans may thus diffuse over the administration of African affairs, repelling the more able, highly qualified, and ambitious White administrators. Quite apart from this possibility, the very size of the bureaucracy, which grows rapidly as its powers of control are extended, makes it difficult to recruit on the basis of qualifications consistent with responsibility and powers. The powers themselves are such that it is inconceivable that the requisite qualifications for their exercise could be found in sufficient volume to man the administrative posts. These powers include the right to deny occupational opportunity, choice of residence, and freedom of movement. They include the right of exile by administrative process, and the routine debasement of human dignity.

Here lies the basic incongruity in the positions of the White members of the African affairs bureaucracy. Their positions, as compared with similar positions in other government and municipal bureaucracies, are not more highly rewarded, nor do they enjoy more prestige (perhaps less, as I have suggested). Yet they carry incomparably greater powers. Contact with the officials of this bureaucracy is inescapable for the African, and the contact is most frequent with the lower levels of the bureaucracy, where there is maximum incongruity between the position, qualifications, prestige, and rewards of the bureaucrat on the one hand, and power over the lives of Africans on the other. I am thinking of the Superintendent of a location and the wide powers the Superintendent exercises over the residents, whatever their educational and occupational qualifications; or the policeman with the right to humiliate Africans by the calculated demand for the production of papers, or the right to debase African parents before their children by the raiding of homes in the early hours of the morning; or the Native Commissioner in a rural area, by training and perspective a minor administrator, but by position and by the powers vested and sometimes usurped almost an Oriental despot.

Weber[5] states it as a general proposition that: "The hatred and the distrust of the subjects, which is common to all patrimonialism, in China as everywhere turned above all against the lower levels of the hierarchy, who came into the closest practical contact with the population." The African stereotypes of the Afrikaner discussed above are some evidence of the applicability of this generalization to South African society. In the case of the African professional, there is the added element of a complicated interplay between two sets of status incongruities. The

5. Max Weber, *The Religion of China* (Glencoe, Free Press, 1951), p. 133.

incongruities in the status of the African professional confront the status incongruities of the White lower bureaucrat.

The lower bureaucrat is deficient in qualifications and economic rewards, but endowed with civic rights and extensive authority over the person and personality of the African. This imbalance between rewards, qualifications, and power in the position of the petty bureaucrat is accentuated in contact with the African professional, who has precisely the qualifications and perhaps the possessions the White bureaucrat lacks. It is a challenge to his position, and there seems to be a temptation in this situation for the petty bureaucrat to use, and abuse, his powers to the full, as if to root out the incongruity. He exaggerates the authority of his own position, and makes meaningless the achievement of the African, not only denying him recognition but debasing the dignity of his personality. By an exaggerated exercise of power, he compensates for his own status deficiencies, and the temptation to behave in this way is especially strong for those who occupy the lowest positions in the bureaucracy, where the status deficiencies are most marked. The situation is similar to that expressed in the observation, ascribed to Cape Coloreds, that the "pure White" is all right, with the implication that it is mainly the dark-colored, the doubtful, White man who acts out an aggressive racial superiority.

The research files give many accounts of the debasement of African professionals and university students at the hands of the lower bureaucracy. There are encounters with the police, detention at the police station, or arrest under the pass laws. Some of the episodes reveal deliberate humiliation, rough and contemptuous handling, cynical corruption, a calculated unreasonableness, or determination to persecute. Then there are the routine practices of many officials—the deliberate discourtesy, the bullying and swearing, and the interminable waiting. An African may not originate action, because this implies superiority, nor is it consistent with racial status that a White person should serve a non-White. Hence the African may be deliberately ignored for long periods, while the lumpen-bureaucrat is conspicuously doing nothing. This conspicuous leisure emphasizes contempt, and also that the lumpen-bureaucrat does not serve him. When he finally originates attention for the African, it may be done rudely, emphasizing again that he is master and the African a servant. Any show of "cheek" invites persecution. And outside of the civil service, shop and office workers have their comparable techniques and resources for asserting superiority—such as the arsenal of terms of address, "boy," "girl," "John," "Jim," and "Nanny." I am not suggesting that all policemen and petty officials persecute Africans, nor that all members of the African bourgeoisie have suffered traumatic experiences at their hands, but only that these patterns of behavior are so general as to constitute part of the style of African life. They are so pervasive that even the most exalted of the African bourgeoisie, the priest, the doctor, or the lawyer is likely to bear the stigmata of race.

It is inevitable that the members of the African bourgeoisie should react with deep resentment against this degradation of their status, and that they should seek to set aside a system which imposes such humiliating conditions of living. The situation is all the more wounding because the accomplished African, who is denied the human civic status accorded the meanest of White men, receives an exaggerated acclaim from his fellow Africans.

The type of conflict between the sharply contrasted status of White petty bureaucrat and of African bourgeoisie is merely a special, and extreme, case of a more general type of conflict. If we accept a doctrine of universal human rights, then there is an inherent incongruity in the racial position of the African worker or peasant, denied the full expression of the personal rights and dignity which inhere in the human status. And, conversely, the swollen grandeur of the rights enjoyed by White persons, in relation to fellow human beings of different color, tends to dehumanize the status of White man. This grandeur promotes an arrogance, a disregard for the human rights of others, and hence a diminution of the human status of the White man himself. Again, there is a complementary relationship, inflation of the status of the White man to king size, deflation of the status of the Black man to minor, ward, inferior: hypertrophy and atrophy.

I have assumed throughout that the specific character of the occupational milieu will influence political choice, but I do not mean to imply an occupational determination of political attitudes. Other factors, such as the status incongruity of the bourgeoisie, or the shared oppression of all Africans in South Africa, or the continent-wide emancipation of Africans may be of far greater significance. And even among Africans of the same occupation, there are marked differences in political ideology, though within certain limits, which mostly include the rejection of apartheid and racial subordination. Nevertheless, it seems likely that the occupational milieu, reflecting life chances and style of life, will enter as an important element in, though not a determinant of, the ideological perspectives of the bourgeoisie.

The occupations here treated as bourgeois vary in many respects relevant to race relations and political ideology. They vary in the type of setting they provide—an individual setting in the case of the doctor in private practice, or a group setting as for the African teacher or nurse. And they vary in the opportunity for interracial contact. Thus an African clergyman in the Methodist Church has occasion for contact with White fellow clergymen, while most African teachers are confined within a racial, and, I assume, an increasingly tribal, work environment. In the case of the teachers, the combination of a group setting and group exclusiveness seems likely to promote a social effervescence and an intensity of involvement in times of crisis. I am thinking, for example, of Durkheim's analysis of an Australian corroboree, and the way in which the coming together and the acting in unison generate the sentiment of a force far transcending the individual. It is the presence in some measure of these elements which partly explains the intense political involvement at the University of Fort Hare and in the non-White humanities section of the University of Natal.

The occupations also vary in the opportunities they offer for personal advancement and in the extent of exposure to competition. African doctors and lawyers have perhaps the most favorable opportunities, and they are little exposed to competition. The trader may now hope for his Eldorado, but he is in an ambiguous position with reference to competition. Theoretically enjoying or about to enjoy a monopoly of trade in his own area, in practice he experiences a most intense competition, and this competition is expressed in racial terms. The African minister of religion in a White-controlled English denomination is in some measure in a directly competitive relationship with his White brothers, and this competition has a racial cast. To the extent that he is able to achieve equality in stipend and executive responsibility by constitutional means within the Church, racially cooperative relations are likely to gain in strength. African teachers are not in competition with teachers of other races, but are subject to considerable competition among themselves. The rewards are modest, even with the greater number of appointments to supervisory posts and the recent advances in salary. The discrepancy between competition and reward must certainly be a source of frustration.[6]

The occupations also vary in their relationship to the wider society. The occupational milieu may be in a state of harmony or tension with other institutional aspects. This was a major theme in the analysis of the occupational milieus, and offered such contrasts as doctrinal tensions with White domination but practical adjustment in the case of the English churches, and doctrinal harmony but practical tensions in the case of the African schools. Related to this is the distinction between instrumental and self-expressive occupational roles. The occupational role may be detached as it were from the individual and handed over

6. Generally in the African states, the teaching profession seems to offer relatively poor inducements. The Commission on the Process of Educational Planning at the Conference of African States on the Development of Education in Africa, held at Addis Ababa in May 1961, noted the decline of interest in teaching, particularly in the young African states, where the senior administrative posts, political life, and diplomatic careers drew many teachers away from the profession, and recommended that steps be taken to improve the status conditions of teachers both with regard to salaries and the standing of the African teacher (UNESCO/ED/181, pp. 37–42).

to the control of others for purposes they define, or it may offer scope for self-expression. And this purpose or scope may be confined within racial limits or permitted universal extension. Thus the African teacher or civil servant is in many respects an instrument for the racial policies of alien rulers, while the African doctor is to some extent his own master, with opportunity for self-expression in the service of universal values. This distinction is partly related to that of intercalary positions, which, in the case of the Durban Advisory Boards, seemed to influence behavior toward oscillation between submission and belligerence.

The above distinctions by no means exhaust the range of variation in occupational milieu, and yet even in terms of these distinctions the differences are considerable, as shown for example in profiles of the professions of teacher and lawyer. The teacher works in a racially exclusive group setting, under strong competition for modest rewards, in a profession of declining prestige. He cannot influence policy, and he is denied a fully creative role. He is employed as an agent for an alien power, and for alien objectives, harmonized with the politics of apartheid and in tension with the aspirations of many of his own people. The lawyer by contrast follows a profession of high prestige and reward, in an individual setting, but obliged by the very nature of his calling to work with members of other racial groups. He expresses himself in the type of practice he builds, and, though many of his cases flow from racial discrimination, he can control to some extent tension with the wider society. He is not obliged to accept political leadership, however well qualified he may be, as a lawyer, for the role, nor need he be involved in legal political causes. His position is not inherently political, as is that of the teacher.

Very different influences may be expected to arise from these sharp contrasts between occupations. And yet the common elements in the occupational situation, as in the general social situation, may be of equal or even greater significance for political outlook. African professionals and traders share the same racial status which extends to virtually all aspects of life, and imposes on their occupations two basic conditions grounded in race. The first is that over and above the general controls applicable to all sections of the population, Africans are specifically subject to racial regulation and control. This may arbitrarily impose a discrimination in salary, as in the case of the medical interns; or a sudden frustration of legitimate aspiration, as when a lawyer or a trader is required to move from city premises into a location; or special racial conditions of employment, as for teachers; or a racial barrier to opportunity; or a racial ceiling on reward. Whatever the form of this racial control and regulation, it is imposed by rulers of another race, in their own interests, and links occupational freedom with emancipation from racial domination.

A second condition is like the torment of Tantalus, a phrase I use not to hurl abuse at apartheid but to describe the display of the glittering prize and its withdrawal. This condition would have been present in some measure in any event. The economic development of the country is such that Africans inevitably advance, and share, albeit most unequally, in the new developments. And the greater the advance, the greater the impatience with arbitrary restraint. This is a common observation, that the drive to revolutionary change comes from those strata which experience an enhancement of life, rather than those still deeply imbedded in their misery and poverty. There is an anticipatory movement into the new Eden, and a deeper anger at exclusion.

Apartheid heightens this tension between anticipation and reality. The Government is driven, by the need for moral justification and for African acceptance, to boost the rewards of separate development. But it dare not grant these rewards, lest African advancement undermine Afrikaner power or diminish Afrikaner profit. And rising Afrikaner profits have been accompanied by rising aspirations and great reluctance to share these profits. Hence as in the case of trading, the Government oscillates: it entices and denies, gives and deprives. And this may be sharp torment, particularly for Africans in the higher occupations, rendering the continued racial domination intolerable.

The subjects of this study, with few exceptions, reject apartheid. As a political ideology of Afrikaner nationalism, apartheid is hardly compatible with the interests of the African bourgeoisie. Though it may offer regulated opportunity for limited advancement under racial control, the opportunity is modest: Africans are the beneficiaries of the ideology rather than the practice of apartheid, which affords them small inducement. "Self-government" in the Transkei and other Bantustans may offer some immediate enhancement of satellite life chances, but again of modest proportions. The South African Government represents the interests of Whites, and it is accountable to strata close to Africans in occupation and rural background—relatively unskilled workers demanding privileged and protected standards of living and the reservation of occupations, and new rising petty capitalist classes demanding a racial monopoly of the more favorable opportunities in trade and industry, their appetites growing with what they feed upon. The Government dare not make a substantial allocation for African development from its own resources, nor dare it seriously deprive White merchants and industrialists of prospective profits in the development of the Bantustans, or expose them, or White workers, to African competition. Much as the Bantustans must be subordinated politically to safeguard the power of the South African Government, so too must they be subordinated economically to control competition and to enhance White commercial and industrial interests. Indeed the apartheid system of border industries seems to provide for the efficient exploitation of cheap African labor, expressing in another form the increasing dependence of Whites upon African labor as a result of industrialization. It means a different pattern of integration, with some decentralization of industry, and not racial separation at all.

Even if international agencies were to make funds available for the development of backward African areas, so that there need be no diminution of South African "White" funds for this purpose; and even if White South Africans were to accept fully the principle of African entitlement in African areas, apartheid would still not accord with the interests of the African bourgeoisie. Its members would need to find their fulfillment in backward undeveloped areas, within a refurbished tribal milieu, which they reject. And they would need to accept philosophically, or even as morally justified, the reservation to Whites of most of the area of South Africa and virtually all its towns and industries, and a status of aliens in the land of their ancestors. The situation reproduces the old discriminations. The relationship of the Bantustans to "White" South Africa is that of the urban African locations to the cities, or of the squatter's shack to the owner's farmhouse. It is inconceivable that Africans would be immune to the conspicuous deprivation of living in an African pondokkie behind the White man's mansion, or that the leaders of the independent African states would accept the loss of the most highly developed resources on the continent of Africa to what they would regard as a successor state of colonial oppressors.

But the strength of apartheid, and its significance for the political choices and life chances of the African bourgeoisie, should not be underestimated. As the crisis sharpens, outside pressure groups representing industrial interests, or expressing in disguised form the widespread color prejudices of Western society, bring support to the South African Government both locally and abroad. They are now trying to propagate a more favorable image of apartheid. In their proposals for an ultimate solution, the formula may change to support of partition, not apartheid. By a curious nuance, partition may reproduce apartheid and yet divest it of any suggestion of moral turpitude, since partition seeks the solution of radical separation as an evil made necessary by the avoidance of the greater evil of civil war, whereas apartheid finds moral purpose in the separation itself.

Support from the West has been an appreciable factor in sustaining apartheid. To this must be added the internal divisions among Africans themselves. Inevitably some members of the African bourgeoisie are attracted by the immediate rewards of apartheid, and may acquire a vested interest in its maintenance. Apartheid works along lines of natural cleavage for the traditionally oriented Africans and, indeed, even for the Westernized—the cleavage of tribal loyalties—and it provides an institutional basis in tribal neighborhoods, schools, and university colleges for tribalism. The strength of the Government is thus augmented by external supports and some fragmentation of Africans in tribal entities or as the recipients or nonrecipients of benefits.

Class distinctions afford another basis for fragmentation of Africans. The divisions between the educated and the uneducated, the urban and the rural, are appreciable, and apartheid makes use of these divisions. It advances the interests of the traditionally oriented and of peasants against the Western urban bourgeoisie. It offers some opportunity for individual mobility but seeks to embed it within the tribal matrix. It plays African chiefs against African politicians and African intellectuals, projecting images of the latter as the agents of Communism or as otherwise subversive of traditional authority.

Class distinctions among Africans might have entered into the structure of South African society in a very different way if policy had encouraged greater integration of the African bourgeoisie with Whites. The circumstances were favorable to this development. There was a marked class differentiation of the educated with an anticipatory socialization and identification with Whites, acquisition of their culture and rejection of the tribal, and the enjoyment of certain exemptions, conferring a special intermediate status. In some measure the policy of the opposition United Party is apparently designed to foster an African middle class sharing common interests with Whites and bound in loyalty to them. Thus the United Party opposed the Bantu Laws Amendment Bill as being in conflict with the fundamental tenets of its policy, since under the provisions of the Bill there could be no development of a Native middle class in the urban areas.[7] Underlying this policy is the assumption that an African middle class, having a stake in the society, would act as a stable and conservative force. This may be so, provided that its members acquire a substantial interest in the status quo—economic opportunities and assets and a social and civic status comparable with those of White professionals, traders, and entrepreneurs. But it is highly doubtful that the United Party could contemplate so radical a step toward nonracialism. Indeed, though it represents a more mature paternalist phase of capitalism, the United Party begins to merge with the National Party as racial tensions forge White solidarity, thus rendering its policies even more suspect in African political circles. Educated Africans often refuse to distinguish between the United Party and the National Party, in part as an expression of contempt, and not so much because they do not see a distinction. In

7. *Hansard, House of Assembly Debates,* No. 15, May 6, 1963, col. 5366.

part the rejection serves to assert that Africans must depend on themselves for liberation: it is partly for this reason too that clichés of vilification are directed against White liberals, whose policies might otherwise be highly persuasive.

The policy of a qualified franchise proposed by the Progressive Party provides a basis for class identification transcending race. It is specially relevant for the African bourgeoisie, whose members would immediately form a privileged enfranchised stratum, and under other conditions it might have been a means for an evolutionary movement to a democratic society. But there has been a generation of disillusionment with evolutionary policies in circumstances which brought the extinction of the African franchise rather than its progressive extension, and the repudiation by the Government of many past obligations inconsistent with its ideology. The effect has been to undermine the sense of confidence and continuity necessary for the acceptance of an evolutionary policy, and to encourage the appraisal of the qualified franchise as a device for strengthening White domination and emasculating the liberatory movement. The qualified franchise is apparently anathema to the leaders of the main African political organizations. Nevertheless, if it were backed by political power it might very well have some appeal for those sections of the African bourgeoisie who feel that their position is threatened by the antagonism of uneducated or semieducated Africans, or who feel that their achievements merit special recognition.

As it is, class distinctions and tribal divisions are dominated by the overriding racial conflict. Government policy rests on the primacy of race as the basic determinant of the life chances of the individual. Women are equally subjected to regulation, and increasingly involved in political struggle. The racial definition is inescapable, implacable. Non-Whites cannot enter into the upper strata of South African society, or circulate among its elite. The mobility of the individual and the circulation of the elite depend ultimately on the destruction of the racial barriers. And since these barriers are imposed by massive force, and since constitutional avenues of change are closed to Africans, and since the Government has so perfected suppression that only extreme measures offer hope, the situation becomes revolutionary. The African political organizations begin to mobilize for the violent overthrow of the apartheid system of race relations, and in the process they themselves move toward racial exclusiveness, as shown by the emergence of the Pan-Africanist Congress and by changes within the African National Congress toward the Africanist ideology. Thus the struggle is given an even more specifically racial stamp. The probability of great violence increases because of the affinity between racialism and violence. The Government mobilizes its forces and racial civil war threatens.

Many observers feel that civil war is an inevitable consequence of an irreconcilable conflict in values. Some discern a therapeutic virtue in the violence as the traumatic condition of social change. These expectations of violence and these comfortable assessments of its beneficial consequences may actually encourage violence. They need careful appraisal for this reason, and all the more so because the violence may take the form of great carnage and not simply of a little "bloodletting," as it is sometimes phrased. The anticipation of violence clearly rests on very strong evidence, but it seems to place too great an emphasis on the irreconcilability of values, and on violence as the only mechanism of change. In particular, there appears to be an overestimate of the Government's commitment to racialism and an underestimate of the forces of nonracialism.

The strength of commitment to an ideology or to the mores is difficult to assess. In historical retrospect, seemingly rigid values have often proved remarkably flexible. There may even be a greater appearance of rigidity at the moment of change. Certainly the ideology of apartheid has profoundly changed. And even though the solid core of systematic racial exploitation remains, the Government cannot fail to realize the potential threat of its Bantustan policy. Indeed, much of the handling of this policy suggests panic behavior, perhaps a last desperate attempt to salvage apartheid. The commitment to capitalism may be much stronger for many of the leaders than the commitment to apartheid. To the extent that apartheid serves capitalism, there is no problem, as perhaps in the mining and textile industries which the Government encourages. But apartheid is in tension with the mature industrial development of the country's resources, and there may very well be a readiness, in certain strata of Afrikaner society, to abandon a system of race relations once it ceases to be profitable.

Moreover, the power of nonracialism in South African society is by no means negligible. It is obscured by an excessive prominence given to racialism in chronicles which seek out the dramatic and the violent rather than the routine and the cooperative. In fact, daily life is characterized by innumerable acts of cooperation between persons of different race in every sphere of life, vastly in excess of the violent encounters. This is not to deny that the balance between racialism and nonracialism, and between conflict and cooperation, may suddenly be transformed by a conflagration which sweeps aside many established customs. In life itself, as in the chronicles of life, violence commands a potent role and a seemingly respected status. But the great network of social relationships established across the barriers of race over three centuries of contact still offers the hope of nonviolent and nonracial solutions.

Because of this network, much of South African life is marked either by the coexistence of racialism and nonracialism or the ambivalence between them. There is ambivalence within the Pan-Africanist Congress and the African National Congress. The commitment to a democratic ideology, which accorded for many years with the ideal and material interests of Africans, persists. There are a number of reasons, historically, for the strength of this commitment. Many of the African leaders were devout Christians, dedicated to Christianity in a deep and sincere way, more so than some of their White brothers, who were to the manner born. Second, until recent years, the idea of Africans taking control was remote, and hopes thus centered in the democratization of the entire society. Another element of ambivalence enters here, because, no doubt, there was also the realization that a democratic suffrage would ensure a dominant African influence. Third, the aspirations of educated Africans were directed away from their traditional culture, and toward Western European culture: there was a tendency to identify with White people. Fourth, Africans have suffered under racialism, and their own suffering, and the very monstrousness of racialism, serve as correctives. Also, of course—and again there is an ambiguity—suffering under racialism provokes counterracialism. And finally, the possibility of effective struggle was bedeviled by tribalism. From the very inception of the Union of South Africa, the political struggle of Africans was associated also with a struggle against tribalism. In their nature, tribalism and racialism are kindred. Logically the rejection of the one implies the rejection of the other. There is, of course, an alternate possibility, that anti-White racialism might be used to weld together the tribes. Racialism and African unity are to say the least compatible, but when the struggle itself is based on group exclusiveness, there is the inherent danger of reversion to tribalism.

Political loyalties still cut across the racial cleavages. Leaders of the African National Congress continue to work with non-African political leaders, and the recent admission of a White member to the revolutionary council of the Pan-Africanist Congress is not perhaps without significance. Sabotage has its interracial following. The proscription lists of persons arrested without trial, detained, and confined to their homes or otherwise persecuted are interracial. Even apartheid exhibits an ambivalence between the reality of systematic racial discrimination and the ideology of separate development. And as industrialization fosters greater interdependence, the apartheid Utopia of racial separation becomes an increasingly remote fantasy.

The many and repressive laws testify to the strength of nonracialism. Apartheid certainly engenders racialism, but it also promotes the reaction of nonracialism. The dialectic in South African life consists not only in the antithesis between White racialism and Black racialism, but also in the antithesis between racialism and nonracialism. In church and sport, and modestly even in politics, apartheid has given an impetus to racial integration. In many circles there are persons deeply committed to democratic ideals, with a commitment of tried strength, forged under the most exacting conditions. The racial composition of the country, a population of five million non-Africans, offers powerful argument for racial accommodation. And minority groups of Indians and Coloreds are not likely to seek salvation in the nationalism of either Afrikaners or Africans. Moreover the Africans themselves, being a majority group on an African continent, responding with vitality and enthusiasm to the new experiences of Western urban life, and optimistic about their ultimate destiny, may prove more generous to people of other race than the fearful minority group of Afrikaners.

Above all, the power of nonracialism rests in the universal values of the higher tribunals of the conscience, expressed in the declarations of World churches, in the Charter of the United Nations, and in the ethos of the contemporary world. By contrast, apartheid is a relic of colonialism, of purely transient significance. The triumph of more universal values can hardly be in doubt. The manner of this triumph is, however, uncertain, whether lives must be wantonly squandered in great human misery before a moral order is established. These universal values are not foreign to South African society: they act within it, and they can be highly effective, even against the power of the State, when strongly sanctioned, as by the faith of deep religious conviction, or, more concretely, by international tribunals, as in the organization of sport. Since apartheid undermines the institutional supports of non-racialism in South Africa, deliberately eradicating nonracialism under heavy repression, and since it deforms many of its subjects to its own infirmity, external sanctions have a crucial role. It is not a matter of imposing something foreign to the South African way of life. Three centuries of contact have laid a basis for racial cooperation. It is apartheid which is an anachronism, foreign to the contemporary structure of South African society, requiring the massive mobilization of force for its momentary maintenance, as it precipitates the country into a civil war between the races. And it is in effective sanctions by international agencies against the violence of racial domination, and in effective support for the principles of nonracialism, that there may be some hope of a nonviolent resolution of the conflict.

Notes on Procedures

I DERIVED much of the background material for this study from participation in South African society over many years, and research interests in race relations and stratification, political ideology, and techniques of change. My own position was of some help. Since my students were of varied background and race, I was inevitably exposed to a process of interracial education. Involvement in issues affecting race relations provided relevant experience and contacts in the political and welfare fields. And I formed many friendships in different groups, and gained a measure of acceptance in interracial circles. The general knowledge gathered in this way served as an introduction to the research topics but not as a systematic foundation. In particular, I lacked knowledge of the growth of African professional life. I tried to make good this deficiency in some measure, but much research is needed and my own work is quite preliminary. From an historical point of view, I think it would be valuable to select specific periods, and to analyze the occupations in their interrelations with each other and with other aspects of the structure of the society, rather than in segments, occupation by occupation, as I have done in Part III.

The empirical study of the Durban African bourgeoisie is based on the analysis of records and on observation and interview. The volume of recorded material is considerable, notwithstanding loss, destruction, and impounding of records. The trading files of the Durban Bantu Administration Department were of particular value, though covering only the later years, and I also had access to the minutes of the African Football Association and the Durban Teachers' Association, to municipal records, bluebooks, *Hansards,* reports, journals, and newspapers. The sources are given in the text. Most of the quoted materials were rechecked from the text to the original source. In the few cases where this was not possible, the item is indicated by an asterisked footnote.

The period of research, one of profound social change, provided many valuable opportunities for observation. I attended the inaugural meeting of the Pan-Africanist Congress in Durban, a meeting which almost dissolved in chaos after probing questions into race attitudes and a demonstration by supporters of the African National Congress, and I was present when Chief Luthuli, President of the A.N.C., debated political ideology with one of the Africanist leaders. My research assistants followed the dispute between the Russians and the Japanese in the meetings of the Football Association. We attended the course for African traders and their graduation ceremony, and indeed so far as possible all public events relevant to the research. Durban, for all its pluralism, is a relatively compact city, and it was not difficult to encompass the important developments.

The main source of new material was from interviews of different types, namely:—

1. A small number of life histories, in which I personally sought new perspectives and an understanding of these perspectives in the context of the respondent's own history.

2. Interviews with key persons in the different milieus, such as sports administrators, municipal officials, Advisory Board leaders, senior personnel in the nursing services, hospital supervisors, and leaders in Lamont Location.

3. Relatively intensive interviews with members of the different occupations. These were intended to cover the background of the individual, his training, work situation, class perspectives, religious attitudes, race attitudes, and political outlook. Not all these topics were necessarily discussed. The approach varied a great deal, depending on the specific problems of a particular milieu, what the individual himself wished to communicate, the rapport between him and the interviewer, omissions on the part of the interviewer—sometimes inadvertent and sometimes deliberate, and decisions as to the particular aspects of the interview to be developed with a specific category of respondents. Initially interviewers studied political affiliations, but later, as the situation deteriorated, questions were directed rather to the assessment of political ideologies. Though most respondents still seemed ready to give their political affiliations, sometimes political discussion was entirely omitted. In general, the interview approach was open and flexible, attempting to follow the interests and involvements of the persons interviewed. Sometimes what was designed as an intensive interview emerged as a brief sketch, but many of the interviews were rich and rewarding.

4. Specifically focused fact-collecting interviews—as, for example, interviews designed to secure the demographic characteristics of Advisory Board members or traders—sometimes linked with other topics, such as the assessment of their experiences in the Advisory Boards.

5. Questionnaire schedules, used only for the schoolchildren, teachers, and nurses. Questionnaires were administered to a representative sample of Durban schoolchildren, in the manner described in the text, and they themselves entered their answers to questions dealing with demographic data, rating of occupations, and their occupational hopes and expectations. The procedures were probably adequate for the type of information gathered. In the case of the teachers, the long questionnaire which follows at the end of this section was administered by dialogue, with the interviewer recording and probing the answers. There were some exceptions to this, where the schedules were left with the respondents and completed by them, or where there was little or no probing into the answers. The nurses at the two main hospitals studied were handed a much shorter version of the teachers' schedule, which they com-

pleted themselves while assembled. In a third small hospital, which contributed only a few schedules, the documents were made available for the nurses to complete at their leisure. The responses in the nurses' schedules were somewhat denuded of content, in sharp contrast to the richness of many of the teachers' schedules. I think the explanation lies partly in the fact that Africans, and perhaps South Africans in general, are not domesticated to filling in questionnaires, and partly that African culture still emphasizes the verbal rather than the written skills. African respondents are not fully trained to written culture, but they are often vivid, expansive, and highly cultivated in conversation.

There was a good deal of variation in the quality of the data for different occupations, in consequence of differences in numbers, availability, and rapport. We did not establish rapport with civil servants, and the traders, apart from a few leaders, were guarded in their interviews. It proved difficult to meet individually with the nurses. By arrangement with the hospital supervisors, my wife met the nurses in the hospital, mainly in groups. More information was secured for the mission hospital, which provided much of the questionnaire material, than for the two provincial hospitals.

The problem of representativeness hardly arose for occupations such as law, medicine, journalism, the ministry in the established denominations, or social work, the numbers involved being so small. The sample taken of university students was relatively large but not random—31 of the 85 African medical students in 1960 (excluding students in the preliminary year, with one inadvertent exception), selected from the different years and so far as possible including African class leaders, and 25 of the 75 African students in the humanities section at the time of the interviews in 1959, both undergraduates (18) and graduates (7). Teaching, nursing, and trading are sufficiently populous occupations for sampling. However, the samples of these occupations used in the present study are *not* representative. In the case of the teachers, our interest lay mainly in the highly qualified teachers or those working for higher qualifications (which is to say, mainly men with a T3 teacher's certificate), and not in the numerous women teachers resting on the low qualification of T4. Hence in the intensive interviews, we interviewed the more highly qualified teachers, and in the questionnaire study we interviewed 11 of the 12 graduate teachers in the main teaching circuit in Durban and included two additional graduate teachers, one temporarily in the area and one on leave, but thought it beside our purpose to keep adding interviews with women teachers of T4 qualification. Even so, the latter constitute 40 per cent of the sample. The distribution of the 248 teachers in the Durban South Circuit of Durban in 1960 and in the sample is given below. This circuit includes most of the teachers in Durban. According to figures supplied by the inspector of the Durban North Circuit in March 1961, there were 97 teachers in his circuit in Durban. Our sample was about 30 per cent of African teachers in Durban, drawn from 20 schools of all types. Where there is a high degree of unanimity among the teachers, as in the rejection of certain aspects of apartheid, this can be taken as fairly representative of the outlook of Durban teachers.

In the case of the nurses at the mission hospital, the procedure was that nurses not on ward duty at an appointed time completed the questionnaires. At the large provincial hospital, the schedules were given to two classes of 25 nurses in all, a minute fraction of the African nursing population of the hospital. The small provincial hospital yielded 14 questionnaires by a process of self-selection. These materials were supplemented by group discussions with nurses and by interviews with the matrons of the three hospitals, the superintendents of two of the hospitals, and individual nurses.

In the case of the African traders, the compiling of a rough census and distribution was one of the products of the research, and took much time. Even then, the census was far from accurate. Sampling could have been postponed to this stage. Instead we proceeded to interview traders, selecting different trades, and most of the areas of African trade—the two city markets and traders in the city area, trading stalls in the hostels, shops in the locations, in Cato Manor, and in the small area of African freehold ownership. We omitted peddlers, but interviewed some of the traders operating from carts. I think that these interviews, supplemented by some observation of trading, attendance at the classes for traders, analysis of records, and discussions with municipal personnel, African leaders, and members of the Durban Junior Chamber of Commerce, provide a basis for presenting a fair picture of African trade in Durban, though again the sample interviewed was drawn quite imprecisely.

It is clear that on the basis of these interview materials it is difficult to generalize with accuracy about the bourgeoisie of Durban. However, I should add that the question of representativeness is secondary where one attempts to analyze what elements might enter into such social phenomena as political ideologies, or the type of influence on political ideology which might be expected

Universe and sample of African teachers—Durban South Circuit, Durban, 1960

			UNIVERSE			
Sex	Unqua-lified	T4	T3J	T3S	University degree	Total
Male	3	30	49	6	7	95
Female		126	18	4	5	153
Total	3	156	67	10	12	248
			SAMPLE			
Sex	Unqua-lified	T4	T3J	T3S	University degree	Total
Male		9	26	4	7	46
Female		40	4	3	6	53
Total		49	30	7	13	99

Based on data supplied by the Inspector, 1960.
T4   = Standard VI plus three years further training.
T3 Junior = Standard VIII plus two years teacher training.
T3 Senior = Matriculation plus two years teacher training.

to flow from the social situation of the African professional, or the possible social consequences of a particular class situation.

My research assistants and I conducted most of the interviews, turning to others mainly for help in difficulty, or where we planned many interviews, as in the case of the teachers. A health educator assisted in the interviews with the nurses, until my wife took over. I received help from graduate students in the few interviews with civil servants, social workers, and authors; from a teacher and a social science graduate in the interviews with teachers; from a university student in some interviews with members of the African Congregational Church; and from a second teacher, from whom I hoped for better rapport with traders, and deeper insight into their perspectives. In Lamont Township, which I selected as an area of special study, I was fortunate to have the help of the Institute of Family and Community Health.

[I am indebted to Dr. P. L. van den Berghe for his help in drafting this schedule.]

Code Number . . . . . .

This is a survey of the teaching profession. Our aims are purely scientific and your answers will be completely confidential.

1. Name of school where you teach _____
2. Which standard do you teach? _____
3. What is your sex? _____
4. What is your age? _____
5. What is your home language? _____
6. What other languages do you speak? _____
7. What is your province and place
   of birth? _____
8. Please list all the jobs you have held to this date, with the place and dates of employment.

   Job   *Place of Work*   *From . . . . To . . . .*

9. What is your religious denomination? _____
10. How often do you go to Church? _____
11. What is your feeling about religion?

    and the contribution of the missionaries?

    and the role of the Church in South Africa to-day?

12. What are your teaching qualifications? _____
13. Where did you go to school? _____
14. Where did you do your teacher training? _____
15. Are you studying further?   Yes_____ No_____
    If so, for what? _____
    If not, are you planning to study further?
    (For what?) _____
16. What is (or was) your father's occupation? _____
17. What is the last standard your father
    completed at school? _____
18. Does (or did) your father speak a European
    language? How fluently? _____
19. What is (or was) your father's
    religious denomination? _____

Code Number . . . . . .

20. Does he (did he) hold any office
    in the Church? If so, what? _____

21. What is (or was) your mother's occupation? _____

22. What is the last standard your mother
    completed in school? _____

23. What is (or was) your mother's
    religious denomination? _____

. . . .

25. Please list your brothers and sisters both dead and alive and the last standard
    they completed at school.

First Name	*Sex*	*Age*	*Last Standard Completed*

26. What is your marital status?
    (Check one)   Married_____
                             Single_____
                             Widower_____
                             Divorced_____

        If Married:

27. Was your marriage civil, religious,
    or customary? _____

28. How long have you been married? _____

29. What is your wife's (or husband's)
    present occupation? _____

30. What was her (his) occupation
    when you married? _____

31. What is the last standard your spouse
    completed in school? _____

32. Does your spouse speak a European
    language? How fluently? _____

33. What language do you most
    frequently speak with your spouse? _____

34. What is the mother tongue of
    your spouse? _____

35. What is the religious denomination
    of your spouse? _____

36. How many children do you have? _____

37. Please list your children with their age and sex:

First Name	*Age*	*Sex*

38. In respect of those sons who have already
    completed their education,
    (a) What standard did they reach? _____
            and
    (b) What occupation are they following? _____

Code Number . . . . . .

39. In respect of those sons who are still at
    school,
    (a) What standard of education would
        you like them to reach?   _____
    (b) What occupation would you like
        them to follow?   _____

. . . .

44. Why did you enter the teaching profession?
45. Have your views about teaching changed since you have been a practising
    teacher?   Yes_____   No_____
    If yes, then how and why?
46. Are there any other occupations you would have preferred to have entered?
    Which ones?
47. What are the three things you *like* most about teaching?
48. What are the three things you *dislike* most about teaching?
49. Which qualities are most important in a *man*? Here are 14 cards, each
    giving a particular quality. Please arrange them in order of importance,
    the most important at the top, then the next in importance and so on.

        Wealth   Hard Work
        Physical Strength   Independence
        Generosity   Honesty
        Professional Training   Sociability
        Respect for Authority   Thrift
        Shrewdness   Intelligence
        Courage   Good Looks

50. Do you think
    (a) that a man should act in accordance with the judgment of his friends
        and colleagues:
        or
    (b) that a man should act according to his own independent judgment
        even if it conflicts with that of his friends and colleagues.
                        Indicate your choice   (a)_____ or (b)_____
51. (a) Do you admire systematic hard work, even at the expense of the enjoy-
        ment of life:
        or
    (b) Do you think that a man should not allow his work to interfere with
        the enjoyment of life?
                        Indicate your choice   (a)_____ or (b)_____
52. Which qualities are most important in a *woman*? Please arrange these 14
    cards in order of importance.

        Physical Strength   Courage
        Generosity   Sociability
        Hard Work   Honesty
        Intelligence   Respect for Authority
        Good Looks   Independence
        Professional Training   Thrift
        Wealth   Shrewdness

53. Do you feel that African education has improved or worsened in the last 20 years? In what ways?

54. How would you say the children you are teaching to-day compare with the children when you were at school?

55. How would you describe the racial attitudes of the older school children to-day?
     And their political attitudes?

56. Think of the three people you see most of socially. (Please note down their names on a separate sheet of paper.)
     Now what are their occupations?
     Their standards of education?
     And their religious denominations?

57. How does a fellow African introduce you to strangers?

58. (If married) Do you and your wife normally go visiting together?

59. If you have visitors to a meal at your home, do you all sit down together?

60. If you were describing the Africans of Durban to a stranger, how would you classify them?

61. Do you think there are any class differences among Africans in Durban?

62. If there are any classes, how many are there and how would you describe them?

63. The name of an occupation is written on each of these 16 cards. Please put at the top the occupation you think is most highly respected, then the second most highly respected. and so on.

Artist	Lawyer
Clerk	Nurse
Doctor	Minister of Religion
Trader	Factory Worker
Civil Servant	Teacher
Carpenter	Social Worker
Herbalist	University Lecturer
Labourer	Farmer

64. In advising a good all-round student, what considerations would you advance to help him choose an occupation?

65. Please list the clubs, organisations and societies (religious, social, cultural, recreational and public) to which you belong.

Club, Organisation or Society	*Member Since*	*Office Held*

66. What are the characteristics of the white man? Do you draw a distinction between English speaking and Afrikaans speaking? If so, what?

67. What are the characteristics of the Indian?

68. Please rate the following groups:
    (a) In order of intelligence
        Xhosas _____
        Indians _____
        Sothos _____

English Speaking Europeans ——————————————
Zulus   ——————————————
Afrikaans Speaking Europeans ————————————

(b) In order of honesty:
Afrikaans Speaking Europeans ————————————
Zulus   ——————————————
English Speaking Europeans ——————————————
Sothos   ——————————————
Indians   ——————————————
Xhosas   ——————————————

(c) In order of human kindness
Indians   ——————————————
Zulus   ——————————————
English Speaking Europeans ——————————————
Xhosas   ——————————————
Afrikaans Speaking Europeans ————————————
Sothos   ——————————————

(d) In order of respect for authority
English Speaking Europeans ——————————————
Afrikaans Speaking Europeans ————————————
Sothos   ——————————————
Zulus   ——————————————
Indians   ——————————————
Xhosas   ——————————————

69. Both the African National Congress and the Pan African Congress have been banned for one year.
    (a) What do you regard as the main differences in their policies?
    (b) How would you assess their policies?

70. If everything happened as you would like to see it happen, what would your solution be to the South African race problem over the next twenty years?

71. As things are going now, what do you think will happen in South Africa in the next 20 years?

72. Looking back over the last 20 years, do you think the racial situation in South Africa has improved or worsened? In what ways?

73. Franchise (vote) should be:
    (a) Limited to the whites;
    (b) Limited to matriculants regardless of race;
    (c) Limited to persons having completed Standard VI, regardless of race;
    (d) Universal on the principle of one man—one vote.

74. The future of South Africa should take the line of:
    (a) Separate development along ethnic lines;
    (b) Economic integration with a social colour bar;
    (c) A non-racial society with equal opportunities to all and no colour bar;
    (d) Control by Africans as the majority group.

Code Number . . . . . .

75. The economy of a country should:
    (a) be left entirely to free enterprise;
    (b) be controlled to some extent by the state;
    (c) have complete state ownership of all commerce and industry.
76. In South Africa one should:
    (a) keep and revive the tribal way of life;
    (b) let the tribal way of life alone, without either encouraging or discouraging it;
    (c) spread education, soil conservation, health services, etc. without trying to destroy the tribal way of life as a whole;
    (d) destroy the tribal way of life and introduce the Western way of life as fast as possible.
77. The medium of instruction in schools should be:
    (a) the mother tongue throughout primary and secondary school;
    (b) the mother tongue through Standard VI, thereafter instruction in a European language;
    (c) the mother tongue through Standard II, thereafter instruction in a European language;
    (d) a European tongue throughout the school system.
78. Of the two European languages, English and Afrikaans:
    (a) both should be stressed equally in the schools;
    (b) English should be given more emphasis;
    (c) Afrikaans should be given more emphasis;
    (d) only English should be taught;
    (e) only Afrikaans should be taught.
79. Are you buying the home in which you live?
80. Do you own any property?
81. Views on intermarriage
Comments (General)

NURSE'S SCHEDULE

This is a survey of the nursing profession, carried out at the University of Natal. Our aims are purely scientific, and your answers will be completely confidential.

1. What is your province and place of birth? _____
2. What is your age? _____
3. What is your home language? _____
4. When did you come to this hospital? _____
5. What is your professional qualification in nursing? (Please place an X in the appropriate square.)
   Have you passed the First Year Training?

Code Number . . . . . .

Have you passed the Second Year Training?
Have you passed the Third Year Training?
Are you a Staff Nurse?
Are you a Sister?

6. What was the highest standard you reached
   at school or at University? _____

7. At what secondary or high school did you
   study? Please give the name of the school. _____

8. What is (or was) your father's occupation? _____

9. What is the highest educational standard
   your father completed? _____

10. What is (or was) your father's religion? _____

11. What is (or was) your mother's occupation? _____

12. What is the highest educational standard
    your mother completed? _____

13. What is (or was) your mother's religion? _____

14. What is your religion? _____

15. Are you married or single? _____

16. If married, what is
    (a) Your husband's occupation _____
    (b) His highest educational standard _____
    (c) His religion _____
    (d) His home language _____
    (e) How much lobola was paid? _____
    (f) What occupation would you like
        for your sons? _____
    (g) What occupation would you like
        for your daughters? _____

17. If you are engaged to be married, what is
    (a) Your future husband's occupation? _____
    (b) His highest educational standard? _____
    (c) His religion _____
    (d) His home language _____
    (e) How much lobola is to be paid? _____

18. Why did you decide to take up nursing? _____

19. Is there any other occupation you would
    rather have taken up? If so, what occupation? _____

20. Did you have any other occupation
    before nursing?   Yes_____ No_____
    If yes, then what occupation? _____

21. Have you worked in any other hospital
                        Yes_____ No_____

22. If you have worked in another hospital,
    please give the name of the hospital?

23. How does that hospital compare with
    McCord's Hospital
    (Please answer fully.)

Code Number . . . . . .

24. Suppose that a friend came and asked you
to advise her whether she should take up
nursing. What advice would you give her and why?

25. (a) What kind of person do you think would make the ideal nurse?
(b) What do you think are the worst qualities for a nurse?

26. To what societies, clubs, religious and sporting associations do you belong?

27. What is the position of an educated woman in African society? What are
her problems? How is she treated (a) by uneducated African men, (b) by
educated African men, (c) by uneducated African women, (d) by educated
African women. (PLEASE ANSWER FULLY)

28. Think of your three best friends (men) outside the hospital.
(a) What are their occupations?
(b) What is their standard of education?

29. Think of your three best friends (women) outside the hospital.
(a) What are their occupations?
(b) What is their standard of education?

30. Do you have any problems in working with people of a different race?
(Please answer fully.)

31. If everything happened as you would like to see it happen, what would
your solution be to the South African race problem over the next twenty
years?

32. As things are going now, what do you think *will* happen in South Africa
in the next twenty years?

33. What are your views on intermarriage between people of different race?

34. Is there anything else you would like to add to help us understand the
nursing profession?

Notes on Tsotsis

ANTHONY NGUBO comments that the use of the word *tsotsi* has undergone a change in meaning. According to the new meaning of the word, the group referred to in the text as the "location boys" would now be the tsotsis. Tsotsis in Durban make a fine distinction between themselves and those who indulge in violence. The tendency is to reserve the word "tsotsi" for the smart "location boys" who tend to avoid violence because this would expose them to the police, thus interfering with their sly ways of making a living. Tsotsis tend to identify with the younger members of the African bourgeoisie, whom they consider not "starchy" and therefore "non-'scuse me." The words "tsotsi" and " 'scuse me" are descriptive of behavior patterns and are considered morally "neutral" by the tsotsis. " 'Scuse me" people are those members of the African bourgeoisie who are particularly concerned with the rules of etiquette and correct behavior, that is, imitators of White middle-class behavior.

Some of the tsotsis boast a higher standard of education than a good many African teachers. Because of their education, they have the social graces that are necessary for participation in the social activities of the bourgeoisie. *Amagxagxa*, on the other hand, have little or no education.[1] The group Vilakazi refers to as amagxagxa, or *abaqhafi*, is the same group that tsotsis call *abaxhaka*. Abaxhaka tend to be crude, violent, and culturally rootless. They try to emulate tsotsis, but lack the education and the polish of the "location boys." Both the tsotsis and the abaxhaka are criminal elements of city communities, but differ in that abaxhaka tend to engage in crimes of violence whereas the tsotsis, although not completely nonviolent, tend to commit crimes that call for special operational skills. They approximate white-collar criminals.

Vilakazi's genesis of the tsotsis does not take cognizance of the fact that amagxagxa are what the tsotsis call abaxhaka. The same group was known in the late 1930s and early '40s as *olayitha*, who were noted for their violence. Tsotsis, on the other hand, are as much a product of mission schools as the bourgeoisie with whom they share a common culture.

1. Cf. A. Vilakazi, *Zulu Transformations* (Petermaritzburg, University of Natal Press, 1962), pp. 76–78.

Notes on Hypocrisy

THESE NOTES on hypocrisy are an attempt to explain why informants stereotype the English as hypocrites and not the Afrikaners. If an informant is prepared to offer group steretoypes, Afrikaners would seem as likely a target as the
English. Apartheid bears heavily on Africans, and they often expose the contradictions between the professions and practices of apartheid, precisely a situation
in which the description hypocrisy might seem not inappropriate. I think the
explanation is to be found in a more careful examination of the nature of hypocrisy. Its main elements are as follows:

1. There is a pretence which does not accord with the true motives of action.
A person protests that he holds a particular belief whereas in fact he holds a
different belief; or he acts in a way which is different from the belief he proclaims; or he appears to act in a way which is different from the way in which
he is actually acting.

2. The pretence proclaims or implies or insinuates a moral value—some noble
principle, the self-sacrifice of a friend or the humanity of democratic values.
Thus the charge of hypocrisy would not be made against a widow who pretends
that she is wealthy when in fact she is not.

3. The values are shared and that is why the pretence seduces.

4. The pretence is plausible. It must appear to be the noble thing it is represented to be. The hypocrite must be distinguished from the boaster, whose
pretence is blatant and puts us on our guard, while the hypocrite insinuates his
noble virtue subtly and indirectly.

5. The individual is deceived by the pretence and acts on it to his disadvantage.

6. He acts upon it innocently and morally.

7. The whole complex of hypocrisy inures to the advantage of the hypocrite.

8. The pretence is deliberate, Machiavellian, designed to ensnare.

9. The hypocrite is an object of admiration, until his hypocrisy is exposed.

If we take the point of view of an educated African, I think we can now
understand why the charge of hypocrisy is not made against Afrikaners in
relation to apartheid. There is a pretence which does not accord with the true
motives of action. The pretence implies (possibly) a moral value, that of
separate development. The whole complex of apartheid inures to the benefit of
the people who impose it, and it is part of a deliberate plan designed to attract
Africans. The other elements are missing. The educated African does not desire
the Afrikaner form of separate development, and hence there are no shared

values in the pretence. The pretence is not plausible: informants attach little importance to the rationalizations of apartheid, since they are experiencing the reality. The rationalizations are a play for Whites; non-Whites see the issues more bluntly. Hence if the informant acts upon the pretence, it is not done innocently, but cynically to extract an advantage. And, finally, informants do not admire the Afrikaner and do not wish to model themselves on him.

APPENDIX D

Tables

TABLE 1. Growth of secondary industry in South Africa, in relation to
geographical national income and urbanization
of Whites and Africans, 1921–60

Year	1921	1936	1951	1958–60
Contribution to national income				
Secondary industries	12.2%	15.7%	22.3%	24.6%[1]
Primary industries				
(mining and agricultural)	38.9%	34.5%	30.8%	25.0%[1]
Net national average income				
(£million at 1938 prices)	156.6	348.8	730.1	913.1[2]
In urban areas				
White population	59.6%	68.0%	78.4%	80.0%
African population	14.0%	18.4%	27.2%	30.0%

Sources: Union Statistics for 50 years, Union of South Africa, Government Printer, 1961, pp. S-3
and A-10. Provisional figures for urban population in 1960 are derived from the first results of the
Population Census, 1960: net national average income from S. T. van der Horst, "The Economic
Implications of Political Democracy," *Optima* (supplement), June 1960.
   1. Provisional figures for 1959.
   2. Annual income for 1959.

TABLE 2. Paternal occupations of a sample population of African nurses, teachers, and traders in 1959–60, and general occupational distribution of African men in 1951—Durban Magisterial District

Occupational category	Durban African men[1]	Fathers' occupations (in per cent)		
		Teachers[2]	Nurses[4]	Traders[7]
1. Professional, technical, and related workers	.4 ⎫	26 ⎫	27 ⎫	9 ⎫
2. Managers, administrators, and officials	.3 ⎬ 2.4	2 ⎬ 34	8 ⎬ 44	15 ⎬ 29
3. Clerical, office, and related workers	1.0 ⎪	3 ⎪	8 ⎪	4 ⎪
4. Salesmen and related workers	.7 ⎭	3 ⎭	1 ⎭	1 ⎭
5. Farmers	1.4	13	10	20
6. Mine, quarry, and related workers	.7			
7. Workers in operating transport occupations	3.5	3	1	1
8. Craftsmen	65.3 ⎫	7 ⎫	11 ⎫	7 ⎫
9. Laborers and factory workers	⎬ 90.3	32[3] ⎬ 43	20[5] ⎬ 33	15 ⎬ 27
10. Services and related workers	25.0 ⎭	4 ⎭	2 ⎭	5 ⎭
11. Others, including unemployed and unidentifiable (or not known, in case of fathers) or no information	1.7	7	12[6]	23
Total per cent	100.0	100	100	100

1. Source: Special Tabulation—1951 Union Census
2. Total sample—99.
3. Four factory workers were classified with the laborers; they might in fact have been skilled operatives. The 32% for category 9 has been rounded off from 31.3%.
4. Based on total sample of 149 nurses. The distribution for the McCord nurses alone is similar: 40%, first four census categories; 27%, craft, laboring, and service; 19%, other, etc.; 13%, farmers; 1%, transport.
5. Includes 5% factory workers.
6. Father's occupation is often not known, reflecting disorganization of African life.
7. Classification of the paternal occupations of the 75 traders in the sample proved difficult. In 11% of the cases, the relevant information was not collected. In the remaining 12% (category 11), informants had either not known their fathers, or the information given did not permit of precise classification. Chiefs were also grouped under category 11. The classification of farmer was not satisfactory, since it includes subsistence peasant farmers, as well as farmers of substance who had many head of cattle, or cultivated sugar cane. The line between the craftsman and the independent businessman could not easily be drawn. Policemen were classified with service workers, and indunas with laborers.

TABLE 3. Paternal occupations of a sample African population of Durban students in Standard V, Standard IX, and of all students in the arts and allied faculties (1959), and of students at the Medical School of the University of Natal (1960), and general occupational distribution of African men in 1951—Durban Magisterial District

	Fathers' occupations (in per cent)				
				University of Natal	
Occupational category	Durban African men	Stand-ard V[1]	Stand-ard IX[1]	Arts and allied faculties[2]	Medical School[3]
1. Professional, technical, and related workers	.4 ⎫	5 ⎫	12 ⎫	29 ⎫	42 ⎫
2. Managers, administrators, and officials	.3 ⎪ 2.4	4 ⎪ 27	7 ⎪ 37	8 ⎪ 46	11 ⎪ 63
3. Clerical, office, and related workers	1.0 ⎪	18 ⎭	18 ⎭	8 ⎪	8 ⎪
4. Salesmen and related workers	.7 ⎭			1 ⎭	2 ⎭
5. Farmers	1.4			13	10
6. Mine, quarry, and related workers	.7				
7. Workers in operating transport occupations	3.5			3	1
8. Craftsmen	65.3 ⎫	16 ⎫	22 ⎫	4 ⎫	1 ⎫
9. Laborers and factory workers	⎪ 90.3	52 ⎪ 68	41 ⎪ 63	27 ⎪ 35	5 ⎪ 16
10. Services and related workers	25.0 ⎭			4 ⎭	10 ⎭
11. Others, including unemployed and unidentifiable (or not known, in case of fathers)	1.7	5		3	10
Total per cent	100.0	100	100	100	100

1. The Standard IX students in the sample, numbering 191 (99 boys and 92 girls), were enrolled at 4 secondary schools, 2 being Bantu Community Schools, 1 a Government Bantu School, and the fourth a private Catholic School, thus covering the range of secondary schools in Durban. The Standard V children were chosen from the same schools, plus one additional school, a Bantu Community School. The Standard V sample numbered 216 (116 boys and 100 girls).

2. The total number of students was 75.

3. Based on 83 of the 85 African medical students (excluding 23 preliminary year students). Information as to occupation relates to fathers *or* guardians.

TABLE 4 (a). Occupations of friends of male and female teachers
in sample population, Durban, 1960

Occupation	Friends of male teachers (in per cent)	Friends of female teachers (in per cent)
Professional	73 (53 teachers)	75 (45 teachers)
Clerical, managerial, sales personnel, students	20	10
Factory workers, laborers, and domestic servants	5	3
Housewives		5
Others	2	7
Total per cent	100[1]	100[2]

1. Based on information for 134 choices of a possible 138. One schedule was blank and one gave
information for only two instead of the three friends the schedule requested.
2. Based on information for 156 friends (one schedule was blank).

TABLE 4 (b). Occupations of male and female friends of nurses
at McCord Zulu Hospital, Durban, 1961

Occupations	Male friends (in per cent)	Female friends (in per cent)
Professional	52	70 (34 nurses)
Clerical, managerial, sales personnel, and students	33	13
Factory workers and laborers	5	6
Housewives		5
Others	10	6
Total per cent	100[1]	100[1]

1. Occupations given for 226 men and 237 women. There were 96 informants, each asked to
name three friends; full replies would have elicited the names of 288 persons in each column.

TABLE 5 (a). Education of friends of male and female teachers
in sample population, Durban, 1960

Education	Friends of male teachers (in per cent)	Friends of female teachers (in per cent)
Standard VIII and below	15	24
Standard IX, X, teaching certificate, and nursing and other diplomas	67	63
Degrees	18	13
Total per cent	100[1]	100[2]

1. Based on 129 statements of education of friends.
2. Based on 143 statements.

TABLE 5 (b). Education of male and female friends of nurses
at the McCord Zulu Hospital, 1961

Education	Male friends (in per cent)	Female friends (in per cent)
Standard VIII and below	24	38
Standard IX, X, teaching certificate, and nursing diplomas	50	55
Studying for degree	5	3
Degrees	21	4
Total per cent	100[1]	100[2]

1. Information for 225 male friends.
2. Information for 235 female friends.

TABLE 6. Religious affiliation of Africans in Durban (1951 Census) and of
teachers, nurses, medical students, and traders (1959–1961)

Religious denomination	Africans[3] in Durban (in per cent)	Teachers[4] (in per cent)	Nurses[5] (in per cent)	Medical[6] students (in per cent)	Traders[7] (in per cent)
Anglican and Church of England in South Africa	9	17	20	28	11
Catholic	16	25	8	6	12
Lutheran	5	7	8	7	7
Methodist	12	23	25	28	13
Presbyterian	1	4	7	7	
(grouped subtotal)	43	76	68	76	43
American Board[1] complex		14	17	8	21
Minor sects and separatist churches	43	6	4	7	17
(Traders grouped subtotal)					38
Heathen, quasi-religious, none	10				
Other[2]	4	3	6	5	8
No or inadequate information or no church affiliation		1	5	4	11
Total per cent	100	100	100	100	100

1. The American Board complex includes the Bantu Congregational Church, and two churches which separated from it, the African Congregational Church and the Zulu Congregational Church. We were not sufficiently aware of the distinction between these churches, and thus did not probe informants' replies. American Board or African Congregational seems to have been used loosely by informants.

2. Denominations, listed by the Census, not falling within the category of minor sects and separatist churches; e.g. the few members of the Dutch Reformed Churches were classified in this category.

3. Special Tabulation, 1951 Union Census.

4. Based on a sample of 99 teachers in Durban (1960).

5. Total sample of 149 nurses (1961). Religious affiliation of the McCord nurses is similar, with 70% in established denominations, and 16% in the American Board complex, and no heathen.

6. Eighty-three African students registered at the Medical School, University of Natal, 1959.

7. Based on a sample of 75 traders.

TABLE 7. Occupation, education, and religious affiliation of executive members and representatives of the Durban and District African Football Association, 1924–60

(a) OCCUPATION

Professional	Managerial, self-employed	Clerical	Salesmen	Other	No information	Total
31	13	33	4	4	18	103

(b) EDUCATION

Below Junior Certificate	Junior Certificate	Teachers' Certificates		Standard X	Degree	No information	Total
		T4	T3				
16	15	15	6	15	9	27	103

(c) RELIGION

American Board complex	Major denominations				Sects	No information	Total
	Anglican	Catholic	Lutheran	Methodist			
23	8	8	4	21	3	36	103

Source: Analysis by my research assistant, Bernard Magubane. The relevant information could not always be obtained and there is some unreliability in the data, since use had to be made of informants and a long period of time is involved.

TABLE 8. Rating of occupations by African schoolchildren in Standards V and IX, and by African teachers, men and women, Durban, 1959–60.

Occupations	Primary school Standard V	Secondary school Standard IX	Teachers Men	Women
Doctor	1	1	1	1
University lecturer	2	3	3	5
Minister of religion	3	4	5	2
Nurse	4	6	6	6
Lawyer	5	2	2	3
Teacher	6	5	4	4
Social worker	7	10	7	7
Clerk	8	8	10	8
Trader	9	11	8	11
Civil servant	10	12	9	9
Carpenter	11	13	14	13
Artist	12	7	12	10
Farmer	13	9	11	12
Herbalist	14	14	13	15
Factory worker[1]		15	15	14
Laborer	15	16	16	16

Prodecure. The school children were asked to arrange a set of index cards bearing the names of different occupations, in the order in which they enjoyed prestige, and to give their reasons for first and last ranking. To illustrate what was meant, they were first asked to rank four minerals in terms of prestige (copper, gold, silver, and coal), and they ranked them as follows: gold, silver, copper, and coal. They were then told that the occupations given on the cards could be ranked in the same way, no doubt an encouragement to use earnings as the criterion. The Standard V children were instructed in Zulu, the Standard IX children in English. The sample of teachers was also handed a set of index cards and asked: "Please put at the top the occupation you think is most highly respected, then the second most highly respected, and so on." This in effect called for the informants' views as to the prestige of an occupation within the community. Some informants showed by their comments that they were distinguishing between their own ratings and community ratings. Most apparently gave their own evaluation.

[1] The factory worker was not included for rating by the Standard V children.

TABLE 9. Racial distribution of government and municipal Trading licenses,
Durban, 1930–62

Year	Europeans Actual	Per cent	Indians Actual	Per cent	Africans Actual	Per cent	Total
1930	3,931	76.02	1,165	22.52	75	1.46	5,171
1934	4,349	57.38	3,147	41.54	82	1.08	7,578
1938	5,449	58.34	3,767	40.31	127	1.35	9,343
1942	5,817	54.50	4,667	43.72	190	1.78	10,674
1946	6,731	54.29	5,327	42.98	339	2.73	12,397
1950	8,203	51.15	7,266	45.30	570	3.55	16,039
1954	9,718	53.94	7,756	43.06	541	3.00	18,015
1958	10,374	54.35	8,202	42.97	512	2.68	19,088
1962	10,478	53.97	8,161	42.04	776	3.99	19,415

Source: Licensing Officer's Annual Reports.

Note: The number of licenses is not equivalent to the number of traders, since African traders in beer halls and municipal markets who deal with non-Europeans are exempt from licenses, and since a trader may hold more than one license. In 1959, the Durban Bantu Administration Department furnished a list of traders—134 in the locations, 309 in the beer halls, 61 in the meat markets, and 89 outside the locations and municipal institutions, making a total of 593. These figures require adjustment: the licensing department shows a greater number of licenses in certain trades than the municipal list, as, for example, 25 licensed laundries as against 5, and 3 cartage contractors as against none. Checking against municipal and government licenses, a rough estimate of the number of traders in 1959 would be about 650, or about 800 including hawkers and peddlers. This excludes illegal traders, unlicensed craftsmen, roadside vendors of offal, and vendors of home produce.

TABLE 10. Teachers' ratings of races by intelligence, honesty, human kindness, and respect for authority

Race	Intelligence		Honesty		Human kindness		Respect for authority		All qualities	
	Average	Rank order	Average	Rank order	Average	Rank order	Average	Rank order	Average	Rank order
Afrikaner	4.6	6	3.9	4	5.5	6	4.8	6	4.7	6
English	1.7	1	2.6	2	3.1	3	2.9	2	2.5(8)	2
Indian	3.4	3	4.9	6	3.4	4	3.4	4	3.8	4
Sotho	4.0	5	3.0	3	2.7	2	3.4	3	3.3	3
Xhosa	3.3	2	4.9	5	3.9	5	4.4	5	4.1	5
Zulu	4.0	4	1.7	1	2.4	1	2.1	1	2.5(5)	1
Total	21.0		21.0		21.0		21.0		21.0	
Per cent giving[1] ratings	71		78		80		83		78	
Per cent rejecting	25		13		13		12		16	

[1] I excluded such answers as "All the same except . . ." or "Zulus more kind" without other specification.

Bibliography

Annual Survey of Race Relations in South Africa, Johannesburg, South African Institute of Race Relations.

Banton, Michael P., *West African City*, London, Oxford University Press, 1960.

Brandel-Syrier, Mia, *Black Women in Search of God*, London, Butterworth, 1962.

Brausch, G. E. J., "The Problem of Elites in the Belgian Congo," *International Social Science Bulletin*, vol. 8, 1956.

Brett, E. A., *African Attitudes: A Study of Social, Racial and Political Attitudes of Some Middle Class Africans*, Johannesburg, South African Institute of Race Relations, 1963.

Brookes, E. H., *The History of Native Policy in South Africa*, Pretoria, Van Schaik, 1927.

—— and J. B. Macaulay, *Civil Liberty in South Africa*, New York, Oxford University Press, 1958.

Burrows, J. R., *The Population and Labour Resources of Natal*, Pietermaritzburg, Natal Town and Regional Planning Reports, vol. 6, 1959.

Christian Council of South Africa, *The Christian Citizen in a Multi-Racial Society*, Cape Province, 1949.

Comhaire, J., "Some Aspects of Urbanization in the Belgian Congo," *American Journal of Sociology*, vol. 62, 1956.

Conference of African States on the Development of Education in Africa, Paris, UNESCO/ED/181.

Draper, Mary, *Sport and Race in South Africa*, Johannesburg, South African Institute of Race Relations, 1963.

Edwards, G. Franklin, *The Negro Professional Class*, Glencoe, Free Press, 1959.

Emerson, Rupert, *From Empire to Nation*, Cambridge, Harvard University Press, 1960.

Epstein, Arnold L., *Politics in an Urban African Community*, Manchester, University Press, 1958.

Forman, Lionel, *Chapters in the History of the March to Freedom*, Cape Town, New Age Publication, 1959.

Frazier, Franklin, *Black Bourgeoisie*, Glencoe, Free Press, 1957.

Gluckman, Max, *Custom and Conflict in Africa*, Oxford, Blackwell, 1955.

Goldthorpe, J. E., "Educated Africans: Some Conceptual and Terminological Problems," in *Social Change in Modern Africa*, ed. A. Southall, London, Oxford University Press, 1961.

Hellman, Ellen, "Some Comments on Bantu Education," *Race Relations Journal*, vol. 28, 1961.

Hopkinson, T., "Deaths and Entrances: The Emergence of African Writing," *Twentieth Century*, April 1959.

Horrell, Muriel, "The 'Pass Laws'," Johannesburg, South African Institute of Race Relations, 1960.

Horwood, O. P. F., "Some Aspects of Urban African Employment in the Durban Area," *Race Relations Journal*, vol. 25, 1958.

————, "The Private Budget of the Urban Native," *Optima*, September 1962.

Institute for Social Research, *Baumannville, A Study of an Urban African Community*, Cape Town, Oxford University Press, 1959.

International Commission of Jurists, *South Africa and the Rule of Law*, Geneva, 1960.

International Ecumenical Study Conference, *Dilemmas and Opportunities*, Geneva, World Council of Churches, 1959.

Jabavu, D. D. T., *The Black Problem*, Lovedale, Book Department, 1920.

————, *The Segregation Fallacy and Other Papers*, Lovedale, Book Department, 1928.

————, "Bantu Grievances," in *Western Civilization and the Natives of South Africa*, ed. I. Schapera, London, Routledge, 1934.

Jabavu, Noni, *Drawn in Colour*, London, Murray, 1960.

Jordan, A. C., "The Political and Cultural Aspirations of the Southern Africans as Reflected in Xhosa Literature," unpublished seminar paper.

Kuper, Hilda, *Indian People in Natal*, Pietermaritzburg, University of Natal Press, 1960.

Kuper, Leo, *Passive Resistance in South Africa*, New Haven, Yale University Press, 1957.

————, Hilstan Watts, and Ronald L. Davies, *Durban: A Study in Racial Ecology*, New York, Columbia University Press, 1958.

Landis, Elizabeth S., "South African Apartheid Legislation," *Yale Law Journal*, vol. 71, 1961–62.

Legum, Colin, "The Roots of Violence," *Observer*, May 5, 1963.

————, "The Gathering Storm," *Observer*, May 12, 1963.

Lewin, Julius, "The Legal Status of African Women," *Race Relations Journal*, vol. 26, 1959.

Lombard, J. A., "The Determination of Racial Income Differentials in South Africa," Durban, Institute for Social Research, University of Natal, 1962.

Luthuli, Albert J., *Let My People Go*, New York, McGraw-Hill, 1962.

MacQuarrie, J. W., "The African in the City: His Education," Durban, South African Institute of Race Relations, NR.130/1960.

————, "The Bantu Education Act and its Implementation," Durban, South African Institute of Race Relations, NRC.84/58.

Magubane, Bernard, "Sport and Politics in an Urban African Community," unpublished dissertation for the master's degree, Durban, University of Natal, 1963.

Mayer, Philip, *Townsmen or Tribesmen*, Cape Town, Oxford University Press, 1961.

Meisel, J. H., *The Myth of the Ruling Class*, Ann Arbor, University of Michigan Press, 1958.

Mitchell, J. C., "The African Middle Class in British Central Africa," in *Development of a Middle Class in Tropical and Sub-tropical Countries*, Brussels, INCIDI, 1956.

Mkele, Nimrod, "The Emergent African Middle Class," *Optima*, December 1960.

Mokitimi, S. M., "African Religion," in *Handbook of Race Relations in South Africa*, ed. Ellen Hellmann, Cape Town, Oxford University Press, 1949.

Molema, S. M., *The Bantu: Past and Present,* Edinburgh, Green, 1920.

Mphahlele, Ezekiel, *Down Second Avenue,* London, Faber and Faber, 1959.

———, *The African Image,* London, Faber and Faber, 1962.

Munger, E. S., *African Field Reports 1952–61,* Cape Town, Struik, 1963.

Ngubane, Jordan K., *An African Explains Apartheid,* New York, Praeger, 1963.

Nkosi, Lewis, "African Fiction," *Africa Report,* October 1962.

Nursing Services for 15 Million People, South African Government Information Service, Pretoria, 1961.

Nyembezi, C. L. S., *A Review of Zulu Literature,* Pietermaritzburg, University of Natal Press, 1961.

Pauw, B. A., *Religion in a Tswana Chiefdom,* London, Oxford University Press, 1963.

———, *The Second Generation,* Cape Town, Oxford University Press, 1961.

Pellegrin, Ronald J. and Frederick L. Bates, "Congruity and Incongruity of Status Attributes," *Social Forces,* vol. 38, 1959.

Phillips, Ray E., *The Bantu in the City,* Lovedale, Lovedale Press, 1938.

Pons, V. G., N. Xydias and P. Clément, "Social Effects of Urbanization in Stanleyville, Belgian Congo," in *Social Implications of Industrialization and Urbanization in Africa South of the Sahara,* Paris, UNESCO, 1956.

Progress of the Bantu Peoples towards Nationhood, The, No. 3, New York, South African Government Information Office, 1960.

Rautenbach, P. S., "The Impact of the Bantu on the Location of Industry and Bantu Reserves," Johannesburg, National Development Foundation, 1960.

Reader, D. H., *The Black Man's Portion,* Cape Town, Oxford University Press, 1961.

Report of the Commission on Native Education 1949–51, Pretoria, Government Printer, U.G.53/1951.

Report of the Commission of Enquiry into Riots in Durban, Pretoria, Government Printer, U.G. 36/1949.

Report of the Commission for the Socio-Economic Development of the Bantu Areas in the Union of South Africa, 1954–56, Pretoria, Government Printer, 1956.

Report of the Fort Hare Commission, Lovedale, Lovedale Press, 1955.

Report of the Interdepartmental Committee on the Social, Health and Economic Conditions of Urban Natives, Pretoria, Government Printer, 1942.

Report of the Native Economic Commission, 1930–32, Pretoria, Government Printer, U.G.22/1932.

"Report on Unrest in Pondoland," Johannesburg, South African Institute of Race Relations, RR.152/60.

Reyburn, Lawrence, *African Traders, Their Position and Problems in Johannesburg's South-Western Townships,* Johannesburg, South African Institute of Race Relations, RR. 83/60.

Sadie, J. L., "Bantu Population Growth and Distribution of Goods," Johannesburg, National Development Foundation of South Africa, 1960.

Samuels, L. H., "Bantu Economic Growth and Capital Development," Johannesburg, National Development Foundation of South Africa, 1960.

Sandor, *The Coming Struggle for South Africa,* Fabian Tract 345, London, Fabian Society, June 1963.

Sherwood, Rae, "Motivation Analysis: A Comparison of Job Attitudes among African and American Professional and Clerical Workers," *Proceedings of the South African Psychological Association,* 1956–57, No. 7/8.

———, "The Bantu Civil Servant," unpublished report; publication forbidden by the South African Government.

Skota, T. D. Mweli, ed. and comp., *The African Yearly Register,* Johannesburg, Esson and Co., 1932.

Social Implications of Industrialization and Urbanization in Africa South of the Sahara, Paris, UNESCO, 1956.

Steenkamp, W. F. J., "Bantu Wages in South Africa," *South African Journal of Economics,* June 1962.

Sundkler, B. G. M., *The Concept of Christianity in African Independent Churches,* Durban, Institute for Social Research, University of Natal, 1958.

———, *Bantu Prophets in South Africa,* London, Oxford University Press, 1961.

Tambo, Oliver, "Passive Resistance in South Africa," a paper delivered in Washington at a conference of the American Society of African Culture, April 1963.

Union Statistics for Fifty Years, Pretoria, Bureau of Census and Statistics, 1960.

University of South Africa, "Patterns of Income and Expenditure in the Urban Bantu Townships near Pretoria," *baNtu,* December 1961.

van den Berghe, P. L., "Race Attitudes in Durban, South Africa," *Journal of Social Psychology,* vol. 27, 1962.

———, *Caneville,* Middletown, Wesleyan University Press, 1964.

van der Horst, S. T., "A Note on the Native Labour Turnover and the Structure of the Labour Force in the Cape Peninsula," *South African Journal of Economics,* vol. 25, 1957.

———, "The Economic Implications of Political Democracy," *Optima* (Supplement), June 1960.

van Selms, A., "The Communion of the Saints and the Colour Problem," in *Delayed Action,* ed. A. S. Geyser and others, Pretoria, Craft Press, dist. by N. G. Kerkboekhandel, 1960.

Vilakazi, Absolom, "A Reserve from Within," *African Studies,* vol. 16, 1957.

———, *Zulu Transformations,* University of Natal Press, Durban, 1962.

Villiers, F. J. de, "Financing of Bantu Education," Johannesburg, South African Institute of Race Relations, RR.64/61.

Visser 't Hooft, W. A., *The Ecumenical Movement and the Racial Problem,* Paris, UNESCO, 1954.

Weber, Max, *The Religion of China,* Glencoe, Free Press, 1951.

Wilson, Gordon, "Mombasa—A Modern Colonial Municipality," in *Social Change in Modern Africa,* ed. A. Southall, London, Oxford University Press, 1961.

Wilson, Monica, *The Coherence of Groups,* Durban, Institute for Social Research, University of Natal, 1962.

——— and Archie Mafeje, *Langa: A Study of Social Groups in an African Township,* Cape Town, Oxford University Press, 1963.

Wolff, Kurt H., *The Sociology of Georg Simmel*, Glencoe, Free Press, 1950.
Ziervogel, D., "The Development of the Literature of the South African Bantu," in *Bantu Language and Literature*, Union Festival Committee, Bloemfontein, 1960.

Index